visions of the bigbuilding danced in their heads ... Drew

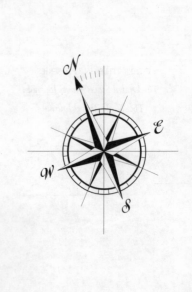

THE TRAVELER'S
ATLAS
A Geographic Handbook

Table of Contents

Legend 7
World Political 8
World Physical 10
World Time Zones 12

Europe 14
British Isles 18
France - Spain 20
North Central 22
South Central 24
Balkan Peninsula 25
London METRO & DOWNTOWN 26
Paris METRO & DOWNTOWN 28
Amsterdam - The Hague - Rotterdam 30
Antwerp - Brussels 31
Berlin METRO & DOWNTOWN 32
Essen - Dortmund - Düsseldorf 34
Frankfurt / Prague 35
Copenhagen / Stockholm 36
Bern / Zurich 37
Lisbon / Barcelona 38
Madrid 39
Rome / Milan 40
Rome DOWNTOWN 41
Budapest / Vienna 42
Athens / Istanbul 43

Africa and Middle East 44
Tel Aviv - Yafo - Jerusalem / Cairo 50
Pretoria - Johannesburg 51

Northern Asia - Russia 52
Moscow METRO 56
Moscow DOWNTOWN / St. Petersburg 57

Southern Asia 58
Taipei / Manila 62
Bangkok / Singapore 63
Jakarta / Delhi - New Delhi 64
Bombay / Calcutta 65

Far East 66
Tokyo METRO & DOWNTOWN 68
Osaka - Kyoto - Kobe 70
Osaka / Kyoto DOWNTOWN 71
Seoul 72
Beijing 73
Shanghai 74
Hong Kong 75

Australia - New Zealand 76
Sydney 78
Melbourne 79

Pacific 80

Polar Regions 82

South America 84
Lima / Santiago 87
Buenos Aires METRO & DOWNTOWN 88
Caracas / Bogotá 90
Rio de Janeiro 91
São Paulo METRO & DOWNTOWN 92

Caribbean 94

Mexico - Central America 96
Mexico City 98
Guadalajara 99

Canada 100
Toronto 104
Ottawa / Quebec 105
Montréal 106
Winnipeg / Vancouver 107

United States 109
New England 114
New York State 116
Middle Atlantic States 118
Southeastern States 120
Florida - Puerto Rico 122
Midwestern States 124
North Central States 126
South Central States 128
Rocky Mountain States 130
California - Nevada 132
Northwestern States 134
Alaska 136
Hawaii 137
Boston METRO & DOWNTOWN 138
New York DOWNTOWN & METRO 141
Philadelphia 144
Pittsburgh 146
Baltimore 147
Washington, D.C. METRO & DOWNTOWN 148
Cleveland 150
Cincinnati 151
Atlanta 152
Orlando 153
Tampa - St. Petersburg 154
Miami - Fort Lauderdale 155
Detroit 156
Milwaukee / Indianapolis 157
Chicago METRO & DOWNTOWN 158
Minneapolis - St. Paul 161
Kansas City / St. Louis 162

New Orleans / San Antonio 163
Dallas - Fort Worth 164
Houston 166
Denver 167
Phoenix 168
San Diego 169
Los Angeles METRO & DOWNTOWN 170
San Francisco DOWNTOWN 173
San Francisco Bay 174
Seattle - Tacoma 176
Portland / Honolulu 177

National Parks & Interstates 178
Yellowstone National Park 180
Grand Teton National Park 181
Yosemite National Park 182
Grand Canyon National Park 183
Cape Cod 184
Acadia National Park 186
Cape Hatteras 187
Florida Keys 188

Appendix
Traveler's Notes 189
International Dialing Codes 201
U.S. & Canadian Area Codes 204
Toll-Free Numbers 206
International Travel 207
Country Information 208
U.S. Foreign Embassies 209
U.S. Road and Air Distances 210
International Air Distances 212
U.S. Weather 214
International Weather 216
Weights and Measures 218
Perpetual Calendar 220

Index 222

Legend

General

―――――― International boundary

―――――― Internal political boundary

- - - - - - Undefined/disputed boundary

· · · · · · · Boundary in water

⊛ National capital

★ State or provincial capital

· Other city or town.
City or town type size is an indication of the relative size or importance of the city or town.

Political / Physical

Elevations in meters and feet above sea level.

Elevation range varies from map to map.

Regional Maps

―――――― Limited access highway...

―――――― Other main route

UNITED STATES ONLY

- - - - - - Unpaved road

- - - - - - Ferry

Subject states

Non subject states

Large built up area

Park

National or state forest

Military reservation

Indian reservation

City Maps

═══════ Limited access highway...

= = = = = : ...under construction

―――――― Other main route

▪▪▪▪▪▪▪ Tunnel

- - - - - - Ferry

Approximate built up area

○ Point of interest

· City or town.
Settlements not located with a black circle are districts or communities that are part of a larger city.

Park Maps (United States)

═══════ Limited access highway (Interstate, toll road etc.)

―――――― Other main route

· · · · · · Scenic Route

- - - - - - Trail

⊗ Road closed in winter

- - - - - - Ferry

National Park

Other park

National or state forest

Military reservation

Indian reservation

▲ Campsite

⧉ Skiing

● Point of interest

7

World POLITICAL

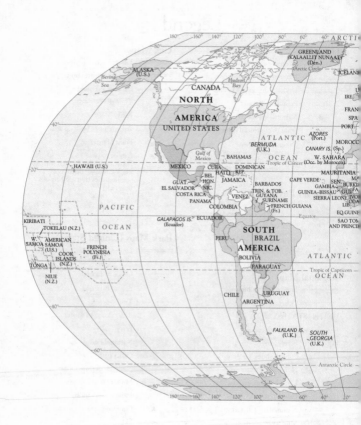

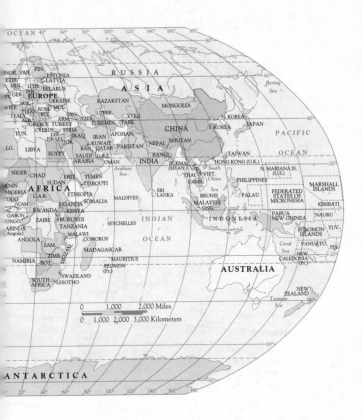

World PHYSICAL

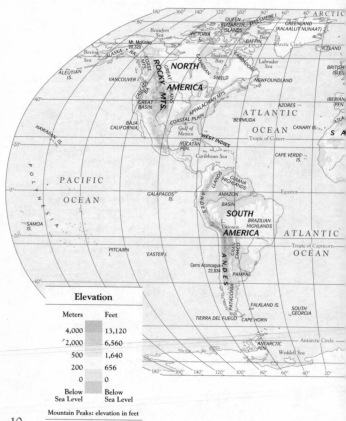

Elevation

Meters	Feet
4,000	13,120
2,000	6,560
500	1,640
200	656
0	0
Below Sea Level	Below Sea Level

Mountain Peaks: elevation in feet

World Time Zones

The World is divided into 24 time zones, beginning at the Prime Meridian, which runs through Greenwich, England. The twelve zones east and twelve zones west of the Prime Meridian meet halfway around the globe at the International Date Line.

Traveling in an easterly direction, the time of day moves ahead one hour for each zone crossed. Traveling west, time falls behind one hour per zone. At the International Date Line a traveler gains one day crossing in an easterly direction, and loses one day traveling west.

The table below the map can be used to quickly compare times of day between places. The vertical columns of the table correspond with the time zones on the map, and are color coordinated with their respective zones. Gray shading is added to the table to mark a change between days of the week ("Monday" is symbolized with gray shading; "Sunday" and "Tuesday" have no shading). By reading horizontally across the table the time of day in each zone can be compared. For example, if it is noon in New York on Monday, it is 5:00 p.m. Monday in London and 2:00 a.m. Tuesday in Tokyo.

Note that times shown are "standard time". Adjustments are necessary when "daylight saving time" is used.

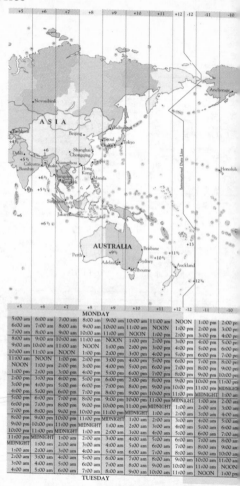

| MONDAY | | | | | | | | | |
+5	+6	+7	+8	+9	+10	+11	+12 -12	-11	-10
5:00 am	6:00 am	7:00 am	8:00 am	9:00 am	10:00 am	11:00 am	NOON	1:00 pm	2:00 pm
6:00 am	7:00 am	8:00 am	9:00 am	10:00 am	11:00 am	NOON	1:00 pm	2:00 pm	3:00 pm
7:00 am	8:00 am	9:00 am	10:00 am	11:00 am	NOON	1:00 pm	2:00 pm	3:00 pm	4:00 pm
8:00 am	9:00 am	10:00 am	11:00 am	NOON	1:00 pm	2:00 pm	3:00 pm	4:00 pm	5:00 pm
9:00 am	10:00 am	11:00 am	NOON	1:00 pm	2:00 pm	3:00 pm	4:00 pm	5:00 pm	6:00 pm
10:00 am	11:00 am	NOON	1:00 pm	2:00 pm	3:00 pm	4:00 pm	5:00 pm	6:00 pm	7:00 pm
11:00 am	NOON	1:00 pm	2:00 pm	3:00 pm	4:00 pm	5:00 pm	6:00 pm	7:00 pm	8:00 pm
NOON	1:00 pm	2:00 pm	3:00 pm	4:00 pm	5:00 pm	6:00 pm	7:00 pm	8:00 pm	9:00 pm
1:00 pm	2:00 pm	3:00 pm	4:00 pm	5:00 pm	6:00 pm	7:00 pm	8:00 pm	9:00 pm	10:00 pm
2:00 pm	3:00 pm	4:00 pm	5:00 pm	6:00 pm	7:00 pm	8:00 pm	9:00 pm	10:00 pm	11:00 pm
3:00 pm	4:00 pm	5:00 pm	6:00 pm	7:00 pm	8:00 pm	9:00 pm	10:00 pm	11:00 pm	MIDNIGHT
4:00 pm	5:00 pm	6:00 pm	7:00 pm	8:00 pm	9:00 pm	10:00 pm	11:00 pm	MIDNIGHT	1:00 am
5:00 pm	6:00 pm	7:00 pm	8:00 pm	9:00 pm	10:00 pm	11:00 pm	MIDNIGHT	1:00 am	2:00 am
6:00 pm	7:00 pm	8:00 pm	9:00 pm	10:00 pm	11:00 pm	MIDNIGHT	1:00 am	2:00 am	3:00 am
7:00 pm	8:00 pm	9:00 pm	10:00 pm	11:00 pm	MIDNIGHT	1:00 am	2:00 am	3:00 am	4:00 am
8:00 pm	9:00 pm	10:00 pm	11:00 pm	MIDNIGHT	1:00 am	2:00 am	3:00 am	4:00 am	5:00 am
9:00 pm	10:00 pm	11:00 pm	MIDNIGHT	1:00 am	2:00 am	3:00 am	4:00 am	5:00 am	6:00 am
10:00 pm	11:00 pm	MIDNIGHT	1:00 am	2:00 am	3:00 am	4:00 am	5:00 am	6:00 am	7:00 am
11:00 pm	MIDNIGHT	1:00 am	2:00 am	3:00 am	4:00 am	5:00 am	6:00 am	7:00 am	8:00 am
MIDNIGHT	1:00 am	2:00 am	3:00 am	4:00 am	5:00 am	6:00 am	7:00 am	8:00 am	9:00 am
1:00 am	2:00 am	3:00 am	4:00 am	5:00 am	6:00 am	7:00 am	8:00 am	9:00 am	10:00 am
2:00 am	3:00 am	4:00 am	5:00 am	6:00 am	7:00 am	8:00 am	9:00 am	10:00 am	11:00 am
3:00 am	4:00 am	5:00 am	6:00 am	7:00 am	8:00 am	9:00 am	10:00 am	11:00 am	NOON
4:00 am	5:00 am	6:00 am	7:00 am	8:00 am	9:00 am	10:00 am	11:00 am	NOON	1:00 pm
TUESDAY									

World Time Zones

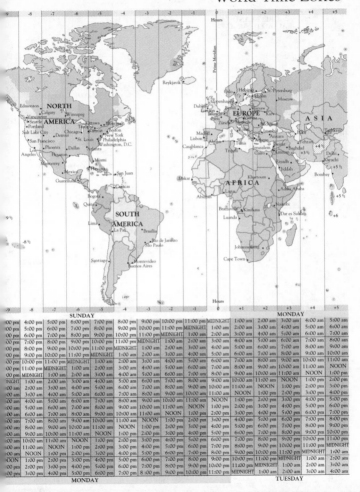

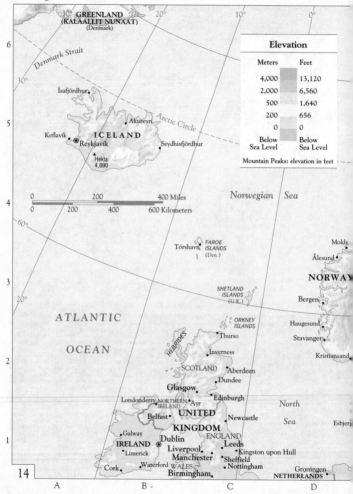

GREENLAND (KALAALLIT NUNAAT) (Denmark)

Denmark Strait

Ísafjördhur

Akureyri

Keflavík • • Reykjavík **ICELAND** Seydhisfjördhur

Arctic Circle

Hekla 4,890

Elevation

Meters	Feet
4,000	13,120
2,000	6,560
500	1,640
200	656
0	0
Below Sea Level	Below Sea Level

Mountain Peaks: elevation in feet

Norwegian Sea

0   200   400 Miles
0   200   400   600 Kilometers

Molde

Ålesund

NORWAY

Tórshavn **FAROE ISLANDS** (Den.)

Bergen

ATLANTIC

OCEAN

SHETLAND ISLANDS (U.K.)

Haugesund

Stavanger

ORKNEY ISLANDS

Thurso

Kristiansand

HEBRIDES

Inverness

North

SCOTLAND

Aberdeen

Dundee

Glasgow

Edinburgh

Sea

Londonderry NORTHERN IRELAND • Ayr

Belfast

UNITED

Newcastle

Esbjer

Galway

KINGDOM

IRELAND ⊛ Dublin

ENGLAND

Liverpool • Leeds

Kingston upon Hull

Limerick

Manchester • Sheffield

Groningen

Cork

Waterford WALES

Nottingham

Birmingham

NETHERLANDS

14

A   B   C   D

10°   20°   30°   40°   70°   50°

Barents   Sea

NORTH CAPE

Vardø

Hammerfest

• Tromsø   • Ivalo   Murmansk•

L A P L A N D   KOLA PENINSULA

• Narvik   • Kiruna   Apatity•

• Bodø   *White Sea*   Arkhangelsk•

Mo-i-Rana   • Rovaniemi   Belomorsk•

Namsøs   Kemi   • Luleå   *Lake Onega*

rondheim   Skellefteå   Oulo   Petrozavodsk•

• Östersund   FINLAND

• Umeå   Kokkola   Kuopio   *Lake Ladoga*

• Sundsvall   Vassa   Joensuu•   60°

aldhøpiggen   SWEDEN   Jyväskylä   LAKE REGION

098

llehammer   Tampere   Lahti

• Gävle   Pori   Turku   Helsinki   Kotka   Vyborg

)slo   • Borlänge   ÅLAND IS. (Fin.)   *Gulf of Finland*   St. Petersburg

• Drammen   Karlstad   • Uppsala   Tallinn   Novgorod   RUSSIA

kien   • Örebro   Stockholm   ESTONIA   Tver•

Vänern   Norrköping   Parnu   Tartu•   *Lake Peipus*   Pskov•   Moscow

Vättern   Linköping   *Sea*   *Gulf of Riga*   Riga

• Jönköping   GOTLAND (Swe.)   LATVIA

• Göteborg   Växjö   ÖLAND   Ventspils   Daugavpils•   Vitsyebsk•   Smolensk•

lborg   Halmstad   Kalmar   Liepaja•   *Baltic*   LITHUANIA   Vilnius   Minsk   BELARUS   Bryansk•

JTLAND   Helsingborg   Klaipeda•   Kaunas   RUSSIA   PLAIN

Århus   Copenhagen   BORNHOLM (Den.)   Kaliningrad   Mahilyow•

Odense•   Malmö   Gdansk   Hrodna   Minsk   Homyel•

Kiel   Rostock   Szczecin   POLAND   Bialystok•

übeck   Hamburg   Bydgoszcz   NORTHERN   EUROPEAN

remen   GER.

15

E   F   G   H

6   5   4   1

Europe SOUTHERN

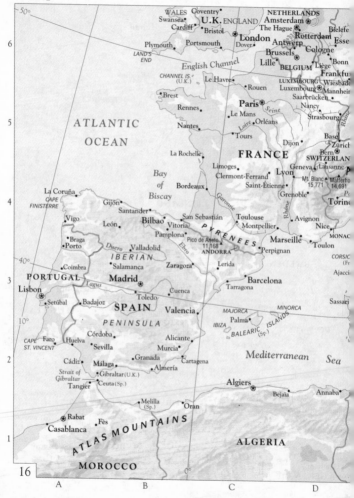

*The Former Yugoslav Republic of Macedonia
** Serbia and Montenegro have formed a joint independent state
referred to as Yugoslavia, but this entity has not been formally
recognized by the United Nations.

British Isles

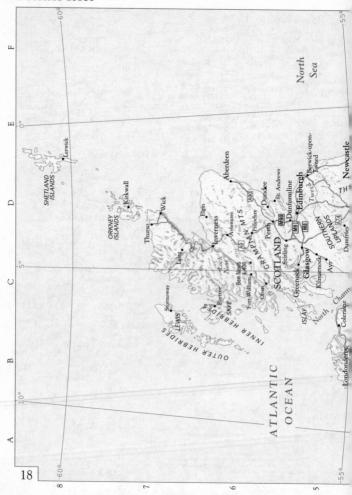

ATLANTIC OCEAN

North Sea

SHETLAND ISLANDS
Lerwick

ORKNEY ISLANDS
Kirkwall

Thurso
Wick
Lairg
Elgin
Aberdeen
Inverness
Aviemore
Pitlochry
St. Andrews
Dundee
Dunfermline
Berwick-upon-Tweed
Newcastle
Edinburgh
Tweed
TH
Loch Ness
GRAMPIAN MTS.
A9
A90
Perth
M90
Stirling
M9
M8
SOUTHERN UPLANDS
Dumfries
A74
Portree
SKYE
Ben Nevis
4406
Fort William
Oban
SCOTLAND
Greenock
Glasgow
Ayr
Kilmarnock
LEWIS
Stornoway
OUTER HEBRIDES
INNER HEBRIDES
ISLAY
North. Chann.
Coleraine
Londonderry

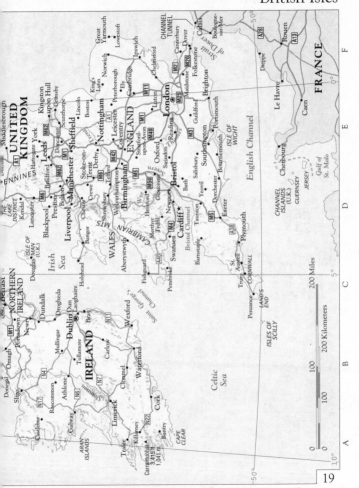

France - Spain

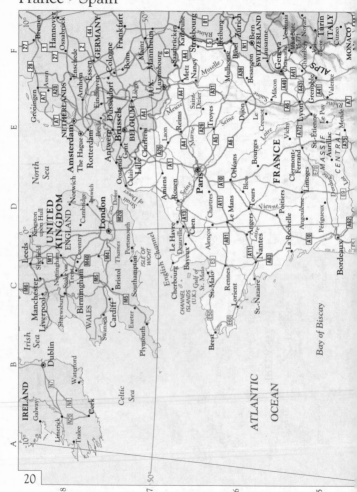

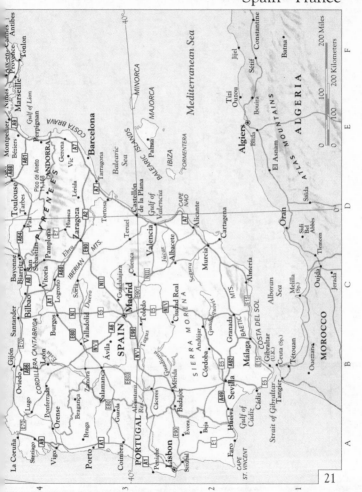

Europe NORTH CENTRAL

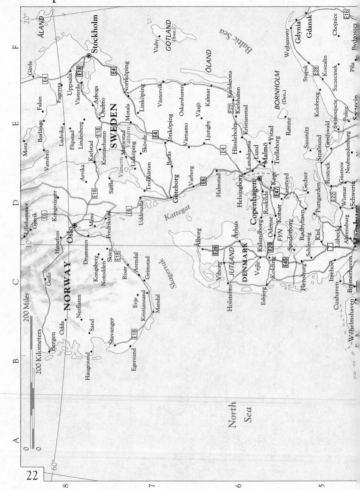

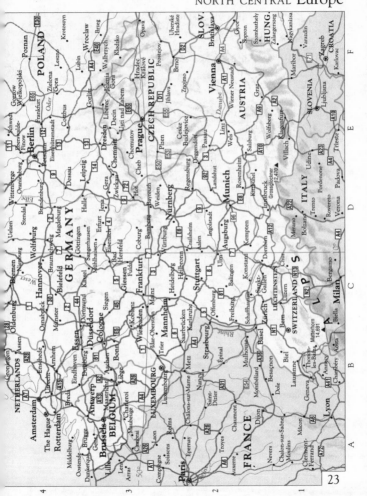

23

Europe SOUTH CENTRAL

Balkan Peninsula

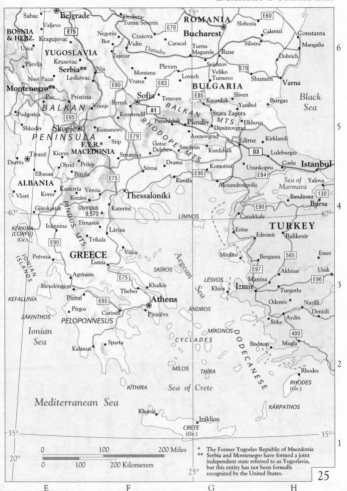

* The Former Yugoslav Republic of Macedonia
** Serbia and Montenegro have formed a joint independent state referred to as Yugoslavia, but this entity has not been formally recognized by the United States.

London UNITED KINGDOM

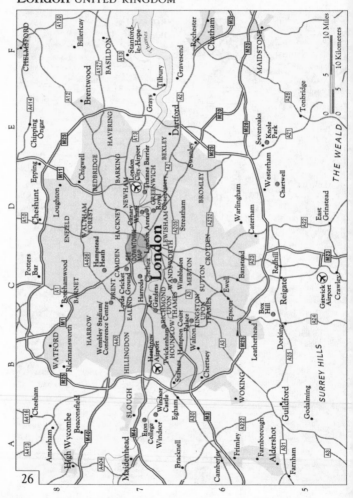

26

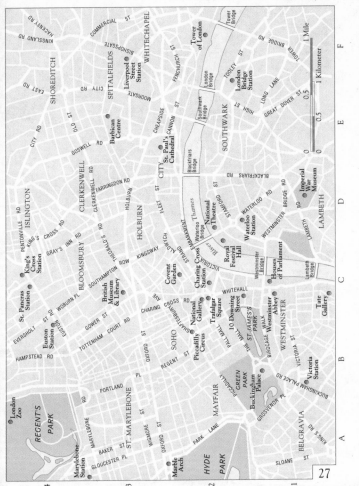

Tower Bridge

HACKNEY RD
KINGSLAND RD
COMMERCIAL ST
BISHOPSGATE
SPITALFIELDS
WHITECHAPEL
EAST RD
CITY RD
SHOREDITCH
OLD ST
CITY RD
GOSWELL RD
Barbican Centre
CLERKENWELL RD
CLERKENWELL
FARRINGDON RD
GRAY'S INN RD
ISLINGTON
PENTONVILLE RD
KING'S CROSS RD
PENTONVILLE
HOLBORN
Liverpool Street Station
MOORGATE
CHEAPSIDE
CANNON ST
CITY
St. Paul's Cathedral
FENCHURCH ST
Tower of London
London Bridge
TOOLEY ST
London Bridge Station
LONG LANE
GREAT DOVER ST
HIGH ST
SOUTHWARK
Southwark Bridge
Blackfriars Bridge
BLACKFRIARS RD
FLEET ST
HOLBORN
HOLBORN
ALDWYCH
Waterloo Bridge
River Thames
EMBANKMENT
National Theatre
STAMFORD ST
WATERLOO RD
Waterloo Station
WESTMINSTER BRIDGE RD
Imperial War Museum
LAMBETH
LAMBETH
KINGSWAY
STRAND
Charing Cross Station
Royal Festival Hall
VICTORIA EMBANKMENT
Westminster Bridge
Lambeth Bridge
Houses of Parliament
KING'S CROSS RD
King's Cross Station
St. Pancras Station
EVERSHOLT ST
Euston Station
EUSTON RD
WOBURN PL
SOUTHAMPTON ROW
THEOBALD'S RD
BLOOMSBURY
British Museum & Library
GOWER ST
TOTTENHAM COURT RD
CHARING CROSS RD
SHAFTESBURY AVE
Covent Garden
SOHO
CHARING CROSS
National Gallery
Trafalgar Square
WHITEHALL
10 Downing Street
PALL MALL
THE MALL
WESTMINSTER
Westminster Abbey
VICTORIA ST
Tate Gallery
HAMPSTEAD RD
OXFORD ST
REGENT ST
PL
PORTLAND
MARYLEBONE RD
ST. MARYLEBONE
WIGMORE ST
OXFORD ST
Marble Arch
Piccadilly Circus
PICCADILLY
MAYFAIR
PARK LANE
GREEN PARK
ST. JAMES'S PARK
BIRDCAGE WALK
Buckingham Palace
GROSVENOR PL
BUCKINGHAM PALACE RD
Victoria Station
BELGRAVIA
KING'S RD
SLOANE ST
London Zoo
REGENT'S PARK
BAKER ST
MARYLEBONE
GLOUCESTER PL
Marylebone Station
HYDE PARK

1 Mile
1 Kilometer
0.5
0.5
0

27

F
E
D
C
B
A

4
3
2
1

Paris FRANCE

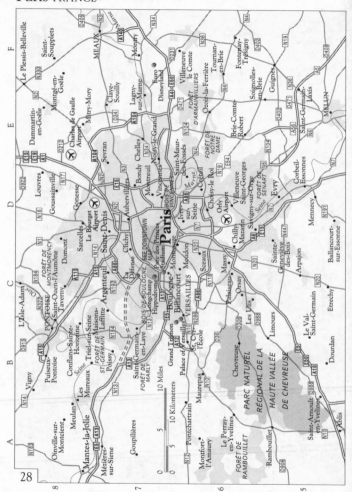

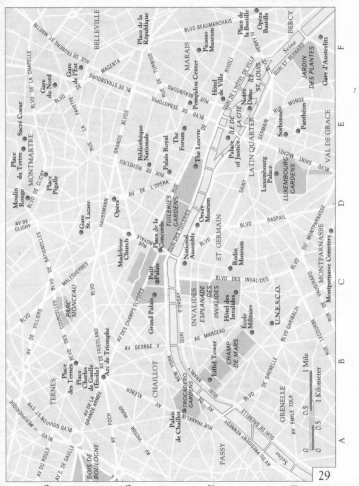

Amsterdam - The Hague - Rotterdam NETHERLANDS

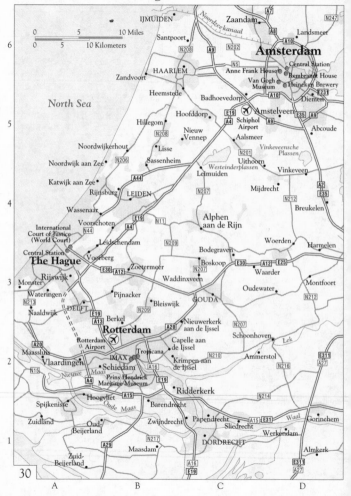

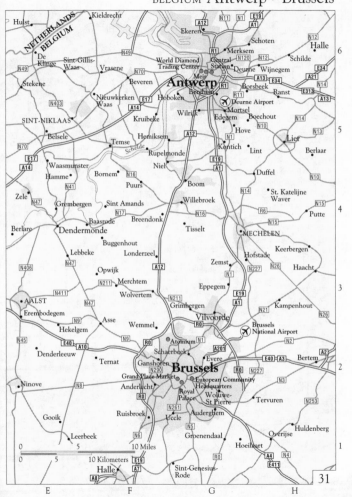

Hulst · Kieldrecht · · N11 · N1 · E19 · A1

NETHERLANDS
BELGIUM · Ekeren · · N12 · Halle
Schoten · Schilde
De · Sint-Gillis- · R1 · Merksem · N120 · N12 · N34
Klinge · Waas · N49 · World Diamond · Central · Deurne · Wijnegem · E34
N49 · Vrasene · N70 · Trading Center · Station · N13 · E34 · N14 · E313
Stekene · Beveren · Meir · Borsbeek · Ranst · A13
Antwerp · Berchem · R11
N403 · Nieuwkerken · E17 · Hoboken · Deurne Airport · Boechout · N14
Waas · A14 · Mortsel
SINT-NIKLAAS · Kruibeke · Wilrijk · Edegem · N10
Belsele · Hemiksem · Hove · Lier · Berlaar
N70 · Temse · A12 · Kontich · Lint · N13
E17 · Schelde · Rupelmonde · N10
A14 · Waasmunster · Niel · E19 · Duffel
Hamme · Bornem · A1
N41 · Puurs · Boom · N14 · St. Katelijne
Zele · N47 · Grembergen · Sint Amands · Waver · N15
N17 · Willebroek · R6 · Putte
Baasrode · Breendonk · N16 · N15
Berlare · Dendermonde · Tisselt · MECHELEN
Buggenhout · Hofstade · Keerbergen
Lebbeke · Londerzeel · Zemst · N227 · N26 · Haacht
N406 · N47 · Opwijk · A12 · N1
N411 · Merchtem · N211 · Eppegem · E19 · N21 · Kampenhout
AALST · N47 · Wolvertem · Grimbergen · A1 · N26
Erembodegem · Asse · Vilvoorde
N9 · Wemmel · R0 · Brussels
Hekelgem · Atomium · N1 · National Airport
N45 · E40 · N9 · R0 · Schaerbeek · A201 · E40 · A3 · Bertem · A2
A10 · Ganshoren · N290 · **Brussels** · R0 · N227
Denderleeuw · Ternat · Grand Place Market · European Community · N3
Ninove · N8 · Anderlecht · Royal · Headquarters · Tervuren · N253
R0 · Palace · Woluwe-
Gooik · Ruisbroek · N261 · Uccle · St Pierre · Auderghem
N6 · Groenendaal · Overijse · Huldenberg
Leerbeek · N5 · Hoeilaart · A4 · N4
0 — 5 — 10 Miles · R0
0 — 5 — 10 Kilometers · E19 · Sint-Genesius- · E411
Halle · A7 · Rode
A8

31

E · F · G · H

Berlin GERMANY

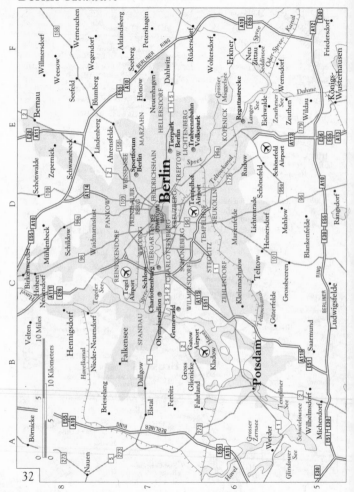

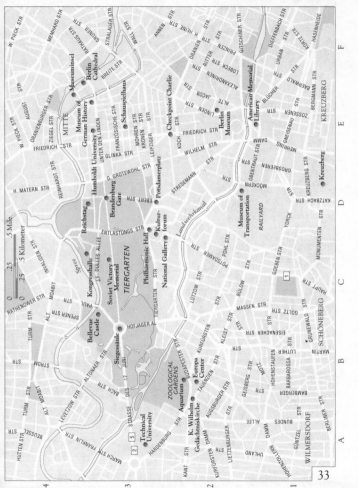

GERMANY **Berlin**

W PIECK STR
MEINHARD STR
RATHAUS STR
GRÜNER STR
STRALAUER STR
WALL STR
ANNEN STR
H HEINE STR
ORANIEN STR
RITTER STR
PRINZEN STR
GITSCHINER STR
DIEFFENBACH STR
KORTE STR
HASENHEIDE

W PIECK STR
ORANIENBURGER STR
AUGUST STR
ZIEGEL STR
FRIEDRICH STR

Museuminsel
Berlin Cathedral
BREITE STR

Museum of German History
MITTE
Schauspielhaus
FRANZÖSISCHE STR
Checkpoint Charlie
ALEXANDRINEN STR
ALTE JACOB STR
LINDEN STR
American Memorial Library
URBAN STR
BAERWALD STR
KREUZBERG

H MATERN STR
REINHARDT STR
Humboldt University
UNTER DEN LINDEN
GLINKA STR
MOHREN STR
KRONEN STR
LEIPZIGER STR
Berlin Museum
KOCH STR
WILHELM STR
FRIEDRICH STR
ZOSSENER STR
BLÜCHER STR
BERGMANN STR

Reichstag
Brandenburg Gate
O. GROTEWOHL STR
Potsdamerplatz
EBERT STR
STRESEMANN STR
OBENTRAUT STR
MEHRING DAMM
GNEISENAU STR
GROSSBEEREN STR
Kreuzberg

.5 Mile
.25
.5 Kilometer
.25
0

Kultur- forum
Philharmonic Hall
ENTLASTUNGS STR
Landwehrkanal
Museum of Transportation
RAILYARD
KREUZBERG STR
KATZBACH STR
YORCK STR
MONUMENTEN STR

Kongresshalle
J.F. DULLES ALLEE
Spree
INVALIDEN STR
TIERGARTEN
National Gallery
TIERGARTEN STR
LÜTZOW STR
POTSDAMER STR
POHL STR
GOEBEN STR

RATHENOWER STR
MOABIT
ALT MOABIT
PAUL STR
SPENER STR
Bellevue Castle
ALTONAER STR
Soviet Victory Memorial
BACH STR
HOFJAGER AL
Siegessäule
DES 17 JUNI
STRASSE
HARDENBURG STR
BUDAPESTER STR
KURFÜRSTEN STR
KLEIST STR
MASSEN STR
BÜLOW STR
EISENACHER STR
GOLTZ STR
MARTIN LUTHER STR
GRUNEWALD STR
HAUPT STR
SCHÖNEBERG

TURM STR
ALT MOABIT
STROM STR
LEVETZOW STR
TURM STR
BEUSSEL STR
HÜTTEN STR
STR
MARCH STR
FRANKLIN STR
SALZUFER
Technical University
KANT STR
ZOOLOGICAL GARDENS
Aquarium
K. Wilhelm Gedächtniskirche
Europa Center
TAUENZIEN STR
AUGSBURGER STR
KURFÜRSTEN DAMM
LIETZENBURGER STR
NÜRNBERGER
ANSBACHER
GEISBERG STR
HOHENSTAUFEN STR
BARBAROSSA STR
BAMBERGER STR
HOHENZOLLERN DAMM
GÜNTZEL STR
BUNDES ALLEE
UHLAND STR
BERLINER STR
WILMERSDORF

33

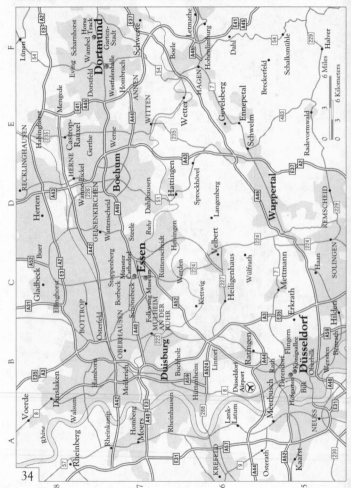

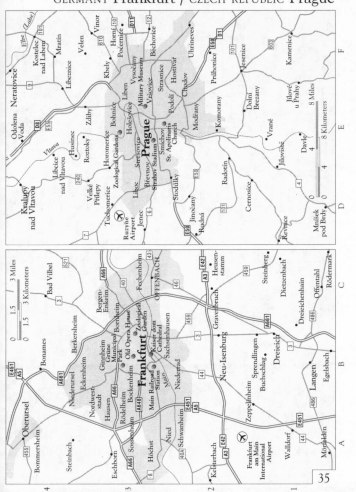

Copenhagen DENMARK / Stockholm SWEDEN

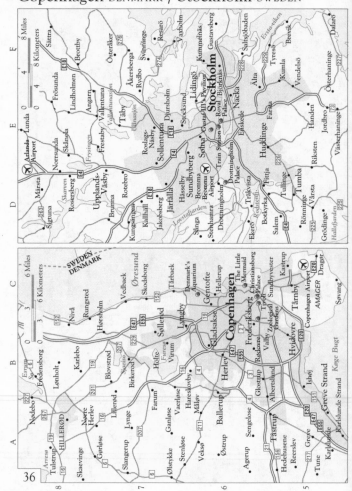

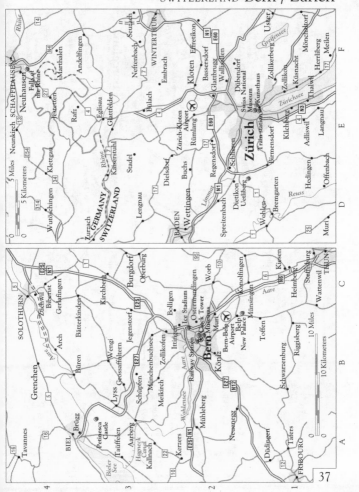

Lisbon PORTUGAL / Barcelona SPAIN

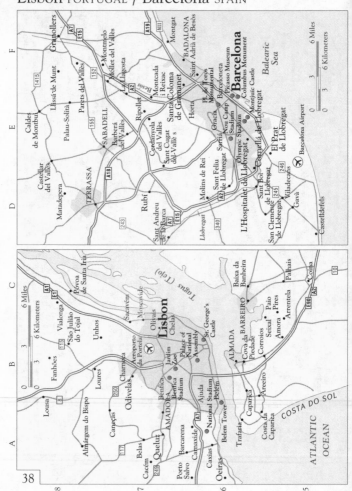

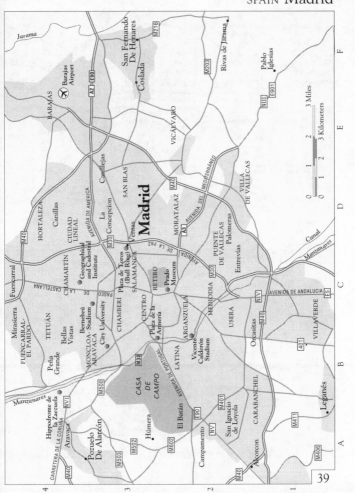

39

Rome / Milan ITALY

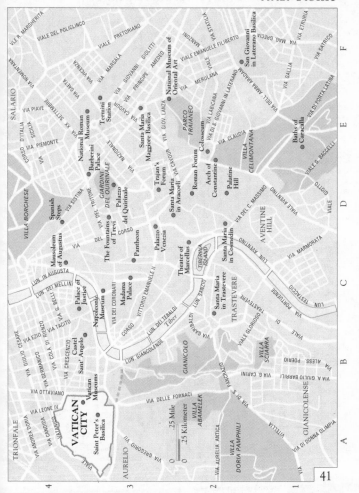

Budapest HUNGARY / Vienna AUSTRIA

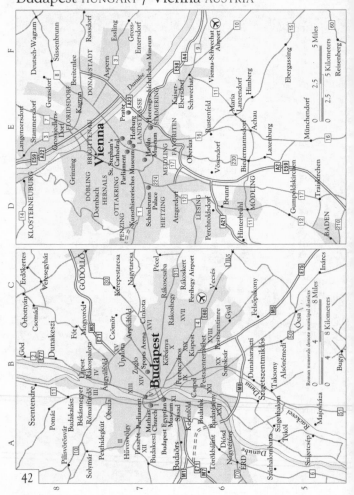

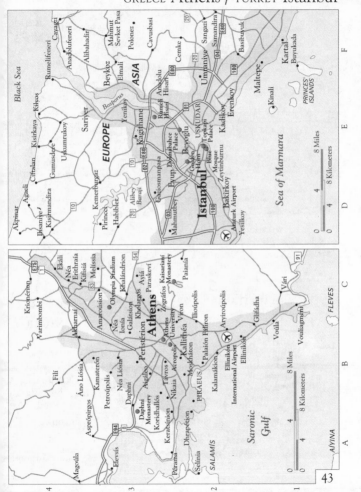

Africa NORTHERN

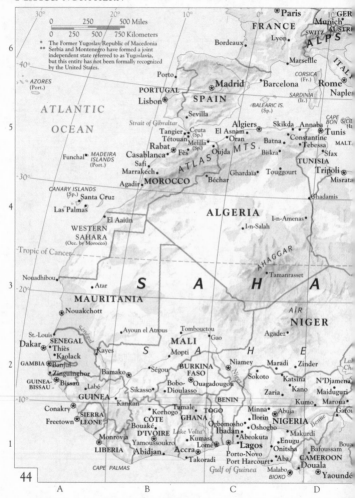

ATLANTIC OCEAN

AZORES (Port.)

MADEIRA ISLANDS (Port.)
Funchal

CANARY ISLANDS (Sp.)
Santa Cruz
Las Palmas

0   250   500 Miles
0   250   500   750 Kilometers

* The Former Yugoslav Republic of Macedonia
** Serbia and Montenegro have formed a joint
independent state referred to as Yugoslavia,
but this entity has not been formally recognized
by the United States.

Paris
FRANCE
Bordeaux
Lyon
Munich
SWITZ. AUSTRI
ALPS
Marseille
Porto
CORSICA (Fr.)
Rome
Naples
PORTUGAL
Lisbon
Madrid
SPAIN
Barcelona
SARDINIA (It.)
Sevilla
BALEARIC IS. (Sp.)
Strait of Gibraltar
Algiers
Skikda
Annaba
CAPE BON
Tunis
SICIL (It.)
Tangier
Ceuta (Sp.)
El Asnam
Tétouan
Melilla (Sp.)
Oran
Constantine
MALT.
Rabat
Fès
Oujda
Batna
Tebessa
Sfax
Casablanca
TUNISIA
Safi
Biskra
ATLAS
Ghardaïa
Touggourt
Tripoli
Marrakech
Béchar
Misrata
Agadir
MOROCCO
Ghadamis
El Aaiún
WESTERN SAHARA (Occ. by Morocco)
ALGERIA
I-n-Amenas
I-n-Salah
Tropic of Cancer
Nouadhibou
Atar
AHAGGAR
Tamanrasset
S   A   H   A   R   A
MAURITANIA
Nouakchott
AIR
NIGER
St.-Louis
Ayoun el Atrous
Tombouctou
Agadez
Dakar
SENEGAL
Thiès
Kayes
Gao
Kaolack
MALI
Niamey
Maradi
Zinder
GAMBIA
Banjul
Mopti
N'Djamena
GUINEA-BISSAU
Bissau
Bamako
Ségou
BURKINA FASO
Sokoto
Katsina
Kano
Maiduguri
Zinguinchor
Labé
Sikasso
Bobo-Dioulasso
Ouagadougou
Zaria
Maroua
GUINEA
Kankan
BENIN
TOGO
Minna
Abuja
Kumo
Conakry
SIERRA LEONE
Korhogo
Tamale
GHANA
Ogbomosho
Ilorin
Oshogbo
NIGERIA
Gato
Freetown
Bouaké
CÔTE D'IVOIRE
Kumasi
Ibadan
Abeokuta
Enugu
Makurdi
Bafoussam
Monrovia
Yamoussoukro
Lake Volta
Lomé
Lagos
Onitsha
Aba
Boua
LIBERIA
Abidjan
Accra
Porto-Novo
Malabo
CAMEROON
Douala
CAPE PALMAS
Takoradi
Port Harcourt
BIOKO
Yaoundé
Gulf of Guinea

44

A   B   C   D

30°   20°   10°   0°   10° GER
40°
5
30°
Tropic of Cancer
20°
3
10°
2
10°
1

Africa SOUTHERN

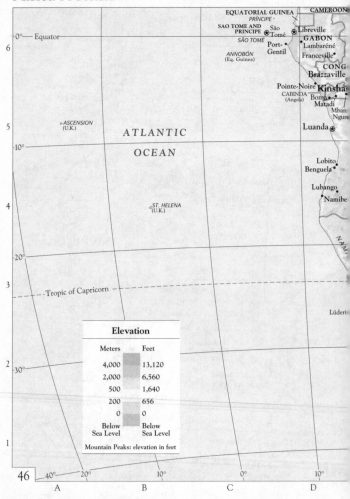

EQUATORIAL GUINEA   CAMEROON

PRÍNCIPE
SAO TOME AND
PRINCIPE   São Tomé   Libreville
SÃO TOMÉ   GABON
Port-   Lambaréné
Gentil   Franceville

ANNOBÓN
(Eq. Guinea)

CONG
Brazzaville   Kinsha

Pointe-Noire
CABINDA   Boma
(Angola)   Matadi
Mban
Ngun

Luanda

Lobito
Benguela

Lubango
Namibe

0° — Equator

6

ASCENSION
(U.K.)   ATLANTIC

5   OCEAN

-10°

ST. HELENA
(U.K.)

4

NAM

-20°

3

-Tropic of Capricorn-

Lüderi

Elevation

Meters		Feet
4,000		13,120
2,000		6,560
500		1,640
200		656
0		0
Below Sea Level		Below Sea Level

Mountain Peaks: elevation in feet

2

-30°

1

46   -40°   -20°   10°   0°   10°

A   B   C   D

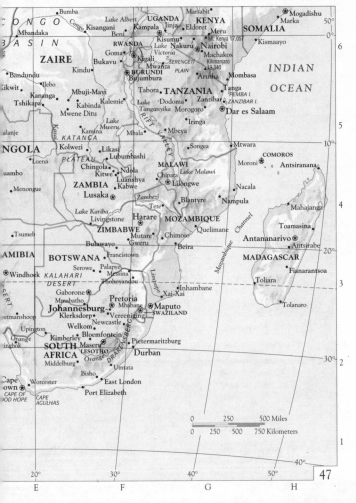

Bumba

CONGO Congo Kisangani Kampala Jinja Eldoret Marsabit Mogadishu
Mbandaka Lake Albert UGANDA KENYA Marka
BASIN Beni Kisumu Meru SOMALIA
RWANDA Goma Lake Nakuru Nairobi Mt. Kenya 17,057
ZAIRE Bukavu Kigali Victoria Machakos Kismaayo
Bandundu Ilebo Kindu BURUNDI SERENGETI Arusha Kilimanjaro Mombasa
Kikwit Bujumbura PLAIN 19,340 INDIAN
Kananga Mbuji-Mayi Tabora TANZANIA Tanga OCEAN
Tshikapa Kabinda Kalemie Lake Dodoma Zanzibar PEMBA I.
Mwene Ditu Tanganyika Morogoro ZANZIBAR I.
alanje Lake Dar es Salaam
Kamina Mweru Mbala RIFT Iringa
NGOLA KATANGA Mbeya VALLEY
Kolwezi Likasi Songea Mtwara
Luena Lubumbashi Moroni COMOROS
uambo PLATEAU Chingola Ndola MALAWI Antsiranana
Menongue Kitwe Luanshya Chipata Lake Malawi Nacala
ZAMBIA Kabwe Lilongwe
Lusaka Zambezi Blantyre Nampula
Lake Kariba Tete MOZAMBIQUE Mahajanga
Tsumeb Livingstone Harare Quelimane
Bulawayo ZIMBABWE Chimoio Antananarivo Toamasina
AMIBIA BOTSWANA Francistown Mutare Beira Antsirabe
Gweru MADAGASCAR
Windhoek KALAHARI Serowe Palapye MOZAMBIQUE Fianarantsoa
eetmanshoop DESERT Messina Limpopo Channel Toliara
Gaborone Thohoyandou Inhambane
Upington Mmabatho Xai-Xai Tolanaro
Orange Johannesburg Pretoria Maputo
ingbok Klerksdorp Mbabane SWAZILAND
Kimberley Welkom Vereeniging
Bloemfontein Newcastle
SOUTH Maseru Pietermaritzburg
AFRICA LESOTHO Durban
Cape Middelburg Orange Umtata
own Bisho DRAKENSBERG
OOD HOPE Worcester East London
CAPE OF CAPE Port Elizabeth
GOOD HOPE AGULHAS

0 250 500 Miles
0 250 500 750 Kilometers

50°
0°
6
5
10°
4
20°
3
2
30°
1
40°

20° 30° 40° 50°
E F G H

47

Middle East

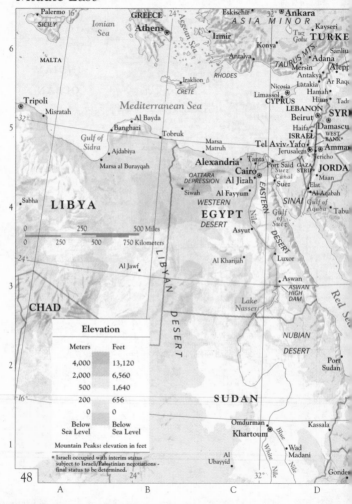

Palermo
SICILY
MALTA
Tripoli
Misratah
Sabha
LIBYA
CHAD
Al Jawf

Ionian Sea
GREECE
Athens
Iraklion
CRETE
Mediterranean Sea
Al Bayda
Banghazi
Gulf of Sidra
Ajdabiya
Marsa al Burayqah

Eskisehir
ASIA MINOR
Ankara
Kayseri
Izmir
Konya
TURKE
Antalya
TAURUS MTS.
Sanliu
Adana
Alepp
RHODES
Mersin
Antakya
Latakia
Ar Raqq
Nicosia
CYPRUS
Limassol
Hamah
Tadr
Hims
LEBANON
SYR
Beirut
Haifa
Damascu
Tobruk
Tel Aviv-Yafo
WEST BANK
Amman
Marsa Matruh
Jerusalem
Jericho
ISRAEL
JORDA
Alexandria
Tanta
GAZA STRIP
Cairo
Port Said
Maan
QATTARA DEPRESSION
Al Jizah
Suez Canal
Elat
Siwah
Al Fayyum
Suez
Al-Aqabah
WESTERN
Gulf of Aqaba
Tabu
EGYPT
SINAI
DESERT
Gulf
Asyut
EASTERN
of
Suez
Al Kharijah
DESERT
Luxor
Red Sea
Aswan
ASWAN HIGH DAM
Lake Nasser
LIBYAN
NUBIAN
DESERT
DESERT
Port Sudan
SUDAN
Omdurman
Kassala
Khartoum
Blue
Wad Madani
White
Nile
Al Ubayyid
Gonder

0   250   500 Miles
0   250   500   750 Kilometers

Elevation

Meters	Feet
4,000	13,120
2,000	6,560
500	1,640
200	656
0	0
Below Sea Level	Below Sea Level

Mountain Peaks: elevation in feet

* Israeli occupied with interim status
subject to Israeli/Palestinian negotiations -
final status to be determined.

48

A   B   C   D

Erzurum • Mt. Ararat 16,853 • AZERBAIJAN • Ashgabat • TURKMENISTAN • KOPET MTS.
Lake Van • AZER. • Ardabil • Caspian Sea
• Diyarbakir • Tabriz • Aras • Gorgan • Mashhad
• Orumiyeh • Lake Urmia • Rasht • Qazvin • ELBURZ MTS. • Sari
• Hasakah • Mosul • Tehran • Mt. Damavand 18,606 • Herat
• Karkuk • Irbil • Hamadan • Qom • Kashan • DASHT-E KAVIR • AFGHANISTAN
• Bayji • Bakhtaran • Khorramabad • IRAN • Birjand • Farah
Abu • IRAQ • Baqubah • Esfahan • Zabol
• Ar Ramadi • Baghdad • Al Hillah • Yazd
• Karbala • An Najaf • Ad Diwaniyah • Ahvaz • Kerman • Zahedan
SYRIAN • An Nasiriyah • Abadan • Shiraz • PAKISTAN
DESERT • Al Basrah • KUWAIT • Bandar-e Bushehr • Iranshahr
AN NAFUD • Kuwait • Persian Gulf • Bandar-e Abbas • Strait of Hormuz
• Hail • AD DAHNA • Ad Dammam • Al Khasab • OMAN • Jask • Bandar Beheshti
• Buraydah • Manama • BAHRAIN • Dubayy • Gulf of Oman
• Riyadh • Al Mubarraz • Doha • Abu Dhabi • Suhar
• Al Hufuf • QATAR • Al Buraymi • Muscat
• Harad • UNITED ARAB EMIRATES • Ibri • Sur
• Medina • JABAL TUWAYQ • SAUDI ARABIA • OMAN • MASIRAH
ddah • Mecca • At Taif • ARABIAN • RUB AL KHALI
• As Sulayyil • Dawkah • Arabian Sea
• Abha • PENINSULA • Salalah
RITREA • Sanaa • Saywun • Sayhut
• Massawa • Al Hudaydah • Al Mukalla
Asmara • Taizz • Ahwar • YEMEN
• Bab al Mandab • Aden • SOCOTRA (Yemen)
THIOPIA • DJIBOUTI • Gulf of Aden • SOMALIA

Tel Aviv - Yafo - Jerusalem ISRAEL / Cairo EGYPT

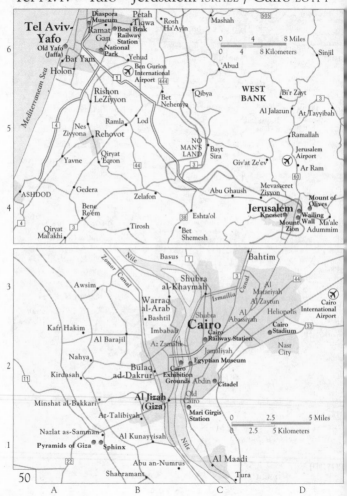

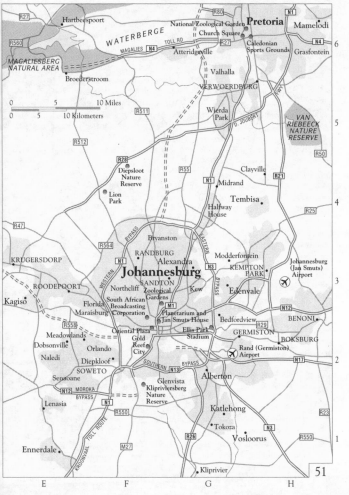

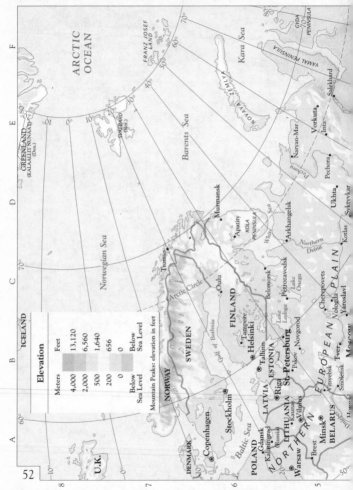

Elevation

Meters	Feet
4,000	13,120
2,000	6,560
500	1,640
200	656
0	0
Below Sea Level	Below Sea Level

Mountain Peaks: elevation in feet

ARCTIC OCEAN

FRANZ JOSEF LAND

GYDA PENINSULA

Kara Sea

YAMAL PENINSULA

Salekhard

GREENLAND (KALAALLIT NUNAAT) (Den.)

SPITSBERGEN (Nor.)

NOVAYA ZEMLYA

Vorkuta

Inta

Barents Sea

Naryan-Mar

Pechora

Norwegian Sea

Murmansk

Apatity

KOLA PENINSULA

White Sea

Arkhangelsk

Ukhta

Syktyvkar

Northern Dvina

Kotlas

ICELAND

Tromsø

Arctic Circle

Oulu

FINLAND

Belomorsk

Petrozavodsk

Lake Onega

Cherepovets

EUROPEAN PLAIN

Vologda

Yaroslavl

NORWAY

SWEDEN

Gulf of Bothnia

Tampere

Helsinki

Lake Ladoga

Novgorod

Tver

Moscow

Tallinn

ESTONIA

St. Petersburg

Pskov

Rzhev

Smolensk

Stockholm

Riga

LATVIA

DENMARK

Copenhagen

Baltic Sea

LITHUANIA

Kaunas

Vilnius

Minsk

BELARUS

U.K.

POLAND

Gdansk

Kaliningrad (Russia)

NORTHERN

Warsaw

Brest

52

Asia NORTHEASTERN

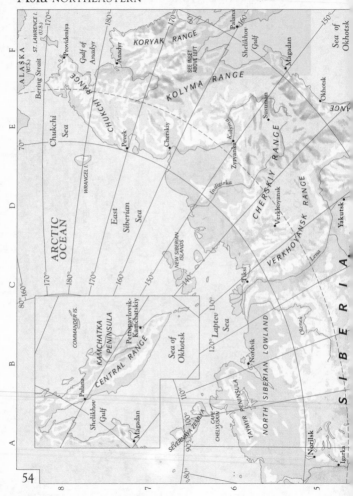

Gulf of Anadyr
KORYAK RANGE
Palana
Shelikhov Gulf
Magadan
Sea of Okhotsk

Providentya
ST. LAWRENCE I. (U.S.)
ALASKA (U.S.)
Bering Strait
CHUKCHI RANGE
Anadyr
KOLYMA RANGE
SEE INSET ABOVE LEFT

Okhotsk

Chukchi Sea
Pevek
Cherskiy
Kolyma
Zyryanka
Susuman
CHERSKIY RANGE

WRANGEL I.
East Siberian Sea
Indigirka
Verkhoyansk
VERKHOYANSK RANGE
Yakutsk

ARCTIC OCEAN
NEW SIBERIAN ISLANDS
Lena

Tiksi

COMMANDER IS.
KAMCHATKA PENINSULA
Petropavlovsk-Kamchatskiy
CENTRAL RANGE
Sea of Okhotsk

Laptev Sea
Nordvik
Olenek

S I B E R I A

Palana
Shelikhov Gulf
Magadan

TAYMYR PENINSULA
CAPE CHELYUSKIN
SEVERNAYA ZEMLYA
NORTH SIBERIAN LOWLAND
Norilsk
Igarka

54

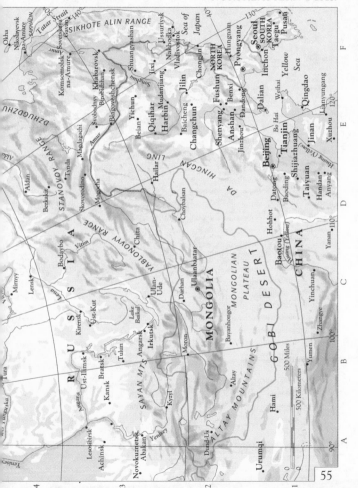

Obha
Nikolayevsk-na-Amure
Tatar Strait
SAKHALIN
Sovetskaya Gavan
SIKHOTE ALIN RANGE
Sea of Japan
JAPAN

F

Komsomolsk-na-Amure
Khabarovsk
Bikin
Bjobidzhan
Blagoveshchensk
Shuangyashan
Jiamusi
Suizhong
Jixi
Mudanjiang
Vladivostok
Ussuriyska
Nakhodka
Chongjin
Hungnam
Pyongyang
NORTH KOREA
Seoul
Inchon
Taegu
Pusan
SOUTH KOREA
Yellow Sea

Yichun
Jilin
Fushun
Benxi

Komsomolsk-na-Amure
Amur
Magdagachi
Svobodny
Skovorodino
Yichun
Beian
Qiqihar
Harbin
Baicheng
Changchun
Shenyang
Anshan
Jinzhou
Dandong
Dalian
Weihai
Qingdao
Lianyungang

E

DZHUGDZHUR
STANOVOY RANGE
Aldan
Berkakit
Tynda
Amur
Hailar
DA HINGGAN LING
Beijing
Tangshan
Tianjin
Jinan
Xuzhou

120°

D

Aldan
YABLONOVYY RANGE
Chita
Vitim
Choybalsan
Hohhot
Datong
Baoding
Shijiazhuang
Taiyuan
Handan
Anyang
CHINA

Mirnyy
Bodaybo
Lensk
Kirensk
Ust-Kut
Chita
Ulan-Ude
Lake Baikal
Darhan
Ulaanbaatar
MONGOLIA
MONGOLIAN PLATEAU
GOBI DESERT
Baotou
Yellow River
Yinchuan
Yanan
Huang (Yellow)

110°

C

RUSSIA
Ust-Ilimsk
Bratsk
Kansk
Angara
Tulun
Irkutsk
SAYAN MTS
Bayanhongor
Moron
Zhangye
Yumen

100°

B

500 Miles
500 Kilometers

Tura
Leosibirsk
Achinsk
Abakan
Novokuznetsk
Yenisey
Kyzyl
Altay
ALTAY MOUNTAINS
Dund-Us
Hami
Urumqi

90°

A

55

4   3   2   1

MOSCOW RUSSIA

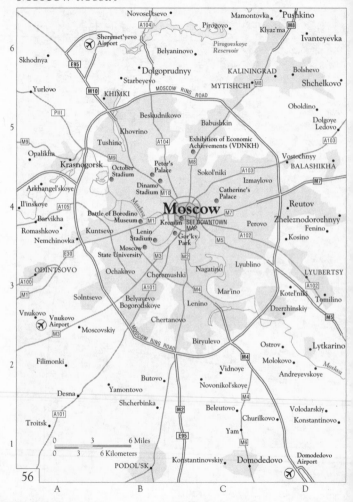

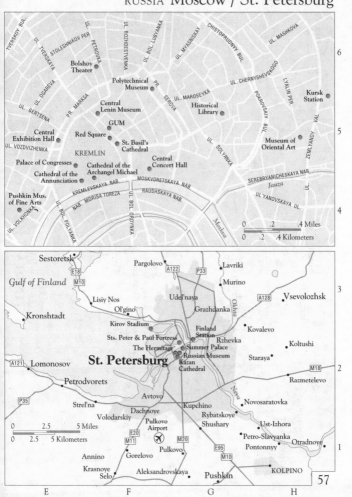

Moscow map labels:

TVERSKOY BUL.
UL. TVERSKAYA
UL. STOLESHNIKOV PER.
UL. OGAREVA
UL. GERTSENA
UL. PETROVKA
PR. MARKSA
UL. ROZHDESTVENKA
UL. BOL. LUBYANKA
UL. MYASNISKAY
PR. SEROVA
CHISTOPRUDNYY BUL.
UL. MAROSEYKA
UL. CHERNYSHEVSKOGO
UL. MASHKOVA
LYALIN PER.
PONROVSKIY BUL.
ZEMLYANOY VAL

Bolshoy Theater
Polytechnical Museum
Central Lenin Museum
GUM
Central Exhibition Hall
Red Square
Historical Library
Kursk Station
St. Basil's Cathedral
KREMLIN
UL. VOZDVIZHENKA
Palace of Congresses
Cathedral of the Annunciation
Cathedral of the Archangel Michael
Central Concert Hall
UL. SOLYANKA
Museum of Oriental Art
SEREBRYANICHESKAYA NAB.
Jauza
Pushkin Mus. of Fine Arts
KREMLEVSKAYA NAB.
MOSKVORETSKAYA NAB.
KREMLEVSKAYA NAB.
NAB. MORISA TOREZA
RAUSHSKAYA NAB.
UL'YANOVSKAYA UL.
UL. VOLKHONKA
UL. BOL. POLYANKA
UL. BOL. ORDYNKA
Moskva

0   .2   .4 Miles
0   .2   .4 Kilometers

St. Petersburg map labels:

Sestoretsk
Gulf of Finland
Pargolovo
Lavriki
E18
A122
P33
M10
Murino
A128
Vsevolozhsk
Lisiy Nos
Udel'naya
Ol'gino
Grazhdanka
Okha
Kronshtadt
Kirov Stadium
Sts. Peter & Paul Fortress
Finland Station
Rzhevka
Kovalevo
Koltushi
The Hermitage
Summer Palace
St. Petersburg
Russian Museum
Kazan Cathedral
Staraya
A121
Lomonosov
M18
Petrodvorets
Novosaratovka
Razmetelevo
P35
Strel'na
Avtovo
Dachnoye
Kupchino
Nevа
Volodarskiy
Rybatskoye
Ust-Izhora
Pulkovo Airport
Shushary
Petro-Slavyanka
Otradnoye
E20
M11
M20
Pontonnyy
E95
Annino
Gorelovo
Pulkovo
M10
Krasnoye Selo
Aleksandrovskaya
Pushkin
KOLPINO

0   2.5   5 Miles
0   2.5   5 Kilometers

57

E   F   G   H

Asia SOUTHWESTERN

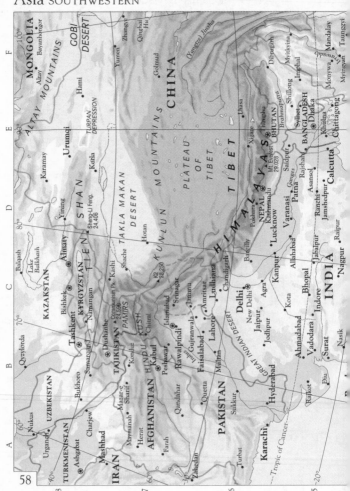

58

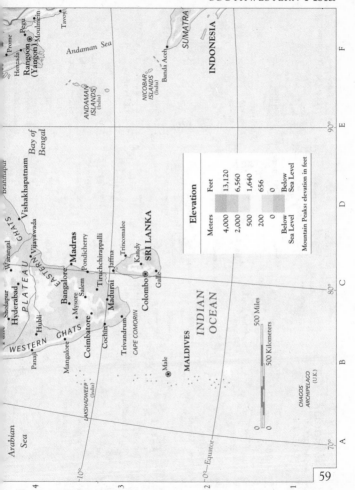

Prome • Pegu
Henzada •
Rangoon ✸ Moulmein
(Yangon)

Tavoy •

Andaman Sea

SUMATRA

INDONESIA

Banda Aceh •

NICOBAR
ISLANDS
(India)

ANDAMAN
ISLANDS
(India)

Bay of
Bengal

Brahmapur •

Vishakhapatnam

EASTERN GHATS

Warangal •
Vijayawada
Madras
Pondicherry
Tiruchchirappalli
Jaffna
Trincomalee
Kandy SRI LANKA
Colombo ✸
Galle

Elevation	
Meters	Feet
4,000	13,120
2,000	6,560
500	1,640
200	656
0	0
Below Sea Level	Below Sea Level

Mountain Peaks: elevation in feet

Sholapur •
Hyderabad •
PLATEAU
Bangalore •
Mysore •
Salem •
Madurai •

Panaji •
Hubli •

Mangalore •

WESTERN GHATS

Coimbatore •

Cochin •

Trivandrum •

CAPE COMORIN

INDIAN
OCEAN

• Male
MALDIVES

LAKSHADWEEP
(India)

Arabian
Sea

500 Miles

500 Kilometers

CHAGOS
ARCHIPELAGO
(U.K.)

Equator

Arabian
Sea

90°

80°

70°

10°

0°

Asia SOUTHEASTERN

60

MONGOLIA

MONGOLIAN PLATEAU

GOBI DESERT

CHINA

Yinchuan

Baotou

Hohhot

Datong

Shenyang
Fushun
Benxi
Anshan

Jinzhou

Dandong

NORTH KOREA

Hungnam

Pyongyang

Seoul
Inchon

SOUTH KOREA

Taegu

Pusan

Sea of Japan

Korea Strait

JAPAN

Tokyo
Yokohama
Nagoya
Kyoto
Kobe
Osaka

HONSHU

Hiroshima
Kitakyushu
Nagasaki
Kumamoto
Kagoshima

SHIKOKU
Kochi

KYUSHU

PACIFIC OCEAN

Tropic of Cancer

Beijing

Tianjin

Dalian

Weihai

Qingdao

Jinan

Shijiazhuang

Taiyuan
Handan
Anyang

Baoding

Zhengzhou

Luoyang

Nanyang
Xiangfan

Xuzhou

Grand Canal Lianyungang

Bo Hai

Yellow Sea

Hefei

Nanjing

Suzhou
Wuhu

Shanghai

Hangzhou
Ningbo

Wenzhou

East China Sea

Taipei

Taichung

TAIWAN

Kaohsiung

RYUKYU ISLANDS (Japan)

OKINAWA
Naha

Taiwan Strait

LUZON

Laoag

Baguio

Luzon Strait

Lanzhou

Xian

Baoji

Yanan

Wuhan

Yichang

Changde

Dongting Hu

Changsha

Shaoyang

Hengyang

Nanchang

Poyang Hu

Jingdezhen

Chang (Yangtze)

Huang (Yellow)

Ganzhou

Fuzhou

Xiamen

Shantou

Guangzhou

Hong Kong (U.K.)

Macau (Port.)

Chengdu

Chongqing

Zigong

Zunyi

Guiyang

Guilin

Liuzhou

Wuzhou

Nanning

Zhanjiang

Haikou

HAINAN

Gulf of Tonkin

Haiphong

Hanoi

Xichang

Panzhihua

Panzhihua

Kunming

Gejiu

Pingxiang

Mekong

Xining

Elevation

Meters	Feet
4,000	13,120
2,000	6,560
500	1,640
200	656
0	0
Below Sea Level	Below Sea Level

Mountain Peaks: elevation in feet

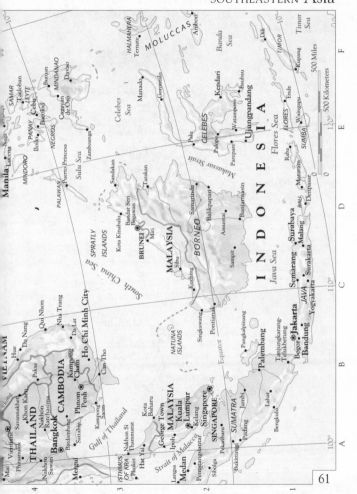

Taipei TAIWAN / Manila PHILIPPINES

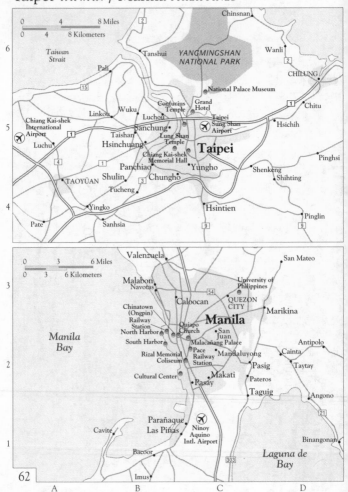

0   4   8 Miles
0   4   8 Kilometers

Chinsnan

2

Taiwan Strait

6

Tanshui

YANGMINGSHAN NATIONAL PARK

Wanli

Pali

2

CHILUNG

15

National Palace Museum

1   Chitu

Linkou   Wuku   Luchou   Confucius Temple   Grand Hotel

Chiang Kai-shek International Airport

Taipei   Sung Shan Airport

Hsichih

Luchu   1   Taishan   Sanchung   Lung Shan Temple   Taipei

5

4   1   Hsinchuang   Chiang Kai-shek Memorial Hall

Pinghsi

Panchiao   Yungho   Shenkeng   Shihting

TAOYÜAN   Shulin   3   Chungho

Tucheng

Yingko   Hsintien

4   Pate   Sanhsia   9   Pinglin

Hsinten   9

---

0   3   6 Miles
0   3   6 Kilometers

Valenzuela   San Mateo

3

Malabon   54   University of Philippines

Navotas   Caloocan   QUEZON CITY

Chinatown (Ongpin) Railway Station   Marikina

North Harbor   Quiapo Church   Manila   San Juan

Manila Bay   South Harbor   Malacañang Palace   Antipolo

Pace Railway Station   Mandaluyong   Cainta

Rizal Memorial Coliseum   Makati   Pasig   Taytay

2

Cultural Center   Pasay   Pateros   Angono

Taguig   21

Parañaque   Las Piñas   Ninoy Aquino Intl. Airport   Binangonan

Cavite   1

Bacoor   Laguna de Bay

303

62   Imus

A   B   C   D

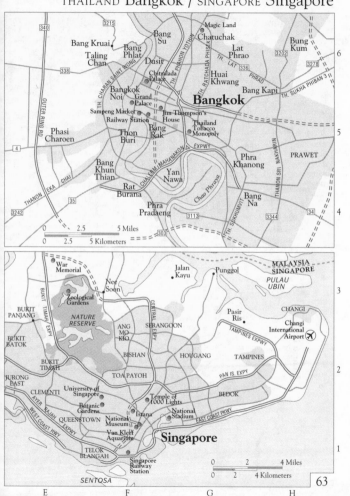

Jakarta INDONESIA / Delhi - New Delhi INDIA

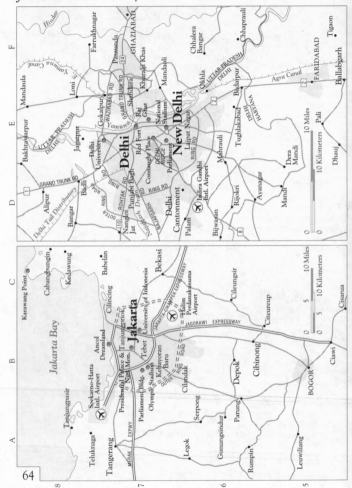

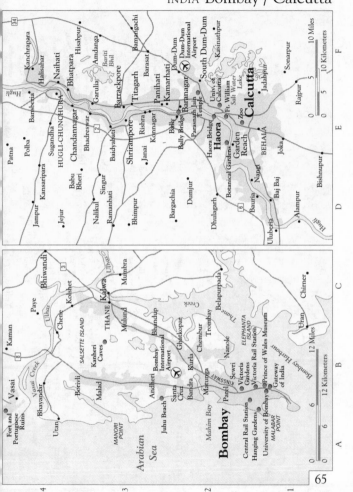

Far East

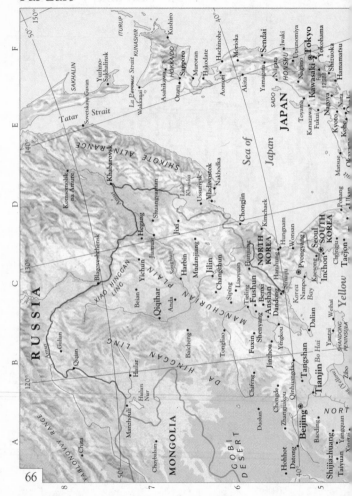

66

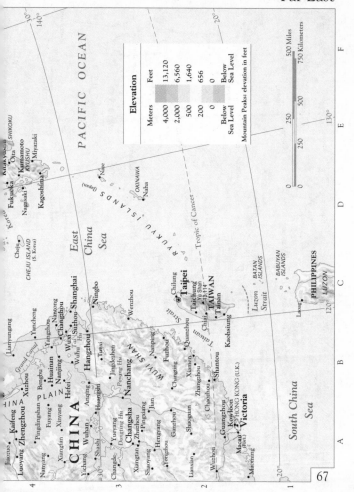

PACIFIC OCEAN

East China Sea

South China Sea

Elevation

Meters	Feet
4,000	13,120
2,000	6,560
500	1,640
200	656
0	0
Below Sea Level	Below Sea Level

Mountain Peaks: elevation in feet

0   250   500 Miles
0   250   500   750 Kilometers

KANTO-YAMA
SHIKOKU
Kii-Saki
Fukuoka • Oita • Kumamoto
Nagasaki • KYUSHU
Korea Kagoshima • Miyazaki
Cheju
CHEJU ISLAND
(S. Korea)

Naze

OKINAWA
Naha
(Japan)

R Y U K Y U   I S L A N D S

Tropic of Cancer

Lianyungang
Yancheng
Suzhou Shanghai
Grand Canal Changzhou
Yangzhou Wuxi
Huainan Nantong Tai Hu
Xinyang Nanjing Wuhu Suzhou Hangzhou Ningbo
Hefei Tai Hu
Bengbu
Pingdingshan
Fuyang
Nanyang
Anqing
Huangshi
Wuhan
Yichang
Shashi
Changde Dongting Hu
Xiangtan Zhuzhou
Shaoyang
Yongzhou Hengyang
Lianjiang
Maoming

Jingdezhen
Poyang Hu
Nanchang
Pingxiang
Ji'an
Ganzhou
Shaoguan

Tunxi
Nanping
Changting
Zhangzhou

WUYI SHAN

Wenzhou

Chilung
Taipei
Taichung Yu Shan 13,114
Chiai TAIWAN
Tainan
Kaohsiung

Taiwan Strait

Fuzhou
Quanzhou
Xiamen
Zhangzhou
Shantou

Guangzhou
Kowloon
Victoria HONG KONG (U.K.)
Macau (Port.)
Wuzhou

Lanzou
Luoyang Kaifeng
Zhengzhou
Xuzhou

CHINA

PLAIN

CHINA

Changsha

Lianyungang

Ningbo

Lúzon Strait
Lanao
BATAN ISLANDS
BABUYAN ISLANDS
LUZON
PHILIPPINES

140°
130°
120°

30°
20°

A   B   C   D   E   F
1   2   3   4

Tokyo JAPAN

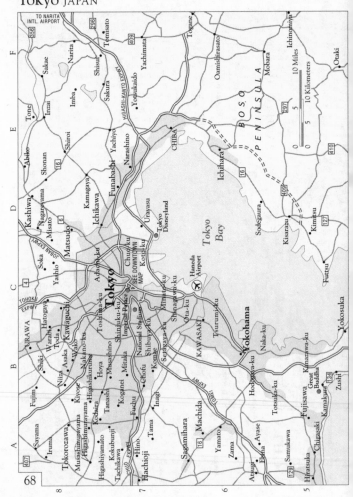

68

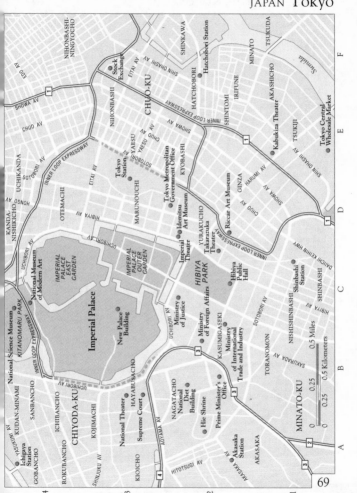

Osaka - Kyoto - Kobe JAPAN

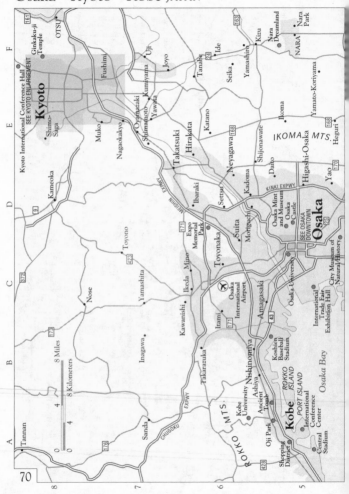

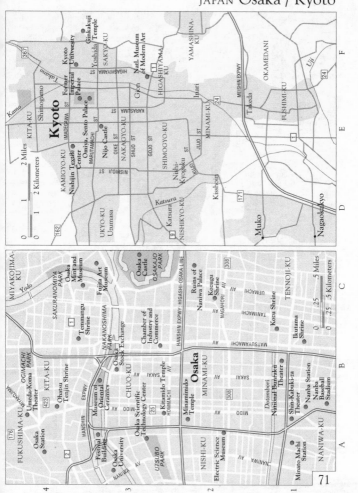

Kyoto

KITA-KU
KAMIGYO-KU
UKYO-KU
Uzumasa
NAKAGYO-KU
SHIMOGYO-KU
Nishi-Kyogoku
NISHIKYO-KU
SAKYO-KU
HIGASHIYAMA-KU
YAMASHINA-KU
MINAMI-KU
FUSHIMI-KU
OKAMEDANI

Takano
Kamo
Shirogawo
Katsura

Ginkakuji Temple
Kyoto University
Yoshida Temple
Natl. Museum of Modern Art
Gion
Inari
Former Imperial Palace
Omiya, Sento Palace
Nijo Castle
Nishijin Textile Center

MADEGAWA ST
IMADEGAWA ST
MARUTAMACHI
OIKE ST
SHIJO ST
GOJO ST
JUJO ST
KARASUMA ST
HORIKAWA ST
NISHIOJI ST

Kisshoin
Takeda
Muko
Nagaokakyo

MEISHIN EXPWY
367
162
9
24
171
Uji

0 1 2 Miles
0 1 2 Kilometers

Osaka

MIYAKOJIMA-KU
FUKUSHIMA-KU
KITA-KU
CHUO-KU
NISHI-KU
MINAMI-KU
TENNOJI-KU
NANIWA-KU

Yodo
SAKURANOMIYA PARK
NAKANOSHIMA PARK
OSAKAJO PARK
UTSUBO PARK
OGIMACHI PARK

Osaka Castle
Osaka Mint and Museum
Fujita Art Museum
Temmangu Shrine
Osaka Stock Exchange
Chamber of Industry and Commerce
Ruins of Naniwa Palace
Korugu Shrine
Kozu Shrine
Ikutama Shrine
Minamimido Temple
Kitamido Temple
Museum of Oriental Ceramics
Osaka Scientific Technology Center
Festival Building
Osaka University
Umeda-Koma Theater
Ohatsu Tenjin Shrine
Osaka Station
National Bunraku Theater
Dotombori
Shin-Kabuki-za Theater
Nanba Station
Namba Baseball Stadium
Electric Science Museum
Minato Machi Station

HANSHIN EXPWY
HANSHIN EXPWY: HIGASHI-OSAKA LINE
MIDO AV
SAKAI AV
NAGAHORI AV
MATSUYAMACHI AV
TANIMACHI AV
UEMACHI AV
HOMMACHI AV
NANIWA AV
NAGAHORI

176
2
423
25
308

0 .25 .5 Miles
0 .25 .5 Kilometers

71

Seoul SOUTH KOREA

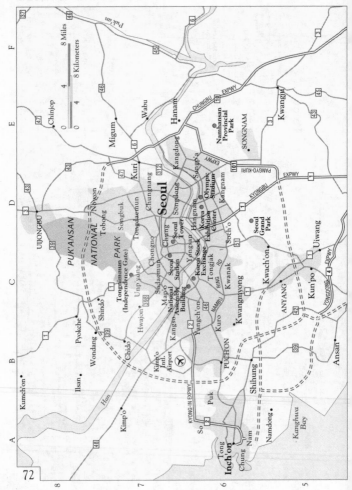

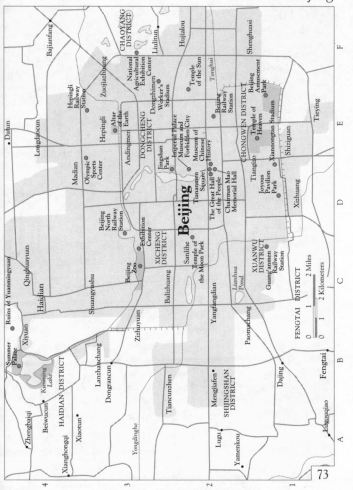

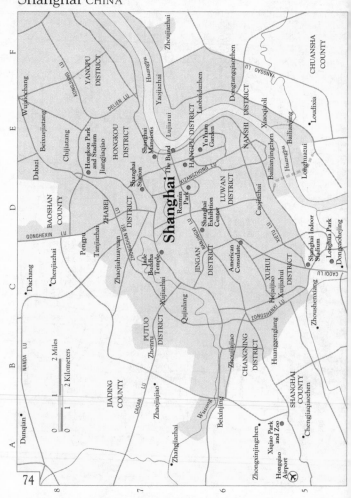

Shanghai CHINA

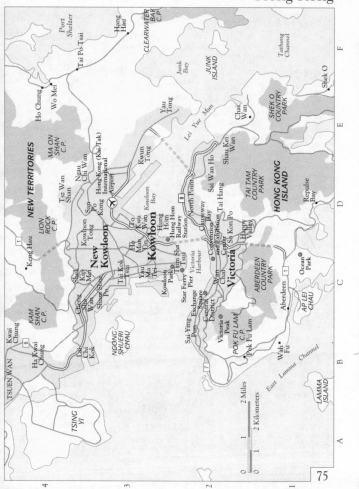

Australia - New Zealand - New Guinea

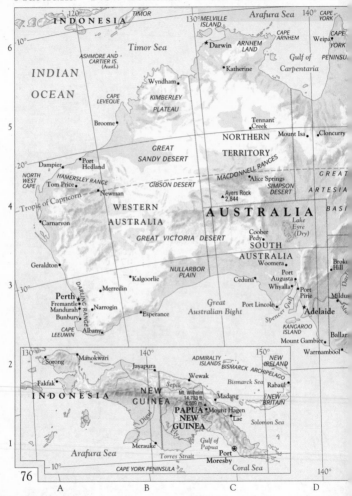

New Guinea - New Zealand - Australia

SEE INSET
BELOW LEFT

SOLOMON
ISLANDS

150°

160°

170°

10°

6

Elevation

Meters	Feet
4,000	13,120
2,000	6,560
500	1,640
200	656
0	0
Below Sea Level	Below Sea Level

Mountain Peaks: elevation in feet

Coral Sea

Great Barrier Reef

rns

Townsville

Charters
Towers

Bowen

Mackay

DIVIDING

Emerald

Rockhampton

Gladstone

ngreach

Bundaberg

JEENSLAND

Maryborough

arleville

Roma

Gympie

Toowoomba

Brisbane

Southport

Lismore

Moree

Grafton

Bourke

NEW

Tamworth

Armidale

Port Macquarie

OUTH

Dubbo

Taree

VALES

Orange

Newcastle

Griffith

Sydney

igga Wagga

Canberra

Wollongong

lbury

AUSTL. CAP. TERR.

endigo

Mt. Kosciusko
7,310

CTORIA

Melbourne

elong

ss Strait

RANGE

GREAT

DIVIDING

RANGE

20°

5

PACIFIC

OCEAN

*NORFOLK
ISLAND*
(Australia)

30°

4

3

*Tasman
Sea*

Whangarei

Auckland

Hamilton

Tauranga

NORTH ISLAND

New Plymouth

Rotorua

NEW ZEALAND

Gisborne

Cook
Strait

Napier

Nelson

Palmerston
North

Greymouth

Wellington

SOUTHERN ALPS

Mt. Cook
12,349

Timaru

SOUTH ISLAND

Christchurch

Devonport

Launceston

Queenstown

Hobart

TASMANIA

40°

2

Dunedin

Invercargill

STEWART ISLAND

0	250	500	750 Miles
0	250	500	750	1,000 Kilometers

150°

160°

170°

180°

1

77

E

F

G

H

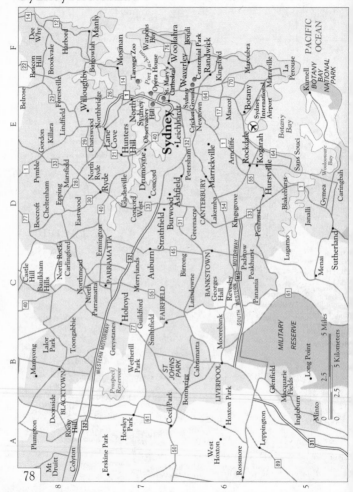

Sydney AUSTRALIA

78

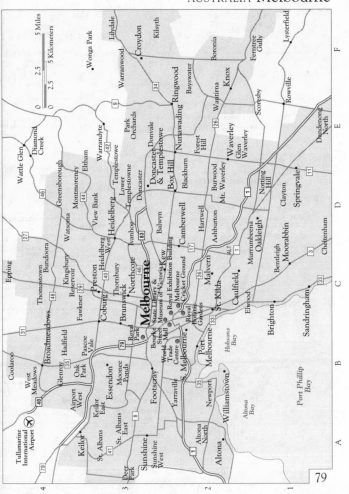

Pacific

NORTH PACIFI

JAPAN
Tokyo

MIDWAY ISLAND (U.S.)
HAWAIIAN ISLAN

NORTHERN MARIANA ISLANDS (U.S.)

WAKE ISLANDS (U.S.)

GUAM (U.S.)

MARSHALL ISLANDS

RATAK CHAIN

RALIK CHAIN

Koror
YAP ISLANDS
PALAU

PALMYRA ATOLL (U.S.)

CAROLINE   ISLANDS
Palikir
FEDERATED STATES OF MICRONESIA

Majuro

HOWLAND ISLAND (U.S.)
BAKER ISLAND (U.S.)

JARVI ISLAN (U.S.)

Tarawa

Javapura
PAPUA NEW GUINEA
NEW IRELAND
Yaren
NAURU
KIRIBATI
PHOENIX ISLANDS
KIRIBATI

Ambon
NEW GUINEA
Madang Rabaul
INDONESIA
Merauke
Mt. Wilhem
14,793
Lae NEW BRITAIN
Port Moresby
BOUGAINVILLE
SOLOMON ISLANDS
Honiara
TUVALU
Funafuti
TOKELAU (N.Z.)

Arafura Sea
MELVILLE ISLAND
CAPE YORK
WALLIS AND FUTUNA
W. SAMOA
AMERICAN SAMOA (U.S.)
Apia Pago Pago

AUSTRALIA
GREAT DIVIDING RANGE
Coral Sea
VANUATU
NEW CALEDONIA (Fr.)
Port-Vila
Suva
FIJI
TONGA
NIUE (N.Z.)
Nukualofa
COOK ISLAND (N
Avar

Nouméa

Brisbane

NORFOLK ISLAND (AUST.)
KERMADEC ISLANDS (N.Z.)

Adelaide
Mt. Kosciusko
7,310
Sydney
Canberra
Melbourne
Tasman Sea
NORTH ISLAND
Auckland
SOUTH

Bass Strait
TASMANIA
NEW ZEALAND
Christchurch
Mt. Cook
12,349
SOUTH ISLAND
Wellington
CHATHAM ISLANDS (N.Z.)

STEWART ISLAND
AUCKLAND ISLANDS (N.Z.)

80

A   B   C   D

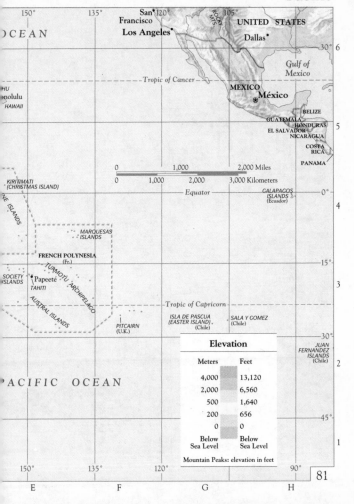

150° 135° 120° 105°

San
Francisco
Los Angeles•

OCEAN

ROCKY MTS.

UNITED STATES

Dallas•

30° 6

Gulf of
Mexico

─ Tropic of Cancer ─

HU
onolulu
HAWAII

MEXICO
México ⊛

BELIZE

GUATEMALA
HONDURAS
EL SALVADOR
NICARAGUA

COSTA
RICA

PANAMA

0		1,000		2,000 Miles	
0	1,000	2,000		3,000 Kilometers	

KIRITIMATI
(CHRISTMAS ISLAND)

─ Equator ─

GALAPAGOS
ISLANDS
(Ecuador)

0° 4

NE ISLANDS

MARQUESAS
ISLANDS

FRENCH POLYNESIA
(Fr.)

15° 3

SOCIETY
ISLANDS •Papeete
TAHITI

TUAMOTU ARCHIPELAGO

AUSTRAL ISLANDS

─ Tropic of Capricorn ─

ISLA DE PASCUA
(EASTER ISLAND)
(Chile)

SALA Y GOMEZ
(Chile)

30°

PITCAIRN
(U.K.)

JUAN
FERNANDEZ
ISLANDS
(Chile)

2

PACIFIC   OCEAN

Elevation

Meters	Feet
4,000	13,120
2,000	6,560
500	1,640
200	656
0	0
Below Sea Level	Below Sea Level

Mountain Peaks: elevation in feet

45° 1

150° 135° 120° 90°

E   F   G   H

Arctic

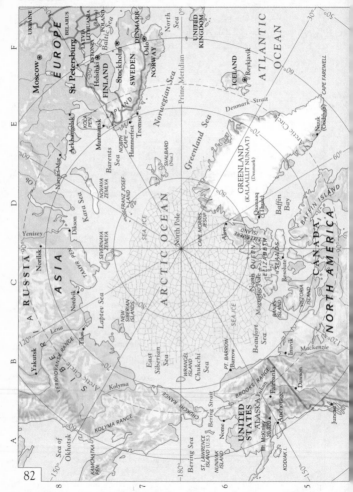

Antarctic

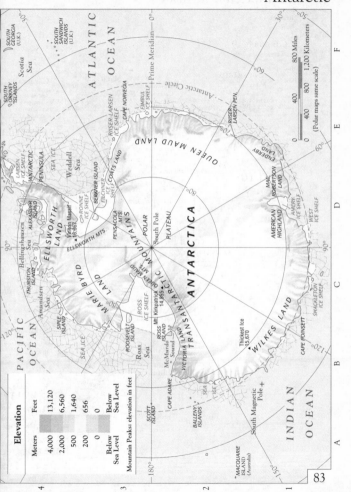

Elevation

Meters	Feet
4,000	13,120
2,000	6,560
500	1,640
200	656
0	0
Below Sea Level	Below Sea Level

▲ Mountain Peaks: elevation in feet

ATLANTIC OCEAN

SOUTH GEORGIA (U.K.)

SOUTH SANDWICH ISLANDS (U.K.)

Scotia Sea

SOUTH ORKNEY ISLANDS

Prime Meridian

Antarctic Circle

RISER-LARSEN ICE SHELF

CAPE NORVEGIA

FIMBUL ICE SHELF

RISER-LARSEN PEN.

QUEEN MAUD LAND

ENDERBY LAND

Weddell Sea

LARSEN ICE SHELF

ANTARCTIC PENINSULA

BERKNER ISLAND

COATS LAND

FILCHNER ICE SHELF

RONNE ICE SHELF

Vinson Massif 16,066

PENSACOLA MTS.

POLAR PLATEAU

South Pole

ANTARCTICA

MAC ROBERTSON LAND

AMERY ICE SHELF

WEST ICE SHELF

AMERICAN HIGHLAND

ALEXANDER ISLAND

Bellingshausen Sea

ELLSWORTH LAND

ELLSWORTH MTS.

QUEEN MAUD MTS.

TRANSANTARCTIC MOUNTAINS

WILKES LAND

SHACKLETON ICE SHELF

CAPE POINSETT

THURSTON ISLAND

Amundsen Sea

MARIE BYRD LAND

SIPLE ISLAND

SEA ICE

ROSS ICE SHELF

Mt. Kirkpatrick 14,855

Thickest Ice ▲ 15,670

PACIFIC OCEAN

ROOSEVELT ISLAND

Ross Sea

McMurdo Sound

VICTORIA LAND

CAPE ADARE

SEA ICE

SCOTT ISLAND

BALLENY ISLANDS

South Magnetic Pole +

INDIAN OCEAN

*MACQUARIE ISLAND (Australia)

| | | 400 | 800 Miles |
| 0 | 400 | 800 | 1,200 Kilometers |

(Polar maps same scale)

83

South America NORTHERN

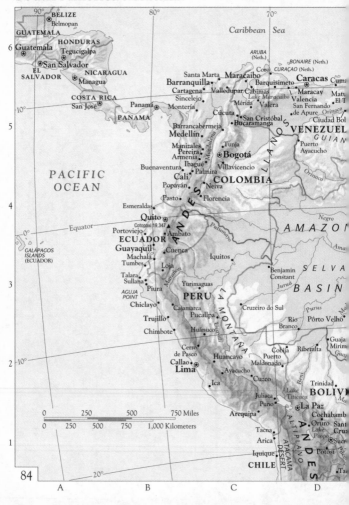

Caribbean Sea

PACIFIC OCEAN

BELIZE
Belmopan
GUATEMALA
⊛Guatemala
HONDURAS
Tegucigalpa⊛
⊛San Salvador **NICARAGUA**
EL SALVADOR ⊛Managua
COSTA RICA
San José⊛ Panamá
PANAMA

Santa Marta Maracaibo Coro
Barranquilla Valledupar Cabimas Barquisimeto **Caracas** Cumá
Cartagena Mérida Lake Maracaibo Valencia Maracay Matu
Sincelejo Valera San Fernando El T
Montería de Apure Orinoco
Cúcuta San Cristóbal Ciudad Bol
Barrancabermeja ⊛Bucaramanga **VENEZUELA**
Medellín GUIAN
Manizales Tunja Puerto
Pereira ⊛**Bogotá** Ayacucho
Armenia Ibagué Villavicencio
Buenaventura Palmira Orinoco
Cali **COLOMBIA**
Popayán Neiva
Pasto Florencia

ARUBA (Neth.)
BONAIRE (Neth.)
CURAÇAO (Neth.)

LLANOS

Negro

Esmeraldas
Quito⊛
Cotopaxi 19,347
Portoviejo **ECUADOR** Ambato
Guayaquil Cuenca
Machalá Loja Iquitos
Tumbes Marañón
Talara Benjamin
Sullana Piura Yurimaguas Constant Jurúa
AGUJA POINT **PERU**
Chiclayo Cajamarca Cruzeiro do Sul Purús
Trujillo Pucallpa Rio Pôrto Velho
Chimbote Huánuco Branco

AMAZON
SELVA
BASIN

Equator

GALAPAGOS ISLANDS (ECUADOR)

LA MONTAÑA
Putumayo

Cerro
de Pasco Huancayo Cobija Riberalta Guaja
Callao Puerto Mirim
Lima⊛ Ayacucho Maldonado Guaj
Ica Cuzco Beni
Juliaca Lake Trinidad **BOLIVI**
Puno Titicaca
Arequipa ⊛**La Paz** Cochabamb
Lake Oruro Sant
Tacna Poopó Cruz
Arica **ALTIPLANO** Sucr
ATACAMA Potosí
Iquique **DESERT** **ANDES**
CHILE Ta

| 0 | 250 | 500 | 750 Miles |
| 0 | 250 | 500 | 750 | 1,000 Kilometers |

84

A   B   C   D

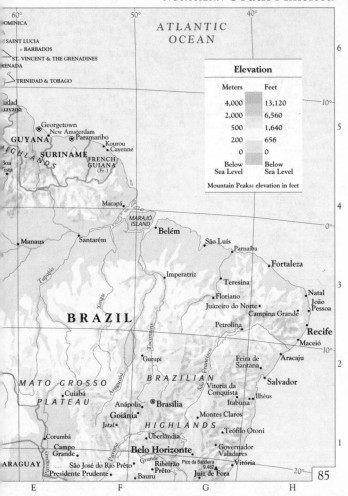

ATLANTIC
OCEAN

60°　　　　　　50°　　　　　　40°

DOMINICA
SAINT LUCIA
BARBADOS
ST. VINCENT & THE GRENADINES
GRENADA
TRINIDAD & TOBAGO

udad
uayana

Georgetown
New Amsterdam
GUYANA
Paramaribo
Kourou
SURINAME
Cayenne
FRENCH
GUIANA
(Fr.)

3oa
ista

Macapá

MARAJÓ
ISLAND
Belém

Manaus
Santarém
São Luís
Parnaíba
Fortaleza

Imperatriz
Teresina
Floriano
Natal
Juàzeiro do Norte
João
Pessoa
Campina Grande
Petrolina
Recife
Maceió

BRAZIL

Gurupi
Feira de
Santana
Aracaju
BRAZILIAN
Salvador
MATO GROSSO
Vitória da
Conquista
Ilhéus
Cuiabá
PLATEAU
Anápolis
Brasília
Itabuna
Goiânia
Montes Claros
Jataí
HIGHLANDS
Teófilo Otoni
Corumbá
Uberlândia
Campo
Grande
Governador
Valadares
Belo Horizonte
Pico da Bandeira
9,482
ARAGUAY
São José do Rio Prêto
Vitória
Ribeirão
PARAGUAY
Presidente Prudente
Prêto
Juiz de Fora
Bauru

Elevation

Meters	Feet
4,000	13,120
2,000	6,560
500	1,640
200	656
0	0
Below Sea Level	Below Sea Level

Mountain Peaks: elevation in feet

6

10°

5

4

0°

3

10°

2

1

20°

E　　　F　　　G　　　H

South America SOUTHERN

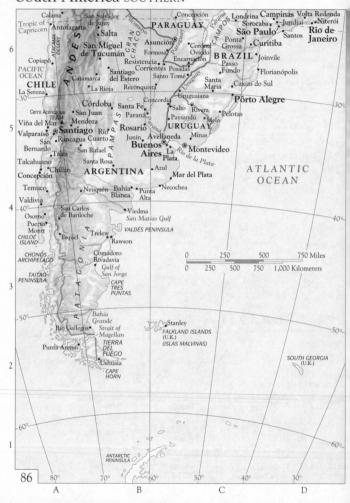

Calama
San Salvador de Jujuy
Tropic of Capricorn
Antofagasta
Salta
San Miguel de Tucumán
Copiapó
PACIFIC OCEAN
Catamarca
Santiago del Estero
CHILE
La Serena
La Rioja
Córdoba
Cerro Aconcagua 22,834
San Juan
Santa Fe
Viña del Mar
Mendoza
Valparaíso
San Bernardo
Rancagua
Rosario
Santiago
Río
Junín
Cuarto
Buenos Aires
Talcahuano
Talca
San Rafael
Santa Rosa
La Plata
Concepción
Chillán
ARGENTINA
Azul
Temuco
Neuquén
Bahía Blanca
Punta Alta
Necochea
Valdivia
Mar del Plata
Osorno
Puerto Montt
San Carlos de Bariloche
Viedma
San Matías Gulf
CHILOÉ ISLAND
Trelew
VALDÉS PENINSULA
CHONOS ARCHIPELAGO
Esquel
Rawson
TAITAO PENINSULA
Comodoro Rivadavia
Gulf of San Jorge
CAPE TRES PUNTAS
PATAGONIA
Bahía Grande
Río Gallegos
Strait of Magellan
Stanley
FALKLAND ISLANDS (U.K.) (ISLAS MALVINAS)
Punta Arenas
TIERRA DEL FUEGO
SOUTH GEORGIA (U.K.)
Ushuaia
CAPE HORN

GRAN CHACO
Pilcomayo
Concepción
PARAGUAY
Asunción
Formosa
Paraná
Coronel Oviedo
CAMPOS
Londrina
Campinas
Volta Redonda
Niterói
Jundiaí
São Paulo
Rio de Janeiro
Ponta Grossa
Curitiba
Santos
BRAZIL
Joinvile
Resistencia
Corrientes
Posadas
Encarnación
Santo Tomé
Passo Fundo
Florianópolis
Reconquista
Santa Maria
Caxias do Sul
Concordia
Uruguay
Paraná
Salto
Rivera
Pôrto Alegre
Paysandú
Melo
Pelotas
URUGUAY
Minas
Avellaneda
Montevideo
Río de la Plata

ATLANTIC OCEAN

ANDES
PAMPAS

ATACAMA DESERT

ANTARCTIC PENINSULA

0	250	500	750 Miles
0	250	500	750	1,000 Kilometers

86

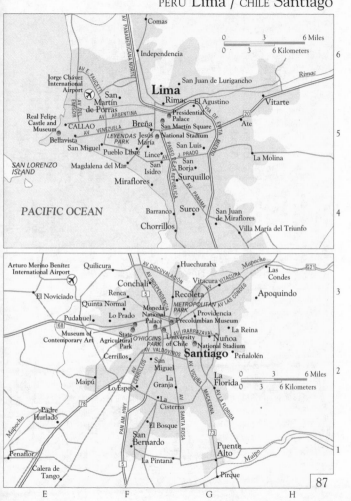

87

Buenos Aires ARGENTINA

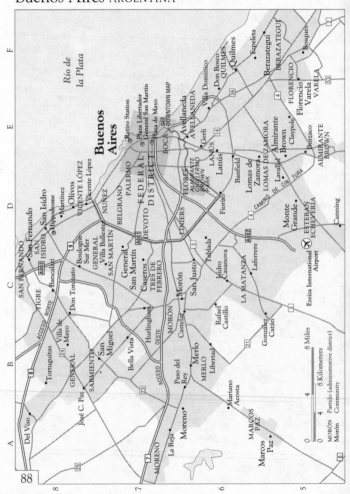

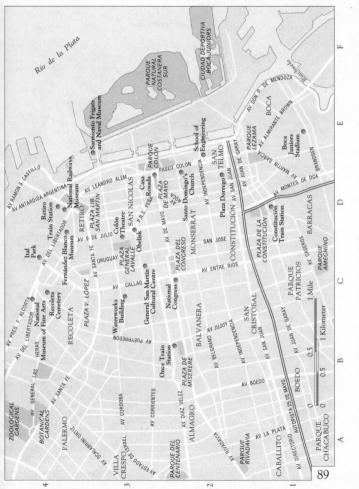

Rio de la Plata

PARQUE NATURAL COSTANERA SUR

CIUDAD DEPORTIVA BOCA JUNIORS

Riachuelo

F

E

AV RAMON S. CASTILLO

AV DON P. DE MENDOZA

BOCA

Sarmiento Frigate and Naval Museum

AV ANTARTIDA ARGENTINA

National Railways

School of Engineering

Parque Lezama

Boca Juniors Stadium

AV ALMIRANTE BROWN

AV MARTIN GARCIA

BRANDSEN

Retiro Train Station

AV DEL LIBERTADOR

AV LEANDRO ALEM

PARQUE COLON

PASEO COLON

SAN TELMO

AV MONTES DE OCA

RETIRO

PLAZA LIB. SAN MARTIN

Casa Rosada

PLAZA DE MAYO

AV INDEPENDENCIA

Plaza Dorrego

BARRACAS

D

Fernández Blanco Museum

Colón Theatre

SAN NICOLAS

P.A.S. PEÑA

Santo Domingo's Church

AV JUAN DE GARAY

AV PRES. F. ALCORTA

Ital Park

AV 9 DE JULIO

AV SANTA FE

Obelisk

AV DE MAYO

MONSERRAT

SAN JOSE

AV SAN JUAN

CONSTITUCIÓN

PLAZA DE LA CONSTITUCIÓN

Constitución Train Station

PARQUE AMEGHINO

AV CASEROS

PARQUE PATRICIOS

C

AV DEL LIBERTADOR

National Museum of Fine Arts

Recoleta Cemetery

PLAZA GENERAL LAVALLE

AV URUGUAY

AV CALLAO

PLAZA DEL CONGRESO

AV ENTRE RIOS

SAN CRISTOBAL

AV JUJUY

HERAS

RECOLETA

PLAZA V. LOPEZ

Waterworks Building

AV PUEYRREDON

General San Martín Cultural Centre

National Congress

BALVANERA

AV BELGRANO

AV INDEPENDENCIA

AV SAN JUAN

AV JUAN DE GARAY

1 Mile

1 Kilometer

0.5

0.5

0

0

B

ZOOLOGICAL GARDENS

AV GENERAL LAS

AV SANTA FE

PALERMO

AV CORDOBA

AV CORRIENTES

Once Train Station

PLAZA DE MISERERE

AV DIAZ VELEZ

ALMAGRO

AV BOEDO

BOEDO

AV DIRECTORIO

AUTOPISTA 25 DE MAYO

PARQUE CHACABUCO

A

BOTANICAL GARDENS

AV SARMIENTO ORTIZ

VILLA CRESPO

AV ESTADO DE ISRAEL

PARQUE DEL CENTENARIO

AV RIVADAVIA

AV LA PLATA

CABALLITO

PARQUE RIVADAVIA

4

3

2

1

89

Caracas VENEZUELA / Bogotá COLOMBIA

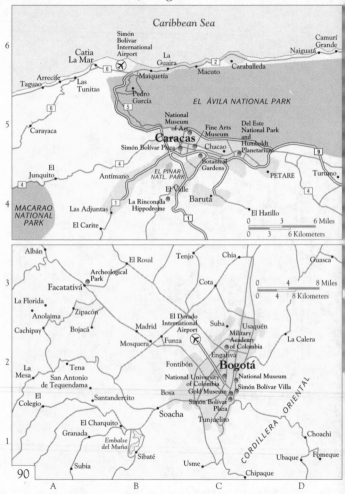

Caracas map labels:

Caribbean Sea

Simón Bolívar International Airport
Catia La Mar
La Guaira
Macuto
Caraballeda
Camurí Grande
Naiguatá
Arrecife
Taguao
Las Tunitas
Maiquetía
Pedro García
EL ÁVILA NATIONAL PARK
Carayaca
National Museum of Art
Fine Arts Museum
Del Este National Park and Humboldt Planetarium
Caracas
Simón Bolívar Plaza
Chacao
El Junquito
Antímano
EL PINAR NATL. PARK
Botanical Gardens
PETARE
Turumo
MACARAO NATIONAL PARK
Las Adjuntas
El Valle
Baruta
El Carite
La Rinconada Hippodrome
El Hatillo

0   3   6 Miles
0   3   6 Kilometers

Bogotá map labels:

Albán
El Rosal
Tenjo
Chía
Guasca
Archeological Park
Facatativá
Cota
0   4   8 Miles
0   4   8 Kilometers
La Florida
Anolaima
Zipacón
Cachipay
Bojacá
Madrid
El Dorado International Airport
Suba
Usaquén
Military Academy of Colombia
La Calera
Mosquera
Funza
Bogotá
Engativá
La Mesa
Tena
San Antonio de Tequendama
Fontibón
National University of Colombia
National Museum
Simón Bolívar Villa
El Colegio
Santandercito
Bosa
Gold Museum
Simón Bolívar Plaza
CORDILLERA ORIENTAL
El Charquito
Granada
Soacha
Tunjuelito
Choachí
Embalse del Muña
Subia
Sibaté
Usme
Ubaque
Fómeque
Chipaque

90

A   B   C   D

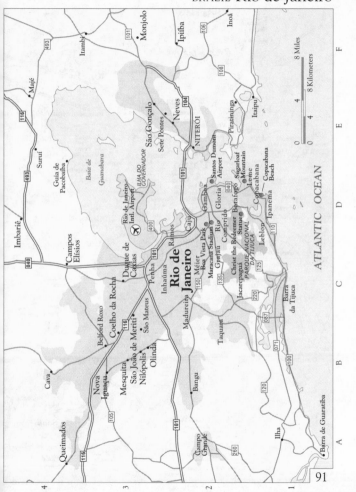

São Paulo BRAZIL

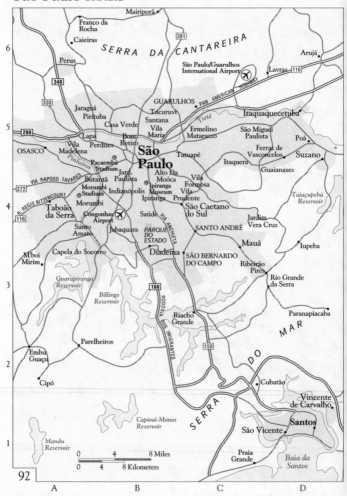

Mairiporã

Franco da Rocha

Caieiras

SERRA DA CANTAREIRA

Perus

São Paulo/Guarulhos International Airport

Arujá

Lavras

PAN AMERICAN HIGHWAY

Jaraguá

Pirituba

GUARULHOS

Tucuruvi

Santana

Vila Maria

Bom Retiro

Ermelino Matarazzo

Itaquaquecetuba

Casa Verde

Tietê

São Miguel Paulista

Poá

Lapa

Vila Madelena

Perdizes

OSASCO

Pinheiros

Pacaembú Stadium

São Paulo

Tatuapé

Itaquera

Ferraz de Vasconcelos

Suzano

Guaianases

Butantã

Jard. Paulista

Alto da Mooca

Ipiranga

Vila Formosa

VIA RAPOSO TAVARES

Morumbi Stadium

Indianópolis

Museum

Vila Prudente

Taiaçupebá Reservoir

R. REGIS BITTENCOURT

Taboão da Serra

Morumbi

Congonhas Airport

Saúde

VIA ANCHIETA

São Caetano do Sul

Jardim Vera Cruz

Santo Amaro

Jabaquara

PARQUE DO ESTADO

SANTO ANDRÉ

Mauá

Iupeba

M'boi Mirim

Capela do Socorro

Diadema

SÃO BERNARDO DO CAMPO

Ribeirão Pires

Rio Grande da Serra

Guarapiranga Reservoir

Billings Reservoir

RODOVIA DOS IMIGRANTES

Paranapiacaba

SERRA

Riacho Grande

Parelheiros

Embu Guaçu

Cipó

Capivai-Monos Reservoir

Cubatão

DO

MAR

Vincente de Carvalho

Santos

Mandu Reservoir

São Vicente

Praia Grande

Baía da Santos

0   4   8 Miles

0   4   8 Kilometers

92

A   B   C   D

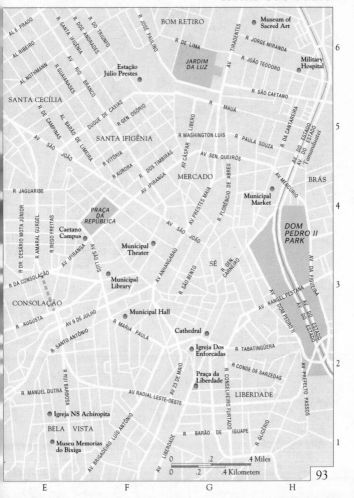

AL. E PRADO
AL. RIBEIRO
R. SANTA IFIGÊNIA
R. DOS ANDRADES
R. DO TRIUNFO
R. JOSÉ PAULINO
BOM RETIRO
Museum of Sacred Art
R. TIRADENTES
R. JORGE MIRANDA
AL. NOTHMANN
AV. RIO BRANCO
R. DE LIMA
R. JOÃO TEODORO
Military Hospital

R. GUAIANASES
Estação Júlio Prestes
JARDIM DA LUZ
AV. TIRADENTES
R. SÃO CAETANO

SANTA CECÍLIA
R. DE CAMPINAS
AL. BARÃO DE LIMEIRA
DUQUE DE CAXIAS
R. GEN. OSÓRIO
SANTA IFIGÊNIA
LIBERO
R. MAUÁ
R. DA CANTAREIRA
AV. DO ESTADO
Tamanduateí

AV. SÃO JOÃO
R. VITÓRIA
R. WASHINGTON LUIS
AV. CÁSPER
R. PAULA SOUZA
AV. DO ESTADO

R. JAGUARIBE
R. AURORA
R. DOS TIMBIRAS
AV. SEN. QUEIRÓS
MERCADO
AV. FLORÊNCIO DE ABREU
AV. MERCÚRIO
BRÁS

R. DR. CESÁRIO MOTA JÚNIOR
R. AMARAL GURGEL
R. REGO FREITAS
AV. IPIRANGA
PRAÇA DA REPÚBLICA
AV. PRESTES MAIA
Municipal Market

Caetano Campus
AV. SÃO JOÃO
DOM PEDRO II PARK

R. DA CONSOLAÇÃO
AV. SÃO LUÍS
Municipal Theater
AV. ANHANGABAÚ
SÉ
R. SÃO BENTO
R. GEN. CARNEIRO
AV. DA FIGUEIRA

CONSOLAÇÃO
Municipal Library
AV. RANGEL PESTANA
AV. DOM PEDRO II
AV. DO ESTADO

R. AUGUSTA
AV. 9 DE JULHO
R. MARIA PAULA
Municipal Hall

R. SANTO ANTÔNIO
Cathedral
R. TABATINGÜERA

R. RUI BARBOSA
R. MANUEL DUTRA
Igreja Dos Enforcadas
R. CONDE DE SARZEDAS
AV. PREFEITO PASSOS

AV. 23 DE MAIO
Praça da Liberdade
R. CONSELHEIRO FURTADO
LIBERDADE

AV. RADIAL LESTE-OESTE
R. GLICÉRIO

Igreja NS Achiropita
AV. LIBERDADE
R. BARÃO DE IGUAPE

BELA VISTA
Museu Memorias do Bixiga
AV. BRIGADEIRO LUÍS ANTÔNIO

0   .2   .4 Miles
0   .2   .4 Kilometers

E   F   G   H

6 5 4 3 2 1

Caribbean

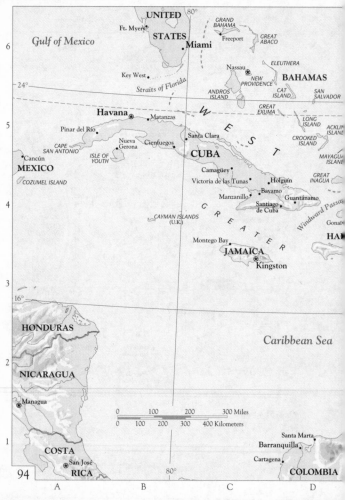

Gulf of Mexico

UNITED STATES

Ft. Myers •
• **Miami**

Key West •

Straits of Florida

GRAND BAHAMA

GREAT ABACO

Freeport •

Nassau ⊛
NEW PROVIDENCE

ELEUTHERA

BAHAMAS

ANDROS ISLAND

CAT ISLAND

SAN SALVADOR

GREAT EXUMA

Havana ⊛   • Matanzas

W   E   S   T

LONG ISLAND

ACKLIN ISLAND

Pinar del Río •

Nueva Gerona •

• Cienfuegos

• Santa Clara

CUBA

CROOKED ISLAND

CAPE SAN ANTONIO

ISLE OF YOUTH

MAYAGU

GREAT INAGUA

• Cancún

MEXICO

COZUMEL ISLAND

• Camagüey

Victoria de las Tunas •

• Holguín

• Bayamo

Manzanillo •

Santiago de Cuba

• Guantánamo

G   R   E   A   T   E   R

Windward Passa

Gonaï

HA

CAYMAN ISLANDS (U.K.)

Montego Bay •

JAMAICA

• **Kingston**

HONDURAS

Caribbean Sea

NICARAGUA

Managua ⊛

| 0 | 100 | 200 | 300 Miles |

| 0 | 100 | 200 | 300 | 400 Kilometers |

Santa Marta •

Barranquilla •

COSTA RICA

San José ⊛

Cartagena •

COLOMBIA

A   B   C   D

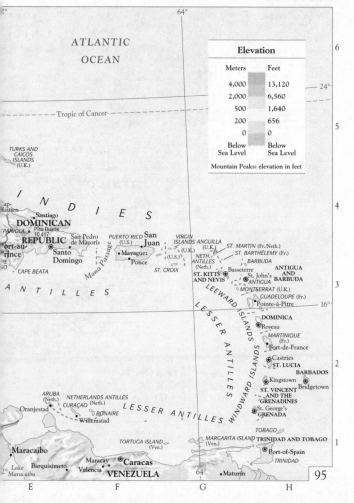

ATLANTIC
OCEAN

Elevation

Meters	Feet
4,000	13,120
2,000	6,560
500	1,640
200	656
0	0
Below Sea Level	Below Sea Level

Mountain Peaks: elevation in feet

-- Tropic of Cancer --

TURKS AND
CAICOS
ISLANDS
(U.K.)

W E S T   I N D I E S

ap-Haïtien

Santiago
DOMINICAN   Pico Duarte
REPUBLIC   10,417   San Pedro
            de Macorís
Port-au-   Santo
Prince   Domingo

CAPE BEATA

PUERTO RICO   San
(U.S.)   Juan   VIRGIN
Mayagüez   ISLANDS   ANGUILLA
Ponce   (U.K.)   (U.K.)   ST. MARTIN (Fr./Neth.)
            Mona Passage   (U.S.)   ST. BARTHÉLEMY (Fr.)
                    ST. CROIX   NETH.   BARBUDA
                              ANTILLES
                              (Neth.)   Basseterre   ANTIGUA
                              ST. KITTS   AND
                              AND NEVIS   St. John's   BARBUDA
                                          ANTIGUA

G R E A T E R   A N T I L L E S

MONTSERRAT (U.K.)

GUADELOUPE (Fr.)
Pointe-à-Pitre

LEEWARD ISLANDS

DOMINICA
Roseau

MARTINIQUE
(Fr.)
Fort-de-France

Castries
ST. LUCIA

LESSER ANTILLES

WINDWARD ISLANDS

BARBADOS
Kingstown   Bridgetown
ST. VINCENT
AND THE
GRENADINES
St. George's
GRENADA

ARUBA
(Neth.)   NETHERLANDS ANTILLES
          CURAÇAO (Neth.)
Oranjestad   LESSER   ANTILLES
          BONAIRE
          Willemstad

TOBAGO

TORTUGA ISLAND   MARGARITA ISLAND TRINIDAD AND TOBAGO
(Ven.)   (Ven.)
                          Port-of-Spain
Maracaibo   TRINIDAD

Barquisimeto Maracay Caracas
Lake   Valencia   Maturín
Maracaibo   VENEZUELA

Mexico - Central America

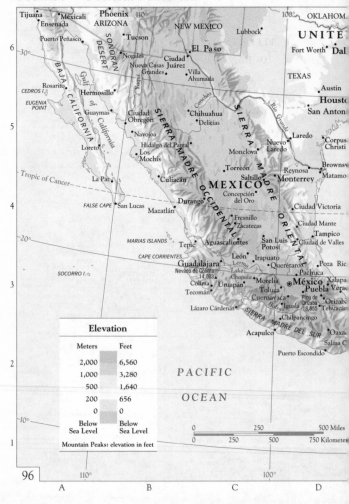

Tijuana • Mexicali • Phoenix • 110° • 100° • OKLAHOMA
Ensenada • ARIZONA • NEW MEXICO • Lubbock • UNITE
Puerto Peñasco • Tucson • El Paso • Fort Worth • Dal
SONORAN DESERT • Nogales • Ciudad Juárez • TEXAS
Nueva Casas • Villa Ahumada • Austin
Grandes • Rosarito • Hermosillo • Houst
CEDROS I. • Chihuahua • San Anton
EUGENIA POINT • Guaymas • Ciudad Obregón • Delicias
Navojoa • Saltillo • Laredo • Corpus
Hidalgo del Parral • Monclova • Nuevo Laredo • Christi
Loreto • Los Mochis • Torreón • Reynosa • Brownsv
La Paz • Culiacán • Saltillo • Monterrey • Matamo
Tropic of Cancer • Concepción del Oro
FALSE CAPE • San Lucas • Durango • Ciudad Victoria
Mazatlán • Fresnillo • Ciudad Mante
Zacatecas • Tampico
MARIAS ISLANDS • Tepic • Aguascalientes • San Luis Potosí • Ciudad de Valles
CAPE CORRIENTES • León • Irapuato • Poza Ric
SOCORRO I. • Guadalajara • Lerma • Querétaro • Pachuca
Nevado de Colima • Lake Chapula • Morelia • México • Xalapa
14,003 • Colima • Uruapan • Toluca • Puebla • Verac
Tecomán • Cuernavaca • Pico de Orizaba • Orizab
Lázaro Cárdenas • Iguala • 18,855 • Tehuacán
Chilpancingo • SIERRA MADRE DEL SUR • Oaxac
Acapulco • Salina C
Puerto Escondido

PACIFIC

OCEAN

Elevation

Meters	Feet
2,000	6,560
1,000	3,280
500	1,640
200	656
0	0
Below Sea Level	Below Sea Level

Mountain Peaks: elevation in feet

0 • 250 • 500 Miles
0 • 250 • 500 • 750 Kilometers

96

110° • 100°

A • B • C • D

Mexico City MEXICO

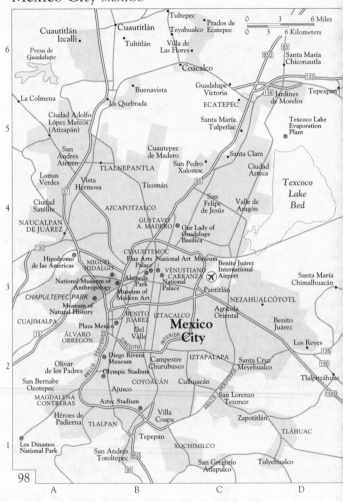

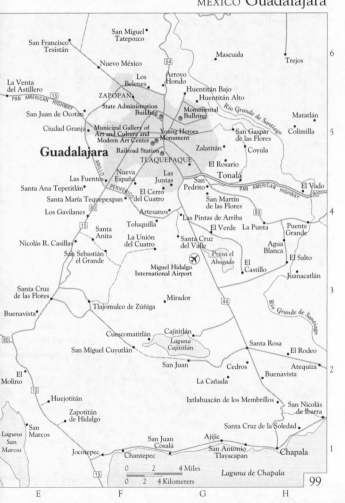

San Francisco
Tesistán

San Miguel
Tatepozco

Mascuala

Trejos

6

Nuevo México

La Venta
del Astillero

PAN AMERICAN HIGHWAY 15

Los
Belenes

ZAPOPAN

State Administration
Building

54

Arroyo
Hondo

Huentitán Bajo

Huentitán Alto

Río Grande de Santiago

Monumental
Bullring

Matatlán

Colimilla

San Juan de Ocotlán

Ciudad Granja

Municipal Gallery of
Art and Culture and
Modern Art Center

Guadalajara

Railroad Station

Young Heroes
Monument

TLAQUEPAQUE

San Gaspar
de las Flores

Zalatitán

El Rosario

Coyula

5

Las Fuentes

Nueva
España

Las
Juntas

San
Pedrito

Tonalá

PAN AMERICAN HIGHWAY

El Vado

90

Santa Ana Tepetitlán

PERIFÉRICO

El Cerro
del Cuatro

San Martín
de las Flores

Santa María Tequepexpan

80

Los Gavilanes

Artesanos

Las Pintas de Arriba

15

Toluquilla

El Verde

La Punta

4

Puente
Grande

Santa
Anita

La Unión
del Cuatro

Santa Cruz
del Valle

Agua
Blanca

El Salto

Nicolás R. Casillas

San Sebastián
el Grande

Miguel Hidalgo
International Airport

Presa el
Ahogado

El
Castillo

Juanacatlán

Santa Cruz
de las Flores

Mirador

44

Río Grande de Santiago

3

Buenavista

80

Tlajomulco de Zúñiga

Cuescomatlán

Cajititlán

Laguna
Cajititlán

Santa Rosa

El Rodeo

San Miguel Cuyutlán

San Juan

Cedros

Buenavista

Atequiza

2

El
Molino

La Cañada

Ixtlahuacán de los Membrillos

San Nicolás
de Ibarra

15

Huejotitán

Zapotitán
de Hidalgo

Santa Cruz de la Soledad

Laguna
San
Marcos

San
Marcos

Jocotepec

Chantepec

San Juan
Cosalá

Ajijic

San Antonio
Tlayacapan

Chapala

15

0   2   4 Miles

0   2   4 Kilometers

Laguna de Chapala

1

99

E   F   G   H

Canada WESTERN

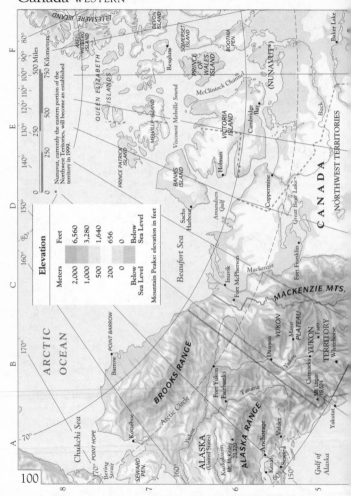

Elevation

Meters	Feet
2,000	6,560
1,000	3,280
500	1,640
200	656
0	0
Below Sea Level	Below Sea Level

Mountain Peaks: elevation in feet

Nunavut, currently the eastern portion of the Northwest Territories, will become an established territory in 1999.

ELLESMERE ISLAND
AXEL HEIBERG ISLAND
DEVON ISLAND
SOMERSET ISLAND
PRINCE OF WALES ISLAND
BOOTHIA PEN.
Resolute
Baker Lake
QUEEN ELIZABETH ISLANDS
McClintock Channel
(NUNAVUT*)
Viscount Melville Sound
MELVILLE ISLAND
VICTORIA ISLAND
Cambridge Bay
PRINCE PATRICK ISLAND
Holman
Back
BANKS ISLAND
Amundsen Gulf
Coppermine
Great Bear Lake
CANADA
NORTHWEST TERRITORIES
Sachs Harbour
Beaufort Sea
Inuvik
Fort McPherson
Fort Franklin
Mackenzie
MACKENZIE MTS.
ARCTIC OCEAN
POINT BARROW
Barrow
Mayo
YUKON PLATEAU
Dawson
YUKON
Faro
Chukchi Sea
BROOKS RANGE
Fort Yukon
Fairbanks
Tanana
Carmacks
YUKON TERRITORY
Whitehorse
Bering Strait
POINT HOPE
Kotzebue
Arctic Circle
Yukon
Mt. Logan 19,524
SEWARD PEN.
ALASKA (United States)
Kuskokwim
Mt. McKinley 20,320
ALASKA RANGE
Anchorage
Valdez
Yakutat
Kenai
Seward
Gulf of Alaska

Miles
0   250   500   750 Miles
0   250   500   750 Kilometers

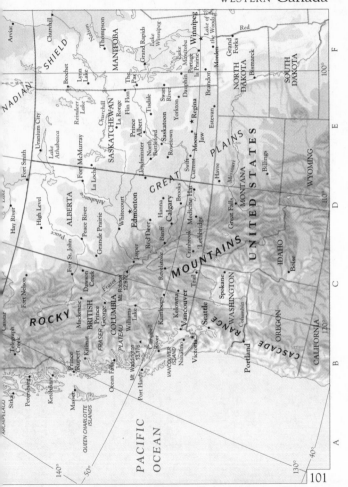

ICELAND

Reykjavík

90°
20°
30°
40°

CAPE FAREWELL

Denmark Strait

Ammassalik

Arctic Circle

Labrador Sea

Qaqortoq

Nuuk
(Godthåb)

Maniitsoq

Sisimiut

Davis Strait

Aasiaat

Qeqertarsuaq

GREENLAND
(KALAALLIT NUNAAT)
(Denmark)

30°

Baffin Bay

40°

Pangnirtung

Iqaluit

Hudson Strait

50°

Foxe
Basin

PRINCE
CHARLES I.

Pond Inlet

Arctic
Bay

BYLOT
ISLAND

Lancaster Sound

DEVON
ISLAND

Grise Fiord

Qaanaaq
(Thule)

Alert

ELLESMERE ISLAND

80°

BAFFIN ISLAND

MELVILLE
PENINSULA

SOUTHAMPTON
ISLAND

Gulf
of
Boothia

Repulse Bay

NORTHWEST TERRITORIES
(NUNAVUT*)

0   250   500
0   250   500   750 Kilometers

500 Miles

* Nunavut, currently the eastern portion of the
Northwest Territories, will become an established...

7   6   5

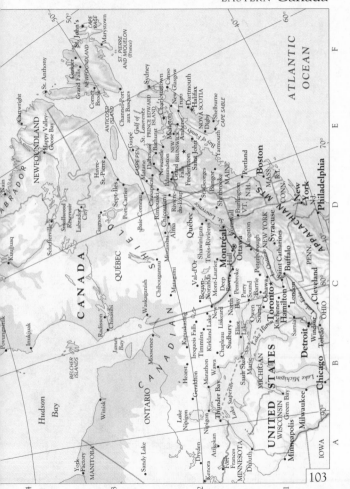

103

Toronto CANADA

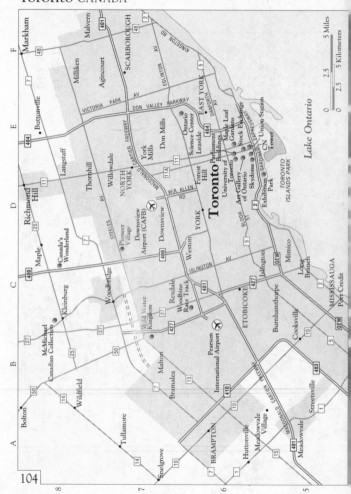

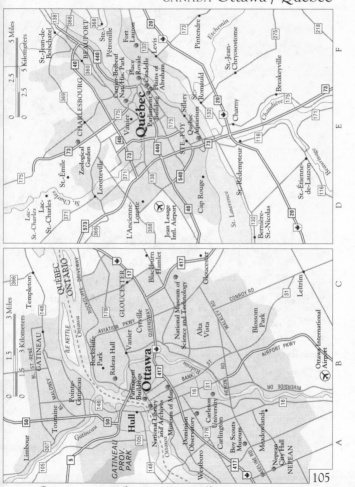

Montréal CANADA

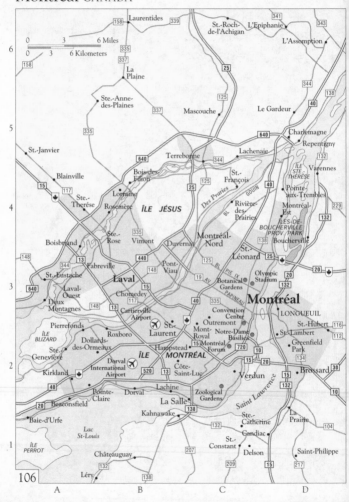

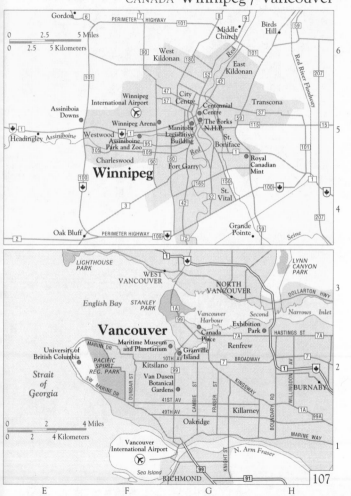

UNITED
STATES

United States WESTERN

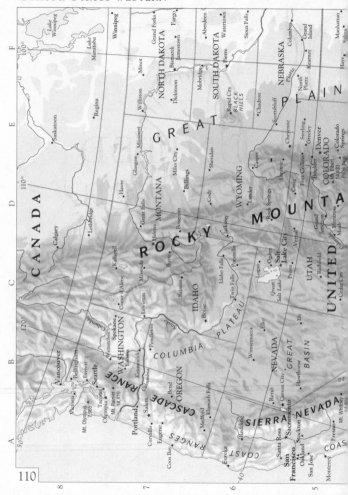

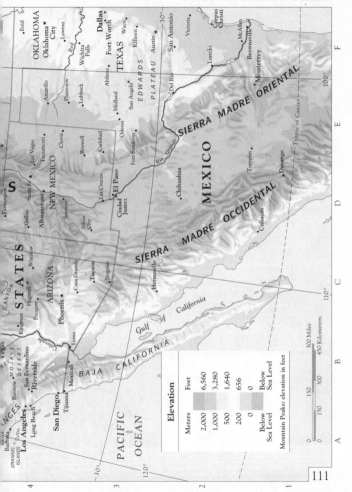

Elevation

Meters	Feet
2,000	6,560
1,000	3,280
500	1,640
200	656
0	0
Below Sea Level	Below Sea Level

★ Mountain Peaks: elevation in feet

300 Miles
450 Kilometers

150
150 300

0
0

United States EASTERN

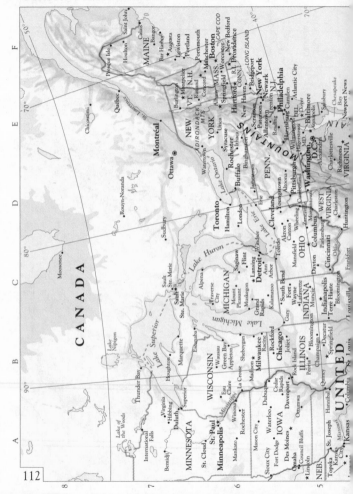

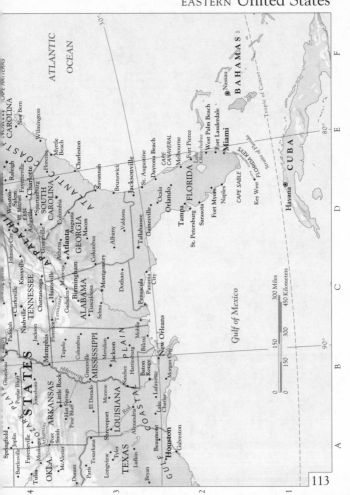

113

New England

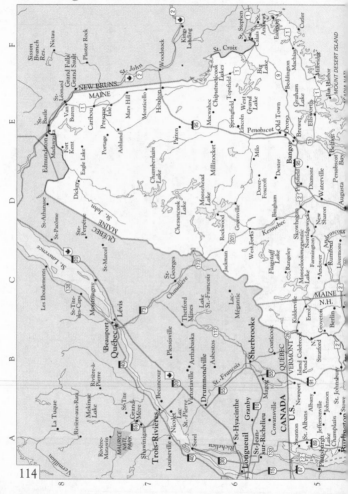

114

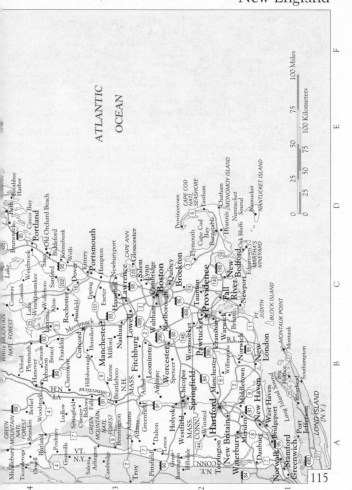

ATLANTIC

OCEAN

115

New York State

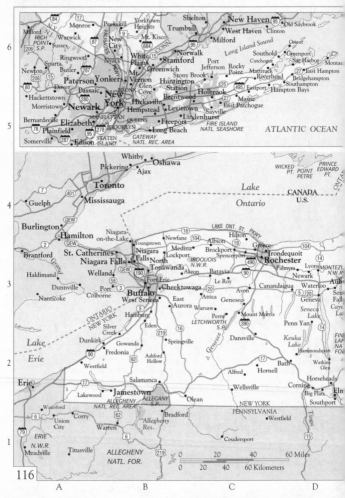

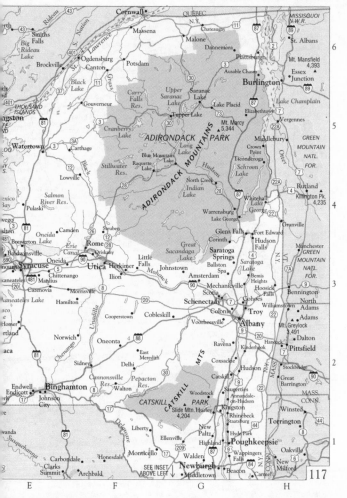

Middle Atlantic States

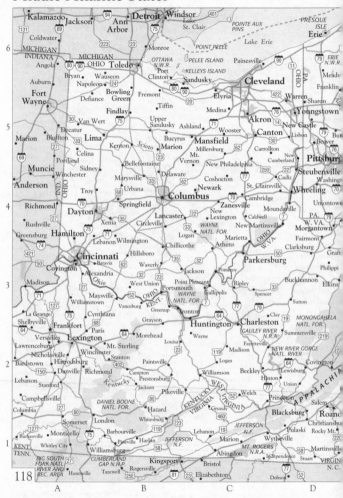

118

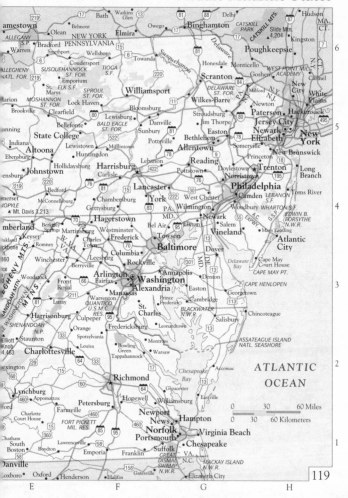

amestown
ALLEGANY S.F.
Belmont
Bath
Watkins Glen
Owego
Delhi
Binghamton
CATSKILL MTS.
Slide Mtn. ▲4,204
CATSKILL PARK
Hudson
MA. CT.
Olean
NEW YORK
Elmira
Warren
Bradford
PENNSYLVANIA
Poughkeepsie
Kingston
Smethport
Wellsboro
Towanda
Honesdale
Monticello
WEST POINT MIL. ACADEMY
Goshen
Coudersport
ALLEGHENY NATL. FOR.
SUSQUEHANNOCK ST. FOR.
TIOGA S.F.
Scranton
DELAWARE ST. FOR.
Milford
New City
Carmel
Emporium
ELK S.F.
St. Marys
SPROUL ST. FOR.
Williamsport
Wilkes-Barre
Newton
White Plains
MOSHANNON ST. FOR.
Lock Haven
Bloomsburg
Stroudsburg
Jim Thorpe
Paterson
Hackensack
Brookville
Clearfield
Lewisburg
Danville
Easton
Bethlehem
Jersey City
Newark
New York
BALD EAGLE ST. FOR.
Sunbury
Allentown
Somerville
Elizabeth
State College
Pottsville
Reading
Princeton
New Brunswick
Altoona
Lewistown
Mifflintown
Lebanon
Harrisburg
Pottstown
Doylestown
Norristown
Trenton
Long Branch
Huntingdon
Hollidaysburg
Carlisle
Lancaster
York
West Chester
Philadelphia
Camden
Toms River
Bedford
Chambersburg
Gettysburg
Wilmington
Newark
Elkton
Salem
Vineland
Atlantic City
Hagerstown
Westminster
Bel Air
Baltimore
Dover
Frederick
Towson
Columbia
Rockville
Annapolis
Arlington
Washington
Alexandria
Easton
Cambridge
Salisbury
Chincoteague
Richmond
ATLANTIC OCEAN
Newport News
Hampton
Norfolk
Portsmouth
Virginia Beach
Chesapeake

0   30   60 Miles
0   30   60 Kilometers

119

Southeastern States

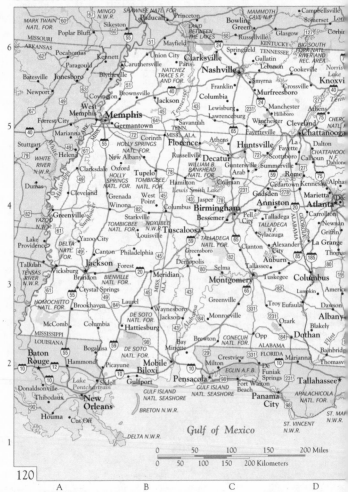

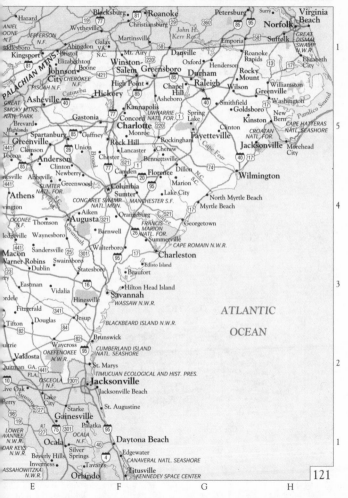

Southeastern States

ATLANTIC

OCEAN

Florida - Puerto Rico

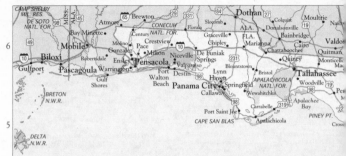

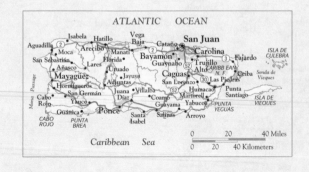

A B C D

ATLANTIC

OCEAN

0   40   80 Miles
0   40   80 Kilometers

Midwestern States

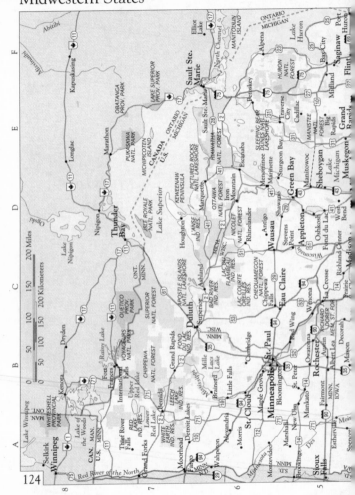

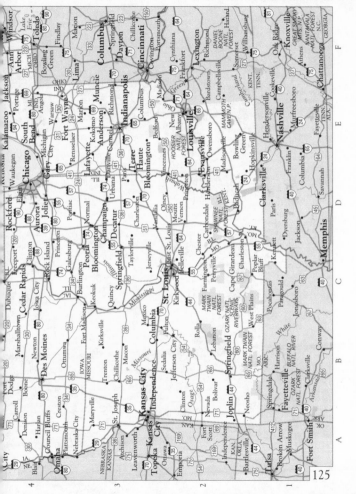

North Central States

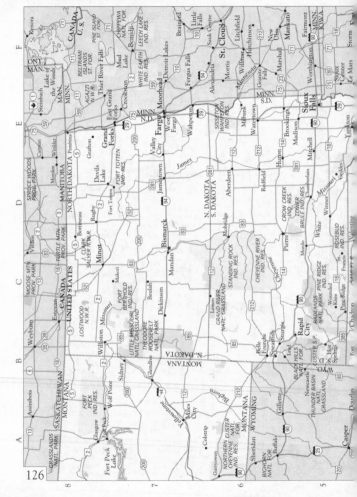

North Central States

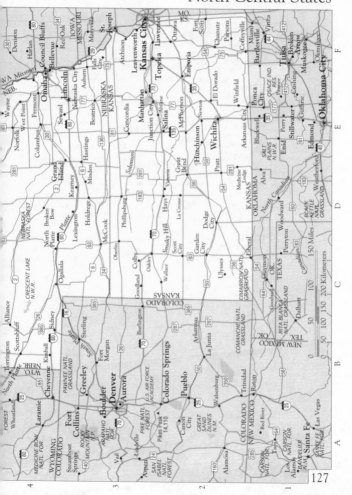

South Central States

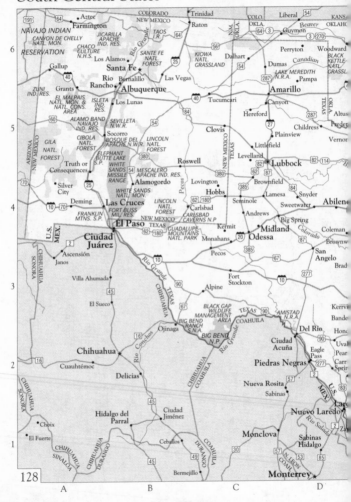

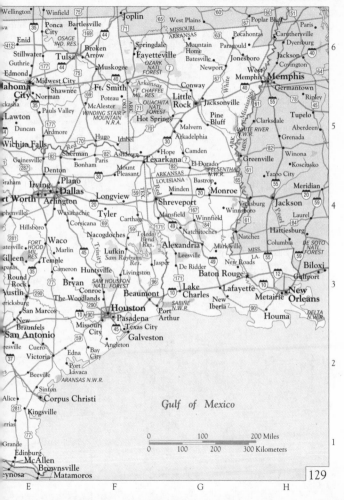

Wellington • Winfield [75]
va   Enid [35] Ponca City Bartlesville
[412] Stillwater OSAGE IND. RES. Broken Arrow
Guthrie [177] Tulsa
Edmond Midwest City [44] [75]
ahoma City Shawnee
cksha [35] Norman McAlester
Lawton Pauls Valley
Duncan Ardmore
Wichita Falls [70] Hugo Idabel

Joplin [65] [71] West Plains
West Plains [60]
Springdale Fayetteville MISSOURI Poplar Bluff [51]
Ft. Smith Mountain Home Pocahontas Caruthersville
Muskogee FT. CHAFEE MIL. RES. Batesville Jonesboro Jackson
Poteau OUACHITA NATL. FOREST Newport [67] West Memphis Covington
Conway Little Rock Memphis
Hot Springs Jacksonville Germantown [78] Ripley
Pine Bluff Clarksdale [45]
Malvern Aberdeen
Atkadelphia WHITE RIVER W.R. Grenada
Camden Greenville Winona • Kosciusko

Gainesville [82] Sherman Paris Texarkana [7] El Dorado FELSENTHAL N.W.R. [82]
Graham [287] Denton Bonham Mount Pleasant ARKANSAS Minden Monroe [65] Yazoo City [55]
Irving Plano LOUISIANA Bastrop Vicksburg Meridian [20]
rt Worth Dallas Longview [59] Shreveport Winnsboro Jackson [59]
Arlington [20] Tyler Mansfield [167] Winnfield [61] Laurel
phenville Waxahachie Carthage Natchitoches Hattiesburg
Hillsboro Corsicana [69] Nacogdoches [59] Alexandria Marksville Columbia DE SOTO NATL. FOREST
Waco Toledo Bend Res. Leesville [49] Natchez MISS.
teville Marlin Lufkin Jasper New Roads LA. [55] Biloxi
Killeen [45] Temple Sam Rayburn Res. De Ridder Baton Rouge Gulfport
apasas Cameron Huntsville Livingston [96] Lafayette [10] [12]
Round Rock [77] Bryan SAM HOUSTON NATL. FOREST Lake Charles New Orleans
Austin The Woodlands Beaumont [10] New Iberia Metairie
ricksburg [290] Conroe SABINE N.W.R. Houma
San Marcos Houston Port Arthur [90] DELTA N.W.R.
New Braunfels Pasadena
San Antonio [10] [90] Missouri City [45] Texas City
resville Cuero Galveston
Victoria Angleton
[37] Edna Bay City
Beeville Port Lavaca
ARANSAS N.W.R.

Alice Sinton
[281] Corpus Christi
Kingsville

rrias
Grande [77]
Edinburg
McAllen
ynosa Brownsville Matamoros

Gulf of Mexico

0   100   200 Miles
0   100   200   300 Kilometers

E   F   G   H

Rocky Mountain States

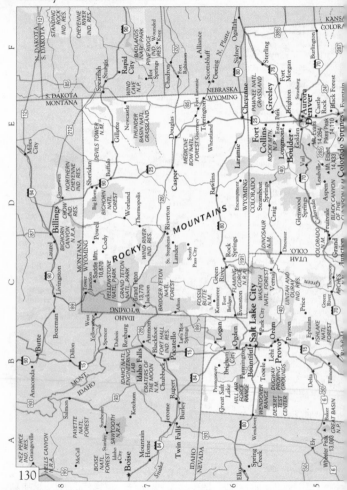

Rocky Mountain States

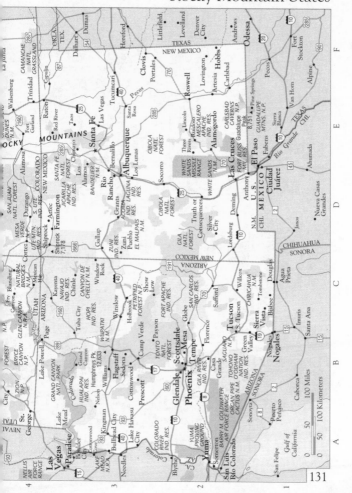

California - Nevada

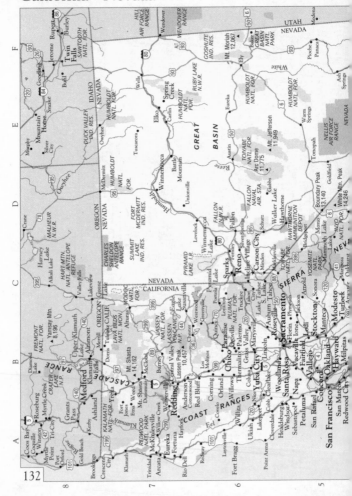

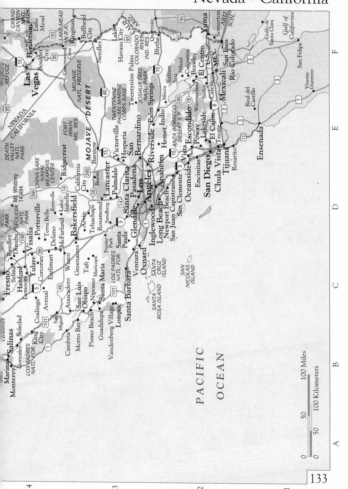

Northwestern States

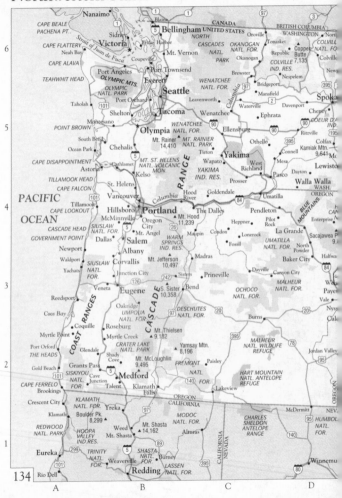

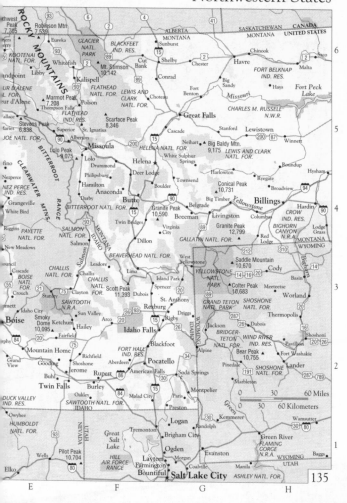

ROCKY MOUNTAINS

thwest Peak 7,705 · Robinson Mtn. 7,539

93 · Robinson Mtn. · 6 · 2 · 4 · 41 · SASKATCHEWAN · CANADA · MONTANA · UNITED STATES

ers City · Eureka · GLACIER NATL. PARK · BLACKFEET IND. RES. · ALBERTA · MONTANA · Sunburst · 15 · Chinook · 2 · Saco · 6

KOOTENAI NATL. FOR. · Whitefish · 2 · Mt. Stimson 10,142 · Cut Bank · Shelby · Chester · Havre · FORT BELKNAP IND. RES. · Malta

andpoint · Libby · Kalispell · 93 · Conrad · Big Sandy · Hays · Fort Peck Lake

UR D'ALENE L. FOR. · eur d'Alene · Marmot Peak 7,208 · Thompson Falls · FLATHEAD NATL. FOR. · Polson · LEWIS AND CLARK NATL. FOR. · Choteau · Fort Benton · Missouri · CHARLES M. RUSSELL N.W.R.

allace · Stevens Peak 6,838 · Superior · FLATHEAD IND. RES. · St. Ignatius · Scarface Peak 8,346 · Great Falls · Stanford · Lewistown · Winnett

JOE NATL. FOR. · 90 · Alberton · Lolo Peak 9,075 · Missoula · 200 · HELENA NATL. FOR. · Cascade · Neihart · Big Baldy Mtn. 9,175 · LEWIS AND CLARK NATL. FOR. · 200 · 87 · Roundup · Hysham · 5

fino · Nezperce · CLEARWATER · Lolo · Drummond · Helena · White Sulphur Springs · Harlowton · Ryegate · Broadview · 94

Grangeville · NEZ PERCE IND. RES. · BITTERROOT RANGE · Philipsburg · Deer Lodge · Townsend · Conical Peak 10,731 · Billings · Hardin

White Bird · Hamilton · Anaconda · Boulder · Belgrade · Big Timber · Yellowstone · Columbus · CROW IND. RES. · 90 · 4

Riggins · PAYETTE NATL. FOR. · Darby · BITTERROOT NATL. FOR. · Butte · Granite Peak 10,590 · Bozeman · Livingston · BIGHORN CANYON · Lodge Grass

New Meadows · SALMON NATL. FOR. · 93 · Twin Bridges · 15 · Virginia City · GALLATIN NATL. FOR. · Granite Peak 12,799 · Red Lodge · 310 · MONTANA · WYOMING

council · Cascade · CHALLIS NATL. FOR. · Salmon · MONTANA · IDAHO · Dillon · BEAVERHEAD NATL. FOR. · 212 · Bighorn · 14

BOISE NATL. FOR. · 55 · 21 · Leadore · West Yellowstone · Saddle Mountain 10,670 · Cody · Basin

mett · Crouch · 75 · Challis · CHALLIS NATL. FOR. · Scott Peak 11,393 · Lima · Island Park · YELLOWSTONE NATL. PARK · 14 · 16 · 20 · Colter Peak 10,683 · Meeteetse · Worland · 20 · 3

Boise · Idaho City · Stanley · Clayton · SAWTOOTH N.R.A. · Dubois · Spencer · 20 · 89 · GRAND TETON NATL. PARK · SHOSHONE NATL. FOR. · Thermopolis · 20

Smoky Dome 10,095 · Ketchum · Sun Valley · Arco · St. Anthony · Rexburg · Rigby · Driggs · Jackson · BRIDGER-TETON NATL. FOR. · Dubois · 287 · 16 · Shoshoni

rphy · 84 · Mountain Home · 75 · Fairfield · Hailey · 20 · 93 · 15 · 26 · IDAHO · WYOMING · Bear Peak 10,755 · WIND RIVER IND. RES. · Pavillion · Fort Washakie · Lander · 20 · 26 · 2

Grand View · Gooding · Richfield · Shoshone · FORT HALL IND. RES. · Idaho Falls · Blackfoot · 34 · Alpine · Pinedale · SHOSHONE NATL. FOR. · 287 · 789

Buhl · Jerome · Rupert · Aberdeen · American Falls · Pocatello · Soda Springs · Marbleton · 191

Twin Falls · Burley · 86 · Montpelier · Green · 0 · 30 · 60 Miles · 0 · 30 · 60 Kilometers

DUCK VALLEY IND. RES. · Oakley · Malad City · 15 · Paris · SAWTOOTH NATL. FOR. IDAHO · Preston · Logan · 30 · Kemmerer · Wamsutter · 80

Owyhee · HUMBOLDT NATL. FOR. · 93 · UTAH · NEVADA · Tremonton · Brigham City · Randolph · Green River · FLAMING GORGE N.R.A. · Baggs · 1

Wells · Pilot Peak 10,704 · Great Salt Lake · Ogden · Evanston · Manila · WYOMING · UTAH · ASHLEY NATL. FOR.

Elko · 80 · HILL AIR FORCE RANGE · Layton · Farmington · Morgan · Coalville · Bountiful · Salt Lake City

135

Alaska

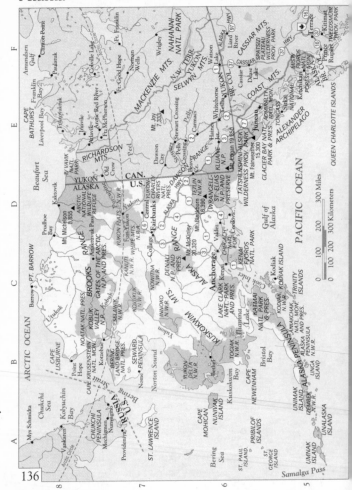

136

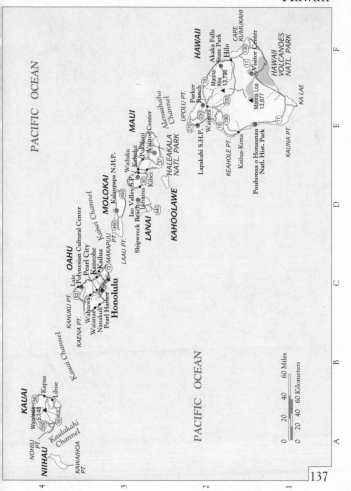

PACIFIC OCEAN

PACIFIC OCEAN

KAUAI
NIIHAU
NOHILI PT.
KAWAIHOA PT.
Waialeale 5,148
Kapaa
Lihue
Kekaha
Kaulakahi Channel

OAHU
KAHUKU PT.
Laie
Polynesian Cultural Center
Kauai Channel
Wahiawa
Pearl City
Kaneohe
Kailua
Nanakuli
Waianae
KAENA PT.
Pearl Harbor
Honolulu
MAKAPUU PT.
LAAU PT.

MOLOKAI
Kalaupapa N.H.P.
Kaiwi Channel

MAUI
Iao Valley S.P.
Wailuku
Kahului
Paia
Lahaina
Puukalani
Visitor Center
Shipwreck Beach
Kihei
LANAI
Alenuihaha Channel

KAHOOLAWE
HALEAKALA NATL. PARK

HAWAII
UPOLU PT.
Parker Ranch
Akaka Falls State Park
Mauna Kea 13,796
Hilo
Waimea
Lapakahi S.H.P.
CAPE KUMUKAHI
KEAHOLE PT.
Kailua-Kona
Mauna Loa 13,677
HAWAII VOLCANOES NATL. PARK
Visitor Center
Puuhonua o Honaunau Natl. Hist. Park
KAUNA PT.
KA LAE

0   20   40   60 Miles
0 20   40   60 Kilometers

A   B   C   D   E   F

4   3   2   1

Boston MASSACHUSETTS

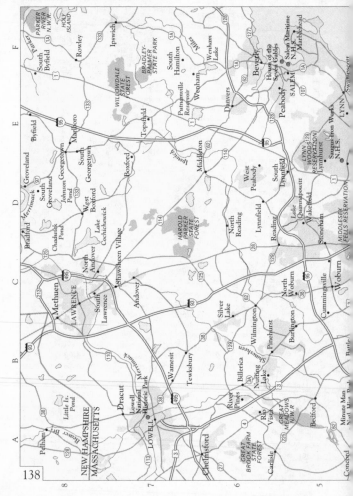

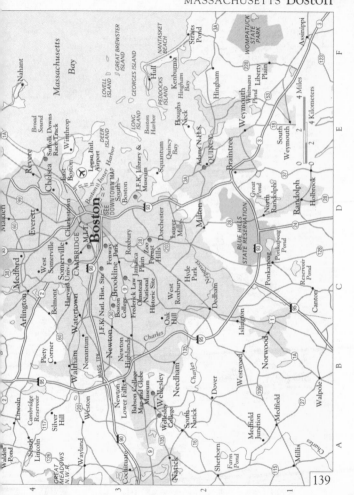

139

Boston MASSACHUSETTS

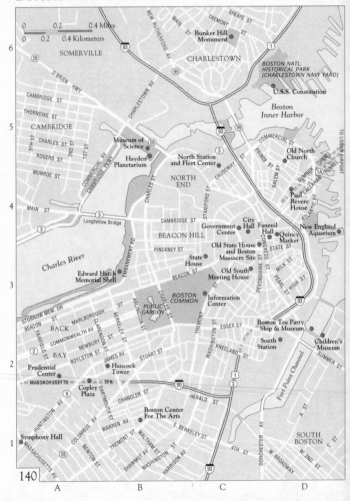

SHEAFE ST

TREMONT ST

NEW RUTHERFORD AV

MAIN ST

Bunker Hill
Monument

CHARLESTOWN

93

99

SOMERVILLE

28

O'BRIEN HWY

CAMBRIDGE ST

THORNDIKE ST

CAMBRIDGE

5TH ST

CHARLES ST

2ND ST

1ST ST

ROGERS ST

MUNROE ST

MAIN ST

CHARLESTOWN AV

CAMBRIDGE PKWY

COMMERCIAL AV

Museum of
Science

Hayden
Planetarium

3

Longfellow Bridge

CHARLES ST

EMBANKMENT RD

NORTH
END

North Station
and Fleet Center

CAUSEWAY ST

STANIFORD ST

CAMBRIDGE ST

Government
Center

City
Hall

Faneuil
Hall

BEACON HILL

PINCKNEY ST

State
House

Old State House
and Boston
Massacre Site

Quincy
Market

STATE ST

Old South
Meeting House

MILK ST

BEACON ST

DEVONSHIRE ST

CONGRESS ST

PEARL ST

HIGH ST

Edward Hatch
Memorial Shell

Charles River

STORROW MEM. DR

BEACON ST

FAIRFIELD ST

2

BOSTON
COMMON

PUBLIC
GARDEN

Information
Center

ARLINGTON ST

CHARLES ST

TREMONT ST

ESSEX ST

WASHINGTON ST

KNEELAND ST

Boston Tea Party
Ship & Museum

South
Station

BACK
BAY

MARLBOROUGH ST

COMMONWEALTH AV

NEWBURY ST

BOYLSTON ST

CLARENDON ST

BERKELEY ST

JAMES AV

STUART ST

Prudential
Center

Hancock
Tower

MASSACHUSETTS TPK

Copley
Plaza

9

CHANDLER ST

HERALD ST

90

HUNTINGTON AV

Symphony Hall

1

MASSACHUSETTS AV

28

COLUMBUS AV

NEWTON ST

WARREN AV

TREMONT ST

SHAWMUT AV

WALTHAM ST

WASHINGTON ST

Boston Center
For The Arts

E. BERKELEY ST

HARRISON AV

93

DORCHESTER AV

W. BROADWAY

SOUTH
BOSTON

W. 2ND ST

4TH ST

A ST

B ST

C ST

SUMNER ST

Fort Point Channel

Children's
Museum

Boston
Inner Harbor

BOSTON NATL.
HISTORICAL PARK
(CHARLESTOWN NAVY YARD)

U.S.S. Constitution

COMMERCIAL ST

PRINCE ST

SALEM ST

Old North
Church

Paul Revere
House

ATLANTIC AV

New England
Aquarium

TO LOGAN AIRPORT

SUMNER TUNNEL

CALLAHAN TUNNEL

1A

93

0   0.2   0.4 Miles

0   0.2   0.4 Kilometers

140

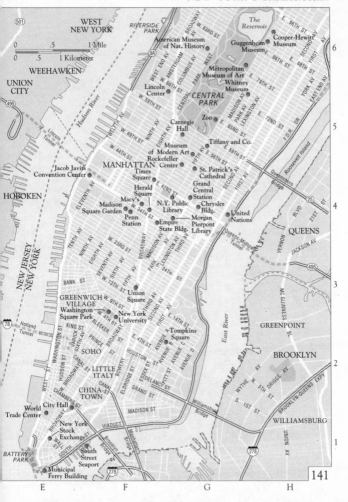

New York NEW YORK

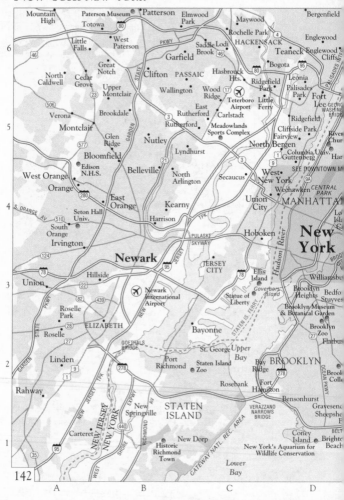

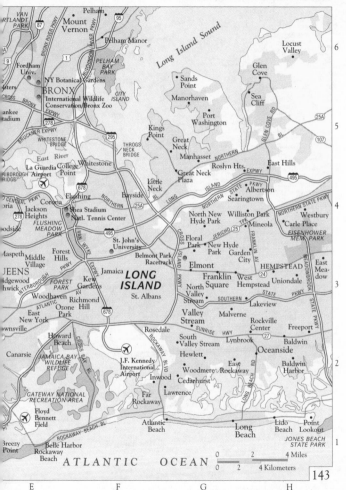

Long Island Sound

ATLANTIC OCEAN

| 0 | 2 | 4 Miles |
| 0 | 2 | 4 Kilometers |

143

E   F   G   H

Philadelphia PENNSYLVANIA

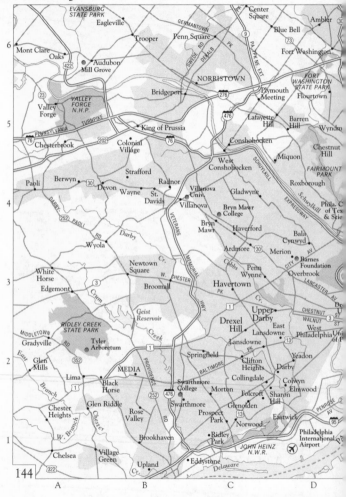

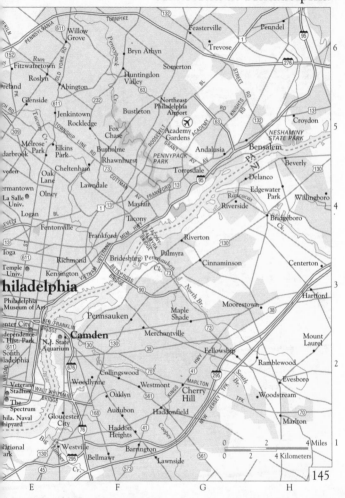

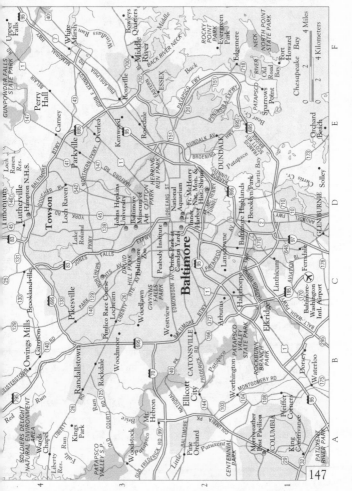

Washington D.C.

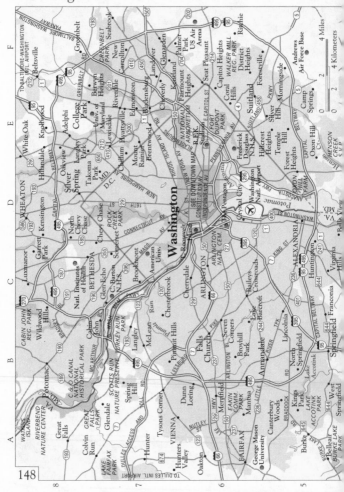

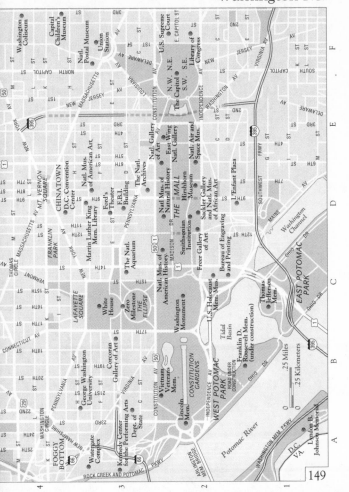

Washington Coliseum

Capital Children's Museum

Natl. Postal Museum

Union Station

U.S. Supreme Court

Library of Congress

N.W. N.E.

The Capitol

S.W. S.E.

Natl. Gallery of Art

East Wing Natl. Gallery

Natl. Air and Space Mus.

D.C. Convention Center

CHINATOWN

Natl. Mus. of American Art

Ford's Theater

F.B.I. Building

The Natl. Archives

Natl. Mus. of Natural History

THE MALL

Hirshhorn Museum

Sackler Gallery and Natl. Mus. of African Art

L'Enfant Plaza

FRANKLIN PARK

Martin Luther King Mem. Library

PENNSYLVANIA

Smithsonian Institution

Freer Gallery of Art

Bureau of Engraving and Printing

Washington Channel

The Natl. Aquarium

Natl. Mus. of American History

MT. VERNON SQUARE

LAFAYETTE SQUARE

THOMAS CIRCLE

White House

Zero Milestone THE ELLIPSE

Washington Monument

U.S. Holocaust Mem. Mus.

Tidal Basin

EAST POTOMAC PARK

Thomas Jefferson Mem.

CONNECTICUT AV

Corcoran Gallery of Art

CONSTITUTION GARDENS

Franklin D. Roosevelt Mem. (under construction)

FOGGY BOTTOM

George Washington University

Vietnam Veterans Mem.

WEST POTOMAC PARK

ROAD UNDER CONSTRUCTION

WASHINGTON CIRCLE

Dept. of State

Lincoln Mem.

INDEPENDENCE AV

CONSTITUTION AV

Kennedy Center for the Performing Arts

Watergate Complex

ARLINGTON MEM. BRIDGE

ROCK CREEK AND POTOMAC PKWY

Potomac River

D.C.

VA.

WASHINGTON MEM. PKWY

Lyndon B. Johnson Memorial

.25 Miles

.25 Kilometers

Cleveland OHIO

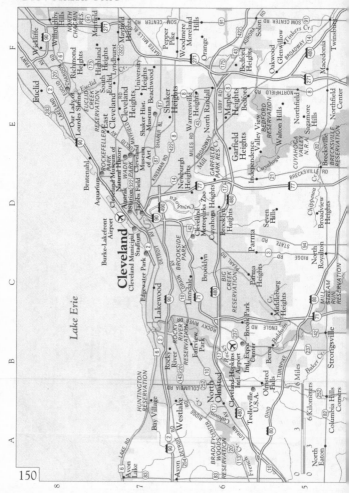

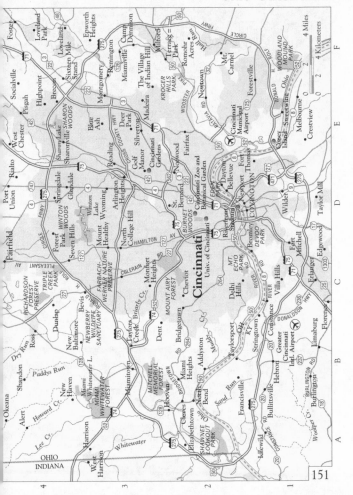

151

Atlanta GEORGIA

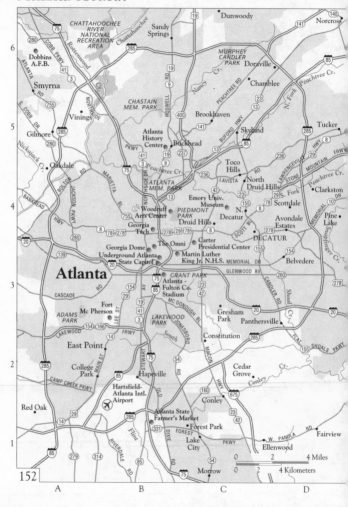

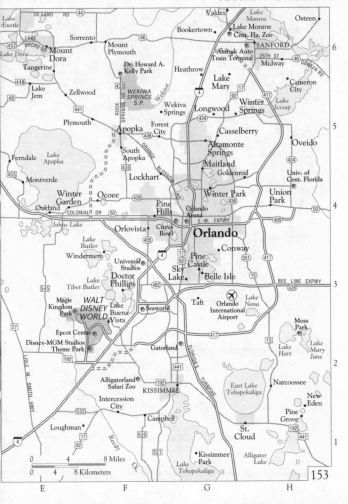

Tampa - St. Petersburg FLORIDA

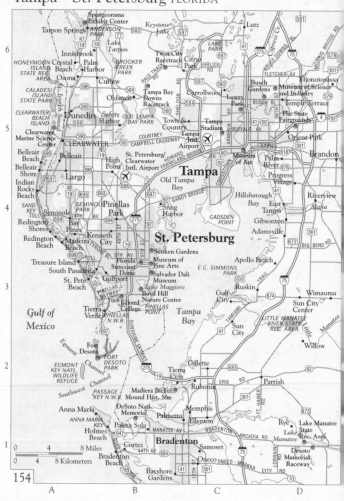

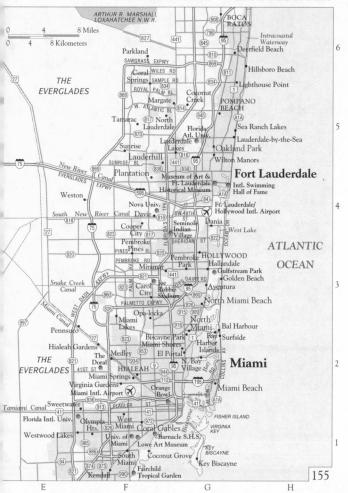

Detroit MICHIGAN

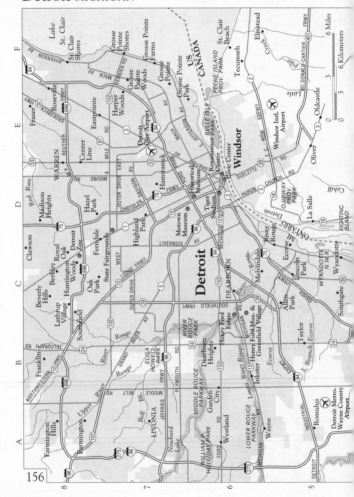

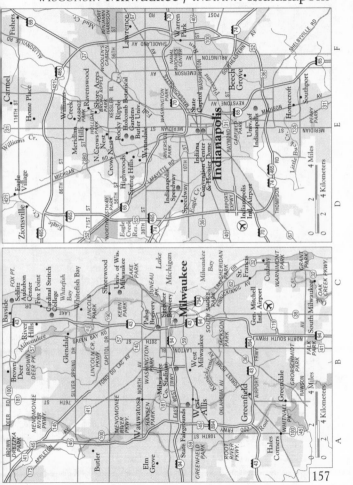

157

Lake Michigan

Carol Beach
Winthrop Harbor
ILLINOIS BEACH STATE PARK
Zion
WAUKEGAN
North Chicago
Great Lakes Naval Training Center
Lake Bluff
Lake Forest
Fort Sheridan
Highwood
Highland Park
Chicago Botanic Garden
Deerfield
Glencoe
Winnetka
Wilmette
Northbrook
Northfield
Glenview
Morton Grove
Niles
Skokie
Lincolnwood
Northwestern Univ.
EVANSTON
Park Ridge
Chicago O'Hare

Russell
Beach Park
Wadsworth
Gurnee
Park City
Green Oaks
Des Plaines
Riverwoods
FOREST PRESERVE
Wheeling
Buffalo Grove
Prospect Heights
Mount Prospect
Arlington Heights
Rosemont
Des Plaines
SKOKIE
N. Branch

Antioch
Lake Marie
Grass Lake
Pistakee Highlands
Fox Lake Hills
Lindenhurst
Old Mill Creek
ROLLINS SAVANNA FOR. PRES.
Gages Lake
Round Lake Beach
Grayslake
Libertyville
Mundelein
Vernon Hills
LAKEWOOD FOREST PRESERVE
Lake Zurich
Palatine
Rolling Meadows
Inverness
DOUGLAS FORESTS PRESERVE
Hoffman Estates
Schaumburg
Streamwood
POPLAR CREEK FOREST PRESERVE
NED BROWN FOR. PRES.
Elk Grove
CHAIN O' LAKES STATE PARK
Fox Lake
Lilymoor
VOLO BOG STATE NAT. AREA
Volo
Island Lake
Wauconda
Tower Lakes
Fox River Grove
Barrington
SPRING LAKE FOREST PRESERVE
CRABTREE FOREST PRESERVE
JOB HWY
NW HWY
HIGGINS
Haines ville
Hainesville

WIS.
ILL.
ROSECRANS
GREEN BAY RD
FOREST PRESERVE
SHERIDAN RD
LAKE HWY
DUNDEE RD
HWY 41
HIGGINS

158

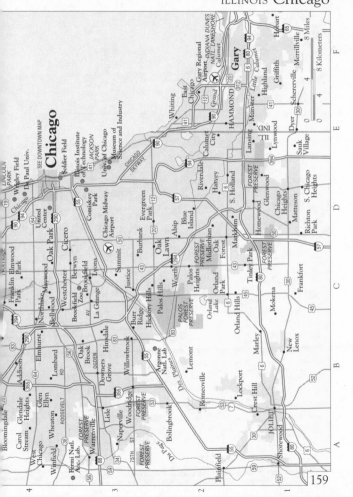

159

Chicago ILLINOIS

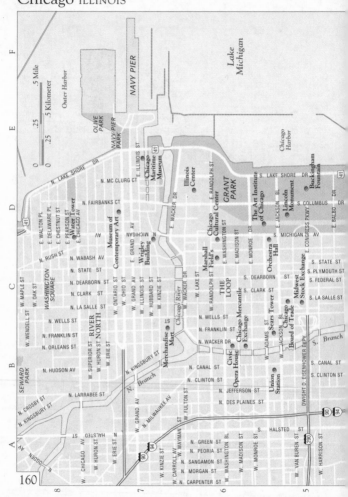

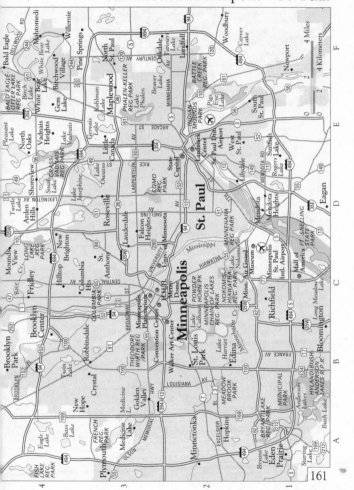

Kansas City / St. Louis MISSOURI

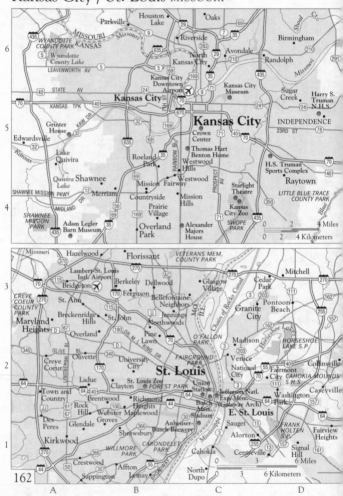

A   B   C   D

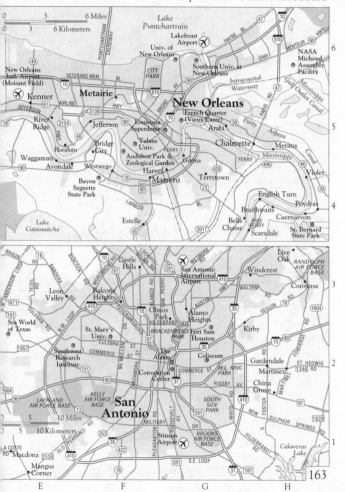

Dallas - Fort Worth TEXAS

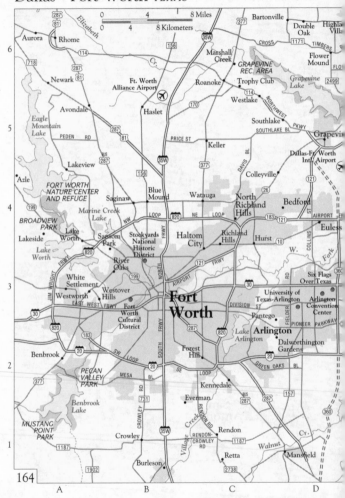

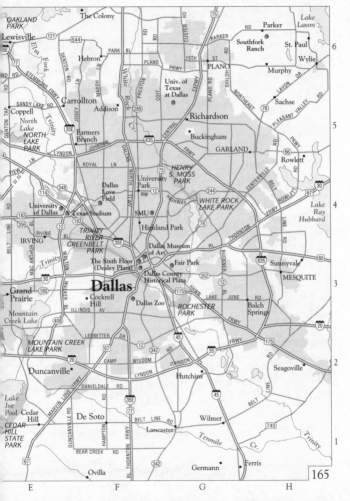

Houston TEXAS

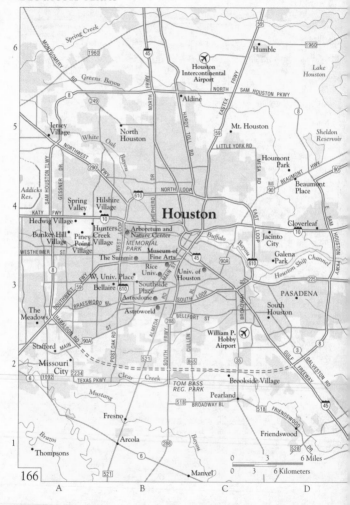

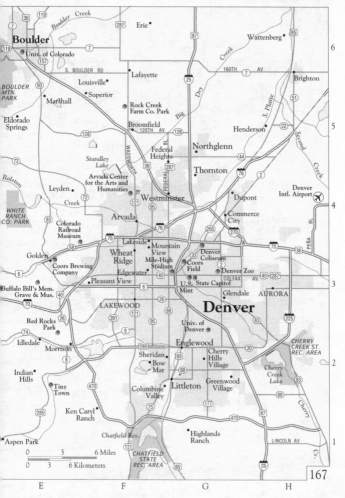

Boulder Creek

Erie

Wattenberg

7 36 119

Boulder

119

Univ. of Colorado

S. BOULDER RD
Lafayette

160TH AV

Brighton

93
BOULDER MTN. PARK
Louisville
Superior

Eldorado Springs

Marshall

Rock Creek Farm Co. Park

Big

Henderson

72

128

Broomfield
120TH AV

128

Northglenn

Standley Lake

Federal Heights

Thornton

Ralston

Leyden

Arvada Center for the Arts and Humanities

Westminster

Dupont

Denver Intl. Airport

58

Creek

72

121

95

Dupont

Commerce City

WHITE RANCH CO. PARK
93

Colorado Railroad Museum

Arvada

76

265

270

Golden

Lakeside

Mountain View

Denver Coliseum

70

6

Coors Brewing Company

Wheat Ridge

Mile-High Stadium

Coors Field

Denver Zoo

Edgewater

Pleasant View

6

40

U.S. Mint

State Capitol

COLFAX AV

Buffalo Bill's Mem. Grave & Mus.
70
40

26

LAKEWOOD

121

88

Denver

Glendale

AURORA

225

Red Rocks Park

74

391

8

95

Univ. of Denver

83

Idledale

285

Englewood

30

CHERRY CREEK ST. REC. AREA

Morrison

8

Sheridan

Cherry Hills Village

Cherry Creek Lake

Indian Hills

Bow Mar

88

Greenwood Village

83

Tiny Town

470

Columbine Valley

Littleton

Ken Caryl Ranch

75

177

87

470

Aspen Park

285

Chatfield Res.

Highlands Ranch

LINCOLN AV

121

CHATFIELD STATE REC. AREA

25

85

0   3   6 Miles
0   3   6 Kilometers

167

E   F   G   H

Phoenix ARIZONA

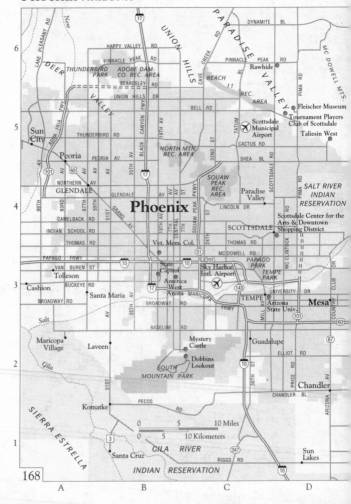

168

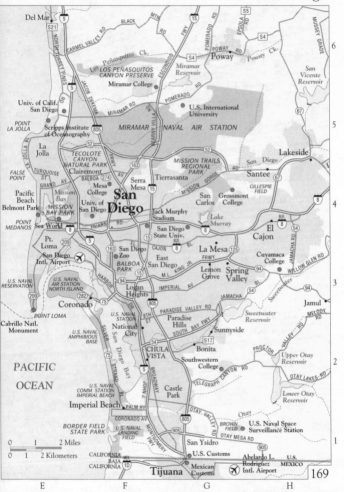

Los Angeles CALIFORNIA

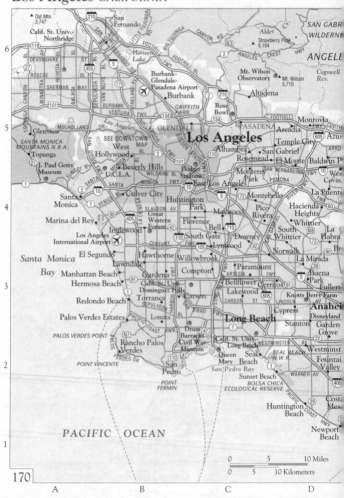

A   B   C   D

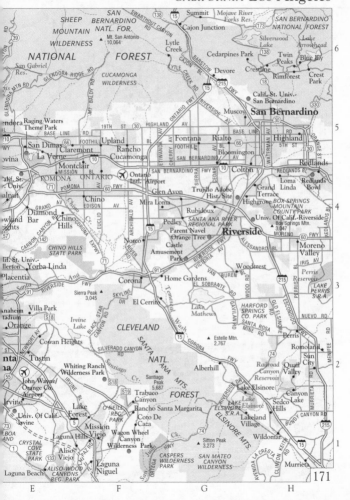

171

Los Angeles CALIFORNIA

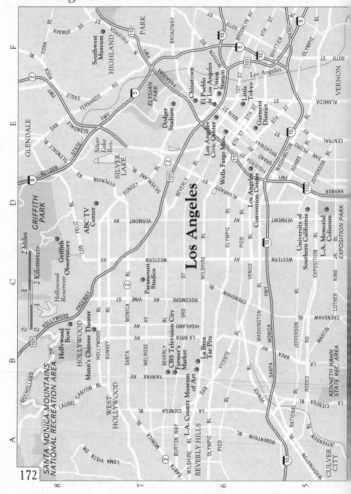

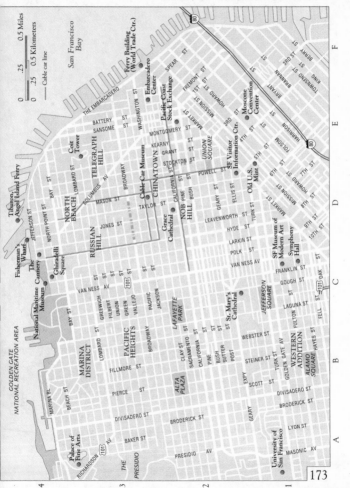

San Francisco Bay

Ferry Building (World Trade Ctr.)

THE EMBARCADERO

Tiburon, Angel Island Ferry

Fisherman's Wharf

Jefferson St

North Point St

Bay St

The Cannery

Ghirardelli Square

National Maritime Museum

Battery St

Sansome St

Washington St

Embarcadero Center

Pacific Coast Stock Exchange

Spear St

Fremont St

Mission St

Howard St

Moscone Convention Center

Bryant St

Harrison

Folsom St

Coit Tower

Telegraph Hill

Lombard St

Columbus Av

Broadway

Montgomery St

Kearny St

Grant Av

Stockton St

Powell St

Market St

Union Square

SF Visitor Information Ctr.

Old U.S. Mint

4th St

5th St

6th St

7th St

8th St

9th St

10th St

Howard St

Mission St

Folsom St

North Beach

Russian Hill

Mason St

Taylor St

Jones St

Cable Car Museum

Chinatown

California St

Pine St

Bush St

Nob Hill

Grace Cathedral

Geary St

Ellis St

Turk St

Leavenworth St

Hyde St

Larkin St

Polk St

Van Ness Av

SF Museum of Modern Art

Symphony Hall

Franklin St

Market St

Gough St

Van Ness Av

Greenwich St

Filbert St

Union St

Green St

Vallejo St

Pacific Av

Jackson St

Lafayette Park

Clay St

Sacramento St

California St

Pine St

Bush St

Sutter St

Post St

Webster St

St. Mary's Cathedral

Jefferson Square

Laguna St

Western Addition

Fulton St

Golden Gate Av

Turk St

Hayes St

Fell St

Oak St

Alamo Square

Fillmore St

Steiner St

Scott St

Expy

Pierce St

Alta Plaza

Pacific Heights

Marina District

Beach St

Bay St

Lombard St

Broadway

Divisadero St

Broderick St

Broderick St

Divisadero St

Geary

Lyon St

Marina Bl

Baker St

Richardson Av

101

The Presidio

Presidio Av

Masonic Av

University of San Francisco

Palace of Fine Arts

Golden Gate National Recreation Area

0 .25 0.5 Miles
0 .25 0.5 Kilometers
—— Cable car line

173

San Francisco Bay CALIFORNIA

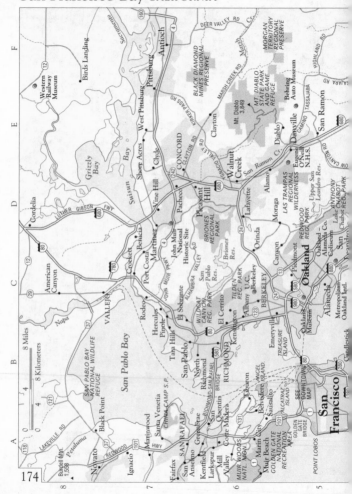

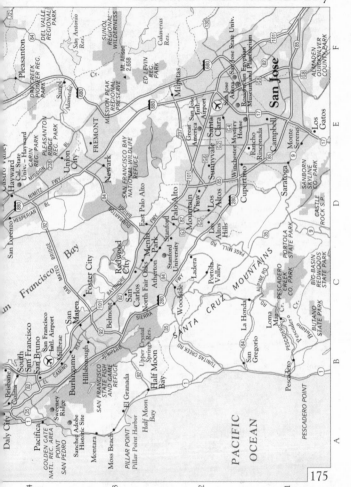

Seattle - Tacoma WASHINGTON

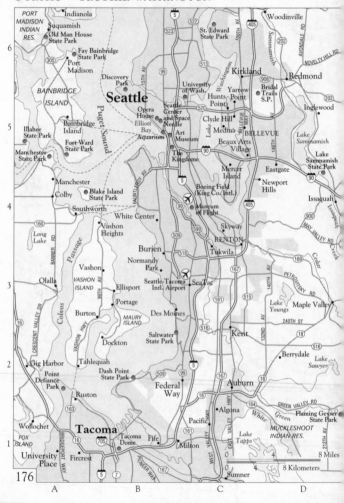

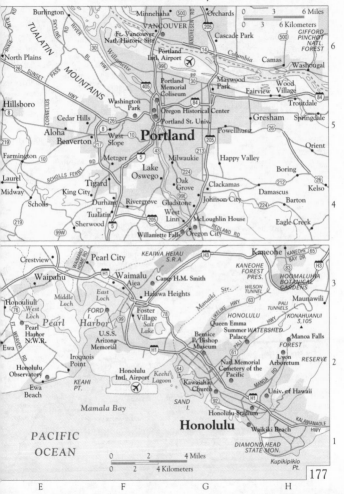

National Parks and Interstates

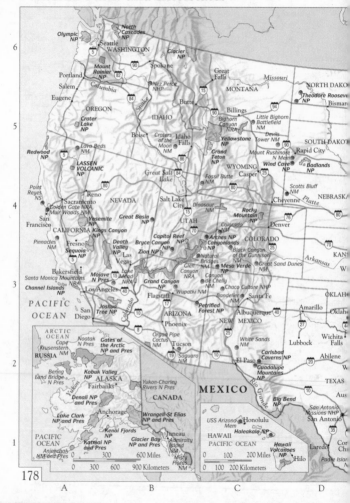

Interstates and National Parks

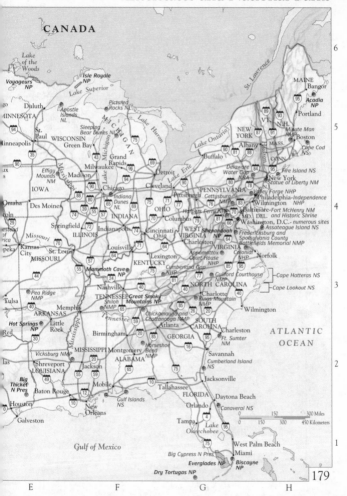

Yellowstone National Park WYOMING

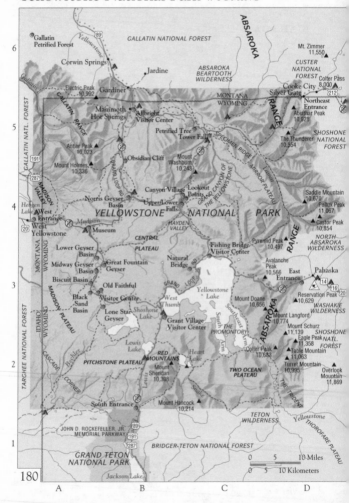

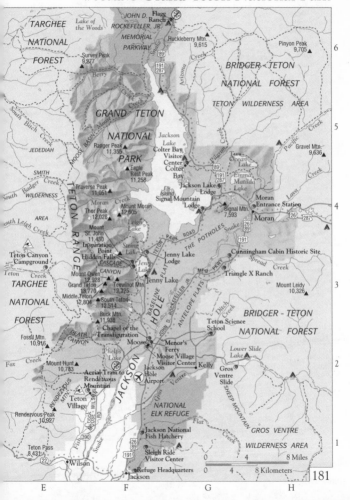

Yosemite National Park CALIFORNIA

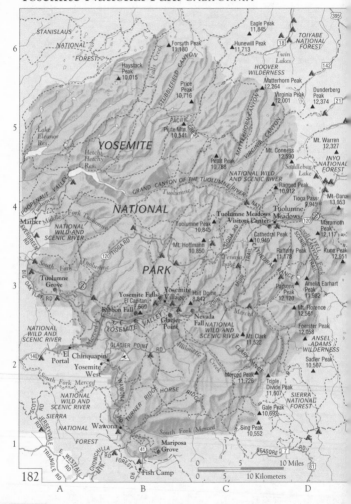

STANISLAUS

NATIONAL

FOREST

Eagle Peak
11,845

TOIYABE
NATIONAL
FOREST

Forsyth Peak
11,180

Hunewill Peak
11,713

Twin
Lakes

HOOVER
WILDERNESS

Haystack
Peak
10,015

Price
Peak
10,716

Matterhorn Peak
12,264

Virginia Peak
12,001

Dunderberg
Peak
12,374

Lake
Eleanor
Res.

Piute Mtn.
10,541

YOSEMITE

Hetch
Hetchy
Res.

Mt. Conness
12,590

Mt. Warren
12,327

INYO
NATIONAL
FOREST

Saddlebag
Lake

Pettit Peak
10,788

NATIONAL WILD
AND SCENIC RIVER

GRAND CANYON OF THE TUOLUMNE RIVER

Tuolumne

NATIONAL

Ragged Peak
10,912

Tioga Pass

Mt. Dana
13,053

PLEASANT VALLEY

North Fork Tuolumne

Middle Fork Tuolumne

NATIONAL
WILD AND
SCENIC RIVER

Mather

Tuolumne Peak
10,845

Tuolumne Meadows
Visitors Center

Tuolumne
Meadows

Cathedral Peak
10,940

Mammoth
Peak
12,117

South Fork Tuolumne

TIOGA RD

Mt. Hoffmann
10,850

Tenaya
Lake

Rafferty Peak
11,178

Kuna Peak
12,951

Tuolumne
Grove

PARK

Amelia Earhart
Peak
11,982

BIG OAK FLAT RD.

NATIONAL
WILD AND
SCENIC RIVER

Yosemite Falls
El Capitan,
7,569

Yosemite
Village

Half Dome
8,842

Parsons
Peak
12,120

Mt. Florence
12,561

Ribbon Fall

YOSEMITE VALLEY

Nevada
Fall

Glacier
Point

NATIONAL
WILD AND
SCENIC RIVER

Mt. Clark
11,522

Foerster Peak
12,058

ANSEL
ADAMS
WILDERNESS

El
Portal

Chinquapin

GLACIER POINT
RD

Illilouette Creek

Sadler Peak
10,567

Yosemite
West

WAWONA RD

South Fork Merced

Merced Peak
11,726

Triple
Divide Peak
11,607

SIERRA

SCOTT RD

JERSEYDALE RD

NATIONAL
WILD AND
SCENIC RIVER

SIERRA

TURNER RIDGE

HORSE RIDGE

CLARK RANGE

Gale Peak
10,693

NATIONAL
FOREST

TRIANGLE RD

NATIONAL

FOREST

Wawona

South Fork Merced

Sing Peak
10,552

E. WESTFALL RD

CHOWCHILLA MTN.

Mariposa
Grove

BEASORE RD

FOREST RD

Fish Camp

0   5   10 Miles

0   5   10 Kilometers

182

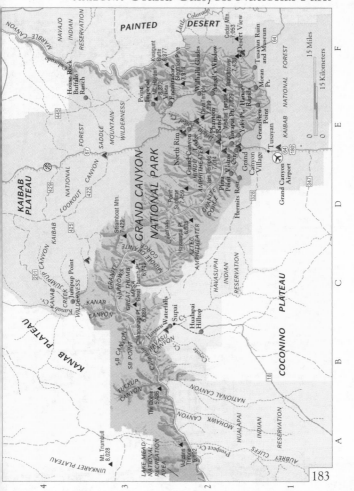

Cape Cod MASSACHUSETTS

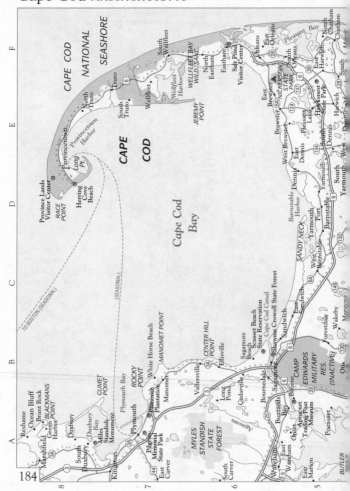

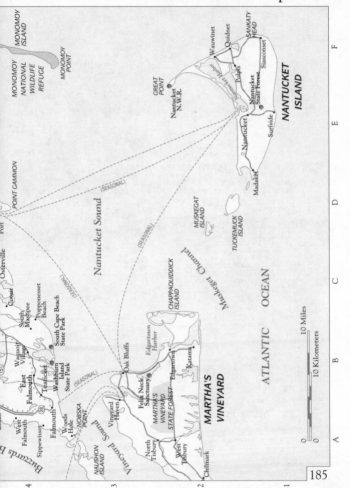

185

Acadia National Park MAINE

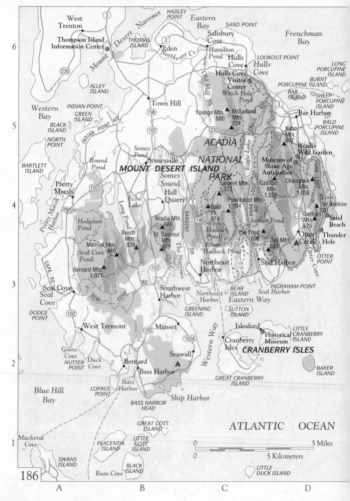

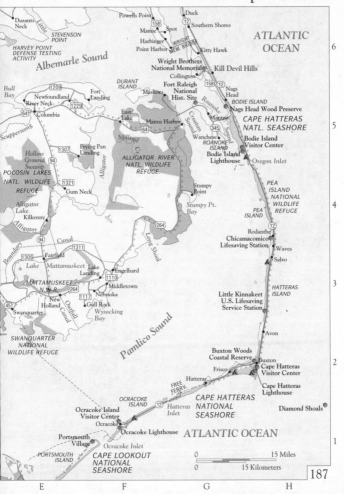

187

Florida Keys FLORIDA

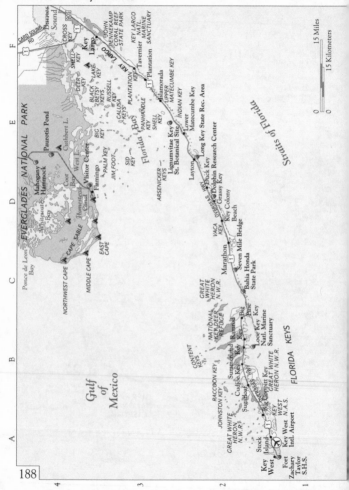

Traveler's Notes

Toll-Free Numbers

Airlines

Air Canada Airlines	800-776-3000
Air France	800-237-2747
Air India	800-442-4455
Air Jamaica	800-523-5585
Alaska Airlines	800-426-0333
Alitalia Airlines *New York**	800-223-5730
American Airlines	800-433-7300
British Airways	800-247-9297
Canadian Airlines	800-426-7000
Continental Airlines	
Domestic	800-525-0280
International	800-231-0856
Delta Air Lines Inc.	
Domestic	800-221-1212
International	800-241-4141
Finnair	800-950-5000
Hawaiian Airlines *Hawaii**	800-367-5320
Iberia Airlines of Spain	800-772-4642
Japan Airlines	800-525-3663
Korean Airlines	800-438-5000
Lufthansa German Airlines	800-645-3880
Northwest Airlines	
Domestic	800-225-2525
International	800-447-4747
Qantas Airways Ltd	800-227-4500
Sabena Belgian World Airlines	800-955-2000
Scandinavian Airlines	800-221-2350
Swissair	800-221-4750
TWA	800-221-2000
United Airlines	800-241-6522
USAir	800-428-4322
Virgin Atlantic Airways	800-862-8621
Varig Brazilian Airlines	800-468-2744
Viasa Venezuelan Intl. *Florida**	800-468-4272

Car Rental

Alamo Rent A Car	800-327-9633
Avis Rent A Car	
Nationwide	800-331-1212
International	800-331-1084
Budget Car & Truck Rental	800-527-0700
Hertz Rent A Car	800-654-3131
Payless Car Rental	800-237-2804
Thrifty Car Rental	800-367-2277

Courier Services

DHL	800-225-5345
Emery Worldwide	800-443-6379
Federal Express	800-238-5355
LEP Profit International	800-241-6690
United Parcel Service (UPS)	800-742-5877

Credit Cards (Lost or Stolen)

American Express	800-528-4800
Diners Club/Carte Blanche	800-234-6377
MasterCard International	800-826-2181
Visa Worldwide	800-336-8472

Hotels, Motels & Resorts

Best Western International	800-528-1234
Clarion Hotels & Resorts *Maryland**	800-252-7466
Comfort Inns & Suites	800-228-5150
Courtyard (by Marriott)	800-321-2211
Days Inns - Hotels/Suites	800-325-2525
Embassy Suites Hotel	800-362-2779
Forte Hotels	800-223-5672
Four Seasons Hotels	800-332-3442
Guest Quarters Suites	800-424-2900
Hampton Inns	800-426-7866
Helmsley Hotels	800-221-4982
Hilton Hotels	800-445-8667
Holiday Inn	800-465-4329
Howard Johnson Hotels & Lodges	800-654-2000
Hyatt Hotels & Resorts	800-228-9000
Marriott Hotels & Resorts	800-228-9290
Nikko Hotels International	800-645-5687
Omni International Hotels	800-843-6664
Princess Hotels International	800-223-1818
Radisson Hotels International	800-333-3333
Ramada Worldwide	800-228-2828
Ritz-Carlton Hotels	800-241-3333
Sheraton Hotels, Inns & Resorts	800-325-3535
Stouffer Renaissance Hotels	800-468-3571
Westin Hotels & Resorts	800-228-3000

Railways

Amtrak-Metroliner	800-523-8720
Conrail	800-228-4661
Metro North	800-638-7646

* Indicates the state within which the above listing is not applicable. For additional information regarding toll-free service for those companies you wish to reach, dial 1-800-555-1212 or check your local directory.

United States Area Codes

Alabama		Illinois		Mississippi	601	Pennsylvania	
Birmingham	205	Centralia	618	**Missouri**		Allentown	610
Mobile	334	Chicago	312	Kansas City	816	Altoona	814
Alaska	907	Lake Bluff	847	St. Louis	314	Harrisburg	717
Arizona		Oak Brook	630, 708	Springfield	417	Philadelphia	215, 610
Phoenix	602	Peoria	309	Sullivan	573	Pittsburgh	412
Tucson	520	Rockford	815	**Montana**	406	**Rhode Island**	401
Arkansas	501	Springfield	217	**Nebraska**		**South Carolina**	
California		**Indiana**		North Platte	308	Charleston	803
Bakersfield	805	Evansville	812	Omaha	402	Greenville	864
Beverly Hills	562	Indianapolis	317	**Nevada**	702	**South Dakota**	605
Fresno	209	South Bend	219	**New Hampshire**	603	**Tennessee**	
Los Angeles	213	**Iowa**		**New Jersey**		Knoxville	423
Oakland	510	Des Moines	515	Newark	201	Memphis	901
Orange	714	Dubuque	319	New Brunswick	908	Nashville	615
Pasadena	818	Sioux City	712	Trenton	609	**Texas**	
Sacramento	916	**Kansas**		**New Mexico**	505	Amarillo	806
San Bernardino	909	Topeka	913	**New York**		Austin	512
San Diego	619	Wichita	316	Albany	518	Dallas	214
San Francisco	415	**Kentucky**		Binghamton	607	Fort Worth	817
San Jose	408	Lexington	606	Buffalo	716	Galveston	409
Santa Rosa	707	Louisville	502	Long Island	516	Houston	713, 281
Colorado		**Louisiana**		New York City		San Antonio	210
Aspen	970	New Orleans	504	*Manhattan*	212, 917	Sweetwater	915
Colorado Springs	719	Shreveport	318	*Brx. Bklyn. Qns.*		Tyler	903
Denver	303	**Maine**	207	*& S.I.*	718, 917	**Utah**	801
Connecticut		**Maryland**		Syracuse	315	**Vermont**	802
Fairfield	203	Baltimore	410	White Plains	914	**Virginia**	
Hartford	860	Hagerstown	301	**North Carolina**		Arlington	703
Delaware	302	**Massachusetts**		Charlotte	704	Richmond	804
Florida		Boston	617	Greensboro	910	Roanoke	540
Bradenton	941	Framingham	508	Raleigh	919	**Washington**	
Ft. Lauderdale	954	Springfield	413	**North Dakota**	701	Olympia	360
Jacksonville	904	**Michigan**		**Ohio**		Seattle	206
Miami	305	Detroit	313	Cincinnati	513	Spokane	509
Orlando	407	Escanaba	906	Cleveland	216	**Washington, D.C.**	202
Tampa	813	Grand Rapids	616	Columbus	614	**West Virginia**	304
Georgia		Lansing	517	Toledo	419	**Wisconsin**	
Atlanta	404	Pontiac	810	**Oklahoma**		Eau Claire	715
Augusta	706	**Minnesota**		Oklahoma City	405	Madison	608
Savannah	912	Duluth	218	Tulsa	918	Milwaukee	414
Smyrna	770	Minneapolis	612	**Oregon**		**Wyoming**	307
Hawaii	808	Rochester	507	Eugene	541		
Idaho	208			Portland	503		

For long distance information, dial (Area Code) 555-1212. When requiring an unknown Area Code for a particular place, dial "O" (local Operator); there is no charge for the call.

International Dialing Codes

The procedure for dialing **Station-to-Station Calls** from the United States is as follows: A - dial 011, the international access code; B - dial the country code number listed below; C - dial the city code number; D - dial the local number. If your central telephone office is not equipped for International Dialing, you must dial "O" [local operator] in order to place a call.

Operator-Assisted Calls for person-to-person, collect, credit card, or calls charged to another number, dial "O" [local operator].

Algeria	213	**Brazil**	55	**Croatia, Rep. of**	385
American Samoa*	684	Belo Horizonte	31	**Cyprus**	357
Andorra	33	Brasília	61	Limassol	5
All Points	628	Recife	81	Nicosia	2
Anguilla**	809	Rio de Janeiro	21	**Czech Republic**	42
Antigua**	809	Sao Paulo	11	Ostrava	69
Argentina	54	**Brunei**	673	Prague	2
Buenos Aires	1	**Bulgaria**	359	**Denmark***	45
Cordoba	51	**Cameroon***	237	**Dominican Rep.****	809
La Plata	21	**Canada****		**Ecuador**	593
Rosario	41	Alberta	403	Cuenca	7
Aruba	297	British Columbia	604	Guayaquil	4
All Points	8	London	519	Quito	2
Australia	61	Manitoba	204	**Egypt, Arab Rep. of**	20
Adelaide	8	Montreal	514	Alexandria	3
Brisbane	7	New Brunswick	506	Aswan	97
Melbourne	3	Newfoundland	709	Cairo	2
Sydney	2	North Bay	705	**El Salvador***	503
Austria	43	Nova Scotia	902	**Eritrea**	291
Graz	316	Ottawa	613	Asmara	1
Linz Donau	70	Prince Edward Island	902	**Ethiopia**	251
Vienna	1	Quebec City	418	Addis Ababa	1
Bahamas**	809	Saskatchewan	306	**Fiji Islands***	679
Bahrain*	973	Sherbrooke	819	**Finland**	358
Barbados**	809	Thunder Bay	807	Helsinki	0
Belgium	32	Toronto (metro)	416	Tampere-Tammerfors	31
Antwerp	3	Toronto (vicinity)	905	**France**	33
Brussels	2	Yukon	403	Bordeaux	56
Ghent	9	**Chile**	56	Grenoble	76
Liege	41	Concepcion	41	Lourdes	62
Belize	501	Santiago	2	Lyon	7
Benin*	229	Valparaiso	32	Marseille	91
Bermuda**	809	**China**	86	Nice	93
Bolivia	591	Beijing	1	Paris	1
Cochabamba	42	Fuzhou	591	**French Antilles***	596
La Paz	2	Ghuangzhou	20	**French Polynesia***	689
Santa Cruz	3	Shanghai	21	**Gabon Republic***	241
Bosnia/Herzegovina	387	**Colombia**	57		
		Barranquilla	58		
		Bogota	1		
		Cali	23		

*City Routing code not required. **International access code not required.

Germany	49	Ireland, Rep. of	353	Liechtenstein	41
Berlin	30	Cork	21	All Points	75
Bonn	228	Dublin	1	Luxembourg*	352
Dusseldorf	211	Galway	91	Macedonia, F.Y.R.	389
Frankfurt (east)	335	Killarney	64	Malawi	265
Frankfurt (west)	69	Limerick	61	Domasi	531
Munich	89	Waterford	51	Malaysia	60
Gibraltar*	350	Wexford	53	Johor Bahru	7
Greece	30	Israel	972	Kuala Lumpur	3
Athens	1	Haifa	4	Mexico	52
Iraklion	81	Jerusalem	2	Acapulco	74
Larissa	41	Nazareth	6	Cancun	98
Salonica	31	Tel Aviv	3	Mexico City	5
Greenland	299	Italy	39	Monterrey	8
Godthaab	2	Bari	80	Tampico	12
Guam*	671	Florence	55	Monaco	33
Guantanamo Bay*	5399	Genoa	10	All Points	93
Guatemala	502	Milan	2	Morocco, Kingdom of	212
Guatemala City	2	Naples	81	Agadir	88
All Other Cities	9	Rome	6	Casablanca	2
Guyana	592	Venice	41	Mozambique	258
Georgetown	2	Ivory Coast, Rep. of*	225	Beira	3
Haiti*	509	Jamaica**	809	Maputo	1
Honduras*	504	Japan	81	Namibia	264
Hong Kong*	852	Kyoto	75	Nepal	977
Hungary	36	Osaka	6	Netherlands	31
Budapest	1	Sapporo	11	Amsterdam	20
Gyor	96	Tokyo	3	Rotterdam	10
Iceland	354	Yokohama	45	The Hague	70
Reykjavik	1	Jordan	962	Netherlands Antilles	599
India	91	Amman	6	Curaçao	9
Bombay	22	Irbid	2	St. Maarten	5
Calcutta	33	Karak	3	New Caledonia*	687
Madras	44	Kenya, Rep. of	254	New Zealand	64
New Delhi	11	Mombasa	11	Auckland	9
Indonesia	62	Nairobi	2	Christchurch	3
Jakarta	21	Korea, Rep. of	82	Hamilton	7
Medan	61	Inchon	32	Nicaragua	505
Iran	98	Pusan	51	Leon	311
Mashad	51	Seoul	2	Managua	2
Tabriz	41	Kuwait*	965	Nigeria, Fed. Rep. of	234
Tehran	21	Lesotho*	266	Lagos	1
Iraq	964	Liberia*	231	Norway*	47
Baghdad	1	Libya	218	Oman*	968
Basra	40	Misurata	51		
		Tripoli	21		

Source: AT&T International Telecommunications Guide

Pakistan	92	
Islamabad	51	
Lahore	42	
Panama, Rep. of*	507	
Papua New Guinea*	675	
Paraguay	595	
Asuncion	21	
Concepcion	31	
Peru	51	
Arequipa	54	
Lima	14	
Trujillo	44	
Philippines	63	
Cebu City	32	
Davao	82	
Iloilo City	33	
Manila	2	
Poland, Rep. of	48	
Crakow	12	
Gdansk	58	
Warsaw	22	
Portugal	351	
Lisbon	1	
Porto	2	
Setubal	65	
Qatar*	974	
Reunion Island*	262	
Romania, Soc. Rep. of	40	
Brasov	68	
Constanta	41	
Russia	7	
Moscow	095	
St. Petersburg	812	
Rwanda*	250	
St. Vincent**	809	
Saipan	670	
San Marino	378	
All Points	549	
Saudi Arabia	966	
Hofuf	3	
Makkah	2	
Riyadh	1	
Senegal Republic*	221	
Sierra Leone	232	
Freetown	22	

Singapore, Rep. of*	65
Slovakia	42
Bratislava	7
Slovenia, Rep. of	386
South Africa, Rep. of	27
Cape Town	21
Durban	31
Johannesburg	11
Spain	34
Barcelona	3
Madrid	1
Seville	5
Valencia	6
Sri Lanka	94
Colombo Central	1
Kandy	8
Suriname, Rep. of*	597
Swaziland	268
Sweden	46
Goteborg	31
Stockholm	8
Vasteras	21
Switzerland	41
Basel	61
Berne	31
Geneva	22
Zurich	1
Taiwan, Rep. of China	886
Kaohsiung	7
Tainan	6
Taipei	2
Tanzania	255
Dar Es Salaam	51
Tanga	53
Thailand	66
Bangkok	2
Burirum	44
Chanthaburi	39
Trinidad & Tobago**	809
Tunisia	216
Tunis	1
Turkey	90
Ankara	312
Istanbul Asya	216
Istanbul Avrupa	212
Izmir	232

Turkmenistan	7
Uganda	256
Entebbe	42
Kampala	41
Ukraine	7
Kiev	044
United Arab Emirates	971
Abu Dhabi	2
Al Ain	3
Dubai	4
United Kingdom	44
Belfast, N. Ire.	232
Birmingham, Eng.	21
Cardiff, Wales	222
Edinburgh, Scot.	31
Glasgow, Scot.	41
Liverpool, Eng.	51
London, Eng. *(inner)*	71
London, Eng. *(outer)*	81
Nottingham, Eng.	602
Prestwick, Scot.	292
Southampton, Eng.	703
Uruguay	598
Mercedes	532
Montevideo	2
Uzbekistan	7
Vatican City	39
All Points	6
Venezuela	58
Barquisimeto	51
Caracas	2
Maracaibo	61
Valencia	41
Virgin Islands**	809
Yemen, Rep. of	967
Amran	7
Zabid	1
Yugoslavia, Fed. Rep.	381
Belgrade	11
Zaire, Rep. of	243
Kinshasa	12
Lubumbashi	2
Zambia	260
Zimbabwe	263
Harare	4

*City Routing code not required. **International access code not required.

International Travel

Passports usually take two weeks or longer to be issued. They are often required for identification and should be carried at all times when traveling abroad. Canada, Mexico and some Caribbean Islands do not require passports.

Places of Issuance: Passport agencies located in major cities; office of a clerk of any Federal court or State court of record, or a judge or clerk of any probate court accepting applications; selected post offices.

Requirements: Applicants 13 years of age or older must apply in person and submit: **1)** Proof of citizenship: old passport or birth certificate; if not available, a notice from the registrar stating that no birth record exists, accompanied by a baptismal or synagogue certificate, hospital birth record, affidavits of persons having knowledge of the facts of birth, or other documentary evidence; citizens not born in the United States must submit certificate of naturalization or citizenship. **2)** Two recent identical photographs, measuring 2" x 2" with image from bottom of chin to top of head not less than 1" nor more than 1 ³/₈", and signed on the back in the center. **3)** Fees totaling $65 for adults 18 years and older, $40 for children. **4)** Proof of identity that contains your signature and readily identifies you by physical description or photograph.

Validity: Adult passports are valid ten years, children's five years, from the date of issue.

Lost Passport: If in the United States, notify the Passport Office of the Department of State, Washington, D.C. 20520. If you are out of the country, notify the nearest United States Consul and the local police authorities.

Visas: You should obtain necessary visas before you leave the United States. Apply directly to the embassies or consulates of the countries you wish to visit or consult with a travel agent. The process may take several weeks for each visa.

Customs: All articles acquired abroad and in your possession at the time of your return must be declared. There is a $400 duty exemption on articles for personal or household use (gifts are considered for personal use) for residents who have stayed abroad 48 hours or more (no minimum from Mexico or the U.S. Virgin Islands);

this exemption is allowed once in 30 days. The next $1,000 worth of merchandise is charged at a flat 10% rate; above $1,400, at the various rates of duty applicable to the articles. When returning from the U.S. Virgin Islands, American Samoa, or Guam, the exemption is $800 and the flat rate of duty is 5% for the next $1,000 worth of merchandise. A written declaration must be presented when the total value exceeds your personal exemption. It is a good idea to save sales slips of all merchandise bought abroad; they will help speed up the process of going through Customs when re-entering the United States.

Antiques are free of duty if proof that they are over 100 years old is provided. **Gifts** shipped to the United States are duty-free if the retail value of not more than $50 is received by one person in one day. **Personal items** acquired abroad and shipped home are not exempt from duty. **Money,** in excess of $5,000, sent out, brought in, or received by mail or any other means requires the filing of Customs form 4790, available from a Customs officer. This amount includes U.S. or foreign currency, travelers checks, money orders, and negotiable instruments or investment securities in bearer form. **Health:** No vaccinations are required to return to the United States from any country. Some countries, however, may require certain immunizations and International Certificates of Vaccination documenting the dates of your inoculations. The booklet "Health Information for International Travel," available from the Superintendent of Documents, U.S. Government Printing Office, Washington, D.C. 20402, provides pertinent information.

An international driving license is required in some countries which do not recognize a U.S. driver's license. Check with the embassy or consulate of the countries in which you plan to drive. It can be obtained at an international automobile club. You will need two passport-size photographs and your valid U.S. license. **Insurance policies** should be checked before leaving home to be sure they provide coverage while abroad. **Electrical converters** may be necessary for the appliance you bring with you. U.S. appliances operate on 110 volts while 90% of the world operates on 220 volts.

Country Information

Country, Capital	Predominant Language(s)	Predominant Religion(s)	Currency
Argentina, *Buenos Aires*	Spanish	Roman Catholic	Peso
Australia, *Canberra*	English	Protestant	Dollar
Austria, *Vienna*	German	Roman Catholic	Schilling
Belgium, *Brussels*	Flemish (Dutch)	Roman Catholic	Franc
Canada, *Ottawa*	English, French	Roman Catholic	Dollar
Chile, *Santiago*	Spanish	Roman Catholic	Peso
China, *Beijing*	Mandarin Chinese	Officially atheist	Yuan
Denmark, *Copenhagen*	Danish	Protestant	Krone
Egypt, *Cairo*	Arabic	Islam	Pound
England, *London*	English	Protestant	Pound
Finland, *Helsinki*	Finnish, Swedish	Protestant	Markka
France, *Paris*	French	Roman Catholic	Franc
Germany, *Berlin*	German	Protestant	Deutschemark
Greece, *Athens*	Greek	Greek Orthodox	Drachma
India, *Delhi*	Hindi, English	Hindu, Islam	Rupee
Ireland, *Dublin*	Irish, English	Roman Catholic	Pound
Israel, *Jerusalem*	Hebrew, Arabic	Jewish	New Shekel
Italy, *Rome*	Italian	Roman Catholic	Lira
Japan, *Tokyo*	Japanese	Buddhist	Yen
Mexico, *Mexico City*	Spanish	Roman Catholic	Peso
Netherlands, *Amsterdam*	Dutch	Roman Catholic	Guilder
Norway, *Oslo*	Norwegian	Protestant	Krone
Peru, *Lima*	Spanish	Roman Catholic	Intis
Philippines, *Manila*	Filipino, English	Roman Catholic	Peso
Poland, *Warsaw*	Polish	Roman Catholic	Zloty
Portugal, *Lisbon*	Portuguese	Roman Catholic	Escudo
Romania, *Bucurest*	Romanian	Orthodox	Lei
Russia, *Moscow*	Slavic	Orthodox	Rouble
Saudi Arabia, *Riyadh*	Arabic	Islam	Riyal
South Africa, *Cape Town*	English	Protestant	Rand
South Korea, *Seoul*	Korean	Buddhism	Won
Spain, *Madrid*	Spanish	Roman Catholic	Peseta
Sweden, *Stockholm*	Swedish	Protestant	Krona
Switzerland, *Bern*	German	Protestant	Franc
Syria, *Damascus*	Arabic	Islam	Pound
Taiwan, *Taipei*	Chinese	Buddhism	Dollar
Thailand, *Bangkok*	Thai	Buddhism	Baht
Turkey, *Ankara*	Turkish	Islam	Pound
Venezuela, *Caracas*	Spanish	Roman Catholic	Bolivar
Zaire, *Kinshasa*	French	Roman Catholic	Zaire

United States Foreign Embassies

Country	Washington, D.C. Address	Telephone [202]	U.S. Embassy
Argentina	1600 New Hampshire Avenue NW 20009	939-6400	Buenos Aires
Australia	1601 Massachusetts Avenue NW 20036	797-3000	Canberra
Austria	3524 International Court NW 20008	895-6700	Vienna
Belgium	3330 Garfield Street NW 20008	333-6900	Brussels
Brazil	3006 Massachusetts Avenue NW 20008	745-2700	Brasilia
Canada	501 Pennsylvania Avenue NW 20001	682-1740	Ottawa
Chile	1732 Massachusetts Avenue NW 20036	785-1746	Santiago
China	2300 Connecticut Avenue NW 20008	328-2500	Beijing
Denmark	3200 Whitehaven Street NW 20008	234-4300	Copenhagen
Egypt	2310 Decatur Place NW 20008	232-5400	Cairo
Finland	3216 New Mexico Avenue NW 20016	363-2430	Helsinki
France	4101 Reservoir Road NW 20007	944-6000	Paris
Germany	4645 Reservoir Road NW 20007	298-4000	Bonn
Great Britain	3100 Massachusetts Avenue NW 20008	462-1340	London
Greece	2221 Massachusetts Avenue NW 20008	939-5800	Athens
India	2107 Massachusetts Avenue NW 20008	939-7000	New Delhi
Ireland	2234 Massachusetts Avenue NW 20008	462-3939	Dublin
Israel	3514 International Drive NW 20008	364-5500	Tel Aviv
Italy	1601 Fuller Street NW 20009	328-5500	Rome
Japan	2520 Massachusetts Avenue NW 20008	939-6700	Tokyo
Korea	2450 Massachusetts Avenue NW 20008	939-5600	Seoul
Mexico	1911 Pennsylvania Avenue NW 20006	728-1600	Mexico
Netherlands	4200 Linnean Avenue NW 20008	244-5300	The Hague
Norway	2720 34th Street NW 20008	333-6000	Oslo
Peru	1700 Massachusetts Avenue NW 20036	833-9860	Lima
Philippines	1617 Massachusetts Avenue NW 20036	483-1414	Manila
Poland	2640 16th Street NW 20009	234-3800	Warsaw
Portugal	2125 Kalorama Road NW 20008	328-8610	Lisbon
Russia	1125 16th Street NW 20036	628-7551	Moscow
Saudi Arabia	601 New Hampshire Avenue NW 20037	342-3800	Riyadh
Singapore	1824 R Street NW 20009	667-7555	Singapore
South Africa	3051 Massachusetts Avenue NW 20008	232-4400	Pretoria
Spain	2700 15th Street NW 20009	265-0190	Madrid
Sweden	600 New Hampshire Avenue NW 20037	944-5600	Stockholm
Switzerland	2900 Cathedral Avenue NW 20008	745-7900	Bern
Syria	2215 Wyoming Avenue NW 20008	232-6313	Damascus
Taiwan	4201 Wisconsin Avenue NW 20016	895-1800	Taiwan
Turkey	1714 Massachusetts Avenue NW 20036	659-8200	Ankara
Venezuela	1099 30th Street NW 20007	342-2214	Caracas
Zaire	1800 New Hampshire Avenue NW 20009	234-7690	Kinshasa

United States Road and Air Distances

Major Cities	Atlanta	Boston	Chicago	Cleveland	Dallas	Denver	Houston	Indianapolis	Kansas City	Los Angeles	Louisville	Miami
Atlanta, GA		1037	674	672	795	1398	789	493	798	2182	382	655
		946	*606*	*554*	*731*	*1208*	*689*	*432*	*693*	*1946*	*321*	*595*
Boston, MA	1037		963	628	1748	1949	1804	906	1391	2779	941	1504
	946		*867*	*563*	*1561*	*1767*	*1597*	*817*	*1257*	*2611*	*829*	*1258*
Chicago, IL	674	963		335	917	996	1067	181	499	2054	292	1329
	606	*867*		*316*	*802*	*901*	*925*	*177*	*403*	*1745*	*286*	*1197*
Cleveland, OH	672	628	335		1159	1321	1273	294	779	2367	345	1264
	554	*563*	*316*		*1021*	*1213*	*1091*	*261*	*695*	*2053*	*304*	*1080*
Dallas, TX	795	1748	917	1159		781	243	865	489	1387	819	1300
	731	*1561*	*802*	*1021*		*645*	*224*	*762*	*460*	*1235*	*732*	*1121*
Denver, CO	1398	1949	996	1321	781		1019	1058	600	1059	1120	2037
	1208	*1767*	*901*	*1213*	*645*		*864*	*989*	*543*	*849*	*1035*	*1716*
Detroit, MI	699	695	266	170	1143	1253	1265	278	743	2073	360	1352
	595	*632*	*235*	*95*	*987*	*1135*	*1076*	*230*	*630*	*1979*	*306*	*1146*
Indianapolis, IN	493	906	181	294	865	1058	987		485	2073	111	1148
	432	*817*	*177*	*261*	*762*	*989*	*845*		*452*	*1815*	*111*	*1021*
Los Angeles, CA	2182	2779	2054	2367	1387	1059	1538	2073	1589		2108	2687
	1946	*2611*	*1745*	*2053*	*1235*	*849*	*1379*	*1815*	*1363*		*1842*	*2342*
Louisville, KY	382	941	292	345	819	1120	928	111	520	2108		1037
	321	*829*	*286*	*304*	*732*	*1035*	*791*	*111*	*491*	*1842*		*911*
Miami, FL	655	1504	1329	1264	1300	2037	1190	1148	1448	2687	1037	
	595	*1258*	*1197*	*1080*	*1121*	*1716*	*964*	*1021*	*1252*	*2342*	*911*	
Milwaukee, WI	761	1050	87	422	991	1029	1142	268	537	2087	379	1416
	669	*860*	*67*	*328*	*853*	*908*	*984*	*238*	*436*	*1756*	*348*	*1259*
Minneapolis, MN	1068	1368	405	740	936	841	1157	485	447	1889	697	1723
	906	*1124*	*334*	*622*	*852*	*693*	*1034*	*503*	*394*	*1536*	*603*	*1501*
Nashville, TN	242	1088	446	513	660	1156	769	279	556	2025	168	897
	214	*943*	*409*	*448*	*631*	*1023*	*657*	*249*	*492*	*1797*	*151*	*806*
New Orleans, LA	479	1507	912	1030	496	1273	356	796	806	1883	685	856
	425	*1367*	*837*	*917*	*447*	*1067*	*305*	*708*	*690*	*1671*	*621*	*674*
New York, NY	841	206	802	473	1552	1771	1608	713	1198	2786	748	1308
	760	*187*	*740*	*425*	*1391*	*1638*	*1417*	*664*	*1113*	*2475*	*662*	*1090*
Philadelphia, PA	741	296	738	413	1452	1691	1508	633	1118	2706	668	1208
	665	*281*	*678*	*363*	*1302*	*1569*	*1324*	*587*	*1039*	*2401*	*576*	*1013*
Phoenix, AZ	1793	2604	1713	1992	998	792	1149	1698	1214	389	1733	2298
	1587	*2300*	*1440*	*1738*	*868*	*589*	*1009*	*1489*	*1043*	*370*	*1506*	*1972*
Portland, OR	2601	3046	2083	2418	2009	1238	2205	2227	1809	959	2320	3256
	2172	*2537*	*1739*	*2046*	*1616*	*985*	*1825*	*1877*	*1481*	*834*	*1950*	*2700*
St. Louis, MO	541	1141	289	529	630	857	779	235	257	1845	263	1196
	484	*1046*	*258*	*487*	*550*	*781*	*667*	*229*	*238*	*1592*	*254*	*1068*
San Francisco, CA	2496	3095	2142	2467	1753	1235	1912	2256	1835	379	2349	3053
	2139	*2704*	*1846*	*2161*	*1465*	*956*	*1635*	*1944*	*1498*	*337*	*1989*	*2585*
Seattle, WA	2618	2976	2013	2348	2078	1307	2274	2194	1839	1131	2305	3273
	2181	*2496*	*1720*	*2021*	*1660*	*1019*		*1866*	*1489*	*954*	*1944*	*2724*
Washington, DC	608	429	671	345	1319	1616	1375	558	1043	2631	582	1075
	533	*413*	*589*	*288*	*1171*	*1464*	*1190*	*476*	*927*	*2288*	*451*	*921*

Road Miles are on the top in roman; Air Miles *are below in italic.*

United States Road and Air Distances

Milwaukee	Minneapolis	Nashville	New Orleans	New York	Philadelphia	Phoenix	Portland	St. Louis	San Francisco	Seattle	Washington, D.C.	Major Cities
761 / *669*	1068 / *906*	242 / *214*	479 / *425*	841 / *760*	741 / *665*	1793 / *1587*	2601 / *2172*	541 / *484*	2496 / *2139*	2618 / *2181*	608 / *533*	Atlanta, GA
1050 / *860*	1368 / *1124*	1088 / *943*	1507 / *1367*	206 / *187*	296 / *281*	2604 / *2300*	3046 / *2537*	1141 / *1046*	3095 / *2704*	2976 / *2496*	429 / *413*	Boston, MA
87 / *67*	405 / *334*	446 / *409*	912 / *837*	802 / *740*	738 / *678*	1713 / *1440*	2083 / *1739*	289 / *258*	2142 / *1846*	2013 / *1720*	672 / *589*	Chicago, IL
422 / *328*	740 / *622*	513 / *448*	1030 / *917*	473 / *425*	413 / *363*	1992 / *1738*	2418 / *2046*	529 / *487*	2467 / *2161*	2348 / *2021*	346 / *288*	Cleveland, OH
991 / *853*	936 / *852*	660 / *631*	496 / *448*	1552 / *1391*	1452 / *1302*	998 / *868*	2009 / *1616*	630 / *550*	1753 / *1465*	2078 / *1660*	1319 / *1171*	Dallas, TX
1029 / *908*	841 / *693*	1156 / *1023*	1273 / *1067*	1771 / *1638*	1691 / *1569*	792 / *589*	1238 / *985*	857 / *781*	1235 / *956*	1307 / *1019*	1616 / *1464*	Denver, CO
353 / *237*	671 / *528*	528 / *457*	1045 / *926*	637 / *509*	573 / *453*	1957 / *1671*	2349 / *1953*	513 / *440*	2399 / *2079*	2279 / *1927*	506 / *383*	Detroit, MI
268 / *238*	586 / *503*	279 / *249*	796 / *708*	713 / *664*	633 / *587*	1698 / *1489*	2227 / *1877*	235 / *229*	2256 / *1944*	2194 / *1866*	558 / *476*	Indianapolis, IN
2087 / *1756*	1889 / *1536*	2025 / *1797*	1883 / *1671*	2786 / *2475*	2706 / *2401*	389 / *370*	959 / *834*	1845 / *1593*	379 / *337*	1131 / *952*	2631 / *2288*	Los Angeles, CA
379 / *348*	697 / *603*	168 / *151*	685 / *620*	748 / *662*	668 / *576*	1733 / *1506*	2320 / *1950*	263 / *254*	2349 / *1989*	2305 / *1944*	582 / *451*	Louisville, KY
1416 / *1259*	1723 / *1501*	897 / *806*	856 / *674*	1308 / *1090*	1208 / *1013*	2298 / *1972*	3256 / *2700*	1196 / *1068*	3053 / *2585*	3273 / *2724*	1075 / *921*	Miami, FL
	332 / *297*	532 / *475*	994 / *903*	889 / *746*	825 / *690*	1751 / *1460*	2010 / *1718*	363 / *317*	2175 / *1845*	1940 / *1694*	758 / *612*	Milwaukee, WI
332 / *297*		826 / *695*	1214 / *1040*	1207 / *1028*	1143 / *980*	1616 / *1276*	1678 / *1426*	552 / *448*	1940 / *1589*	1608 / *1399*	1076 / *908*	Minneapolis, MN
532 / *475*	826 / *695*		517 / *471*	892 / *766*	792 / *675*	1650 / *1448*	2359 / *1972*	299 / *271*	2333 / *1968*	2376 / *1977*	659 / *542*	Nashville, TN
994 / *903*	1214 / *1040*	517 / *471*		1311 / *1182*	1211 / *1088*	1494 / *1301*	2505 / *2051*	673 / *604*	2249 / *1911*	2574 / *2086*	1078 / *954*	New Orleans, LA
889 / *746*	1207 / *1028*	892 / *766*	1311 / *1182*		100 / *94*	2411 / *2153*	2885 / *2454*	948 / *892*	2934 / *2586*	2815 / *2421*	233 / *228*	New York, NY
825 / *690*	1143 / *980*	792 / *675*	1211 / *1088*	100 / *94*		2331 / *2075*	2821 / *2406*	868 / *813*	2866 / *2521*	2751 / *2378*	133 / *134*	Philadelphia, PA
1751 / *1460*	1616 / *1276*	1650 / *1448*	1494 / *1301*	2411 / *2153*	2331 / *2075*		1266 / *1009*	1470 / *1262*	763 / *651*	1437 / *1106*	2256 / *1956*	Phoenix, AZ
2010 / *1718*	1678 / *1426*	2359 / *1972*	2505 / *2051*	2885 / *2454*	2821 / *2406*	1266 / *1009*		2060 / *1708*	636 / *550*	172 / *129*	2754 / *2327*	Portland, OR
363 / *317*	552 / *448*	299 / *271*	673 / *604*	948 / *892*	868 / *813*	1470 / *1262*	2060 / *1708*		2089 / *1735*	2081 / *1709*	793 / *696*	St. Louis, MO
2175 / *1845*	1940 / *1589*	2333 / *1968*	2249 / *1911*	2934 / *2586*	2866 / *2521*	763 / *651*	636 / *550*	2089 / *1735*		808 / *678*	2799 / *2419*	San Francisco, CA
1940 / *1694*	1608 / *1399*	2376 / *1977*	2574 / *2086*	2815 / *2421*	2751 / *2378*	1437 / *1106*	172 / *129*	2081 / *1709*	808 / *678*		2684 / *2306*	Seattle, WA
758 / *612*	1076 / *908*	659 / *542*	1078 / *954*	233 / *228*	133 / *134*	2256 / *1956*	2754 / *2327*	793 / *696*	2799 / *2419*	2684 / *2306*		Washington, DC

All distances in statute miles. To convert to kilometres, multiply by 1.6

International Air Distances

Major Cities	Athens	Bangkok	Berlin	Bombay	Buenos Aires	Capetown	Frankfurt	Hong Kong	Honolulu	London	Madrid	Melbourne
Amsterdam	1349	5707	360	4258	7117	5997	227	5772	7238	222	921	10286
Athens		4930	1121	3209	7269	4957	1123	5316	8337	1488	1474	9297
Bangkok	4930		5351	1870	10490	6301	5305	1076	6610	5929	6334	4579
Beijing	4734	2027	4600	2960	11968	8034	4836	1195	5049	5089	5759	5632
Beirut	719	4272	1689	2527	7695	4794	1762	4756	8520	2151	2190	8579
Berlin	1114	5351		3915	7395	5958	345	5443	7323	580	1162	9929
Bombay	3209	1870	3915		9275	5103	4078	2679	8024	4478	4689	6101
Buenos Aires	7269	10490	7395	9275		4285	7142	11478	7558	6907	6236	7219
Cairo	694	4521	1768	2706	7341	4510	1823	5057	8838	2158	2069	8700
Cape Town	4957	6301	5958	5103	4285		5730	7377	11534	5988	5306	6428
Caracas	5805	10558	5242	9024	3167	6361	5015	10171	6009	4662	4351	9703
Copenhagen	1327	5361	222	3990	7498	6179	421	5392	7088	595	1289	9936
Frankfurt	1123	5305	345	4078	7142	5730		5403	7432	442	1106	9882
Helsinki	1549	4903	689		8061	6490	955	4867	6788	1135	1835	9448
Hong Kong	5316	1076	5443	2679	11478	7377	5403		5557	5986	6556	4605
Honolulu	8337	6610	7323	8024	7558	11534	7432	5557		7241	7874	5501
Istanbul	346	4648	1075	2992	7611	5204	1156	4989	8104	1551	1701	9100
Lima	7309	12241	6893	10389	1958	6074	6659	11415	5938	6315	5907	8052
Lisbon	1771	6651	1442	4982	5964	5201	1164	6862	7821	989	317	11049
London	1488	5929	580	4478	6907	5988	442	5986	7241		786	10508
Madrid	1474	6334	1162	4689	6236	5306	1106	6556	7874	786		10766
Melbourne	9297	4579	9929	6101	7219	6428	9882	4605	5501	10508	10766	
Mexico City	7006	9793	6054	9782	4591	8516	5931	8789	3781	5558	5642	8420
Montreal	4736	8337	3740	7499	5642	7920	3638	7736	4886	3256	3449	10390
Moscow	1387	4394	1001	3132	8369	6277	961	4443	7049	1556	2140	8965
Nairobi	2836	4481	3947	2816	6463	2543	3922	5447	10739	4229	3840	7159
New Delhi	3107	1812	3598	708	9809	5769	3801	2339	7398	4178	4528	6340
New York	4938	8669	3980	7811	5279	7801	4028	8061	4969	3473	3596	10352
Oslo	1625	5395	523		7618	6477	686	5342	6782	718	1485	9934
Paris	1305	5877	549	4367	6857	5782	353	5992	7452	215	652	10442
Rio de Janeiro	6030	9987	6207	8334	6857	3773	6237	11002	8295	5751	5045	8218
Rome	665	5493	735	3837	6929	5231	594	5773	8026	892	849	9940
San Francisco	6792	7930	5673	8406	6455	10248	5709	6904	2397	5369	5806	7850
Shanghai	5301	1797	5231	3117		8062	5708	760		5728	6386	4991
Singapore	5629	887	6167	2427	9870	6007	6119	1608	6728	6747	7079	3767
Stockholm	1524	5141	505	3880	7823	6422	759	5115	6832	892	1613	9693
Tokyo	5924	2865	5557	4196	11411	9155	5533	1792	3860	5956	6704	5070
Vienna	793	5252	323	3701	7353	5656	386	5432	7621	767	1124	9802
Warsaw	994	5032	322	3589	7656	5934	557	5147	7353	901	1425	9609
Zurich	1014	5605	410	4060	7028	6018	177	5775	7605	489	770	10370

All distances in statute miles. To convert to kilometres, multiply by 1.6

International Air Distances

Mexico City	Montreal	Moscow	New York	Paris	Rio de Janeiro	Rome	San Francisco	Singapore	Stockholm	Tokyo	Warsaw	Major Cities
5717	3420	1337	3654	271	5983	804	5465	6526	716	5788	684	Amsterdam
7006	4736	1387	4938	1305	6030	665	6792	5629	1524	5924	994	Athens
9793	8337	4394	8669	5877	9987	5493	7930	887	5141	2865	5032	Bangkok
7722	6470	3627	6867	5138	10778	5059	5934	2754	4156	1305		Beijing
7690	5400	1514	5622	1987	6478	1377	7302	4935	1954	5598	1458	Beirut
6054	4002	1001	3980	549	6207	735	5673	6167	505	5557	322	Berlin
9728	7499	3132	7811	4367	8334	3837	8406	2427	3880	4196	3589	Bombay
4591	5642	8369	5279	6857	1231	6929	6455	9870	7823	11411	7656	Buenos Aires
7687	5424	1770	5598	1973	6153	1325	7436	5143	2135	5937	1614	Cairo
8516	7920	6277	7801	5782	3773	5231	10248	6007	6422	9155	5934	Cape Town
2228	2458	6176	2124	4735	2805	5196	3908	11408	5406	8813	5551	Caracas
5912	3602	971	3857	642	6321	951	5473	6195	340	5415	413	Copenhagen
5931	3638	961	4028	353	6237	594	5709	6119	759	5533	557	Frankfurt
6105	3827	554	4126	1192	6872	1386	5435	5759	248	4872	583	Helsinki
8789	7736	4443	8061	5992	11002	5773	6904	1608	5115	1792	5147	Hong Kong
3781	4886	7049	4969	7452	8295	8026	2397	6728	6832	3860	7353	Honolulu
7087	4792	1087	5022	1400	6378	859	6711	5379	1371	5574	856	Istanbul
2635	3989	7855	3635	6367	2351	6733	4516	11689	7109	9628	7209	Lima
5391	3261	2433	3377	904	4777	1157	5679	7393	1862	6943	1708	Lisbon
5558	3256	1556	3473	215	5751	892	5369	6747	892	5956	901	London
5642	3449	2140	3596	652	5045	849	5806	7079	1613	6704	1425	Madrid
8420	10390	8965	10352	10442	8218	9940	7850	3767	9693	5070	9609	Melbourne
	2305	6671	2086	5723	4769	6365	1889	10331	5932	7036	6335	Mexico City
2305		4397	333	3432	5082	4093	2544	9207	3642	6470	4015	Montreal
6671	4397		4680	1550	7162	1477	5884	5236	764	4663	716	Moscow
9207	7281	3928	7365	4020	5556	3350	9598	4636	4333	6996	3809	Nairobi
9104	6992	2703	7391	4103	8747	3684	7691	2574	3467	3638	3268	New Delhi
2086	333	4680		3638	4805	4293	2574	9539	3939	6757	4271	New York
5703	3406	1024	3686	838	6462	1251	5196	6249	254	5238	665	Oslo
5723	3432	1550	3638		5681	688	5579	6676	964	6054	853	Paris
4769	5082	7162	4805	5681		5704	6621	9776	6638	11535	6453	Rio de Janeiro
6365	4093	1477	4293	688	5704		6259	6231	1255	6140	823	Rome
1889	2544	5884	2574	5579	6621	6259		8449	5372	5148	5854	San Francisco
	7067	4248	7384	5772	1139	5671	6150	2363	4837	6996	4963	Shanghai
10331	9207	5236	9539	6676	9776	6231	8449		5993	3304	5846	Singapore
5932	3642	764	3939	964	6638	1255	5372	5993		5091	530	Stockholm
7036	6470	4663	6757	6054	11535	6140	5148	3304	5091		5346	Tokyo
6316	4014	1039	4233	643	6124	483	5992	6039	798	5689	341	Vienna
6335	4015	716	4271	853	6453	823	5854	5846	530	5346		Warsaw
	3727	1355	3919	296	5820	430	5810	6502	923	5960	643	Zurich

United States Weather

City	Average Monthly Temperatures (Fahrenheit Degrees) and Average Number of Rain Days										
	Jan.		Feb.		Mar.		Apr.		May		June
Albuquerque, NM	35°	3	40°	4	46°	4	56°	3	65°	4	75°	4
Atlanta, GA	42	11	46	10	52	12	62	9	70	9	77	10
Bismarck, ND	8	8	14	7	25	8	43	8	54	10	64	12
Boise, ID	29	12	36	10	41	9	49	8	57	8	65	7
Boston, MA	29	12	30	11	38	12	49	11	59	11	68	11
Buffalo, NY	24	20	24	17	32	16	45	14	55	13	66	10
Charleston, WV	35	15	37	14	45	15	56	14	65	13	72	11
Charlotte, NC	42	10	44	10	51	12	61	9	69	9	76	10
Chicago, IL	24	11	27	10	37	13	50	12	60	11	71	10
Cleveland, OH	27	16	28	15	36	16	48	14	58	13	68	11
Columbia, SC	45	10	48	10	54	11	64	8	72	9	79	10
Concord, NH	21	11	23	10	32	11	44	11	55	12	65	11
Dallas, TX	45	7	49	6	56	7	66	9	74	8	82	6
Denver, CO	33	6	35	6	39	8	49	9	58	10	68	9
Des Moines, IA	19	7	24	7	34	10	50	10	61	11	71	11
Detroit, MI	25	13	27	12	35	13	48	12	58	12	69	11
Honolulu, HI	72	10	72	10	73	9	75	9	77	7	79	6
Indianapolis, IN	28	11	31	12	40	13	52	12	62	12	72	10
Juneau, AK	24	18	28	18	32	18	34	17	47	17	53	16
Los Angeles, CA	55	6	56	6	57	5	59	3	62	1	65	1
Miami, FL	67	7	68	6	71	6	75	6	78	11	81	15
Milwaukee, WI	19	11	23	9	31	12	45	12	54	12	65	11
Minneapolis, MN	12	9	16	7	28	10	45	10	57	12	66	12
Nashville, TN	38	11	41	11	49	12	60	11	69	11	77	10
New Orleans, LA	53	10	56	9	61	9	69	7	75	7	80	10
New York, NY[1]	32	11	33	10	41	12	52	11	62	11	72	10
Oklahoma City, OK	37	5	41	6	48	7	60	28	68	10	77	9
Phoenix, AZ	51	3	55	4	60	3	68	2	76	1	85	1
Pittsburgh, PA	28	16	29	14	38	16	50	13	60	12	69	1
Portland, ME	22	11	23	10	32	11	43	12	53	13	62	11
Portland, OR	38	19	43	16	46	17	51	14	57	12	62	9
St. Louis, MO	31	8	35	8	43	11	57	11	66	11	75	9
Salt Lake City, UT	28	10	33	9	40	10	49	10	58	8	66	6
San Francisco, CA	51	11	53	10	54	9	55	6	57	3	59	1
Seattle, WA	38	19	42	16	44	18	49	14	55	10	60	9
Washington, DC	36	10	37	9	45	11	56	10	66	11	75	9

Airport data except as noted. Temperature is based on standard 30-year period, 1941-1970. Precipitation is based on average number of days with 0.01 inch or more for period of record through 1977.

United States Weather

Average Monthly Temperatures (Fahrenheit Degrees) and Average Number of Rain Days

July		Aug.		Sept.		Oct.		Nov.		Dec.		City
79°	9	77°	10	70°	6	58°	5	45°	3	36°	4	Albuquerque, NM
79	12	78	9	73	7	63	6	52	8	44	10	Atlanta, GA
71	9	69	8	58	7	47	5	29	6	16	8	Bismarck, ND
75	2	72	3	63	4	52	6	40	10	32	12	Boise, ID
73	9	71	10	65	9	55	9	45	11	33	12	Boston, MA
70	10	58	11	62	11	52	11	40	16	28	20	Buffalo, NY
75	13	74	11	68	9	57	9	45	12	36	14	Charleston, WV
79	12	78	9	72	7	62	7	51	7	43	10	Charlotte, NC
75	10	74	8	66	10	55	9	40	10	29	11	Chicago, IL
71	10	70	9	64	10	54	11	42	15	30	16	Cleveland, OH
81	12	80	11	75	8	64	6	54	7	46	9	Columbia, SC
70	10	67	10	60	9	49	8	38	11	25	11	Concord, NH
86	5	86	5	78	7	68	6	56	6	48	6	Dallas, TX
74	9	73	8	64	6	54	5	42	5	36	5	Denver, CO
75	9	73	9	64	9	54	7	38	6	25	7	Des Moines, IA
73	9	72	9	65	9	54	9	41	11	30	13	Detroit, MI
80	8	81	7	80	7	79	9	77	10	74	10	Honolulu, HI
75	9	73	8	66	8	56	8	42	10	31	12	Indianapolis, IN
56	17	54	18	49	20	42	23	33	20	27	21	Juneau, AK
69	1	70	—	69	1	65	2	61	3	56	5	Los Angeles, CA
82	16	83	17	82	17	78	15	72	8	68	7	Miami, FL
70	10	69	9	61	9	51	9	37	10	24	11	Milwaukee, WI
71	10	69	10	59	9	49	8	32	8	18	9	Minneapolis, MN
80	10	79	9	72	8	61	7	48	9	40	11	Nashville, TN
82	15	82	13	78	10	70	6	60	7	55	10	New Orleans, LA
77	11	75	10	68	8	59	8	47	9	36	10	New York, NY[1]
82	7	81	6	73	7	62	6	49	5	40	5	Oklahoma City, OK
91	4	89	5	86	3	72	3	60	2	53	4	Phoenix, AZ
72	11	70	9	64	9	53	10	41	13	31	17	Pittsburgh, PA
68	8	66	9	59	8	49	9	39	12	26	12	Portland, ME
67	4	67	5	62	7	54	13	45	18	41	19	Portland, OR
79	9	77	7	70	9	59	8	45	8	35	10	St. Louis, MO
77	4	75	5	65	5	52	6	39	7	30	9	Salt Lake City, UT
59	—	59	1	62	1	61	4	57	7	52	10	San Francisco, CA
65	5	64	7	60	9	52	14	45	18	41	20	Seattle, WA
79	10	77	9	71	8	60	7	48	8	37	9	Washington, DC

Records vary from 5 to 109 years, averaging about 36 years. ¹City office data. —Less than half a day.
Source: U. S. Bureau of the Census, *Statistical Abstract of the United States: 1979*

215

International Weather*

Country / City	Jan.			Feb.			Mar.			Apr.			May			June		
Argentina, Buenos Aires	85°	63°	7	83°	63°	6	79°	60°	7	72°	53°	8	64°	47°	7	57°	41°	7
Australia, Sydney	78	65	14	78	65	13	76	63	14	71	58	14	66	52	13	61	48	12
Austria, Vienna	34	25	15	38	28	14	47	30	13	58	42	13	67	50	13	73	56	14
Bahamas, Nassau	77	65	6	77	64	5	79	66	5	81	69	6	84	71	9	87	74	12
Belgium, Brussels	40	30	21	44	32	17	51	36	17	58	41	18	65	46	16	72	52	15
Brazil, Rio De Janeiro	84	73	13	85	73	11	83	72	12	80	69	10	77	66	10	76	64	7
Canada, Toronto	30	16	16	30	15	12	37	23	13	50	34	12	63	44	13	73	54	11
Canada, Vancouver	41	32	20	44	34	17	50	37	17	58	40	14	64	46	12	69	52	11
China, Peking	34	14	3	39	18	3	52	30	3	70	45	4	81	55	6	88	64	8
Denmark, Copenhagen	36	28	17	36	28	13	41	31	12	51	38	13	61	46	11	67	52	13
Egypt, Cairo	65	47	1	69	48	1	75	52	8	83	57	4	91	63	2	95	68	0
England, London	43	36	15	44	36	13	50	38	11	56	42	12	62	47	12	69	53	11
France, Paris	43	34	17	45	34	14	54	39	12	60	43	13	68	49	12	73	55	12
Germany, Berlin	35	26	17	37	26	15	46	31	12	56	39	13	66	47	12	72	53	13
Greece, Athens	55	44	16	57	44	11	60	46	11	68	52	9	77	61	8	86	68	4
Hong Kong	64	56	4	63	55	5	67	60	7	75	67	8	82	74	13	85	78	18
India, Delhi	70	44	2	75	49	2	87	58	1	97	68	1	105	79	2	102	83	4
Ireland, Dublin	46	34	13	47	35	10	51	37	10	55	39	11	60	43	10	65	48	11
Israel, Jerusalem	55	41	9	56	42	11	65	46	3	73	50	3	81	57	6	85	60	1
Italy, Rome	52	40	8	55	42	9	59	45	8	66	50	6	74	56	5	82	63	4
Japan, Tokyo	47	29	5	48	31	6	54	36	10	63	46	10	71	54	10	76	63	12
Kenya, Nairobi	77	54	5	79	55	6	77	57	11	75	58	16	72	56	17	70	53	9
Korea, Seoul	32	15	8	37	20	6	47	29	7	62	41	8	72	51	10	80	61	10
Mexico, Acapulco	88	72	1	88	72	0	88	72	0	90	73	0	90	77	3	91	77	13
Mexico, Mexico City	66	42	4	69	43	5	75	47	9	77	51	14	78	54	17	76	55	21
Monaco, Monte Carlo	54	47	5	55	47	5	57	50	7	61	54	5	66	59	5	73	64	4
Morocco, Marrakech	65	40	7	68	43	5	74	48	6	79	52	6	84	57	2	92	62	1
Netherlands, Amsterdam	40	31	22	42	31	19	49	34	16	56	40	16	64	46	14	70	51	14
Norway, Oslo	28	19	15	30	19	12	39	25	9	50	34	11	61	43	10	68	50	13
Philippines, Manila	86	69	6	88	69	3	91	71	4	93	73	4	93	75	12	91	75	17
Portugal, Lisbon	57	46	15	59	47	12	63	50	14	67	53	10	71	55	10	77	60	5
Russia, Moscow	15	3	18	22	8	15	32	18	15	50	34	13	66	46	13	70	51	12
Saudi Arabia, Riyadh	70	46	1	73	48	1	82	56	3	89	64	4	100	72	1	107	77	0
Singapore	86	73	17	88	73	11	88	75	14	88	75	15	89	75	15	88	75	13
Spain, Madrid	47	35	8	52	36	7	59	41	10	65	45	9	70	50	10	80	58	5
Sweden, Stockholm	30	23	16	30	22	14	37	26	10	47	34	11	58	43	11	67	51	13
Switzerland, Geneva	38	29	11	42	30	9	51	36	9	59	42	9	66	49	11	73	55	11
Taiwan, Taipei	66	54	9	65	53	13	70	57	12	77	63	14	83	69	12	89	73	13
Turkey, Istanbul	46	37	18	47	36	14	51	38	14	60	45	9	69	53	8	77	60	6
Venezuela, Caracas	75	56	6	77	56	2	79	58	3	81	60	4	80	62	9	78	62	14

*Average Maximum and Minimum Temperatures and *Days* with 0.04 inches of Precipitation

International Weather*

July			Aug.			Sept.			Oct.			Nov.			Dec.			Country / City
57°	42°	8	60°	43°	9	64°	46°	8	69°	50°	9	76°	56°	9	82°	61°	8	Argentina, Buenos Aires
60	46	12	63	48	11	67	51	12	71	56	12	74	60	12	77	63	13	Australia, Sydney
76	60	13	75	59	13	68	53	10	56	44	13	45	37	14	37	30	15	Austria, Vienna
88	75	14	89	76	14	88	75	15	85	73	13	81	70	9	79	67	6	Bahamas, Nassau
73	54	17	72	54	18	69	51	13	60	45	17	48	38	20	42	32	19	Belgium, Brussels
75	63	7	76	64	7	75	65	11	77	66	13	79	68	13	82	71	14	Brazil, Rio De Janeiro
79	59	10	77	58	9	69	51	12	56	40	11	43	31	13	33	21	13	Canada, Toronto
74	54	7	73	54	8	65	49	9	57	44	16	48	39	19	43	35	22	Canada, Vancouver
88	70	13	86	68	11	79	57	7	68	43	3	48	28	3	37	18	2	China, Peking
71	57	14	70	56	14	64	51	15	54	44	16	45	38	16	40	34	17	Denmark, Copenhagen
96	70	0	95	71	0	90	68	0	86	65	3	78	58	.8	68	50	.1	Egypt, Cairo
71	56	12	71	56	11	65	52	13	58	46	13	50	42	15	45	38	15	England, London
76	58	12	75	58	13	70	53	13	60	46	13	50	40	15	44	36	16	France, Paris
75	57	14	74	56	14	68	50	12	56	42	14	45	36	16	38	29	15	Germany, Berlin
92	73	2	92	73	3	84	67	4	75	60	8	66	53	12	58	47	15	Greece, Athens
87	78	17	87	78	15	85	77	12	81	73	6	74	65	2	68	59	3	Hong Kong
96	81	8	93	79	8	93	75	4	93	65	1	84	52	2	73	46	1	India, Delhi
67	52	13	67	51	12	63	48	12	57	43	11	51	39	12	47	37	14	Ireland, Dublin
87	63	0	87	64	0	85	62	.1	81	59	1	70	53	4	59	45	7	Israel, Jerusalem
87	67	1	86	67	2	79	62	5	71	55	8	61	49	11	55	44	10	Italy, Rome
83	70	10	86	72	9	79	66	12	69	55	11	60	43	7	52	33	5	Japan, Tokyo
69	51	6	70	52	7	75	52	6	76	55	8	74	56	15	74	55	11	Kenya, Nairobi
84	70	16	87	71	13	78	59	9	67	45	7	51	32	9	37	20	9	Korea, Seoul
90	77	14	91	77	13	90	75	16	90	75	9	90	73	2	88	72	1	Mexico, Acapulco
72	53	27	73	54	27	74	53	23	70	50	13	68	46	6	66	43	4	Mexico, Mexico City
78	71	1	78	71	2	74	67	4	68	61	7	61	54	7	56	49	6	Monaco, Monte Carlo
101	67	0	100	68	1	92	63	3	83	57	4	73	49	3	66	42	7	Morocco, Marrakech
72	55	17	71	55	18	67	50	19	57	44	20	48	38	21	42	33	21	Netherlands, Amsterdam
72	55	15	70	53	14	60	46	14	48	38	14	38	31	16	32	25	17	Norway, Oslo
88	75	24	87	75	23	88	75	22	88	74	19	87	72	14	86	70	11	Philippines, Manila
81	63	2	82	63	2	79	62	6	72	58	9	63	52	13	58	47	15	Portugal, Lisbon
73	55	15	72	53	14	61	45	13	48	37	15	35	26	15	24	15	23	Russia, Moscow
107	78	0	107	75	0	102	72	0	94	61	0	84	55	0	70	49	0	Saudi Arabia, Riyadh
88	75	13	87	75	14	87	75	14	87	74	16	87	74	18	87	74	19	Singapore
87	63	2	85	63	3	77	57	6	65	49	8	55	42	9	48	36	10	Spain, Madrid
71	57	13	68	56	14	60	49	14	49	41	15	40	34	16	35	29	17	Sweden, Stockholm
77	58	9	76	58	11	69	53	10	58	44	10	47	37	11	40	31	10	Switzerland, Geneva
92	76	10	91	75	12	88	73	10	81	67	9	75	62	7	69	57	8	Taiwan, Taipei
82	65	4	82	66	4	76	61	7	68	55	11	59	48	14	51	41	18	Turkey, Istanbul
78	61	15	79	61	15	80	61	13	79	61	12	77	60	13	78	58	10	Venezuela, Caracas

*To convert degrees Fahrenheit to degrees Celsius, subtract 32, multiply by 5, and divide by 9.

Weight and Measure Equivalents

Linear Measure

	1 inch	2.54 cm.
12 inches	1 foot	0.3048 m.
3 feet	1 yard	0.9144 m.
5½ yards	1 rod/pole/perch	5.029 m.
40 rods	1 furlong	201.168 m.
8 furlongs or 5,280 ft.	1 statute mile	1.609 km.
3 miles	1 land league	4.83 km.
6,076.115 feet	1 international nautical mile	1.852 km.

Area Measure

	1 sq. inch	6.452 sq. cm.
144 sq. inches	1 sq. foot	0.0929 m²
9 sq. feet	1 sq. yard	0.8361 m²
43,560 sq. feet	1 acre	0.4047 ha.
640 acres	1 sq. mile	259 ha.
1 sq. mile	1 section	259 ha.
36 sections	1 township	9,324 ha.

U.S. Liquid

8 drams	1 ounce or 1.8047 cu. in.	0.0295 l.
4 oz.	1 gill or 7.219 cu. in.	0.1183 l.
4 gills	1 pint or 28.875 cu. in.	0.4732 l.
2 pints	1 quart or 57.75 cu. in.	0.9464 l.
4 quarts	1 gallon or 231 cu. in.	3.7845 l.

U.S. Dry

2 pints	1 quart or 67.20 cu. in.	1.1012 l.
8 quarts	1 peck or 537.61 cu. in.	8.8098 l.
4 pecks	1 bushel or 2,150.42 cu. in.	35.2391 l.

Weight (Avoirdupois)

	1 grain	0.0648 g.
437.5 grains	1 ounce	28.3495 g.
7,000 grains	1 pound or 16 ounces	0.4536 g.
100 pounds	1 hundredweight	45.36 kg.
2,000 pounds	1 short ton	0.9072 t.
2,240 pounds	1 long ton	1.016 t.

Customary U.S. Household

1 teaspoon	⅙ fluid ounce	4.9 ml.
3 teaspoons	1 tablespoon or ½ fluid ounce	14.8 ml.
16 tablespoons	1 cup or 8 fluid ounces	236.6 ml.
2 cups	1 pint or 16 fluid ounces	473.2 ml.
2 pints	1 quart or 32 fluid ounces	946.4 ml.
4 quarts	1 gallon or 128 fluid ounces	3.785 l.

Metric Linear

	1 millimeter	0.03937 in.
10 millimeters	1 centimeter	0.3937 in.
10 centimeters	1 decimeter	3.937 in.
10 decimeters	1 meter	3.2808 ft.
10 meters	1 dekameter	32.808 ft.
10 dekameters	1 hectometer	328.08 ft.
10 hectometers	1 kilometer	0.621 mi.

Metric Area

	1 sq. millimeter	0.00155 in.²
100 millimeters²	1 sq. centimeter	0.15499 in.²
100 centimeters²	1 sq. decimeter	15.499 in.²
100 decimeters²	1 sq. meter	1.196 yd.²
100 meters²	1 sq. dekameter	119.6 yd.²
100 dekameters²	1 sq. hectometer	2.471 acres
100 hectometers²	1 sq. kilometer	0.386 sq. mi. or 247.1 acres

Metric Capacity of Volume

10 milliliters	1 centiliter	0.338 fluid oz.
10 centiliters	1 deciliter	3.38 fluid oz. or 0.1057 liquid qt.
10 deciliters	1 liter	1.0567 liquid qt.or 0.9081 dry qt.
10 liters	1 dekaliter	2.642 gal. or 0.284 bu.
10 dekaliters	1 hectoliter	26.418 gal. or 2.838 bu.
10 hectoliters	1 kiloliter	264.18 gal. or 28.38 bu.

Metric Weight

10 milligrams	1 centigram	0.1543 gr.
10 centigrams	1 decigram	1.5432 gr.
10 decigrams	1 gram	15.432 gr.
10 grams	1 dekagram	0.35274 oz.
10 dekagrams	1 hectogram	3.5274 oz.
10 hectograms	1 kilogram	2.2046 lb.
1,000 kilograms	1 metric ton	2,204.6 lb.

Weight and Measure Conversions

When you know	Multiply by	To Find*	When you know	Multiply by	To Find*
Linear			**Linear**		
inches	25.0	millimeters	millimeters	0.04	inches
inches	2.5	centimeters	centimeters	0.4	inches
feet	30.0	centimeters	centimeters	0.033	feet
feet	0.3	meters	centimeters	0.01	yards
yards	90.0	centimeters	meters	3.3	feet
yards	0.9	meters	meters	1.1	yards
rods	5.0	meters	meters	0.2	rods
miles	1.6	kilometers	kilometers	0.62	miles
Capacity or Volume			**Capacity or Volume**		
teaspoons	5.0	milliliters	milliliters	0.2	teaspoons
tablespoons	15.0	milliliters	milliliters	0.07	tablespoons
fluid ounces	30.0	milliliters	milliliters	0.034	fluid ounces
fluid ounces	0.03	liters	milliliters	0.004	cups
cups	240.0	milliliters	liters	34.0	fluid ounces
cups	0.24	liters	liters	4.2	cups
pints	0.47	liters	liters	2.1	pints
quarts	0.95	liters	liters	1.06	quarts
gallons	3.8	liters	liters	0.26	gallons
busheis	35.0	liters	liters	0.03	bushels
Weight			**Weight**		
ounces	28.0	grams	grams	0.035	ounces
ounces	0.028	kilograms	grams	0.002	pounds
pounds	454.0	grams	kilograms	35.0	ounces
pounds	0.45	kilograms	kilograms	2.2	pounds
short ton	0.9	metric ton	metric ton	1.1	short ton

*Approximately

Temperature Conversions

$$FAHRENHEIT = 9 \times CELSIUS \div 5 + 32$$

32°	50°	75°	100°	125°	150°	175°	200° 212°
0°	10°	23.9°	37.8°	51.7°	65.6°	79.4°	93.3° 100°

$$CELSIUS = FAHRENHEIT - 32 \times 5 \div 9$$

Clothing Size Equivalents

Men's Suits and Overcoats

U. S.	36	38	40	42	44	46
U. K.	36	38	40	42	44	46
Europe	46	48	50	52	54	56

Men's Shoes

U. S.	7½	8	8½	9½	10½	11½	
U. K.	7	7½	8	9	10	11	
Europe	40½	41	42	43	44½	46	

Men's Shirts

U. S.	14	14½	15	15½	16	17
U. K.	14	14½	15	15½	16	17
Europe	36	37	38	39	41	43

Women's Suits and Dresses

U. S.	6	8	10	12	14	16
U. K.	8	10	12	14	16	18
Europe	36	38	40	42	44	46

Women's Shoes

U. S.	6	6½	7	7½	8	8½
U. K.	4½	5	5½	6	6½	7
Europe	36½	37	37½	38	38½	39

Children's Clothes

U. S.		4	6	8	10	12	14
U. K. –Height(")	43	48	55	58	60	62
– Age	4-5	6-7	9-10	11	12	13
Europe –Height (cm)	125	135	150	155	160	165
– Age		7	9	12	13	14	15

Perpetual Calendar

1

SUN	MON	TUE	WED	THU	FRI	SAT
1	2	3	4	5	6	7
8	9	10	11	12	13	14
15	16	17	18	19	20	21
22	23	24	25	26	27	28
29	30	31				

1A

SUN	MON	TUE	WED	THU	FRI	SAT
1	2	3	4	5	6	7
8	9	10	11	12	13	14
15	16	17	18	19	20	21
22	23	24	25	26	27	28
29	30					

2

SUN	MON	TUE	WED	THU	FRI	SAT
				1	2	3	4	5	6
7	8	9	10	11	12	13
14	15	16	17	18	19	20
21	22	23	24	25	26	27
28	29	30	31			

2A

SUN	MON	TUE	WED	THU	FRI	SAT
	1	2	3	4	5	6
7	8	9	10	11	12	13
14	15	16	17	18	19	20
21	22	23	24	25	26	27
28	29	30				

3

SUN	MON	TUE	WED	THU	FRI	SAT
			1	2	3	4	5
6	7	8	9	10	11	12
13	14	15	16	17	18	19
20	21	22	23	24	25	26
27	28	29	30	31		

3A

SUN	MON	TUE	WED	THU	FRI	SAT
			1	2	3	4	5
6	7	8	9	10	11	12
13	14	15	16	17	18	19
20	21	22	23	24	25	26
27	28	29	30			

4

SUN	MON	TUE	WED	THU	FRI	SAT
				1	2	3	4
5	6	7	8	9	10	11
12	13	14	15	16	17	18
19	20	21	22	23	24	25
26	27	28	29	30	31	

4A

SUN	MON	TUE	WED	THU	FRI	SAT
				1	2	3	4
5	6	7	8	9	10	11
12	13	14	15	16	17	18
19	20	21	22	23	24	25
26	27	28	29	30		

5

SUN	MON	TUE	WED	THU	FRI	SAT
					1	2	3
4	5	6	7	8	9	10
11	12	13	14	15	16	17
18	19	20	21	22	23	24
25	26	27	28	29	30	31

5A

SUN	MON	TUE	WED	THU	FRI	SAT
					1	2	3
4	5	6	7	8	9	10
11	12	13	14	15	16	17
18	19	20	21	22	23	24
25	26	27	28	29	30	

6

SUN	MON	TUE	WED	THU	FRI	SAT
					1	2
3	4	5	6	7	8	9
10	11	12	13	14	15	16
17	18	19	20	21	22	23
24/31	25	26	27	28	29	30

6A

SUN	MON	TUE	WED	THU	FRI	SAT
					1	2
3	4	5	6	7	8	9
10	11	12	13	14	15	16
17	18	19	20	21	22	23
24	25	26	27	28	29	30

7

SUN	MON	TUE	WED	THU	FRI	SAT
						1
2	3	4	5	6	7	8
9	10	11	12	13	14	15
16	17	18	19	20	21	22
23/30	24/31	25	26	27	28	29

7A

SUN	MON	TUE	WED	THU	FRI	SAT
						1
2	3	4	5	6	7	8
9	10	11	12	13	14	15
16	17	18	19	20	21	22
23/30	24	25	26	27	28	29

8

SUN	MON	TUE	WED	THU	FRI	SAT
						1
2	3	4	5	6	7	8
9	10	11	12	13	14	15
16	17	18	19	20	21	22
23	24	25	26	27	28	29

Every possible monthly calendar is represented above. In the tables on the following pages you will find the years 1985 through 2010; leap years, having 29 days in February, are in the bold type. On the lines with each year, under the month, is the reference number for the applicable calendar month above. For example, to find the day of the week for April 24, 1989, locate 1989 in the year column; looking across that line, under the **Apr.** column, you will find the reference number 7A; in that numbered calendar month above you will note that April 24, 1989 was a Monday.

Year	Jan.	Feb.	Mar.	Apr.	May	June	July	Aug.	Sept.	Oct.	Nov.	Dec.
1985	3	6A	6	2A	4	7A	2	5	1A	3	6A	1
1986	4	8	7	3A	5	1A	3	6	2A	4	7A	2
1987	5	1A	1	4A	6	2A	4	7	3A	5	1A	3
1988	6	2A	3	6A	1	4A	6	2	5A	7	3A	5
1989	1	4A	4	7A	2	5A	7	3	6A	1	4A	6
1990	2	5A	5	1A	3	6A	1	4	7A	2	5A	7
1991	3	6A	6	2A	4	7A	2	5	1A	3	6A	1
1992	4	8	1	4A	6	2A	4	7	3A	5	1A	3
1993	6	2A	2	5A	7	3A	5	1	4A	6	2A	4
1994	7	3A	3	6A	1	4A	6	2	5A	7	3A	5
1995	1	4A	4	7A	2	5A	7	3	6A	1	4A	6
1996	2	5A	6	2A	4	7A	2	5	1A	3	6A	1
1997	4	8	7	3A	5	1A	3	6	2A	4	7A	2
1998	5	1A	1	4A	6	2A	4	7	3A	5	1A	3
1999	6	2A	2	5A	7	3A	5	1	4A	6	2A	4
2000	7	3A	4	7A	2	5A	7	3	6A	1	4A	6
2001	2	5A	5	1A	3	6A	1	4	7A	2	5A	7
2002	3	6A	6	2A	4	7A	2	5	1A	3	6A	1
2003	4	8	7	3A	5	1A	3	6	2A	4	7A	2
2004	5	1A	2	5A	7	3A	5	1	4A	6	2A	4
2005	7	3A	3	6A	1	4A	6	2	5A	7	3A	5
2006	1	4A	4	7A	2	5A	7	3	6A	1	4A	6
2007	2	5A	5	1A	3	6A	1	4	7A	2	5A	7
2008	3	6A	7	3A	5	1A	3	6	2A	4	7A	2
2009	5	1A	1	4A	6	2A	4	7	3A	5	1A	3
2010	6	2A	2	5A	7	3A	5	1	4A	6	2A	4

Abbreviations

Admin	Administration	GA	Georgia	NF	National Forest
AFB	Air Force Base	Ger	Germany	NH	New Hampshire
Afr	Africa	Gdn(s)	Garden(s)	NG	National Grasslands
AK	Alaska	Govt	Government(al)	NHS	National Historic Site
AL	Alabama	Gr	Greece		
Amer	American	Hdqrs	Headquarters	NHP	National Historical Park
Ant	Antarctica	HI	Hawaii		
AR	Arkansas	Hist	Historic(al)	Nic	Nicaragua
Arg	Argentina	HS	Historic Site	NJ	New Jersey
Arpt	Airport	Hts	Heights	NL	National Lakeshore
Aust	Austria	IA	Iowa	NM	National Monument
Austral	Australia	ID	Idaho	NM	New Mexico
AZ	Arizona	IL	Illinois	N Mem	National Memorial
Bah	Bahamas	IN	Indiana	NMP	National Military Park
Bar	Barbados	Indo	Indonesia		
Bel	Belgium	Info	Information	Nor	Norway
Bldg	Building	Inst	Institution(al)	N Pres	National Preserve
Bol	Bolivia	Intl	International	NP	National Park
Bra	Brazil	IR	Indian Reservation	NRA	National Recreation Area
Brdg	Bridge	Ire	Ireland		
C Arpt	County Airport	Isl	Island	NS	National Seashore
CA	California	Jam	Jamaica	NV	Nevada
Can	Canada	KS	Kansas	NWR	National Wildlife Refuge
Cent Sta	Central Station	KY	Kentucky		
Chan	Channel	LA	Louisiana	NY	New York
CO	Colorado	Lab	Laboratory	Obs	Observatory
Col	Colombia	MA	Massachusetts	OH	Ohio
Conv Ctr	Convention Center	MD	Maryland	OK	Oklahoma
Corp	Corporation	ME	Maine	OR	Oregon
CP	County Park	Mem	Memorial	PA	Pennsylvania
CR	Costa Rica	Mex	Mexico	Pen	Peninsula
CRA	County Recreation Area	MI	Michigan	Phil	Philippines
		Mil	Military	Pk	Peak
CT	Connecticut	MN	Minnesota	PNG	Papua New Guinea
Ctr	Center	MO	Missouri	Prov P	Provincial Park
Czech Rep	Czech Republic	Mon	Monument	Port	Portugal
DC	District of Columbia	Mong	Mongolia	PR	Puerto Rico
DE	Delaware	MS	Mississippi	Pres	Preserve
Dept	Department	MT	Montana	Pt(e)	Point(e)
Dom Rep	Dominican Republic	Mt(s)	Mount / Mountain(s)	R	River
El Sal	El Salvador	Mus	Museum	RA	Recreation Area
Environ	Environment(al)	NAS	Naval Air Station	Res	Reservation
Exh	Exhibition	Natl	National	Rfg	Refuge
Falk Isl	Falkland Islands	NC	North Carolina	RI	Rhode Island
FL	Florida	ND	North Dakota	RR	Railroad
FP	Forest Preserve	NE	Nebraska	RP	Regional Park
Fr	France	Neth	Netherlands	R Pres	Regional Preserve
				Rus	Russia

Abbreviations *(cont.)*

S Afr	South Africa	Sta	Station	*Uru*	Uruguay
SC	South Carolina	Stad	Stadium	UT	Utah
Sd	Sound	Str	Strait	VA	Virginia
SD	South Dakota	SU	State University	*Ven*	Venezuela
SF	State Forest	Svc	Service	Vol	Volcano
SHM	State Historical Monument	*Swe*	Sweden	VT	Vermont
		Switz	Switzerland	WA	Washington
SHP	State Historical Park	*Syr*	Syria	*WI*	West Indies
SHS	State Historic Site	Tech	Technology	WI	Wisconsin
SM	State Monument	Term	Terminal	WMA	Wildlife Management Area
SNA	State Natural Area	Terr	Territory		
SP	State Park	TN	Tennessee	WR	Wildlife Refuge
Sq	Square	TX	Texas	WV	West Virginia
SRA	State Recreation Area	U	University	WY	Wyoming
St(e)	Saint(e)	UK	United Kingdom	*Yug*	Yugoslavia

Index

A

Aachen, 23 **B3**
Aalen, 23 **D2**
Aalsmeer, 30 **C5**
Aalst, 31 **E3**
Aarberg, 37 **A3**
Aasiaat, 102 **C7**
Aba, 44 **D1**
Abadan, 49 **F4**
Abakan, 55 **A3**
Abassiya, 50 **C3**
Abbeville, SC 121 **E4**
ABC TV Ctr, CA 172 **D8**
Abcoude, 30 **D5**
Abdin, 50 **C2**
Abéché, 45 **E2**
Abelardo L Rodriguez Intl Arpt, 169 **H1**
Abeokuta, 44 **C1**
Aberdeen, *Austral* 75 **C1**
Aberdeen, ID 135 **F2**
Aberdeen, MS 129 **H5**
Aberdeen, SD 110 **F6**, 126 **D6**
Aberdeen, UK 14 **C2**, 18 **D6**

Aberdeen Country Park, 75 **C1**
Aberystwyth, 19 **C3**
Abha, 49 **E2**
Abiathar Pk, WY 180 **D5**
Abidjan, 44 **B1**
Abiko, 68 **E8**
Abilene, KS 127 **E2**
Abilene, TX 111 **F3**, 128 **D4**, 178 **D2**
Abingdon, VA 118 **C1**, 121 **E6**
Abington, PA 145 **E6**
Abitibi R, 124 **F8**
Ablis, 28 **A5**
Abramtsevo, 56 **D5**
Absaroka Beartooth Wilderness, MT 180 **C6**
Absaroka Range, MT 180 **C6**
Abu an-Numrus, 50 **B1**
Abu Dhabi, 49 **G3**
Abu Ghaush, 50 **C4**
Abu Kamal, 49 **E5**
Abud, 50 **C6**
Abuja, 44 **D1**
Academy Gdn, PA 145 **G5**
Acadia NP, ME 114 **F5**, 179 **H5**, 186 **C5**

Acadia Wild Gdn, ME 186 **D5**
Acapulco, 96 **C2**
Accomac, VA 119 **G2**
Accra, 44 **C1**
Achau, 42 **E6**
Achinsk, 55 **A3**
Acilia, 40 **B4**
Acklins Isl, 94 **D5**
Acoma IR, NM 131 **D3**
Acropolis, 43 **B2**
Ad Dahna, 49 **F4**
Ad Dammam, 49 **F4**
Ad Diwaniyah, 49 **F5**
Adachi-Ku, 68 **C7**
Adams, MA 115 **A3**, 117 **H3**
Adams NHS, MA 139 **E2**
Adams Park, GA 152 **A3**
Adamsville, FL 154 **D4**
Adana, 48 **D6**
Addis Ababa, 45 **G1**
Addison, IL 159 **B4**
Addison, TX 165 **F5**
Addyston, OH 151 **B2**
Adelaide, 76 **D3**, 80 **A3**
Adelphi, MD 148 **E8**
Aden, 49 **F1**

Adirondack Mts, 112 **E6**
117 **G4**
Adirondack Park, NY
117 **G5**
Adjuntas, 122 **B2**
Adliswil, 37 **E1**
Admiralty Island NM, AK
136 **E5**, 178 **B1**
Admiralty Islands, 76 **C2**
Adobe Dam CRA, AZ
168 **B6**
Adriatic Sea, 17 **F4**, 24 **D4**
Aegean Sea, 17 **H3**, 25 **G3**
48 **C6**
Aerial Tram to Rendezvous
Mt, WY 181 **F2**
Aeroporto da Portela,
38 **B7**
Affori, 40 **B2**
Affton, MO 162 **B1**
Afghanistan, 49 **H6**, 58 **A7**
Africa, 44 – 48
Afton, WY 130 **C7**
Agacli, 43 **D4**
Agadez, 44 **D2**
Agadir, 44 **B4**
Agawam R, MA 184 **A6**

223

Agazzi NWR, MN 126 E8
Agerup, 36 A6
Agincourt, 104 F7
Agra, 58 C6
Agrate, 40 D3
Agricola Oriental, 98 C3
Agrigento, 24 C1
Agrínion, 25 E3
Agua Blanca, 99 H4
Agua Prieta, 131 C1
Aguadilla, 122 A2
Aguascalientes, 96 C4
Aguja Pt, 84 B3
Ahaggar, 44 D3
Aharnes, 43 B4
Ahmadabad, 58 B5
Ahrensburg, 22 D5
Ahrensfelde, 32 E7
Ahumada, 131 E1
Ahvaz, 49 F5
Ahwar, 49 F1
Aiea, HI 177 F3
Aigáleo, 43 B2
Aiken, SC 121 F4
Aïr, 44 D3
Airport West, 79 B4
Aix-en-Provence, 21 F4
Ajaccio, 16 D3, 24 A4
Ajax, 116 B4
Ajdabiya, 48 B5
Ajijic, 99 G1
Ajuda, 38 A6
Ajusco, 98 B2
Akasaka, 69 B2
Akasaka Sta, 69 A2
Akashicho, 69 F1
Akersberga, 36 F7
Akharnaf, 43 B4
Akhisar, 25 H3
Akita, 66 F6
Akpinar, 43 D4
Akron, NY 116 C3
Akron, OH 112 D5, 118 C5
Akureyn, 14 B5
Al Amarah, 49 F5
Al Aqabah, 48 D4

Al Barajil, 50 B2
Al Basrah, 49 F5
Al Bayda, 45 E4, 48 B5
Al Buraymi, 49 G3
Al Fashir, 45 F2
Al Fayyum, 45 F4, 48 C4
Al Hasakah, 49 E6
Al Hillah, 49 E5
Al Hudaydah, 49 E1
Al Hufuf, 49 F3
Al Jawf, 45 E3, 48 B3
Al Jizah, 45 F4, 48 C4
Al Kasab, 49 G4
Al Kharijah, 45 F3
Al Kunayyisah, 50 B1
Al Mubarraz, 49 F4
Al Mukalla, 49 F1
Al Qadarif, 45 G2
Al Ubayyid, 45 F2, 48 C1
Alabama, 97 F6, 113 C5,
   120 C2, 179 F2
Alabama R, 120 C3
Alachua, FL 123 E5
Alameda, CA 174 C5
Alameda Park, 98 B3
Alamo, CA 174 C6
Alamo, The, TX 163 G2
Alamo Band Navajo IR,
   NM 128 A5
Alamo Hts, TX 163 G3
Alamo Sq, CA 173 B1
Alamogordo, NM 128 B4,
   131 E2
Alamosa, CO 127 A2,
   131 E4
Alampur, 65 D1
Åland Isl, 15 F3, 22 F8
Alaska, 100 A6, 136,
   178 A2
Alaska Falls SP, HI 137 F2
Alaska Peninsula, AK
   136 B5
Alaska Peninsula NWR, AK
   136 B5
Alaska Range, 100 A6,
   136 C6
Albacete, 21 C2

Albán, 90 A3
Albania, 17 G3, 25 E4,
   45 E6
Albany, Austral 76 A2
Albany, CA 174 C6
Albany, GA 113 D3, 120 D3
Albany, NY 112 E6,
   117 H2, 179 G5
Albany, OR 134 B3
Albany, VT 114 B5
Albemarle Sd, NC 187 E6
Alberhill, CA 171 G2
Albert Lea, MN 124 B5
Alberta, 101 D4
Alberton, MT 135 E5
Alberton, S Afr 51 G2
Albertsland, 36 B5
Albertson, NY 143 H4
Albi, 21 D4
Albion, NY 116 C4
Alboranse, 21 C1
Ålborg, 15 E2, 22 D6
Albright Visitor Ctr, WY
   180 B5
Albuquerque, NM 111 D4
   128 B6, 131 E3, 178 C3
Albury, 77 E3
Alcántara Reservoir, 21 B3
Alcorcon, 39 A1
Aldan, 55 D4
Aldan R, 55 E4
Aldershot, 26 A5
Aldine, TX 166 B5
Aleksandrovskaya, 57 F1
Alencon, 20 D6
Alenuihaha Chan, HI
   137 E2
Aleppo, 48 D6
Alert, Can 82 D6, 102 A8
Alert, OH 151 A4
Alessandria, 24 A5
Ålesund, 14 D3
Alexander Archipelago,
   101 A4, 136 E5
Alexander City, AL 120 D3
Alexander Isl, 83 D4

Alexandra, 51 G3
Alexandria, Egypt 45 F4,
   48 C5
Alexandria, KY 118 A3
Alexandria, LA 113 A3,
   129 G4
Alexandria, MN 124 A6,
   126 F6
Alexandria, VA 112 E5,
   119 F3, 148 C5
Alexandroúpolis, 25 G4
Alfred, NY 116 C2
Algeria, 16 C1, 21 E1,
   44 C4
Alghero, 24 A3
Algiers, 16 C2, 21 E2,
   44 C5
Algona, WA 176 C1
Alhambra, CA 170 C5
Alibahadir, 43 F4
Alicante, 21 D2
Alice, TX 129 E2
Alice Springs, 76 C4
Alipur, 64 D8
Aliso Viejo, CA 171 E1
Aliso-Wood Canyons RP,
   CA 171 E1
Alkali Lake, OR 132 C8
Allahabad, 58 C5
Allegany SP, NY
   116 B2, 119 E6
Allegheny C Arpt, PA
   146 C5
Allegheny Mts, WV 119 E3
Allegheny NF, PA 116 B1,
   119 E6
Allegheny NRA, PA 116 B1
Allegheny Obs, PA 146 B7
Allegheny Reservoir, PA
   116 B1
Allegheny R, 119 D5
Allen Park, MI 156 C5
Allentown, PA 112 E6,
   119 G5
Alley Isl, ME 186 A5
Alliance, NE 127 C4,
   130 F6

Alligator Lake, NC 187 **E4**

Alligator River, NC 187 **E4**

Alligator River NWR, NC 187 **F5**

Alligatorland Safari Zoo, FL 153 **F2**

Allison Park, PA 146 **C8**

Alma, 103 **D2**

Alma-Ata, 59 **C8**

Almada, 38 **B6**

Almaden Quicksilver CP, CA 175 **F1**

Almagro, 89 **A2**

Almárgem do Bispo, 38 **A8**

Almería, 16 **B2**, 21 **C2**

Almirante Brown, 88 **E5**

Almkerk, 30 **D1**

Aloha, OR 177 **E5**

Alorton, IL 162 **C1**

Alpena, MI 112 **C6**, 124 **F6**

Alpharetta, GA 120 **D4**

Alphen aan den Rijn, 30 **C4**

Alpine, TX 128 **C3**, 131 **F1**

Alpine, WY 155 **E4**

Alps, 20 **F5**, 23 **C1**, 24 **B6**, 44 **D6**

Alsip, IL 159 **D2**

Alsónémedi, 42 **B5**

Alsopakony, 42 **C5**

Alta, 36 **F6**

Alta Plaza, CA 173 **B2**

Alta Vista, 105 **B2**

Altadena, CA 170 **C5**

Altamont, OR 132 **B8**

Altamonte Springs, FL 153 **G5**

Altamura, 24 **D3**

Altar of the Earth, 73 **E3**

Altay, 55 **B2**, 58 **F8**

Altay Mts, 55 **A2**, 58 **E8**

Altiplano, 84 **D1**

Altlandsberg, 32 **F7**

Altmannsdorf, 42 **E7**

Alto Da Moóca, 92 **B4**

Alton, NH 115 **C4**

Altona, 79 **A2**

Altona Bay, 79 **A2**

Altona East, 79 **A2**

Altona North, 79 **A2**

Altoona, PA 112 **D5**, 119 **E5**

Alturas, CA 132 **C7**, 134 **C1**

Altus, OK 128 **D5**

Alva, FL 123 **B3**

Alva, OK 127 **E1**, 129 **E6**

Álvaro Obregón, 98 **A2**

Ama, LA 163 **E5**

Amadora, 38 **A7**

Amagasaki, 70 **C5**

Amarillo, TX 111 **E4**, 128 **D5**, 178 **D3**

Amaroúsion, 43 **C3**

Amazon Basin, 84 **D4**

Amazon R, 84 **D3**

Ambato, 84 **B4**

Ambler, PA 144 **D6**

Ambon, 61 **F2**, 80 **A4**

Amdanga, 65 **F3**

Amelia Earhart Pk, CA 182 **D3**

American Canyon, CA 174 **C8**

American Consulate, 74 **C6**

American Falls, ID 135 **F2**

American Highland, 83 **D1**

American Mem Library, 33 **E1**

American Mus of Natural History, NY 141 **G6**

American Samoa, 80 **D3**

American U, DC 148 **C7**

American West Arena, AZ 168 **B3**

Americus, GA 120 **D3**

Amersham, 26 **A8**

Amery Ice Shelf, 83 **D1**

Amherst, Can 103 **E2**

Amherst, MA 115 **B2**

Amiens, 20 **D7**

Amistad NRA, TX 128 **D3**

Amman, 48 **D5**

Ammassalik, 102 **E7**

Ammerstol, 30 **C2**

Ammon, ID 130 **B7**

Amora, 38 **B5**

Amritsar, 58 **C6**

Amstelveen, 30 **D5**

Amsterdam, Neth 16 **D6**, 20 **E8**, 23 **B4**, 30 **D6**

Amsterdam, NY 117 **G3**

Amsterdam Cent Sta, 30 **D6**

Amtrak Auto Train Term, FL 153 **H6**

Amtrak Sta, OH 150 **D7**

Amu Darya R, 53 **C1**

Amundsen Gulf, 100 **D6**, 136 **F8**

Amundsen Sea, 83 **C4**

Amuntai, 61 **D2**

Amur R, 55 **E3**, 66 **A2**

An Nafud, 49 **E4**

An Najaf, 49 **E5**

An Nasiriyah, 49 **F5**

Anaconda, MT 130 **B8**, 135 **F4**

Anadolufeneri, 43 **F4**

Anadoluhisari, 43 **E3**

Anadyr, 54 **F7**

Anaheim, CA 133 **D2**, 170 **D3**

Anaheim Stad, CA 171 **E3**

Anaktuvuk Pass, AK 136 **D8**

Anápolis, 85 **F1**

Añasco, 122 **A2**

Anatakya, 48 **D6**

Anchorage, AK 82 **A5**, 100 **A6**, 136 **C6**, 178 **B1**

Ancient Tomb, 70 **B5**

Ancol Dreamland, 64 **B8**

Ancona, 17 **E4**, 24 **C4**

Anda, 66 **C7**

Andalusia, PA 145 **G5**

Andaman Islands, 59 **E3**

Andaman Sea, 59 **F3**

Andelfingen, 37 **F3**

Anderlecht, 31 **F2**

Anderson, CA 132 **B7**

Anderson, IN 118 **A4**, 125 **E3**

Anderson, SC 121 **E5**

Anderson Park, FL 154 **B6**

Andes, 84 **B4**, 84 **D1**, 86 **A6**

Andheri, 65 **B3**

Andijon, 53 **E1**

Andingmen, 73 **E3**

Andorra, 16 **C3**, 21 **E4**

Andover, ME 114 **C5**

Andover, MA 138 **C7**

Andrews, TX 128 **C4**, 131 **F2**

Andrews AFB, MD 148 **F6**

Andreyevskoye, 56 **D2**

Andria, 24 **D3**

Andros Isl, 94 **C5**

Androscoggin R, ME 114 **D5**

Andújar, 21 **B2**

Ang mo Kio, 63 **F2**

Angara R, 55 **B3**

Angarn, 36 **E8**

Angarsk, 55 **B3**

Angeles, 60 **D5**

Angel's Window, AZ 183 **E2**

Angers, 20 **D6**

Angleton, TX 129 **F2**

Angola, 47 **E5**

Angola, IN 118 **A6**, 125 **E4**

Angono, 62 **D2**

Angoulême, 20 **D5**

Anguilla, 95 **G4**

Ángyálföld, 42 **B7**

Anheuser-Busch Brewery, MO 162 **C1**

Aniakchak NM & Pres, AK 136 **C5**, 178 **A1**

Ankara, 45 **F5**, 48 **D5**

Ann Arbor, MI 112 **C6**, 118 **B6**, 125 **F4**

Anna Maria, FL 123 **B3**, 154 **A1**

Annaba, 16 **D2**, 24 **A1**, 44 **D5**

Annandale, VA 148 **B5**

Annandale-on-Hudson, NY 117 **G2**

Annapolis, MD 112 **E5**, 119 **G3**

Anne Frank House, 30 D6
Annecy, 23 B1
Annen, 34 F7
Annino, 57 F1
Anniston, AL 120 D4
Annobón, 46 C6
Ano Liosia, 43 B4
Anolaima, 90 A3
Anqing, 67 B3
Ansan, 72 B5
Ansel Adams Wilderness, CA 182 D2
Anshan, 55 E2, 60 C8, 66 C6
Antalya, 48 C6
Antananarivo, 47 H4
Antarctic Pen, 83 E4
Antarctica, 83
Antelope Flats, WY 181 G3
Anthony, NM 131 D1
Anticosti Isl, 103 E3
Antigo, WI 124 D6
Antigua & Barbuda, 95 H3
Antímano, 90 B4
Antioch, CA 174 F7
Antioch, IL 158 B8
Antipolo, 62 D2
Antler Pk, WY 180 A5
Antofagasta, 86 A6
Antsirabe, 47 H3
Antsiranana, 47 H4
Antwerp, 16 D6, 20 E7, 23 B3, 31 G6
Anyang, 55 D1, 60 B7, 67 A4, 72 C5
Anza-Borrego Desert SP, CA 133 E2
Aomori, 66 F6
Aosta, 23 B1, 24 A5
Apalachee Bay, FL 122 D5
Apalachicola, FL 122 C5
Apalachicola R, FL 120 D2, 122 C6
Apatity, 15 G5, 52 D6
Apennine, 24 C4
Apennines Mts, 17 E4

Apia, 80 D3
Apollo Beach, FL 154 D3
Apopka, FL 123 F4, 153 F5
Apoquindo, 87 H3
Apostle Islands NL, WI 124 C7, 179 E5
Appalachian Mts, 103 D1, 112 E5, 118 D2, 120 D5
Appio, 40 C5
Appleton, WI 112 B6, 124 D5
Appomattox, VA 119 E2
Appomattox Court House NHP, VA 179 G3
Aptucxet Trading Post Mus, MA 184 B5
Aqmola, 53 E3
Aqtau, 53 B2
Aqtobe, 53 C3
Aquarium, OH 150 D7
Aquarium, WA 176 B5
Ar Ram, 50 D5
Ar Ramadi, 49 E5
Ar Raqqah, 48 D6
Arab, AL 120 C4
Arabi, LA 163 G5
Arabian Pen, 49 F3
Arabian Sea, 49 H2, 59 A4
Aracaju, 85 H2
Arafura Sea, 76 A1, 76 C6, 80 A4
Araguaia R, 85 F2
Aral, 53 D2
Aral Sea, 53 C2
Arapaho NF, CO 127 A3
Aransas NWR, TX 129 F2
Aras R, 49 F6
Arashiyama, 70 E8
Aravaca, 39 A4
Arboga, 22 E8
Arboretum & Nature Ctr, TX 166 B4
Arbutus, MD 147 C2
Arc de Triomphe, 29 B3
Arc Dome, NV 132 E6
Arcadia, CA 170 D5

Arcadia, FL 123 E3
Arcata, CA 132 A7
Arch, 37 B4
Archbald, PA 117 F1
Archer, FL 123 E5
Arches NP, UT 130 C5, 178 C4
Arco, ID 135 F3
Arcola, TX 166 B1
Arctic Bay, 102 A6
Arctic Circle, 82, 100 A7, 102 D7, 136 A8
Arctic NWR, AK 136 D8
Arctic Ocean, 100 B8, 136 B8
Arctic Red River, 136 E8
Ardeatino, 40 C5
Ardebil, 49 F6
Arden Hills, MN 161 D4
Ardmore, OK 129 E5
Ardmore, PA 144 C3
Arecibo, 122 B2
Areeiro, 38 B6
Arendal, 22 C7
Arequipa, 84 C1
Arese, 40 B3
Arezzo, 24 B4
Arganzuela, 39 C2
Argenteuil, 28 C7
Argentina, 86 B4
Argonne Natl Lab, IL 159 B2
Århus, 15 E2, 22 D6
Arica, 84 C1
Arizona, 96 B6, 111 C4, 131 B2, 178 B3
Arizona Creek, WY 181 G6
Arizona SU, AZ 168 C3
Arkadelphia, AR 129 G5
Arkansas, 97 E6, 113 B4, 129 G5, 179 E3
Arkansas City, KS 127 F2
Arkansas R, 110 E5, 113 A4, 125 B1, 127 C2, 129 F6, 131 E4, 178 D3
Arkhangelsk, 15 H5, 52 D5, 82 E8

Arkhange l'skoye, 56 A4
Arlanda Arpt, 36 D8
Arlington, MA 139 C4
Arlington, TX 129 E4, 164 D2
Arlington, VT 115 A3
Arlington, VA 119 F3, 148 C6
Arlington Conv Ctr, TX 164 D3
Arlington Hts, IL 158 B5
Arlington Hts, OH 151 D3
Arlington Natl Cemetery, VA 148 C6
Armenia, 45 G5
Armenia, Col 84 C5
Armidale, 77 F3
Arncliffe, 78 E6
Arnhem, 20 E8, 23 B4
Arnhem Land, 76 C6
Arnold, CA 132 C5
Arnold, PA 146 F8
Arpádföld, 42 B7
Arpajon, 28 C5
Arqalyq, 53 E3
Arras, 23 A3
Arrecife, 90 A6
Arrentela, 38 C5
Arroyo, 122 C1
Arroyo Hondo, 99 G6
Arsenicker Keys, FL 188 D3
Art Gallery of Ontario, 104 D6
Art Museum, WA 176 B5
Artesia, NM 131 F2
Arthabaska, 114 B6
Arturo Merino Benítiz Intl Arpt, 87 E3
Aruba, 84 C6, 95 E2
Arujá, 92 D6
Arusha, 47 G6
Arvada, CO 167 F4
Arvada Ctr for the Arts & Humanities, CO 167 F4
Arviat, 101 F4
Arvika, 22 D8
Arvin, CA 133 D3

Aryiroupolis, 43 B2

As Sulayyil, 49 F2

Asahikawa, 66 F7

Asaka, 68 B8

Asansol, 58 E5

Asbestos, 114 B6

Ascensión, 128 A3

Ascension Isl, 46 A5

Ascoli Piceno, 24 C4

Asenovgrad, 25 G5

Ash Springs, NV 132 F5

Ashburton, 79 D2

Ashdod, 50 A4

Ashdown, AR 129 F5

Asheboro, NC 121 G5

Asheville, NC 113 D4, 121 E5

Ashfield, 78 D6

Ashford Hollow, NY 116 B2

Ashgabat, 49 G6, 53 B1

Ashiya, 70 B6

Ashkhbad, 58 A8

Ashland, CA 175 D4

Ashland, ME 114 E7

Ashland, OH 118 C5

Ashland, OR 132 A8

Ashland, WI 124 C6

Ashley NF, UT 135 G1

Ashmore & Cartier
Islands, 76 B6

Asia, 58 – 61, 66

Asia Minor, 48 C6

Asmara, 45 G2, 49 E1

Aspen, CO 127 A3, 130 D5

Aspen Park, CO 167 E1

Aspern, 42 F7

Aspropirgos, 43 A3

Assab, 45 G2

Assateague Island, MD
119 H2

Assateague Island NS, MD
179 H4

Asse, 31 F3

Assemblé Nationale, 29 C2

Assen, 20 F8, 23 B4

Assiniboia, 126 A8

Assiniboine Park & Zoo,
107 F5

Assinippi, MA 139 F1

Asti, 24 A5

Astor, FL 123 F5

Astoria, NY 143 E4

Astoria, OR 134 B4

Astrakhan, 53 B3

Astrodome, TX 166 B3

Astroworld, TX 166 B3

Asunción, 86 B6

Aswan, 45 G3, 48 D3

Aswan High Dam, 48 D3

Asyut, 45 F4, 48 C4

At Taif, 49 E2

At Talibiyah, 50 B1

At Tayyibah, 50 D5

Atacama Desert, 84 D1,
86 A6

Atsugi, 68 A6

Atar, 44 A3

Atascadero, CA 133 C4

Ataturk Arpt, 43 D2

Atbarah, 45 G3

Atchison, KS 125 A3,
127 F3

Ate, 87 G5

Atequiaza, 99 H2

Athabasca R, 101 D3

Athens, AL 120 C5

Athens, GA 113 D4,
121 E4

Athens, Gr 17 H2, 25 F3,
43 B3, 45 F5, 48 B6

Athens, OH 118 C4

Athens, TN 120 D5, 125 F1

Athens U, 43 B3

Atherton, CA 175 C3

Athlone, 19 B4

Athol, MA 115 B3

Atikokan, 103 A2

Atizapán, 98 A5

Atlanta, GA 97 F6, 113 D4,
120 D4, 152 A3, 179 G2

Atlanta-Fulton Co Stad,
GA 152 B3

Atlanta History Ctr, GA
152 B5

Atlanta Mem Park, GA
152 B4

Atlanta State Farmer's
Market, GA 152 B1

Atlantic Beach, FL 123 F6

Atlantic Beach, NY 143 G1

Atlantic City, NJ 112 F5,
119 H4

Atlantic Coastal Plain,
113 E4

Atlantic Ocean, 16 A5,
20 B6, 85 G6, 86 C5,
95 F6, 97 H6, 103 F1

Atlas Mts, 16 A1, 21 E1,
44 C5

Atlavik, 136 E8

Atmore, AL 122 B6

Atomium, 31 G2

Atteridgeville, 51 G6

Attica, NY 116 C3

Atwater, CA 132 C5

Atyrau, 53 C3

Atzgerdorf, 42 D7

Auberry, CA 133 C4

Aubervilliers, 28 D7

Aubre Cliff, AZ 183 A1

Auburn, AL 120 D3

Auburn, Austral 78 C7

Auburn, CA 132 C6

Auburn, IN 118 A6

Auburn, ME 115 D4

Auburn, NE 127 F3

Auburn, NY 116 D3

Auburn, WA 176 C2

Auckland, 77 H2, 80 C2

Auckland Islands, 80 C1

Auderghem, 31 G1

Audubon, NJ 145 F1

Audubon, PA 144 A6

Audubon Park & Zoolog-
ical Gdn, LA 163 F5

Augsburg 17 E5, 23 D2

Augusta, GA 113 D4

Augusta, ME 112 F7,
114 D5

Augusta, SC 121 F4

Aurelio, 40 C5, 41 A3

Aurillac, 20 E5

Aurora, CO 127 A3, 130 E5,
167 H2

Aurora, IL 125 D4

Aurora, TX 164 A6

Ausable Chasm, NY 117 H6

Austin, MN 124 B5

Austin, NV 132 E6

Austin, TX 96 D5, 111 F3,
129 E3, 178 D2

Austral Islands, 81 E3

Australia, 76 C4, 80 A3

Australian Capital Terr,
77 E3

Austria, 17 E5, 23 E2,
24 C6, 44 D6

Autodrome, 40 C3

Auxerre, 23 A2

Avalanche Pk, WY 180 D3

Avalon, PA 146 B7

Avarua, 80 D3

Avellaneda, 86 B5, 88 E6

Avellino, 24 C3

Avenal, CA 133 C4

Aventine Hill, 41 D1

Aventura, FL 155 C5

Aviemore, 18 D6

Avignon, 16 D4, 20 E5

Ávila, 21 B3

Avon, NY 116 C3

Avon, NC 187 H3

Avon, OH 150 A6

Avon Lake, OH 150 A7

Avon Park, FL 123 F3

Avondale, LA 163 E4

Avondale, MO 162 C6

Avondale, TX 164 A5

Avondale Estates, GA
152 D4

Avtovo, 57 F2

Awsim, 50 B3

Axel Heiberg Isl, 100 F8

Ayacucho, 84 C2

Ayagoz, 53 F2

Ayanagar, 64 D6

Ayase, 68 A6

Aydin, 25 H3
Ayers Rock, 76 C4
Ayiá Paraskeví, 43 C3
Ayoun el Atrous, 44 B2
Ayr, 14 C1, 18 C5
Azcapotzalco, 98 B4
Azerbaijan, 45 H5, 49 E6
Azle, TX 164 A4
Azores, 44 A6
Aztec, NM 131 D4, 128 A6
Aztec Amphitheater, AZ
  183 C2
Aztec Stad, 98 B1
Azul, 86 B4

B

Baasrode, 31 F4
Bab el Mandab, 49 E1
Babelan, 64 C8
Babson College Map &
  Globe Mus, MA 139 B3
Babu Bheri, 65 D3
Babushkin, 56 C5
Babuyan Isl, 67 C1
Back Bay, MA 140 A2
Back R, 100 E5
Backbone Mt, MD 119 E3
Baclaran, 62 C1
Bacolod, 61 E4
Bacoor, 62 B1
Bad Hersfeld, 23 C3
Bad River IR, WI 124 C6
Bad Vilbel, 35 C4
Badajoz, 16 A3, 21 B2
Badalona, 38 F6
Badarpur, 64 E6
Baden, Aust 42 D5
Baden, Switz 37 D2
Badhoevedorp, 30 C5
Badlands NP, SD 126 C5,
  130 F7, 178 D5
Badli, 64 D8
Badu, 91 E2
Baetic Mts, 21 C2
Baffin Bay, 82 D5, 102 B7

Baffin Isl, 82 D5, 102 B6
Bafoussam, 44 D1
Baggio, 40 B1
Baggs, WY 135 H1
Baghdad, 45 H5, 49 E5
Bagladesh, 58 E5
Baguio, 60 D3
Bahamas, 94 D6, 97 H5
Bahía Blanca, 86 B4
Bahía Grande, 86 B3
Bahla Honda SP, FL 188 C2
Bahrain, 45 H4, 49 F4
Bahtim, 50 C3
Baicheng, 55 E2, 66 B2
Baidyabati, 65 E3
Baie-Comeau, 103 D3
Baie-d'Urfe, 106 A1
Baileys Crossroads, VA
  148 C6
Bailianjing, 74 E5
Bailianjingzhen, 74 E5
Bainbridge, GA 120 D2,
  122 D6
Bainbridge Isl, WA 176 A5
Bainbridge SP, Fay, WA
  176 A6
Baixa da Banheira, 38 C6
Bajianfang, 73 F4
Baj Baj, 65 D1
Baja California, 96 A5,
  111 B3
Baker, NV 130 A5, 132 F6
Baker City, OR 134 D3
Baker Isl, 80 D4
Baker Isl, ME 186 D2
Baker Lake, 100 F5
Bakersfield, CA 111 B4,
  133 D3, 178 A3
Bakhtaran, 49 F5
Bakhtawarpur, 64 E8
Bakirkoy, 43 D2
Baku, 45 H6, 53 B2
Bal Harbour, FL 155 G2
Bala Cynwyd, PA 144 D4
Balashikha, 56 D5
Balboa Park, CA 169 F3

Balch Springs, TX 165 H3
Balcone Hts, TX 163 F3
Bald Eagle, MN 161 F4
Bald Eagle SF, PA 119 F5
Bald Eagle-Otter Lake RP,
  MN 161 E4
Baldwin, NY 143 H2
Baldwin, PA 146 C5
Baldwin Harbor, NY 143 H2
Baldwin Park, CA 170 D5
Baldwinsville, NY 117 E3
Balearic Islands, 16 C2,
  21 E3, 44 C5
Balearic Sea, 21 E3
Balgowlah, 78 F8
Bali, 61 D1
Balikesir, 25 H4
Balikpapan, 61 D2
Balingen, 23 C2
Balizhuang, 73 C2
Balkan Mts, 25 G5
Balkan Pen, 17 G4, 25 E5
Balkash, 58 C8
Ballabgarh, 64 F5
Ballarat, 76 D2
Balleny Isl, 83 A2
Ballerup, 36 A6
Ballston Spa, NY 117 G3
Bally, 65 E2
Bally Bridge, 65 E2
Ballymena, 18 C5
Balqash, 53 E2
Balsas R, 96 D3
Baltic Sea, 15 F2, 22 F6,
  52 A6, 82 F7
Baltimore, MD 112 E5,
  119 G3, 147 C2, 179 H4
Baltimore Highlands, MD
  147 D2
Baltimore Mus of Art, MD
  147 D3
Baltimore-Washington
  Intl Arpt, MD 147 C1
Baltimore Zoo, MD 147 C3

Balvanera, 89 B2
Balwyn, 79 D3
Bamako, 44 B2
Bamangachi, 65 F3
Bambari, 45 E1
Bamberg, 23 D3
Bancalari, 88 C8
Banda Aceh, 59 F2
Banda Sea, 61 F2
Bandar Beheshti, 49 H4
Bandar Seri Begawan,
  61 D3
Bandar-e Abbas, 49 G4
Bandar-e Bushehr, 49 F4
Bandel, 65 E4
Bandelier NM, NM 127 A1,
  131 D3, 178 C3
Bandera, TX 128 D3
Bandirma, 25 H4
Bandra, 65 A2
Bandundu, 47 E6
Bandung, 61 B1
Banff, 101 D2
Banfield, 88 E6
Bang Kapi, 63 H6
Bang Khun Thian, 63 F5
Bang Kruai, 63 F6
Bang Na, 63 H4
Bang Phlat, 63 F6
Bang Su, 63 F6
Bangalore, 59 C4
Bangar, 64 D8
Banghazi, 45 E4, 48 B5
Bangkok, 61 A4, 63 G5
Bangkok Noi, 63 F5
Bangor, UK 19 D3
Bangor, ME 103 D2,
  112 F7, 114 E5, 179 H6
Bangrak, 63 F5
Bángu, 91 B2
Bangui, 45 E1
Banja Luka, 17 F4, 24 D5
Banjarmasin, 61 D2
Banjul, 44 B2
Bankhead NF, William B,
  AL 120 C4
Banks Isl, 82 C5, 100 D7

Bankstown, 78 **C6**
Bansberia, 65 **E4**
Banska Bystrica, 17 **F5**
Banstead, 26 **C6**
Bantry, 19 **A3**
Baoding, 55 **D1**, 60 **B8**, 66 **A5**
Baoji, 60 **B7**
Baoshan County, 74 **D8**
Baotou, 55 **D1**, 60 **B8**
Baqubah, 49 **E5**
Bar Harbor, ME 112 **F7**, 114 **E5**, 186 **D5**
Bar Isl, ME 186 **D5**
Barabinsk, 53 **F3**
Barajas, 39 **E4**
Barajas Arpt, 39 **F4**
Barangar, 65 **F2**
Barasat, 65 **E5**
Barbados, 85 **E6**, 95 **H2**
Barberá del Vallès, 38 **E7**
Barberini Palace, 41 **D3**
Barbican, 27 **E3**
Barbourville, KY 118 **B3**
Barbuda, 95 **H3**
Barcarena, 38 **A7**
Barcelona, 16 **C3**, 21 **E3**, 38 **E6**, 44 **D6**
Barcelona Arpt, 38 **E5**
Barceloneta, 38 **F6**
Bardstown, KY 118 **A2**, 125 **E2**
Bareilly, 58 **C6**
Barendrecht, 30 **B1**
Barents Sea, 15 **G6**, 52 **E7**, 82 **E7**
Bargachia, 65 **D2**
Bari, 17 **F3**, 24 **D3**
Barking, 26 **D7**
Barletta, 24 **D3**
Barnacle State HS, FL 155 **F1**
Barnaul, 53 **F3**
Barnes Foundation, PA 144 **D3**
Barnes Sd, FL 188 **F4**
Barnet, 26 **C8**

Barnstable, MA 115 **D2**, 184 **D5**
Barnstable Harbor, MA 184 **D5**
Barnstaple, 19 **C2**
Barnwell, SC 121 **F4**
Barquisimeto, 84 **D5**, 95 **E1**
Barra da Tijuca, 91 **C1**
Barracas, 89 **D1**
Barrackpore, 65 **F3**
Barrancabermeja, 84 **C5**
Barranquilla, 84 **C6**, 94 **D1**
Barrarico, 87 **G5**
Barre, VT 115 **B4**
Barreiro, 38 **C6**
Barrie, 103 **C1**
Barrington, IL 158 **A6**
Barrington, NJ 145 **F1**
Barrow, AK 82 **B6**, 100 **B7**, 136 **C8**
Barstow, CA 111 **B4**, 133 **E3**
Bartlesville, OK 113 **A4**, 125 **A1**, 127 **F1**, 129 **F6**
Bartlett, IL 159 **A4**
Bartlett Isl, ME 186 **A4**
Barton, OR 177 **H4**
Barton NHS, Clara, MD 148 **C7**
Bartonville, TX 164 **C6**
Baruta, 90 **C4**
Barvikha, 56 **A4**
Basel, 16 **D5**, 20 **F6**, 23 **B1**, 24 **A6**
Baseline Flat, WY 181 **F3**
Bashtil, 50 **B3**
Basibuyuk, 43 **F2**
Basildon, 26 **F7**
Basin, WY 135 **H3**
Bass Harbor, ME 186 **B2**
Bass Harbor Head, ME 186 **B1**
Bass Str, 77 **E2**, 80 **B2**
Bassersdorf, 37 **F1**
Basseterre, 95 **G3**
Bastia, 24 **B4**
Bastrop, LA 129 **G4**

Basus, 50 **B3**
Bat Yam, 50 **A6**
Batan Isl, 67 **C1**
Batavia, NY 116 **C3**
Batavia, OH 118 **B3**
Batdambang, 61 **A4**
Batesville, AR 120 **A6**, 129 **G6**
Bath, ME 115 **D4**
Bath, NY 116 **D2**, 119 **F6**
Bath, UK 19 **D2**
Baths of Caracalla, 41 **E1**
Bathurst, 103 **E3**
Batna, 21 **F1**, 44 **D5**
Baton Rouge, LA 113 **B3**, 120 **A2**, 129 **G3**, 179 **E2**
Batterkinden, 37 **C3**
Battery Park, NY 141 **E1**
Battle Creek RP, MN 161 **F2**
Battle Green, MA 138 **B5**
Battle Mt, NV 132 **E7**
Batumi, 53 **A3**
Baubau, 61 **F2**
Bauerstown, PA 146 **C7**
Baulkham Hills, 78 **C8**
Bauria, 65 **D1**
Bauru, 85 **F1**
Bay City, MI 124 **F5**
Bay City, TX 129 **F2**
Bay Harbor Islands, FL 155 **G2**
Bay Minette, AL 120 **B2**, 122 **A6**
Bay of Bengal, 59 **E4**
Bay of Biscay, 16 **B4**, 20 **C5**
Bay of Campeche, 97 **E3**
Bay of Fundy, 103 **E2**
Bay Pines, FL 154 **A4**
Bay Ridge, NY 142 **C2**
Bay Village, OH 150 **A7**
Bayamo, 94 **C4**
Bayamon, 122 **C4**
Bayanbayanan, 62 **D3**
Bayanhongor, 55 **C2**, 58 **F8**
Bayji, 49 **E5**
Bayonne, Fr 21 **C4**
Bayonne, NJ 142 **C2**

Bayou Segnette SP, LA 163 **F4**
Bayreuth, 23 **D3**
Bayshore Gdns, FL 154 **B1**
Bayside, NY 143 **F4**
Bayside, WI 157 **B4**
Bayswater, 79 **F2**
Beach Grove, IN 157 **F1**
Beach Park, IL 158 **C8**
Beachwood, OH 150 **F7**
Beacon, NY 117 **G1**
Beacon Hill, Austral 78 **F8**
Beacon Hill, MA 140 **B4**
Beaconsfield, Can 106 **A2**
Beaconsfield, UK 26 **A8**
Bear Isl, ME 186 **C3**
Bear Pk, WY 135 **H2**
Beatrice, NE 127 **E3**
Beatty, NV 133 **E4**
Beaufort, SC 121 **F3**
Beaufort Sea, 82 **B6**, 100 **C4**, 136 **D8**
Beaumont, TX 113 **A3**, 129 **F3**
Beaumont Place, TX 166 **D4**
Beauport, 105 **F3**, 114 **C7**
Beaux Arts Village, WA 176 **C5**
Beaver, PA 118 **D5**
Beaver, UT 130 **B5**
Beaver Creek, AK 136 **D6**
Beaver R, OK 128 **D6**
Beaverhead NF, MT 135 **F3**
Beaverton, OR 177 **F5**
Becancour, 114 **B7**
Béchar, 44 **C4**
Bechler R, 180 **A2**
Bechovice, 35 **F3**
Beckley, WV 118 **C2**
Beddington, ME 114 **E5**
Bedford, IN 125 **E2**
Bedford, OH 150 **E6**
Bedford, PA 119 **E4**
Bedford, TX 164 **D4**
Bedford, VA 119 **E1**
Bedford Hts, OH 150 **F6**
Bedford Res, OH 150 **E5**

Bedford-Stuyvesant, NY 142 D3

Bedfordview, 51 G3

Bedok, 63 H2

Bee Ridge, FL 123 E3

Beecroft, 78 D8

Behala, 65 E1

Behing Auto Mus, CA 174 E5

Beian, 55 E3, 66 C7

Beijing, 55 E1, 60 C8, 66 A5, 73 D2

Beijing Amusement Park, 73 E1

Beijing Exh Ctr, 73 D3

Beijing Railway Station, 73 E2

Beijing Zoo, 73 C3

Beira, 47 G3

Beirut, 48 D5

Beit Sira, 50 C5

Beiwucun, 73 A4

Beixinjing, 74 A6

Beixuejiatang, 74 E8

Beja, 21 A2

Bejaïa, 16 D2

Bekasi, 64 C7

Békásmegyer, 42 A8

Bel Air, MD 119 G4

Belapurpada, 65 C2

Belarus, 15 G1, 52 A5

Belas, 38 A7

Belavista, 93 E1

Belcher Islands, 103 B3

Belém, Bra 85 F4

Belém, Port 38 B6

Beleutovo, 56 C1

Belfast, ME 114 E5

Belfast, UK 14 B1, 19 C4

Belford Roxo, 91 C3

Belgium, 16 D6, 20 E7, 23 A3

Belgrade, MT 135 G4

Belgrade, Yug 17 G4, 25 E6, 45 E6

Belgrano, 88 D7

Belgravia, 27 A1

Belize, 81 H5, 84 A6, 97 F3

Belize City, 97 F3

Bell, CA 170 C4

Bella Vista, 88 B7

Bellair Beach, FL 154 A5

Bellaire, TX 166 B3

Bellavista, 87 F5

Belle Chasse, LA 163 G4

Belle Fourche, SD 126 B6

Belle Harbor, NY 143 E1

Belle Isle, FL 153 G3

Belle Isle Park, MI 156 E6

Belle View, VA 148 D5

Belleair, FL 154 A5

Belleair, VA 148 A5

Belleair Shore, FL 154 A4

Bellefontaine, OH 118 B5

Bellefontaine Neighbors, MO 162 C3

Bellefonte, PA 119 E5

Belleville, Fr 29 F3

Belleville, IL 125 C2

Belleville, NJ 142 B5

Bellevue, KY 151 D2

Bellevue, NE 127 F4

Bellevue, PA 146 B7

Bellevue, WA 176 D5

Bellevue Castle, 33 C3

Bellflower, CA 170 C3

Bellingham, WA 110 B8, 134 B6

Bellingshausen Sea, 83 C4

Bellmawr, NJ 145 F1

Bellows Falls, VT 115 B3

Bellwood, IL 159 C4

Belmont, CA 175 B3

Belmont, MA 139 C4

Belmont, NY 119 F6

Belmont Park, CA 169 E4

Belmont Park Racetrack, NY 143 G3

Belmopan, 84 A6, 97 F3

Belo Horizonte, 85 G1

Belomorsk, 15 G4, 52 C6

Belp, 37 C2

Belrose, 78 E8

Belsele, 31 E5

Beltrami Isl SF, MN 126 F8

Beltsville, MD 148 F8

Belvedere, CA 175 A6

Belvedere, GA 152 D3

Belyayevo Bogorodskoye, 56 B3

Bemidji, MN 112 A7, 124 B7, 126 F7

Bemis Hts, NY 117 H3

Ben Gurion Intl Arpt, 50 B6

Benbrook, TX 164 A2

Bend, OR 110 B7, 134 C3

Bendigo, 77 E2

Bene Re'en, 50 A4

Benevento, 24 C3

Benfica, 38 B7

Benfica Stad, 38 B7

Bengbu, 67 B4

Bengkulu, 61 A1

Benguela, 46 D4

Beni, 47 F6

Beni R, 84 D2

Benicia, CA 174 D7

Benin, 44 C2

Benito Juárez, 98 D2, D3

Benito Juárez Intl Arpt, 98 C3

Benjamin Constant, 84 D3

Bennettsville, SC 121 F5

Bennington, VT 115 A3, 117 H3

Benoni, 51 H3

Benrath, 34 B5

Bensalem, PA 145 H5

Bensenville, IL 159 B4

Bensonhurst, NY 142 D2

Bentleigh, 79 C1

Benue R, 44 D1

Benxi, 55 E2, 60 C8, 66 C6

Berazategui, 88 F5

Berbera, 45 H2

Berchem, 31 G5

Bercy, 29 F1

Berea, OH 150 B5

Berezniki, 53 D4

Bergama, 25 H3

Bergamo, 17 E4, 23 D1, 24 B5

Bergen, 14 D3, 22 B8

Bergen-Enkeim, 35 C3

Bergenfield, NJ 142 D6

Bering Land Bridge Natural Pres, AK 136 B7, 178 A2

Bering Sea, 82 A6, 136 A6

Bering Str, 54 F8, 82 A6, 100 A7, 136 B8

Berkakit, 55 D4

Berkel, 30 B2

Berkeley, CA 174 C6

Berkeley, MO 162 B3

Berkeley, UC, CA 175 C6

Berkeley Springs, WV 119 E4

Berkersheim, 35 B4

Berkley, MI 156 C8

Berkner Isl, 83 D3

Berlaar, 31 H5

Berlare, 31 E4

Berlin, Ger 17 E6, 23 E4, 32 D7, 33

Berlin, NH 114 C5

Berlin Cathedral, 33 F3

Berlin Mus, 33 E2

Bermejillo, 128 B1

Bern, 16 D5, 20 F6, 23 C1, 24 A6, 37 B2

Bern Mus, 37 B2

Bern-Belp Arpt, 37 C2

Bernalillo, NM 128 B6, 131 E3

Bernard, ME 186 B2

Bernardsville, NJ 116 A5

Bernau, 32 E8

Bernebeu Stad, 39 C3

Bernière-St-Nicolas, 105 D1

Berregio, 40 A1

Berry Creek, WY 181 F6

Berrydale, WA 176 D2

Berryville, VA 119 F3

Bertem, 31 H2

Berwick-upon-Tweed, 18 E5

Berwyn, IL 159 C3

Berwyn, PA 144 A4

Berwyn Hts, MD 148 E7

Besançon, 20 F6, 23 B1

Beskudnikovo, 56 B5

Bessemer, AL 120 C4

Bet Nehemya, 50 B5

Bet Shemesh, 50 B4

Bethel, AK 136 B6

Bethel, VT 115 A4

Bethel Park, PA 146 B5

Bethesda, MD 148 C8

Bethlehem, PA 119 G5

Beulah, ND 126 C7

Beveren, 31 F6

Beverly, MA 138 F6

Beverly, NJ 145 H5

Beverly Hills, CA 170 B4, 172 A6

Beverly Hills, FL 121 E1, 123 E4

Beverly Hills, MI 156 C8

Bevis, OH 151 C3

Bexley, 26 E7

Beykoz, 43 F3

Beyoglu, 43 E2

Béziers, 21 E4

Bhadreswar, 65 E3

Bhandup, 65 C2

Bhatpara, 65 F3

Bhayandar, 65 B4

Bhimpur, 65 D3

Bhiwandi, 65 C4

Bhopal, 58 C5

Bhutan, 58 E5

Bialystok, 15 G1

Biberist, 37 C4

Bibliotheque Nationale, 29 E3

Bicutan, 62 C1

Biddeford, ME 115 C4

Biedermannsdorf, 42 E6

Biel, 23 B1, 24 A6, 37 A3

Bielefeld, 16 D6, 23 C4

Biella, 23 C1

Bienville NF, MS 120 B3

Big Baldy Mt, MT 135 G5

Big Basin Redwoods SP, CA 175 C1

Big Bend NP, TX 128 C2, 178 D2

Big Bend Ranch SNA, TX 128 C3

Big Coppitt Key, FL 188 B1

Big Creek Res, OH 150 C6

Big Cypress N Pres, FL 123 F2, 179 G1

Big Flats, NY 116 D2

Big Horn, WY 130 D8

Big Key, FL 188 E4

Big Lake, ME 114 F6

Big Pine, CA 132 D5

Big Pine Key, FL 123 F1, 188 C2

Big Rapids, MI 124 E5

Big Rideau Lake, 117 E6

Big Sandy, MT 135 G6

Big South Fork NRA, TN 118 A1, 120 D6

Big Spring, TX 128 D4

Big Timber, MT 135 G4

Bighorn Canyon NRA, MT 130 D8, 135 H4, 178 C5

Bighorn NF, WY 126 A6, 130 D7

Bighorn R, 126 A6, 135 H3

Bijwasan, 64 D6

Bilbao, 16 B4, 21 C4

Bilk, 34 B5

Billerica, MA 138 B6

Billericay, 26 F8

Billings, MT 101 F1, 110 D7, 130 D8, 135 H4, 178 C5

Biloxi, MS 113 B3, 120 B2, 122 A6, 129 H3

Binangonan, 62 D1

Bingham, ME 115 B3

Binghamton, NY 112 E6, 117 E2, 119 G6

Bioko, 44 D1

Bi'r Zayt, 50 D5

Birch Cliff, 104 F6

Birchwood Village, MN 161 F4

Birds Hill, 107 H6

Birds Landing, CA 174 F8

Birjand, 49 H5

Birkenwerder, 32 C8

Birkerod, 36 B7

Birmensdorf, 37 E1

Birmingham, AL 113 C3, 97 F6, 120 C4, 179 F2

Birmingham, MO 162 D6

Birmingham, UK 14 C1, 19 D3, 20 C8

Birobidzhan, 55 E3

Birrong, 78 C6

Biruyulevo, 56 C2

Bisbee, AZ 131 C1

Biscayne NP, FL 123 G1, 179 G1

Biscayne Park, FL 155 G2

Biscuit Basin, WY 180 A3

Bishan, 63 F2

Bishkek, 53 E1, 58 C8

Bishnupur, 65 D1

Bisho, 47 F2

Bishop, CA 132 D5

Bishop Mus, Bernice P, HI 177 G2

Biskra, 44 C5

Bismarck, ND 101 F1, 110 F7, 126 C7, 178 D5

Bismarck Archipelago, 76 C2

Bismarck Sea, 76 C2

Bissau, 44 A2

Bitola, 25 E4

Bitterroot NF, MT 135 F4

Bitterroot Range, ID 135 E5

Biysk, 53 F3

Bizerte, 24 B1

Björknäs, 36 F6

Black Betsy Keys, FL 188 B4

Black Canyon of the Gunnison NM, CO 130 D5, 178 C3

Black Diamond Mines R Pres, CA 174 F6

Black Forest, CO 130 E5

Black Gap WMA, TX 128 C3

Black Hills, 110 E6

Black Hills NF, SD 126 B5

Black Horse, PA 144 B2

Black Isl, ME 186 A5

Black Isl, ME 186 B1

Black Kettle NG, OK 127 D1, 128 D6

Black Lake, NY 117 F6

Black Pt, CA 174 A8

Black R, NY 117 F4

Black Sand Basin, WY 180 A3

Black Sea, 17 H4, 25 H5, 45 F6, 53 A3

Blackbeard Island NWR, GA 121 F3

Blackburn, 79 D2

Blackburn Hamlet, 105 C3

Blackfeet IR, MT 135 F6

Blackfoot, ID 130 B7, 135 F2

Blackmans Pt, MA 184 A8

Blackpool, 19 D4

Blacksburg, VA 118 D1, 121 F6

Blacktown, 78 B8

Blackwater NWR, MD 119 G3

Blackwell, OK 127 E1

Blad Porcupine Isl, ME 186 D5

Bladensburg, MD 148 F7

Blaenau, OK 127 E1

Blagoveshchensk, 55 E3, 66 C8

Blaine, WA 134 B6

Blainville, 106 A4

Blair, NE 125 A4

Blake Island SP, WA 176 A4

Blakehurst, 78 D5

Blakely, GA 120 D2

Blanding, UT 131 C4

Blankenfelde, 32 D5

Blantyre, 47 G4

Bleiswijk, 30 B3

Blida, 21 E2
Block Isl, RI 115 C1
Bloemfontein, 47 F2
Blois, 20 D6
Bloomfield, NJ 142 B4
Bloomingdale, IL 159 A4
Bloomington, CA 171 G5
Bloomington, IL 112 B5, 125 D3
Bloomington, IN 112 C5, 125 E3
Bloomington, MN 124 B5, 161 C1
Bloomsburg, PA 119 F5
Bloomsbury, 27 C4
Blossom Park, 105 C1
Blountstown, FL 122 C6
Blovstrod, 36 B7
Blue Ash, OH 151 E3
Blue Bell, PA 144, D6
Blue Hill Bay, ME 186 A2
Blue Hills State Reservoir, MA 139 D2
Blue Isl, IL 159 D2
Blue Jay, CA 171 H6
Blue Mosque, 43 E2
Blue Mound, TX 164 B4
Blue Mt Lake, NY 117 G5
Blue Mts, OR 134 D4
Blue Nile R, 45 G2, 48 D1
Bluffton, IN 118 A5
Blumber, 32 E8
Blysk, 53 F3
Blythe, CA 131 A2, 133 F2
Blytheville, AR 120 B6
Bnei Brak Railway Sta, 50 B6
Bo Hai, 66 B5
Bo Hai Bay, 55 E1
Boa Vista, 85 E4
Boa Vista Park, 91 D2
Bobo-Dioulasso, 44 B2
Boca, 88 E7, 89 E1
Boca Raton, FL 123 G2, 155 G6
Boca Juniors Stad, 89 E1
Boccea, 40 B4

Bochum, 34 D7
Bockheim, 35 B3
Bodaybo, 55 C4
Bodegraven, 30 C3
Bodie Isl, NC 187 G5
Bodie Isl Lighthouse, NC 187 C5
Bodie Isl Visitor Ctr, NC 187 H5
Bodø, 15 E5
Bodrum, 25 H2
Boechout, 31 H5
Boedo, 89 B1
Bogalusa, LA 120 A2
Bogor, 61 B1, 64 B5
Bogotá, Col 84 C5, 90 C2
Bogota, NJ 142 C6
Bogotá Archeological Park, 90 B3
Bogotá Natl Mus, 90 C2
Bohnice, 35 E3
Bois de Boulogne, 28 C7, 29 A3
Bois de Vincennes, 28 D7
Bois des Filion, 106 B4
Boisbriand, 106 A4
Boise, ID 101 C1, 110 C6, 130 A7, 135 E3, 178 B5
Boise NF, ID 130 A8, 135 E3
Bojacá, 90 A2
Boksburg, 51 H2
Bolingbrook, IL 159 A2
Bolivar, MO 125 B2
Bolivia, 84 D2
Bollate, 40 B2
Bolligen, 37 C2
Bologna, 17 E4, 24 B5
Bolsa Chica Ecological Reserve, CA 170 C2
Bolshevo, 56 D6
Bol'shoy Theater, 57 E6
Bolton, Can 104 A8
Bolton, UK 19 D4

Bolzano, 23 D1, 24 B6
Bom Retiro, 92 B5, 93 G6
Boma, 46 D5
Bombay, 58 B5, 65 A2
Bombay Intl Arpt, 65 B2
Bombay, U of, 65 A1
Bommersheim, 35 A4
Bonaire, 84 D6, 95 F1
Bonames, 35 B4
Bondi, 78 F6
Bondy, 28 D7
Bonham, TX 129 F5
Bonita, CA 169 G2
Bonita Springs, FL 123 F2
Bonn, 16 D6, 20 F7, 23 B3
Bonners Ferry, ID 135 E6
Bonnyrigg, 78 B6
Bookertown, FL 153 G6
Boom, 31 G4
Boone, IA 125 B4
Boone, NC 121 F6
Boothbay Harbor, ME 115 D4
Boothia Pen, 100 F6
Bor, 25 F6
Borbeck, 34 C7
Bordeaux, 16 C4, 20 D5, 44 C6
Border Field SP, CA 169 F1
Borehamwood, 26 C8
Boring, OR 177 H4
Borivli, 65 B3
Borlange, 15 F3, 22 E8
Bornem, 31 F4
Borneo, 61 D2
Bornheim, 35 C3
Bornholm, 15 F1, 22 E6
Bornicke, 32 A8
Boron, CA 133 D3
Boronia, 79 F2
Borsbeek, 31 H6
Bos en Lommer, 30 D6
Bosa, 90 B2
Boskoop, 30 C3
Bosnia & Herzegovina, 17 F4, 24 D5, 25 E6, 45 E6

Boso Pen, 68 E6
Bosporus, 48 D6
Bosque del Apache NWR, NM 128 A5
Bosques, 88 F5
Boston, MA 103 E1, 112 F6 115 C2, 139 E3, 140, 179 H5
Boston, UK 19 E3
Boston Ctr for the Arts, MA 140 B1
Boston College, MA 139 C3
Boston Common, MA 140 B3
Boston Information Ctr, MA 40 C3
Boston Massacre Site, MA 140 C4
Boston NHP, MA 140 D6
Boston Tea Party Ship & Mus, MA 140 D2
Botafogo, 91 D2
Botanical Gdns, 89 A4
Botany, 78 E6
Botany Bay, 78 E5
Botany Bay NP, 78 F5
Botkyrka, 36 D6
Bottineau, ND 126 D8
Bottrop, 34 C8
Bouaké, 44 B1
Bouar, 44 D1
Boucherville, 106 D4
Bougainville, 80 B4
Bouira, 21 E2
Boulder, CO 127 A3, 130 E5, 167 E6
Boulder, MT 135 F4
Boulder City, NV 131 A3, 133 F4
Boulder Mt Park, CO 167 E5
Boulder Pk, CA 134 B1
Boulogne, 88 C8
Boulogne-Billancourt, 28 C7
Boulogne-sur-Mer, 19 F2

Boundary Canal, NC 187 E3

Boundary Peak, NV 132 D5

Bountiful, UT 130 B6, 135 G1

Bourges, 20 E6

Bourke, 77 E3

Bourke Street Mall, 79 B3

Bourne, MA 184 B5

Bournedale, MA 184 B6

Bournemouth, 19 E2

Bovisa, 40 B2

Bow Mar, CO 167 F2

Bowen, 77 E5

Bowleys Quarters, MD 147 F3

Bowling Green, KY 113 C4, 120 C6, 125 E2

Bowling Green, OH 125 F4, 118 B5

Bowling Green, VA 119 F2

Bowman, ND 130 F8

Box Hill, Austral 79 D2

Box Hill, UK 26 B5

Box Springs Mt CP, CA 171 H4

Boxford, MA 138 E7

Boy Scouts Mus, 105 A2

Boyce Park, PA 146 F7

Boyd Hill Nature Ctr, FL 154 B3

Boydton, VA 119 E1

Boynton Beach, FL 123 G2

Bozeman, MT 110 D7, 130 B8, 135 G4

Brackenridge Park, TX 163 G2

Bracknell, 26 A7

Braddock, PA 146 D6

Bradenburg Gate, 33 D3

Bradenton, FL 123 E3, 154 B1

Bradenton Beach, FL 154 B1

Bradford, MA 138 D8

Bradford, PA 116 B1, 119 E6

Bradford, UK 19 D4

Bradley-Palmer SP, MA 138 F7

Bradley Woods Res, OH 150 A6

Brady, TX 128 D3

Braga, 16 A4, 21 A4

Bragança, 21 B4

Brahmapur, 59 D4

Brahmaputra R, 58 E5

Brainerd, MN 124 B6, 126 F7

Braintree, MA 139 E2

Braithwaite, LA 163 H4

Bramalea, 104 B7

Brampton, 104 A6

Brandenburg, 23 D4

Brandon, Can 101 F2

Brandon, FL 123 E4, 154 D5

Brandon, MS 120 A3

Brandon, VT 115 A4

Brant Rock, MA 184 A8

Brantford, 116 A3

Bras, 93 H4

Brasov, 17 H5

Brasília, 85 F1

Bratenahl, OH 150 E8

Bratislava, 17 F5, 23 F2, 24 D6

Bratsk, 55 B3

Brattleboro, VT 115 B3

Braunschweig, 23 C4

Brawley, CA 133 F2

Bray, 19 C3

Braybrook, 79 A3

Brazil, 85 F3, 86 C6

Brazilian Highlands, 85 G2

Brazos R, TX 128 D4

Brazzaville, 46 D6

Brea, CA 170 D3

Breakeyville, 105 E1, F1

Breckenridge Hills, MO 162 A2

Breckerfeld, 34 F5

Brecksville Res, OH 150 E5

Brecon, OH 151 E4

Breda, 20 E8, 23 B4

Breendonk, 31 F4

Breezy Pt, NY 143 E1

Breitenlee, 42 F8

Bremen, 15 E1, 20 F8, 23 C4

Bremerhaven, 22 C5

Bremgarten, 37 D1

Breña, 87 F5

Brent, 26 C7

Brentwood, MD 148 E7

Brentwood, MO 162 B2

Brentwood, NY 116 B5

Brentwood, PA 146 C5

Brentwood, UK 26 E8

Brescia, 24 B5

Bresso, 40 C2

Brest, 16 B5, 17 G6, 20 B6, 52 A5

Breton NWR, 120 B1, 122 A5

Breukelen, 30 D4

Brevard, NC 121 E5

Brevik, 36 F5

Brevnov, 35 D3

Brewer, ME 114 E5

Brewerton, NY 117 E4

Brewster, MA 184 E5

Brewster, WA 134 C6

Brewton, AL 120 C2, 122 B6

Bridal Trails SP, WA 176 D5

Bridalveil Falls, CA 182 B3

Bridesburg, PA 145 F3

Bridge City, LA 163 F5

Bridgeboro, NJ 145 H4

Bridgehampton, NY 116 D6

Bridgeport, CA 132 D5

Bridgeport, CT 112 F6, 115 A1

Bridgeport, WA 134 C6

Bridger-Teton NF, WY 130 C7, 135 G2, 180 C1, 181 H2

Bridgeton, MO 162 A3

Bridgetown, Bar 95 H2

Bridgetown, OH 151 C2

Bridgeville, PA 146 B5

Brie-Comte-Robert, 28 E6

Brieselang, 32 B7

Brigham City, UT 130 B6, 135 G1

Bright Angel Creek, AZ 183 E2

Brighton, Austral 79 C1

Brighton, CO 130 E5, 167 H6

Brighton, UK 19 F2

Brighton Beach, NY 142 D1

Brigittenau, 42 E7

Brindisi, 24 D3

Briones RP, CA 174 D6

Brisbane, Austral 77 F4, 80 B2

Brisbane, CA 175 B4

Bristol, FL 122 C6

Bristol, NH 115 B4

Bristol, RI 115 C2

Bristol, TN 118 C1, 121 E6

Bristol, UK 16 C6, 19 D2, 20 C7

Bristol, VT 115 A4

Bristol, VA 113 D4

Bristol Bay, AK 136 B6

Bristol Chan, 19 D2

British Columbia, 101 C3

British Columbia, U of, 107 F2

British Isles, 14 C1, 18

British Mus & Library, 27 C3

Brno, 17 F5, 23 F2

Broad Ripple Park, IN 157 E3

Broadmeadows, 79 B4

Broadmoor, CA 175 A4

Broadview, MT 135 H4

Broadview Hts, OH 150 D5

Broadview Park, TX 164 A4

Brochet, 101 F2

Brockport, NY 116 C3

Brockton, MA 115 C2

Brockville, 117 E6

Broederstroom, 51 B3

Broken Arrow, OK 125 **A1** 127 **F1**, 129 **F6**

Broken Bow, NE 127 **D4**

Broken Hill, 76 **D3**

Bromley, KY 151 **D1**

Bromley, UK 26 **D6**

Bromma, 36 **D6**

Bromma Arpt, 36 **D6**

Bronson, FL 123 **E5**

Bronx, NY 116 **B5**, 143 **E5**

Bronx Zoo / Wildlife Conservation Park, NY 143 **E5**

Brook Park, OH 150 **C6**

Brookdale, NJ 142 **B5**

Brooker Creek Park, FL 154 **B6**

Brookfield, IL 159 **C3**

Brookfield Zoo, IL 159 **C3**

Brookhaven, GA 152 **C5**

Brookhaven, MS 120 **A3**

Brookhaven, PA 144 **B1**

Brookings, OR 132 **A8**, 134 **A2**

Brookings, SD 124 **A5**, 126 **E5**

Brooklandville, MD 147 **C4**

Brooklin, 92 **B4**

Brookline, MA 139 **C3**

Brooklyn, NY 116 **B5**, 141 **H2**, 142 **D2**

Brooklyn, OH 150 **C6**

Brooklyn Ctr, MN 161 **B4**

Brooklyn College, NY 142 **D2**

Brooklyn Hts, NY 142 **D3**

Brooklyn Hts, OH 150 **D6**

Brooklyn Mus & Botanical Gdn, NY 142 **D3**

Brooklyn Park, MD 147 **D1**

Brooklyn Park, MN 161 **B4**

Brooklyn Zoo, NY 142 **D2**

Brookmont, MD 148 **C7**

Brooks, 101 **D2**

Brooks AFB, TX 163 **G1**

Brooks Range, 100 **B7**, 82 **B6**, 136 **C8**

Brookside Park, OH 150 **C7**

Brookside Village, TX 166 **C2**

Brooksville, FL 123 **E4**

Brookvale, 78 **F8**

Brookville, PA 119 **E5**

Broomall, PA 144 **B3**

Broome, 76 **B5**

Broomfield, CO 167 **F5**

Brossard, 106 **D2**

Brottby, 36 **F8**

Brown Deer, WI 157 **B4**

Brown Deer Park, WI 157 **B4**

Brown Field, CA 169 **G1**

Brownfield, TX 128 **C4**

Brownsville, NY 143 **E2**

Brownsville, TN 120 **B5**

Brownsville, TX 96 **D5**, 111 **F1**, 129 **E1**

Brownwood, TX 128 **D4**

Broyhill Park, VA 148 **B6**

Brugg, 37 **A3**

Brugge, 23 **A3**

Brugherio, 40 **C2**

Brunei, 61 **D3**

Brunn, 42 **D6**

Brunna, 36 **D7**

Brunswick, Austral 79 **C3**

Brunswick, GA 113 **D3**, 121 **F2**, 123 **F6**

Brussels, 16 **D6**, 20 **E7**, 23 **A3**, 31 **G2**

Brussels Natl Arpt, 31 **G2**

Bruzzano, 40 **B2**, 40 **C2**

Bryan, OH 118 **A6**

Bryan, TX 113 **A3**, 129 **F3**

Bryansk, 15 **H1**, 53 **B4**

Bryanston, 51 **F4**

Bryant Lake RP, MN 161 **A1**

Bryce Canyon NP, UT 131 **B4**, 178 **B4**

Bryn Athyn, PA 145 **F6**

Bryn Mawr, PA 144 **C4**

Bryn Mawr College, PA 144 **C4**

Brzeg, 23 **F3**

Bucaramanga, 84 **C5**

Bucharest, 17 **H4**, 25 **G6**, 45 **F6**

Buchholz, 34 **B6**

Buchs, 37 **E2**

Buchschlag, 35 **B2**

Buckhannon, WV 118 **D3**

Buckhead, GA 152 **C5**

Buckhead Ridge, FL 123 **F3**

Buckingham, TX 165 **G5**

Buckingham Fountain, IL 160 **D5**

Buckingham Palace, 27 **B1**

Bucyrus, OH 118 **B5**

Budafok, 42 **A6**

Budakalász, 42 **B8**

Budakeszi, 42 **A7**

Budaörs, 42 **A6**

Budapest, 17 **F5**, 24 **D6**, 42 **B7**

Budapest Egyptian Mus, 42 **B7**

Budatétény, 42 **A6**

Budge Budge, 65 **D1**

Buena Park, CA 170 **D3**

Buenaventura, 84 **B4**

Buenavista, 98 **B5**, 99 **E3**, 99 **H2**

Buenos Aires, 86 **B5**, 88 **E7**

Buer, 34 **C8**

Buffalo, NY 103 **C1**, 112 **D6** 116 **B3**, 179 **G5**

Buffalo, WY 130 **D7**, 126 **A6**

Buffalo Bill's Mem Grave & Mus, CO 167 **E3**

Buffalo Grove, IL 158 **B6**

Buffalo Natl River, AR 125 **B1**

Buggenhout, 31 **F4**

Bugyi, 42 **B7**

Buhl, ID 132 **F8**, 135 **E2**

Buitenveldert, 30 **D5**

Bujumbura, 47 **F6**

Bukavu, 47 **F6**

Bukhara, 58 **B8**

Bukhoro, 53 **D1**

Bukit Batok, 63 **E3**

Bukit Panjang, 63 **E3**

Bukit Timah, 63 **E2**

Bukittinggi, 61 **A2**

Bülach, 37 **E3**

Bulaq ad-Dakrur, 50 **B2**

Bulawayo, 47 **F4**

Bulgaria, 17 **H4**, 25 **G6**, 45 **E6**

Bull Bay, NC 187 **E5**

Bullittsville, KY 151 **B1**

Bumba, 47 **E6**

Bunbury, 76 **A3**

Bund, The 74 **E7**

Bundaberg, 77 **F4**

Bundorra, 79 **C4**

Bung Kum, 63 **H6**

Bunker Hill Mon, MA 139 **D4**, 140 **C6**

Bunker Hill Village, TX 166 **A4**

Bunnell, FL 123 **F5**

Buona Vista, 63 **E1**

Buraydah, 49 **E4**

Burbank, CA 170 **B5**

Burbank, IL 159 **D3**

Burbank-Glendale-Pasadena Arpt, CA 170 **B6**

Bureau of Engraving & Printing, DC 149 **C2**

Buren, 37 **B3**

Burgas, 17 **H4**, 25 **H5**

Burgdorf, 37 **C3**

Burgos, 21 **C4**

Burholme, PA 145 **F5**

Burien, WA 176 **B3**

Burke Lake Park, VA 148 **A5**

Burke Lakefront Arpt, OH 150 **D7**

Burkesville, KY 118 **A1**

Burkina Faso, 44 **C2**

Burleson, TX 164 **B1**

Burley, ID 130 **A7**, 132 **F8**, 135 **F2**

Burlingame, CA 175 **B4**

Burlington, Can 116 **A4**

Burlington, CO 127 C3, 130 F5

Burlington, IA 125 C3

Burlington, KY 151 B1

Burlington, MA 138 B5

Burlington, OR 177 E6

Burlington, VT 103 D2, 114 A5, 117 H6

Burma, 58 F5

Burnaby, 107 H2

Burnet Woods, OH 151 D2

Burney, CA 132 B7, 134 B1

Burnhamthorpe, 104 C5

Burns, OR 134 C3

Burnt Porcupine Isl, ME 186 D6

Burr Ridge, IL 159 C3

Bursa, 25 H4

Burton, WA 176 B3

Burundi, 47 F6

Burwood, Austral 78 D7

Burwood, Austral 79 D2

Burzaco, 88 E5

Busch Gardens, FL 154 D6

Busch Mem Stad, MO 162 C1

Bushwick, NY 143 E3

Bustleton, PA 145 E5

Buta, 45 F1

Butano SP, CA 175 C1

Butantã, 92 A4

Butler, NJ 116 A6

Butler, PA 118 D5

Butler, WI 157 A3

Butler Pt, MA 184 A5

Butler U, IN 157 E3

Butovo, 56 B2

Butte, MT 110 C7, 130 B8, 135 F4, 178 B5

Buttonville, 104 E8

Buxtehude, 22 C5

Buxton, NC 187 H2

Buxton Woods Coastal Reserve, NC 187 H2

Buyukada, 43 F1

Buyukdere, 43 E3

Buzzards Bay, MA 185 A4

Bydgoszcz, 22 F5

Byfield, MA 138 E8

Bylot Isl, 102 A7

C

C & O Canal NHP, MD 148 B8

Caballito, 89 A1

Cabangbungin, 64 C8

Cabimas, 84 C6

Cabin John, MD 148 B8

Cabin John RP, MD 148 B8

Cabinda, 46 D5

Cable Car Barn & Mus, CA 173 D3

Cabo Rojo, PR 122 A1

Caborca, 131 B1

Cabramatta, 78 B6

Cabrillo NM, CA 169 E3

Cacém, 38 A7

Cáceres, 21 B3

Cachipay, 90 A2

Cadillac, MI 124 E5

Cadiz, OH 118 D4

Cádiz, Spain 16 A2, 21 B1

Caen, 19 E1, 20 D7

Caernarvon, LA 163 H4

Caetamo Campus, 93 F4

Cagayan de Oro, 61 E4

Cagliari, 17 E2, 24 A2

Caguas, 122 C2

Cahokia, IL 162 D4

Cahokia Mounds SHS, IL 162 D2

Caieiras, 92 A6

Cainta, 62 D2

Cairns, 77 E5

Cairo, Egypt 45 F4, 48 C4, 50 C2

Cairo, GA 122 D6

Cairo, IL 113 B4

Cairo Exh Grounds, 50 C2

Cairo Intl Arpt, 50 D3

Cairo Railway Sta, 50 C2

Cairo Stad, 50 D2

Cajamarca, 84 B3

Cajititlán, 99 G2

Cajon Junction, CA 171 G6

Caju, 91 D2

Caladest Island SP, FL 154 A5

Calais, Fr 19 F2, 20 D7

Calais, ME 112 F7, 114 F6

Calama, 86 A6

Calamba, 62 C3

Calarasí, 25 H6

Calcutta, 58 E5, 65 F1

Calcutta Botanical Gdns, 65 E2

Calcutta, U of 65 E2

Calcutta Zoo, 65 E1

Caldes de Montbui, 38 E8

Caldwell, ID 134 D3

Caldwell, OH 118 C4

Caledonian Sports Grounds, 51 H6

Calera de Tango, 87 E1

Calexico, CA 133 F2

Calgary, 101 D2, 110 D8

Calhoun, GA 120 D5

Cali, 84 C4

California, 101 B1, 110 B5, 132, 134 B1, 178 A4

California City, CA 133 D3

California-Irvine, U of, CA 171 E1

California-Riverside, U of, CA 171 H4

California-San Diego, U of, CA 169, E5

California State Polytechnic U, CA 171 E4

California SU Dominguez Hills, CA 170 B3

California SU Fullerton, CA 171 E3

California SU Hayward, CA 175 D4

California SU Long Beach, CA 170 D2

California SU Northridge, CA 170 A6

California SU San Bernardino, CA 171 H5

Calipatria, CA 133 F2

Callao, 84 C2, 87 E5

Callaway, FL 122 C6

Caloocan, 62 C3

Caltanissetta, 24 C1

Calumet City, IL 159 E2

Calusa Keys, FL 188 E3

Camaguey, 94 C4

Camas, WA 177 H6

Camberley, 26 A6

Camberwell, 79 D2

Cambodia, 61 B4

Cambrai, 23 A3

Cambria, CA 133 B4

Cambridge, MD 119 G3

Cambridge, MA 115 C3, 139 C4, 140 A5

Cambridge, MN 124 B6

Cambridge, NY 115 A3

Cambridge, OH 118 C4

Cambridge, UK 19 F3, 20 D8

Cambridge Bay, 100 E6

Camden, AR 129 G5

Camden, ME 114 D5

Camden, NJ 112 E5, 119 H4, 145 E2

Camden, NY 117 F4

Camden, SC 121 F4

Camden, UK 26 C7

Cameron, TX 129 E3

Cameron City, FL 153 H6

Cameroon, 44 D1, 46 D6

Camp Dennison, OH 151 F3

Camp Edwards Mil Res, MA 184 B5

Camp H R Smith, HI 177 G3

Camp Shelby Mil Res, MS 122 A6

Camp Springs, MD 148 C8

Camp Verde, AZ 131 B3

Campamento, 39 A2

Campbell, CA 175 E1

Campbell, FL 153 **F1**

Campbell River, 101 **B3**

Campbellsville, KY 118 **A2**, 120 **D6**, 125 **F2**

Campeche, 97 **E3**

Campestre, 98 **B2**

Campina Grande, 85 **H3**

Campinas, 86 **C6**

Campo Grande, 85 **E1**, 91 **A2**

Campobasso, 24 **C3**

Campos, 86 **C6**

Campos Elísios, 91 **C4**

Campton, KY 118 **B2**

Camurí Grande, 90 **D6**

Can Tho, 61 **B3**

Canaan, NH 115 **B4**

Canada, 100 – 103

Canada Place, 107 **G2**

Canadian R, TX 127 **C1**, 128 **D6**

Canadian Shield, 101 **E4**, 103 **C2**

Canadian Wonderland, 104 **C8**

Canakkale, 25 **G4**

Canandaigua, NY 116 **D3**

Canarsie, NY 143 **E2**

Canary Islands, 44 **A4**

Canary Wharf, 26 **D7**

Canaveral NS, FL 121 **F1**, 179 **G1**

Canberra, 77 **E3**, 80 **B2**

Cancún, 94 **A5**, 97 **F3**

Candiac, 106 **D1**

Candlestick Park, CA 174 **B5**

Caneças, 38 **A7**

Canillas, 39 **D4**

Cannery, The CA 173 **C4**

Cannes, 21 **F4**, 24 **A4**

Canning, 88 **D5**

Cannonsville Reservoir, NY 117 **F4**

Canon City, CO 127 **A2**, 130 **E5**

Canso, 103 **F2**

Cantabrian Mts, 21 **B4**

Canterbury Woods, VA 148 **A5**

Canterbury, Austral 78 **D6**

Canterbury, Austral 79 **D2**

Canterbury, UK 19 **F2**

Canton, MA 139 **C1**

Canton, MS 120 **B3**

Canton, NY 117 **F6**

Canton, OH 112 **D5**, 118 **C5**

Canyon, CA 174 **D5**

Canyon, TX 128 **D5**

Canyon City, OR 134 **D3**

Canyon de Chelly NM, AZ 128 **A6**, 131 **C3**, 178 **C3**

Canyon Lake, CA 171 **H2**

Canyon Village, WY 180 **B4**

Canyonlands NP, UT 131 **C4**, 178 **C4**

Caojiazhai, 74 **D6**

Cap-Haitien, 95 **E4**

Cap Rouge, 105 **D2**

Cap San Antonio, 94 **A5**

Caparica, 38 **B6**

Cape Adare, 83 **B2**

Cape Agulhas, 47 **E2**

Cape Alava, WA 134 **A6**

Cape Ann, MA 115 **C3**

Cape Arnhem, 76 **D6**

Cape Bathurst, 136 **E8**

Cape Beale, 134 **A6**

Cape Beate, 95 **E3**

Cape Bon, 44 **D5**

Cape Canaveral, FL 113 **D2**, 123 **F4**

Cape Chelyuskin, 54 **A6**

Cape Clear, 19 **A2**

Cape Cod, MA 112 **F6**, 184 – 185

Cape Cod Bay, MA 115 **C3**, 184 **D7**

Cape Cod Canal, MA 184 **B6**

Cape Cod NS, MA 115 **D2**, 179 **H5**, 184 **F8**

Cape Comorin, 59 **B3**

Cape Corrientes, 96 **B3**

Cape Disappointment, WA 134 **A5**

Cape Falcon, OR 134 **A4**

Cape Falso, 95 **E3**

Cape Farewell, 82 **F5**, 102 **F6**

Cape Fear R, 121 **G5**

Cape Ferreio, OR 134 **A2**

Cape Finisterre, 16 **A4**

Cape Flattery, WA 134 **A6**

Cape Girardeau, MO 113 **B4** 125 **C2**

Cape Hatteras, NC 113 **F4**

Cape Hatteras Lighthouse, NC 187 **H2**

Cape Hatteras NS, NC 121 **H5**, 179 **H3**, 187 **G2**

Cape Hatteras Visitor Ctr, NC 187 **H2**

Cape Henlopen, DE 119 **H3**

Cape Horn, 86 **B2**

Cape Krusenstern NM, AK 136 **B8**, 178 **A2**

Cape Kumukahi, HI 137 **F2**

Cape Leeuwin, 76 **A2**

Cape Leveque, 76 **B5**

Cape Lisburne, AK 136 **B8**

Cape Lookout NS, NC 179 **H3**, 187 **F1**

Cape Lookout, OR 134 **A4**

Cape May Court House, NJ 119 **H3**

Cape May Pt, NJ 119 **H3**

Cape Mohican, AK 136 **A6**

Cape Morris Jesup, 82 **D6**

Cape Newehham, AK 136 **B6**

Cape Norvegia, 83 **E3**

Cape of Good Hope, 47 **E2**

Cape Palmas, 44 **B1**

Cape Poinsett, 83 **B1**

Cape Race, 103 **F3**

Cape Romain NWR, SC 121 **G4**

Cape Romano, FL 123 **E2**

Cape Sable, Can 103 **E2**

Cape Sable, FL 113 **D2**, 123 **F1**, 188 **D4**

Cape St. Vincent, 16 **A2**, 21 **A2**

Cape San Blas, FL 122 **C5**

Cape Town, 47 **E2**

Cape Tres Puntas, 86 **B3**

Cape York, 76 **D6**, 80 **B3**

Cape York Pen, 76 **B1**

Capela do Socorro, 92 **A3**

Capelle aan den Ijssel, 30 **B2**

Capital Children's Mus, DC 149 **F4**

Capitol, The, DC 149 **F2**

Capitol Hts, MD 148 **F6**

Capitol Reef NP, UT 131 **B4**, 178 **C4**

Capr Nao, 21 **D2**

Capulin, NM 131 **F4**

Caraballeda, 90 **C6**

Carabanchel, 39 **B1**

Caracal, 25 **G6**

Caracas, 84 **D6**, 90 **C5**, 95 **F1**

Caracas Botanical Gdns, 90 **C5**

Caracas Natl Mus of Art, 90 **C5**

Carayaca, 90 **A5**

Carbondale, IL 113 **B4**, 125 **D2**

Carbondale, PA 117 **E1**

Cardiff, 16 **C6** , 19 **D2**, 20 **C7**

Cardinal Stritch College, WI 157 **C4**

Caribbean Sea, 84 **C6**, 94 **D2**, 97 **G3**

Caribou,.ME 114 **E8**

Carin RP, CA 175 **E4**

Caringbah, 78 **D5**

Carle Place, NY 143 **H4**

Carleton U, 105 **B2**

Carlin, NV 132 **E7**

Carlingford, 78 **C8**

Carlington, 105 **A2**

Carlisle, MA 138 **A6**

Carlisle, PA 119 **F4**

Carlisle, UK 18 **D5**

Carlow, 19 **B3**

Carlsbad, NM 111 **E3**, 128 **B4**, 131 **F2**

Carlsbad Caverns NP, NM 128 **C4**, 131 **E2**, 178 **C2**

Carlstadt, NJ 142 **C5**

Carmacks, 100 **B5**

Carmacs, 136 **E6**

Carman, 126 **E8**

Carmel, IN 125 **E3**, 157 **E4**

Carmel, NY 117 **H1**, 119 **H6**

Carnarvon, 76 **A4**

Carnaxide, 38 **A6**

Carnegie, PA 146 **B6**

Carnegie Hall, NY 141 **G5**

Carney, MD 147 **E4**

Carol Beach, WI 158 **C8**

Carol City, FL 155 **F3**

Carol Stream, IL 159 **A4**

Carolina, 122 **C2**

Caroline Islands, 80 **B4**

Carondelet Park, MO 162 **B1**

Carpathian Mts., 17 **G5**

Carrabelle, FL 122 **C5**

Carrara, 24 **B5**

Carrizo Springs, TX 128 **D2**

Carroll, IA 125 **A4**

Carrollton, GA 120 **D4**

Carrollton, OH 118 **C5**

Carrollton, TX 165 **E6**

Carrollwood, FL 154 **C5**

Carry Falls Reservoir, NY 117 **F5**

Carson, CA 170 **C3**

Carson City, NV 110 **B5**, 132 **C6**

Carson NF, NM 127 **A1**

Cartagena, Col 84 **C5**, 94 **D1**

Cartagena, Spain 16 **B2**, 21 **D2**

Carter Presidential Ctr, GA 152 **C3**

Carteret, NJ 142 **A1**

Carthage, NY 117 **F5**

Carthage, TX 129 **F4**

Cartier-Brebeuf NHP, 105 **E3**

Cartierville Arpt, 106 **B3**

Cartwright, 103 **E4**

Carugate, 40 **D3**

Caruthersville, MO 120 **B6**, 129 **H6**

Casa de Campo, 39 **B3**

Casa Grande, AZ 111 **C3**, 131 **B2**

Casa Rosada, 89 **D3**

Casa Verde, 92 **B5**

Casablanca, 16 **A1**, 44 **B5**

Casalotti, 40 **B5**

Cascade, ID 135 **E3**

Cascade, MT 135 **G5**

Cascade Canyon, WY 181 **F3**

Cascade Corner, WY 180 **A2**

Cascade Creek, WY 181 **F3**

Cascade Head, OR 134 **A4**

Cascade Park, WA 177 **G6**

Cascade Range, 101 **B1**, 110 **B7**, 132 **B8**, 134 **B3**

Casco Bay, ME 115 **D4**

Caseros, 88 **C7**

Caserta, 24 **C3**

Caseyville, IL 162 **D2**

Cashion, AZ 168 **A3**

Casper, WY 110 **E6**, 126 **A5** 130 **D7**, 178 **C4**

Caspers Wilderness Park, CA 171 **G1**

Caspian Sea, 45 **H6**, 49 **F6**, 53 **B2**

Cassiar, 101 **C4**, 136 **F6**

Cassiar Mts, 136 **F6**

Castel di Decima, 40 **C4**

Castel di Guido, 40 **A6**

Castel di Leva, 40 **C4**

Castel Porziano, 40 **B4**

Castel Sant'Angelo, 41 **B4**

Castelar, 88 **C6**

Castellar del Vallès, 38 **E8**

Castelldefels, 38 **D5**

Castellón de la Plana, 21 **D3**

Castle Amusement Park, CA 171 **G3**

Castle Hill, 78 **C8**

Castle Hills, TX 163 **F3**

Castle Park, CA 169 **G2**

Castle Rock, CO 130

Castle Rock SP, CA 175 **D1**

Castle Shannon, PA 146 **B5**

Castlebar, 19 **A4**

Castor Peak, WY 180 **D4**

Castries, 95 **H2**

Castro Valley, CA 175 **D4**

Castrop-Rauxel, 34 **E8**

Cat Isl, 94 **D5**

Catamarca, 86 **B6**

Catania, 17 **F2**, 24 **D1**

Cataño, PR 122 **C2**

Catanzaro, 24 **D2**

Cataumet, MA 184 **A5**

Catawba R, NC 121 **E5**

Caterham, 26 **D6**

Catford, 26 **D7**

Cathedral of the Annunciation, 57 **E4**

Cathedral of the Archangel Michael, 57 **F4**

Cathedral Peak, CA 182 **D3**

Cathedral Range, CA 182 **D3**

Catherine's Palace, 56 **C4**

Cathlamet, WA 134 **B4**

Catia la Mar, 90 **A6**

Catonsville, MD 147 **B2**

Catskill, NY 117 **G2**

Catskill Mts, NY 119 **H6**

Catskill Park, NY 117 **G1**, 119 **H6**

Caucagüita, 90 **D5**

Caucasus Mts, 45 **G6**, 53 **A3**

Caulfield, 79 **C2**

Causapscal, 103 **D3**

Causeway Bay, 75 **D2**

Cava, 91 **B4**

Cave Junction, OR 134 **A2**

Cavite, 62 **B1**

Cavusbasi, 43 **F3**

Caxias Belem Tower, 38 **A6**

Caxias do Sul, 86 **C6**

Cayagzi, 43 **F4**

Cayenne, 85 **F5**

Cayman Islands, 94 **B4**, 97 **G3**

Cayuga Lake, NY 116 **D3**

Cazenovia, NY 117 **E3**

CBS TV City, CA 172 **B7**

Ceballos, 128 **B1**

Cebu, 61 **E4**

Cecchignola, 40 **C4**

Cecil Park, 78 **A7**

Cedar City, UT 110 **C5** 131 **B4**

Cedar Falls, IA 125 **B4**

Cedar Grove, GA 152 **C3**

Cedar Grove, NJ 142 **A6**

Cedar Hill, TX 165 **E1**

Cedar Hill SP, TX 165 **E1**

Cedar Hills, OR 177 **F5**

Cedar Isl, NC 187 **E1**

Cedar Key, FL 123 **E5**

Cedar Keys NWR, FL 121 **E1**

Cedar Mt, AZ 183 **F2**

Cedar Park, IL 162 **D3**

Cedar Rapids, IA 112 **B5**, 125 **C4**

Cedarbrook, PA 145 **E5**

Cedarhurst, NY 143 **G2**

Cedarpines Park, CA 171 **G6**

Cedartown, GA 120 **D4**

Cedarville, MA 184 **B6**

Cedros, 99 **H2**

Cedros Isl, 96 **A5**

Ceduna, 76 **C3**

Ceiba, 122 **D2**

Celebes, 61 **E2**

Celebes Sea, 61 **E3**

Celina, OH 118 A5

Celtic Sea, 19 B2, 20 B7

Cemke, 43 F2

Centennial Centre,
107 G5

Centennial Park, MD
147 A2

Center Hill Pt, MA 184 B6

Center Line, MI 156 E8

Center Square, PA 144 C6

Centerton, NJ 145 H3

Centerville, MA 184 C5

Centocelle, 40 C5

Central, AK 136 D7

Central African Republic,
45 E1

Central America, 97

Central Concert Hall,
57 F5

Central Exh Hall, 57 E5

Central Florida, U of, FL
153 H4

Central Florida Zoo, FL
153 G6

Central Lenin Mus, 57 F5

Central Park, NY 141 G5,
142 D4

Central Park Zoo, NY
141 G5

Central Plateau, WY 180 B4

Central Rail Sta, 65 A1

Central Range, 54 B7

Central Russian Upland,
53 B4

Central Siberian Plateau,
55 B4

Central Stad, 70 A5

Central Sta, 31 G6

Central Valley, CA 132 B7

Centre G. Pompidou, 29 E2

Centreville, IL 162 C1

Centro, 39 C3

Centro Simón Bolívar,
90 B5

Century, FL 122 B6

Cerdanyola del Vallès,
38 E7

Cerignola, 24 C3

Cernosice, 35 D2

Cernusco sul Naviglio,
40 D2

Cerrillos, 87 F2

Cerritos, CA 170 D3

Cerro Aconcague, 86 A5

Cerro de Pasco, 84 C2

Cesano Boscone, 40 B1

Cesena, 24 B5

Ceske Budejovice, 23 E2

Ceuta, 16 A2, 21 B1,
44 C5

Chabot RP, Anthony, CA
174 D5

Chacao, 90 C5

Chaco Culture NHP, NM
178 C3

Chaco Culture NHS, NM
128 A6

Chad, 45 E2, 48 A3

Chadron, NE 110 E6,
126 B5, 130 F7

Chadstone, 79 D2

Chagos Archipelago, 59 B1

Chai Wan, 75 E2

Chaillot, 29 B3

Chain O'Lakes SP, IL
158 A8

Chairmen Mao Mem Hall,
73 D2

Challis, ID 135 F3

Challis NF, ID 135 E3,
135 F3

Chalmette, LA 163 G5

Chalon-sur-Saône, 23 B1

Chalons-sur-Marne, 23 B2

Chamartín, 39 C4

Chamberí, 39 C3

Chamberlain, SD 126 D5

Chamberlain Lake, ME
114 D7

Chambersburg, PA 119 F4

Chambéry, 23 B1

Chamblee, GA 152 C6

Champ de Mars, 29 B2

Champaign, IL 112 B5,
125 D3

Chanberly, 20 F5

Chandannagar, 65 E3

Chandigarh, 58 C6

Chandler, AZ 168 D2

Chandrapur, 58 C5

Chang R, 60 C6

Changchun, 55 E2, 66 C6

Changde, 60 B6, 67 A3

Changi, 63 H3

Changi Intl Arpt, 63 H2

Changning District, 74 B6

Changsha, 60 C6, 67 A3

Changting, 67 B2

Changzhi, 67 A4

Changzhou, 67 C4

Channel Islands, CA 111 A4

Channel Islands, UK
16 B6, 19 D1, 20 C7

Channel Islands NP, CA
178 A3

Channel-Port aux Basques,
103 E3

Channel Tunnel, 19 F2

Chantepec, 99 F1

Chanute, KS 127 F2

Chaoyang, 73 F2

Chaoyang District, 73 F3

Chaozhou, 67 B2

Chapala, 99 H1

Chapel Hill, NC 121 G6

Chapel of the Transfigur-
ation, WY 181 F2

Chapleau, 103 B2

Chappaquiddick Isl, MA
185 C2

Chapultepec Park, 98 A3

Chardzhou, 58 A8

Charing Cross Sta, 27 C2

Charjew, 53 C1

Charlemagne, 106 D5

Charleroi, 20 E7, 23 B3

Charles De Gaulle Arpt,
28 E8

Charles Town, WV 119 F4

Charlesbourg, 105 E3

Charleston, IL 125 D3

Charleston, MO 125 C2

Charleston, SC 113 E3,
121 G3, 179 G2

Charleston, WV 112 D5,
118 C3, 179 G4

Charlestown, MA 139 D4,
140 C4

Charleswood, 107 F5

Charleville, 77 E4

Charlotte, NC 113 D4,
121 F5, 179 G3

Charlotte Court House, VA
119 E1

Charlottesville, VA 112 E5,
119 E2

Charlottetown, 103 E2

Charneca, 38 B7

Charny, 105 E2

Charters Towers, 77 E5

Chartres, 20 D6

Chartwell, 26 D5

Chassahowitzka NWR, FL
121 E1

Chastain Mem Park, GA
152 B5

Chateaugay, NY 117 G6

Chateauguay, 106 B1

Chatfield SRA, CO 167 F1

Chatham, MA 115 D2,
184 F5

Chatham, UK 26 F6

Chatham, VA 119 E1

Chatham Islands, 80 D1

Chatswood, 78 E8

Chattahoochee, FL 122 D6

Chattahoochee NF, GA
120 D5

Chattahoochee River NRA,
GA 152 A6

Chattanooga, TN 113 C4,
120 D5, 125 F1

Chatuchak, 63 G6

Chaudière R, 114 C7

Chaumont, 23 B2

Cheb, 23 E3

Checkpoint Charlie, 33 C3

Cheektowaga, NY 116 B3

Chehalis, WA 134 B5

Cheju, 67 **C4**
Cheju Isl, 60 **D7**, 67 **C4**
Chelas, 38 **B7**
Chelles, 28 **E7**
Chelmsford, MA 138 **A6**
Chelmsford, UK 19 **F3**, 26 **F8**
Chelsea, MA 139 **D4**
Chelsea, PA 144 **A1**
Chelsea, UK 26 **C7**
Cheltenham, Austral 78 **D8**
Cheltenham, PA 145 **F5**
Chelyabinsk, 53 **D3**
Chembur, 65 **B2**
Chemnitz, 17 **E6**, 23 **E3**
Chenango R, NY 117 **E2**
Chene, 65 **C4**
Cheney, WA 134 **D5**
Cheng Sha Wan, 75 **B3**
Chengde, 66 **B6**
Chengdu, 60 **A6**
Chengjiaqiaozhen, 74 **A5**
Chenjiazha, 74 **C8**
Chequamegon NF, WI 124 **C6**
Cheraw, SC 121 **F5**
Cherbourg, 19 **E1**, 20 **C7**
Cheremushki, 56 **B3**
Cherepovets, 52 **C5**
Chernovtsy, 17 **G5**
Cherokee NF, NC 120 **D5**, 121 **F6**
Cherry Creek SRA, CO 167 **H2**
Cherry Grove, OH 151 **F1**
Cherry Hill, NJ 145 **G2**
Cherry Hills Village, CO 167 **G2**
Cherrydale, VA 148 **C6**
Cherskiy, 54 **E7**
Cherskiy Range, 54 **E5**
Chertanovo, 56 **B3**
Chertsey, 26 **B6**
Chesapeake, VA 119 **G1**
Chesapeake Bay, 112 **E5**, 119 **G2**

Chesham, 26 **A8**
Cheshunt, 26 **D8**
Chester, CA 132 **B7**
Chester, IL 125 **C2**
Chester, MT 135 **G6**
Chester, SC 121 **F5**
Chester, UK 19 **D3**
Chester, VT 115 **A3**
Chester Hts, PA 144 **A1**
Chesterbrook, PA 144 **A5**
Chesterbrook, VA 148 **C7**
Chesuncook, ME 114 **D7**
Chetenham, 79 **C1**
Chetumal, 97 **F3**
Cheverly, MD 148 **F7**
Cheviot, OH 151 **C2**
Chevreuse, 28 **B6**
Chevy Chase, MD 148 **D8**
Cheyenne, WY 110 **E5**, 127 **B4**, 130 **E6**, 178 **D4**
Cheyenne River, 126 **C6**
Cheyenne River IR, SD 126 **C6**, 130 **F8**
Chhalera Bangar, 64 **F6**
Chhaprauli, 64 **F6**
Chia, 90 **C3**
Chia Keng, 63 **G2**
Chiai, 67 **C2**
Chiang Kai-Shek Intl Arpt, 62 **A5**
Chiang Kai-Shek Mem Hall, 62 **B5**
Chiang Mai, 61 **A4**
Chiba, 68 **E7**
Chibougamau, 103 **C2**
Chicago, IL 103 **B1**, 112 **B5**, 125 **D4**, 159 **E4**, 160, 179 **F4**
Chicago, U of, IL 159 **E3**
Chicago Art Institute, IL 160 **D6**
Chicago Board of Trade, IL 160 **C5**
Chicago Botanic Gdn, IL 158 **D6**
Chicago Civic Opera House, IL 160 **B6**

Chicago Cultural Ctr, IL 160 **D6**
Chicago Hts, IL 159 **D1**
Chicago Maritime Mus, IL 160 **D7**
Chicago Mercantile Exchange, IL 160 **C6**
Chicago Midway Arpt, IL 159 **D3**
Chicago O'Hare Intl Arpt, IL 159 **B4**
Chicamacomico, NC 187 **H4**
Chickamauga & Chatta-nooga NMP, GA 179 **F3**
Chickasha, OK 129 **E5**
Chiclayo, 84 **B3**
Chico, CA 132 **B6**
Chicopee, MA 115 **B2**
Chicoutimi, 103 **D2**, 112 **E8**
Chido, 72 **B7**
Chieti, 24 **C4**
Chifeng, 66 **B6**
Chigasaki, 68 **A5**
Chigwell, 26 **D8**
Chihuahua, 96 **C5**, 111 **D2** 128 **B2**
Chijiatang, 74 **E8**
Chikapanagi Pt, AZ 183 **C3**
Children's Mus, MA 140 **D2**
Childress, TX 128 **D5**
Chile, 84 **C1**, 86 **A6**
Chile, U of, 87 **F2**
Chillán, 86 **A4**
Chillicothe, MO 125 **B3**
Chillicothe, OH 118 **B4**, 125 **F3**
Chillum, MD 148 **E7**
Chilly-Mazarin, 28 **D6**
Chilmark, MA 185 **A2**
Chiloé Isl, 86 **A4**
Chilpancingo, 96 **D3**
Chilung, 62 **D6**, 67 **C2**
Chimayo, NM 131 **E3**
Chimbote, 84 **B2**
Chimoio, 47 **G4**

China, 55 **E1**, 58 **E7**, 60 **A6**, 67 **A4**
China Camp SP, CA 174
China Grove, TX 163 **H2**
China Lake Naval Weap-ons Ctr, CA 133 **D4**
Chinatown, CA 172 **E6**, 173 **D3**
Chinatown, DC 149 **D4**
Chinatown, NY 141 **F2**
Chinatown, Phil 62 **B2**
Chincoteague, MD 119 **H3**
Chingola, 47 **F4**
Chinjop, 72 **E8**
Chinle, AZ 131 **C3**
Chino, CA 171 **F4**
Chino Hills, CA 171 **E4**
Chino Hills SP, CA 171 **E3**
Chinook, MT 135 **H6**
Chinquapin, CA 182 **A2**
Chinsnan, 62 **C6**
Chioggia, 24 **C5**
Chipaque, 90 **C1**
Chipata, 47 **G4**
Chipley, FL 122 **C6**
Chippewa Falls, WI 124 **C6**
Chippewa NF, MN 124 **B7**, 126 **F7**
Chipping Ongar, 26 **E8**
Chiputneticook Lakes, ME 114 **F6**
Chiricahua NM, AZ 131 **C1**
Chirmer, 65 **C1**
Chisasibi, 103 **C3**
Chita, 55 **D3**, 66 **A8**
Chitral, 58 **B7**
Chitralada Palace, 63 **F6**
Chittagong, 58 **E5**
Chittenango, NY 117 **E3**
Chitu, 62 **D5**
Chiyoda-Ku, 69 **A4**
Choachi, 90 **D1**
Chodov, 35 **F3**
Chofu, 68 **B7**
Choisy-le-Roi, 28 **D6**
Choix, 128 **A1**
Chojnice, 22 **F5**

Chomedey, 106 **B3**

Chomutov, 23 **E3**

Chongjin, 55 **F2**, 66 **D6**

Chongju, 66 **C5**

Chongno, 72 **C7**

Chongqing, 60 **A6**

Chongwen District, 73 **E2**

Chonju, 66 **C5**

Chonos Archipelago, 86 **A3**

Chorrillos, 87 **G4**

Choteau, MT 135 **F5**

Chowchilla, CA 132 **C5**

Choybalsan, 55 **D2**, 66 **A7**

Christ the Redeemer Statue, 91 **D2**

Christchurch, 77 **H1**, 80 **C2**

Christiansborg Palace, 36 **C6**

Christiansburg, VA 118 **D1**, 121 **F6**

Chrysler Bldg, NY 141 **G4**

Chuansha County, 74 **F5**

Chubbuck, ID 130 **B7**

Chugach NF, AK 136 **D6**

Chukchi Pen, 136 **A8**

Chukchi Range, 54 **E8**, 82 **A6**

Chukchi Sea, 54 **E8**, 82 **B6**, 100 **A8**, 136 **A8**

Chula Vista, CA 133 **E2** 169 **G2**

Chung, 72 **A6**

Chung Nang, 72 **D7**

Chungho, 62 **B4**

Chuo-Ku, 68 **C7**, 69 **E3**, 71 **B3**

Chur, 23 **C1**

Churchill, 101 **F4**

Churchill R, 101 **E3**

Churilkovo, 56 **D1**

Churubusco, 98 **B2**

Ciampino, 40 **D4**

Ciampino Arpt, 40 **D4**

Ciawi, 64 **B5**

Cibinong, 64 **B6**

Cibola NF, NM 128 **A5**, 131 **D2**, 131 **E3**

Cicero, IL 159 **D4**

Cienfuegos, 94 **B5**

Ciftalan, 43 **D4**

Cilandak, 64 **B7**

Cileungsir, 64 **C6**

Cilincing, 64 **C8**

Cimarron NG, KS 127 **C2**

Cincinnati, OH 112 **C5**, 118 **A3**, 125 **F3**, 151 **C2**, 179 **F4**

Cincinnati, U of, OH 151 **D2**

Cincinnati Gdns, OH 151 **E3**

Cincinnati Municipal Arpt, OH 151 **E2**

Cincinnati Zoo & Botanical Gdn, OH 151 **D2**

Cinecitta, 40 **C5**

Ciniselo Balsamo, 40 **C3**

Cinkota, 42 **C7**

Cinnaminson, NJ 145 **G3**

Cipó, 92 **A2**

Circleville, OH 118 **B4**

Cisaura, 64 **C5**

Citadel, 50 **C2**

Citadelle, 105 **F3**

Citeureup, 64 **B6**

Citrus Bowl, FL 153 **G4**

Citrus Park, FL 154 **C6**

Citta Degli Studi, 40 **C2**

City, 27 **D3**

City Centre, 107 **G5**

City Mus Of Natural History, 70 **D5**

Ciudad Acuña, 128 **D2**

Ciudad Adolfo López Mateos Atizapán, 98 **A5**

Ciudad Azteca, 98 **C4**

Ciudad Bolívar, 84 **D5**

Ciudad Deportiva Boca Juniors, 89 **F2**

Ciudad de Valles, 96 **D4**

Ciudad del Carmen, 97 **E3**

Ciudad Granja, 99 **F5**

Ciudad Guayana, 85 **E5**

Ciudad Jiménez, 128 **B1**

Ciudad Juárez, 96 **B6**, 111D3, 128 **A4**, 131D1

Ciudad Lineal, 39 **D4**

Ciudad Mante, 96 **D4**

Ciudad Obregón, 96 **B5**

Ciudad Real, 21 **C2**

Ciudad Satelite, 98 **A4**

Ciudad Victoria, 96 **D4**

Civitavecchia, 24 **B4**

Clackamas, OR 177 **G4**

Clanton, AL 120 **C3**

Claremont, CA 171 **E5**

Claremont, NH 115 **B4**

Clarion, PA 119 **E5**

Clark Range, CA 182 **C5**

Clarks Summit, PA 117 **E1**

Clarksburg, WV 118 **D3**

Clarksdale, MS 120 **A5**, 129 **H5**

Clarkston, GA 152 **D4**

Clarksville, AR 125 **B1**

Clarksville, TN 113 **C4**, 120 **C6**, 125 **D1**

Claudius, 51 **G6**

Clawson, MI 156 **C8**

Clay, WV 118 **D3**

Claye-Souilly, 28 **E7**

Claypole, 88 **E5**

Clayton, Austral 79 **D1**

Clayton, CA 174 **E6**

Clayton, ID 135 **E3**

Clayton, MO 162 **B2**

Clayville, 51 **H5**

Clearfield, PA 119 **E5**

Clearlake, CA 132 **B6**

Clearwater, FL 123 **E4**, 154 **A5**

Clearwater Bay CP, 75 **F3**

Clearwater Marine Science Ctr, FL 154 **A5**

Clearwater Mts, ID 135 **E4**

Clementi, 63 **E2**

Clemson, SC 121 **E5**

Clerkenwell, 27 **D4**

Clermont-Ferrand, 16 **C4**, 20 **E5**, 23 **A1**

Cleveland, MS 120 **A4**

Cleveland, OH 103 **C1**, 112 **D6**, 118 **C6**, 150 **C7** 179 **G4**

Cleveland, TN 120 **D5**

Cleveland Hts, OH 150 **E7**

Cleveland Hopkins Intl Arpt, OH 150 **B6**

Cleveland Metroparks Zoo, OH 150 **D6**

Cleveland Municipal Stad, OH 150 **D7**

Cleveland Mus of Art, OH 150 **D7**

Cleveland Mus of Natural History, OH 150 **E7**

Cleveland NF, CA 171 **F2**

Cleves, OH 151 **A2**

Clichy, 28 **D7**

Cliffside Park, NJ 142 **D5**

Clifton, NJ 142 **B6**

Clifton Hts, PA 144 **C2**

Clifton Park, MD 147 **D3**

Clinton, CT 116 **D6**

Clinton, IL 125 **D4**

Clinton, MO 125 **A2**

Clinton, NC 121 **G5**

Clinton, SC 121 **E5**

Clinton Pt, 136 **F8**

Cliveden, PA 145 **E4**

Clock Tower, 37 **B2**

Cloisters, The, NY 143 **E5**

Cloncurry, 76 **D5**

Clonmel, 19 **B3**

Clontarf, 78 **F7**

Cloverdale, CA 132 **A6**

Cloverleaf, TX 166 **D3**

Clovis, CA 133 **C4**

Clovis, NM 111 **E4**, 128 **C5** 131 **F3**

Cluj-Napoca, 17 **G5**

Clyde, CA 174 **D7**

Clyde Hill, WA 176 **C5**

CN Tower, 104 **E5**

Coacalco, 98 **B6**

Coalinga, CA 133 **C4**

Coalville, UT 135 **G1**

Coamo, 122 **C1**
Coast Mts, 136 **F5**
Coast Ranges, 110 **A6**, 111 **A4**, 132 **A6**, 134 **A2**
Coaticook, 114 **B6**
Coats Isl, 102 **A5**
Coats Land, 83 **D3**
Coatzacoalcos, 97 **E3**
Cobb, CA 132 **A6**
Cobija, 84 **D2**
Cobleskill, NY 117 **G3**
Coburg, Austral 79 **C3**
Coburg, Ger 23 **D3**
Cochabamba, 84 **D1**
Cochin, 59 **B3**
Cochituate, MA 139 **A3**
Cockrell Hill, TX 165 **F3**
Coco R, 97 **G2**
Cocoa, FL 123 **F4**
Coconino Plateau, AZ 183 **B1**
Coconut Creek, FL 155 **G6**
Coconut Grove, FL 155 **F1**
Cocota, 91 **D3**
Cody, WY 110 **D6**, 130 **D7**, 135 **H3**
Coelho da Rocha, 91 **B3**
Coeur D'Alene, ID 135 **E5**, 110 **C7**
Coeur D'Alene IR, ID 134 **D5**
Coeur D'Alene NF, ID 135 **E5**
Coffeyville, KS 127 **F2**
Cohoes, NY 117 **H3**
Coiba Isl, 97 **G1**
Coimbatore, 59 **B3**
Coimbra, 16 **A3**, 21 **A3**
Coina, 91 **B3**
Coit Tower, CA 173 **E3**
Colby, KS 127 **C3**
Colby, WA 176 **A4**
Coldwater, MI 118 **A6**
Colebrook, NH 114 **B5**
Coleman, TX 128 **D4**
Coleraine, 18 **C5**
Colfax, WA 134 **D5**

Colima, 96 **C3**
Colimilla, 99 **H5**
Collatino, 40 **C6**
College, AK 136 **D7**
College Park, GA 152 **A2**
College Park, MD 148 **E8**
College Pt, NY 143 **E4**
Colleyville, TX 164 **D4**
Collingdale, PA 144 **C2**
Collingswood, NJ 145 **F2**
Collington, NC 187 **G6**
Collinsville, IL 162 **D2**
Colma, CA 175 **A4**
Cologne, 16 **D6**, 20 **F7**, 23 **C3**
Cologno Monzese, 40 **C2**
Colombia, 84 **C4**, 94 **D1**
Colombo, 59 **C3**
Colón, 97 **H1**
Colón Theatre, 89 **D3**
Colonial NHP, VA 179 **G3**
Colonial Village, PA 144 **B5**
Colonie, NY 117 **G3**
Colony, The, TX 165 **F6**
Colorado, 110 **E5**, 127 **A3**, 130 **D5**, 178 **C4**
Colorado NM, CO 130 **D5**, 178 **C4**
Colorado Plateau, 110 **C5**
Colorado River, 110 **D5**, 111 **B4**, 128 **D4**, 130 **D5**, 131 **A3**, 133 **F2**, 178 **B3**, 183 **D2**
Colorado River IR, 131 **A2** 133 **F3**
Colorado Springs, CO 110 **E5**, 127 **A2**, 130 **E3**
Colosseum, 41 **E2**
Colquitt, GA 122 **D6**
Colstrip, MT 126 **A6**
Colter Bay, WY 181 **G4**
Colter Bay Visitor Ctr, WY 181 **G5**
Colter Pass, MT 180 **D6**

Colter Pk, WY 180 **C2**, 135 **G3**
Colton, CA 171 **H4**
Columbia, KY 118 **A1**
Columbia, MD 119 **H4**, 147 **A1**
Columbia, MS 120 **A2**, 129 **H4**
Columbia, MO 112 **B5**, 125 **B3**
Columbia, NC 187 **E5**
Columbia, SC 113 **D4**, 121 **F4**
Columbia, TN 125 **E1**, 120 **C5**
Columbia Hts, MN 161 **C4**
Columbia Park, MN 161 **C3**
Columbia Plateau, 110 **B6**
Columbia R, 101 **C2**, 110 **B7**, 134 **B4**, 178 **B5**
Columbia U, NY 142 **D5**
Columbine Valley, CO 167 **F2**
Columbus, GA 113 **D3**, 120 **D3**
Columbus, IN 125 **E3**
Columbus, MS 113 **B3**, 120 **B4**
Columbus, MT 135 **H4**
Columbus, NE 110 **F5**, 127 **E4**
Columbus, OH 112 **D5**, 118 **C4**, 125 **F3**, 179 **C4**
Columbus Mon, 38 **E6**
Colusa, CA 132 **B6**
Colville, WA 134 **D6**
Colville IR, WA 134 **D6**
Colville Lake, 136 **F8**
Colville NF, WA 134 **D6**
Colvin Run, VA 148 **A8**
Colwyn, PA 144 **C2**
Colyton, 78 **A8**
Coma, 24 **A5**
Comanche NG, CO 127 **B2**, 131 **F4**
Comas, 87 **F6**
Comiskey Park, IL 159 **D3**

Comitán, 97 **E2**
Commander Isl, 54 **B8**
Commerce City, CO 167 **H4**
Communism Park, 53 **E1** 58 **C7**
Como RP, MN 161 **D3**
Comodoro Rivadavia, 86 **B3**
Comoros, 47 **H5**
Compiègne, 23 **A3**
Compton, CA 170 **C3**
Conakry, 44 **A1**
Concepción, 86 **A4**, 86 **C6**
Concepción del Oro, 96 **C4**
Conchalí, 87 **F3**
Conchos R, 96 **C5**
Concord, Austral 78 **D7**
Concord, CA 132 **B5**, 174 **E7**
Concord, MA 138 **A5**
Concord, NH 112 **E6**, 115 **B3**
Concord, NC 121 **F5**
Concord West, 78 **D7**
Concordia, Arg 86 **B5**
Concordia, KS 127 **E3**
Concorezzo, 40 **D3**
Condon, OR 134 **C4**
Conecuh NF, AL 120 **C2**, 122 **B6**
Coney Isl, NY 142 **D1**
Coney Isl, OH 151 **E1**
Conflans-Sainte-Honorine, 28 **C8**
Confucius Temple, 62 **C5**
Congaree R, SC 121 **F5**
Congaree Swamp NM, SC 121 **F4**
Congo, 46 **D6**
Congo Basin, 47 **E6**
Congo R, 47 **E6**
Congonhas Arpt, 92 **B4**
Conical Pk, MT 135 **G4**
Conley, GA 152 **C2**
Connaught Place, 64 **E7**
Connecticut, 103 **D1**, 112 **E6**, 115 **B1**, 179 **H5**

Connecticut R, NH 115 B3

Connell, WA 134 D5

Conrad, MT 135 F6

Conroe, TX 129 F3

Conshohocken, PA 144 C5

Constance, KY 151 C1

Constanta, 17 H4, 25 H6

Constantine, 21 E2, 44 D5

Constitución, 89 D2

Constitución Train Sta, 89 D1

Constitution, GA 152 C2

Constitution Gdns, DC 149 B2

Content Keys, FL 188 B2

Contreras, 98 A1

Convention Ctr, MN 161 C3

Converse, TX 163 H3

Conway, AR 125 B1, 129 G6

Conway, NH 115 C4

Coober Pedy, 76 C4

Cook Inlet, AK 136 C6

Cook Islands, 80 D3

Cook Str, 77 H1

Cooke City, MT 180 D6

Cookeville, TN 120 D6, 125 E1

Cooksville, 104 B5

Coolaroo, 79 B4

Cooper City, FL 155 F4

Cooperstown, NY 117 F3

Coors Brewing Company, CO 167 E3

Coors Field, TX 167 G3

Coos Bay, OR 110 A7, 132 A8, 134 A3

Coot Bay, FL 188 D4

Copacabana, 91 D1

Copacabana Beach, 91 D1

Copenhagen, 15 E1, 22 D6 36 C6, 52 A6

Copenhagen Arpt, 36 C5

Copiapó, 86 A6

Copley Plaza, MA 140 A2

Coppell, TX 165 E5

Copper Butte, WA 134 D6

Coppermine, 100 D6

Coquille, OR 132 A8, 134 A2

Coral Gables, FL 155 F1, 123 G2

Coral Hills, MD 148 E6

Coral Sea, 76 C1, 77 F5, 80 B3

Coral Springs, FL 123 F2, 155 F6

Coraopolis, PA 146 A7

Corbeil-Essonnes, 28 D5

Corbin, KY 120 D6

Corcoran, CA 133 C4

Corcoran Gallery of Art, DC 149 B3

Cordele, GA 121 E3

Cordelia, CA 174 D8

Córdoba Arg 86 B5

Córdoba, Spain 16 B2, 21 B2

Cordova, AK 136 D6

Corfu, 17 G3, 25 E4

Corinth, Gr 17 G2, 25 F3

Corinth, MS 120 B5

Corinth, NY 117 G4

Cork, 14 B1, 19 A3, 20 A8

Corlu, 25 H5

Cormano, 40 B2

Cornaredo, 40 A2

Cornellá de Llobregat, 38 D6

Corner Brook, 103 E3

Corning, CA 132 B6

Corning, NY 116 D2

Cornish, ME 115 C4

Cornwall, 103 D2, 117 F6

Coro, 84 C6

Corona, CA 171 F3

Corona, NY 143 E4

Coronado, CA 169 F3

Coronel Oviedo, 86 C6

Corpus Christi, TX 96 D5, 111 F2, 129 E2, 178 D1

Corrois, 38 B6

Corry, PA 116 A1

Corsica, 16 D3, 24 A4, 44 D6

Corsico, 40 B1

Corte Madera, CA 174 A6

Cortez, CO 131 C4

Cortez, FL 154 B1

Cortland, NY 117 E2

Corumbá, 85 E1

Corvallis, OR 110 A7, 134 B3

Corviale, 40 B5

Corwin Springs, MT 180 A6

Cosenza, 17 F3, 24 D2

Coshocton, OH 118 C4

Coslada, 39 F3

Costa Brava, 21 E4

Costa Da Caparica, 38 A6

Costa Mesa, CA 170 D2

Costa Rica, 81 H5, 84 A5 94 A1, 97 G1

Cota, 90 C3

Côte D'Ivoire, 44 B1

Côte-Saint-Luc, 106 B2

Coto De Caza, CA 171 F1

Cotopaxi, 84 B4

Cotsicana, TX 129 E4

Cottbus, 23 E4

Cottonwood, AZ 131 B3

Cottonwood, CA 132 B7

Cottonwood Cove, NV 131 A3, 133 F4

Cotuit, MA 185 C4

Coubert, 28 E6

Coudersport, PA 116 C1, 119 F6

Council, ID 135 E3

Council Bluffs, IA 112 A5, 125 A4, 127 F4

Countryside, KS 162 B6

Coupeville, WA 134 B6

Cova da Piedade, 38 B6

Covedale, OH 151 C2

Covelo, CA 132 A6

Covent Garden, 27 C2

Coventry, 16 C6, 19 E3, 20 C8

Covina, CA 171 E5

Covington, GA 121 E4

Covington, KY 118 A3, 125 F3, 151 D2

Covington, TN 120 B5, 129 H6

Covington, VA 118 D2

Cowan Hts, CA 171 E2

Cowansville, 114 A5

Coxsackie, NY 117 G2

Coyoacán, 98 B2

Coyote Creek, AZ 183 B2

Coyula, 99 H5

Cozumel Isl, 94 A4, 97 F3

Crabtree FP, IL 158 A6

Crafton, PA 146 B6

Craig, CO 110 D5, 130 D5

Crailsheim, 23 D2

Craiova, 17 G4, 25 F6

Cranberry Isles, ME 186 C2

Cranberry Lake, NY 117 F5

Cranbrook, 101 D2

Crane, OR 132 D8

Crater Lake NP, OR 132 B8, 134 B2, 178 A5

Craters of the Moon NM, ID 130 B7, 178 B5

Crawley, 26 C5

Cregy les Meaux, 28 F7

Cremona, 24 B5

Crescent City, CA 132 A7, 134 A1

Crescent City, FL 123 F5

Crescent Lake NWR, NE 127 C4

Crescenzago, 40 C2

Crest Hill, IL 159 B1

Crest Park, CA 171 H6

Creston, IA 125 A4

Crestview, FL 120 C2, 122 B6

Crestview, HI 177 E3

Crestview, NY 151 E1

Crestwood, MO 162 A1

Crete, 17 H2, 25 G1, 45 E5, 48 B5

Creteil, 28 D6

Creve Coeur, MO 162 A2
Creve Coeur CP, MO 162 A3
Crewe, 19 D3
Crimea, 53 A4
Croatan NF, NC 121 H5
Croatan Sd, NC 187 G5
Croatia, 17 F4, 23 F1,
  24 D5, 45 E6
Crockett, CA 174 C7
Crooked Isl, 94 D5
Crookston, MN 126 E7
Cross City, FL 122 D5
Cross Key, FL 188 F4
Crossville, TN 120 D6
Crotone, 24 D2
Crouch, ID 135 E3
Crow Ctr, MO 162 C5
Crow Creek IR, SD 126 D5
Crow IR, MT 130 D8,
  135 H4
Crowley, TX 164 B1
Crown Pt, NY 117 H5
Crows Nest, IN 157 E3
Croydon, 26 D6
Croydon, Austral 79 F3
Croydon, PA 145 H5
Crum Creek, PA 144 B3
Cruzeiro do Sul, 84 C3
Crystal, MN 161 B4
Crystal, MS 120 A3
Crystal Beach, FL 154 A6
Crystal City, VA 148 A3
Crystal Cove SP, CA 171 E12
Crystal R, FL 123 E4
Csepel, 42 B6
Csillaghegy, 42 B8
Csomád, 42 C8
Csömör, 42 B7
Cuajimalpa, 98 A3
Cuauhtémoc, 98 B3,
  128 A2
Cuautepec de Madero,
  98 C5
Cuautitlán, 98 B6
Cuautitlán Izcalli, 98 A6
Cuba, 94 C5, 97 H4
Cubatão, 92 D2

Cucamonga Wilderness,
  CA 171 F6
Cucuta, 84 C5
Cudahy, WI 157 C1
Cuddy, PA 146 A5
Cudjoe Key, FL 188 B2
Cuenca, Ecuador 84 B3
Cuenca, Spain 16 B3
Cuence, 21 C3
Cuernavaca, 96 D3
Cuero, TX 129 E2
Cuescomatitlán, 99 F2
Cuiabá, 85 E2
Culhuacán, 98 C2
Culiacán, 111 D1
Culliacán, 96 B4
Cullman, AL 120 C4
Culpeper, VA 119 F3
Culver City, CA 170 B4,
  172 A5
Cumaná, 84 D5
Cumberland, MD 112 D5,
  119 E4
Cumberland Gap NHP,
  118 B1, 179 G3
Cumberland Island, GA
  123 F6
Cumberland Island NS, GA
  121 F2, 179 G2
Cumberland R, 125 E2
Cummingsville, MA 138 C5
Cuneo, 24 A5
Cunningham Cabin HS, WY
  181 G3
Cupertino, CA 175 D1
Curacao, 84 D6, 95 F1
Curitiba, 86 C6
Curlew, FL 154 B6
Cusago, 40 A1
Cusano Milanino, 40 B3
Cushing, OK 127 F1
Custer NF, MT 126 A6,
  180 D6
Custer SP, SD 126 B5
Cut Bank, MT 135 F6
Cut Off, LA 120 A1
Cutchogue, NY 116 C6

Cuthbert Lake, FL 188 E4
Cutler, ME 114 F5
Cuttack, 58 D5
Cuxhaven, 22 C5
Cuyahoga Hts, OH 150 D6
Cuyahoga Valley NRA, OH
  150 E5
Cuyamaca College, CA
  169 H3
Cuzco, 84 C2
Cyclades, 17 H2, 25 G2
Cynthiana, KY 118 B3,
  125 F2
Cypress, CA 170 D3
Cyprus, 45 F5, 48 D5
Cyrville, 105 B3
Czech Republic 17 F6,
  23 E3

D

Da Hinggan Ling, 55 D2,
  66 B2
Da Lat, 61 B4
Da Nang, 61 B4
Dabazi, 74 E8
Dachang, 74 C8
Dachnoye, 57 F2
Dadar, 65 B2
Dahl, 34 F6
Dahlhausen, 34 D7
Dahlonega, GA 120 D5
Dahlwitz, 32 F7
Daito, 70 D5
Dajing, 73 B1
Dakar, 44 A2
Dakar, 36 F5
Dalaro, 36 F5
Dalhart, TX 127 C1, 128 C6,
  131 F3
Dalhousie, 103 E3
Dalian, 55 E1, 60 C8,
  66 C5
Dallas, OR 134 B4
Dallas, TX 81 H6, 96 D6,
  111 F3, 129 F4, 165 F3,
  179 E2
Dallas, U of, TX 165 E4

Dallas County Historical
  Plaza, TX 165 G3
Dallas-Fort Worth Intl
  Arpt, TX 164 D5
Dallas Mus of Art, TX
  165 G3
Dallas Zoo, TX 165 F3
Dalles, The, OR 134 C4
Dallgow, 32 B7
Dalton, GA 120 D5
Dalton, MA 115 A3, 117 H2
Dalworthington Gdns, TX
  164 D72
Daly City, CA 175 A4
Damascus, OR 177 H4
Damascus, Syr 45 G5
Dammartin-en-Goele,
  28 E8
Dampier, 76 A5
Danbury, CT 115 A1
Dandenong North, 79 E1
Dandong, 55 E2, 60 C8,
  66 C6
Dania, FL 155 G4
Daniel Boone NF, KY
  118 B2, 121 E6, 125 F2
Dannemora, NY 117 G6
Dansville, NY 116 C2
Danube R 17 F5, 23 E2,
  25 F6, 45 E6
Danvers, MA 138 E6
Danville, CA 174 E5
Danville, IL 125 D3
Danville, KY 118 A2
Danville, PA 119 G5
Danville, VA 113 D4,
  119 E1, 121 G6
Daphni, 43 A3
Daphni Monastery, 43 A3
Dar es Salaam, 47 H5
Darby, MT 135 F4
Darby, PA 144 D2
Darby Creek, 144 B4
Dardanelles, 17 H3, 25 H4
Darhan, 55 C2
Darling Range, 76 A3

Darling R, 76 **D3**

Dartford, 26 **E8**

Dartmouth, 103 **E2**

Darwin, 76 **C6**

Dash Point SP, WA 176 **B2**

Dasht-e Kavir, 49 **G6**

Dasht-e Lut, 49 **G5**

Datong, 55 **D1**, 60 **B8**, 66 **A5**

Datun, 73 **E4**

Daugavpils, 15 **G2**

Dauphin, 101 **F2**

Davao, 61 **F4**

Davenport, IA 112 **B5**

Davenport, WA 134 **D5**

David, 97 **G1**

Davie, FL 155 **F4**

Davis Str, 102 **C6**

Davle, 35 **E1**

Dawkah, 49 **G2**

Dawson, Can 82 **B5**, 100 **B6**

Dawson, GA 120 **D3**

Dawson City, 136 **E7**

Dawson Creek, 101 **C3**

Dawson Range, 136 **E6**

Dayton, KY 151 **D2**

Dayton, OH 112 **C5**, 118 **A4**, 125 **F3**

Dayton, WA 134 **D4**

Daytona Beach, FL 113 **E3**, 121 **F1**, 123 **F5**, 179 **G2**

Dayville, OR 134 **C3**

De Funiak Springs, FL 120 **C2**, 122 **C6**

De Land, FL 123 **F4**

De Paul U, IL 159 **D4**

De Ridder, LA 129 **G3**

De Soto, TX 165 **F1**

De Soto NF, MS 120 **B2**, 122 **A6**, 129 **H4**

Deadwood, SD 130 **F7**

Dealey Plaza, TX 165 **F3**

Dearborn, MI 156 **B6**

Dearborn Hts, MI 156 **B6**

Dease Lake, 136 **F6**

Death Canyon, WY 181 **E2**

Death Valley, CA 110 **B5**

Death Valley NP, CA 133 **E4**, 178 **B3**

Debrecen, 17 **G5**

Decatur, AL 120 **C5**

Decatur, GA 120 **D4**, 152 **C4**

Decatur, IL 112 **B5**, 125 **D3**

Decatur, IN 118 **A5**

Deccan Plateau, 59 **C4**

Decin, 23 **E3**

Decorah, IA 124 **C5**

Dedham, MA 139 **C2**

Dee Why, 78 **F8**

Deep River, 103 **C2**

Deer Key, FL 188 **F4**

Deer Lodge, MT 135 **F4**

Deer Park, Austral 79 **A3**

Deer Park, OH 151 **E3**

Deerfield, IL 158 **C6**

Deerfield Beach, FL 155 **G6**

Defiance, OH 118 **A5**

Deggendorf, 23 **E2**

Del Este NP & Planetario Humboldt, 90 **C5**

Del Mar, CA 169 **E6**

Del Rio, TX 111 **F2**, 128 **D2**

Del Valle, Mex 98 **B2**

Del Valle RP, CA 175 **F4**

Del Viso, 88 **A8**

Delanco, NJ 145 **H4**

Delano, CA 133 **D4**

Delaware, 112 **E5**, 119 **G3**, 179 **H4**

Delaware, OH 118 **B4**

Delaware Bay, 119 **G3**

Delaware R, 117 **F1**, 119 **G6**

Delaware SF, PA 119 **G5**

Delaware Water Gap NRA, PA 179 **G4**

Delft, 30 **A3**

Delhi, India 58 **C6**, 64 **E6**

Delhi, NY 117 **F2**, 119 **G6**

Delhi Cantonment, 64 **D7**

Delhi Hills, OH 151 **C2**

Delhi U, 64 **E8**

Delicias, 128 **B2**, 96 **C5**

Dellwood, MO 162 **B3**

Delray Beach, FL 123 **G2**

Delson, 106 **C1**

Delta, UT 130 **B5**

Delta NF, MS 120 **A3**

Delta NWR, 120 **B1**, 122 **A5**, 129 **H3**

Deltona, FL 123 **F4**

Deming, NM 128 **A4**, 131 **D2**

Demopolis, AL 120 **C3**

Denakil, 45 **G2**

Denali NP & Pres, AK 136 **C7**, 178 **A2**

Denderleeuw, 31 **E2**

Dendermonde, 31 **E4**

Denison, IA 125 **A4**, 127 **F4**

Denizli, 25 **H3**

Denmark, 15 **E1**, 22 **C6**

Denmark Str, 14 **A6**, 82 **E6**, 102 **E8**

Dennis, MA 184 **D5**

Dennis Port, MA 184 **E5**

Denpasar, 61 **D1**

Dent, OH 151 **B3**

Denton, MD 119 **G3**

Denton, TX 129 **E4**

Denver, CO 110 **E5**, 127 **A3**, 130 **E5**, 167 **G3**, 178 **C4**

Denver, U of, CO 167 **G2**

Denver City, TX 131 **F2**

Denver Coliseum, CO 167 **G3**

Denver Intl Arpt, CO 167 **H4**

Denver Zoo, CO 167 **G3**

Department of State, DC 149 **A3**

Depok, 64 **B6**

Dera Mandi, 64 **E5**

Derby, 19 **E3**

Derendorf, 34 **B5**

Des Moines, IA 112 **A5**, 125 **B4**, 179 **E4**

Des Moines, WA 176 **B3**

Des Moines R, IA 124 **A5**

Des Peres, MO 162 **A4**

Des Plaines, IL 158 **C5**

Deschutes NF, OR 134 **C3**

Dese, 45 **G2**

Desert NWR, NV 133 **F4**

Desert Test Ctr, UT 130 **A5**

Desert View, AZ 183 **F2**

Desio, 40 **C3**

Desna, 56 **A2**

Desoto Mem Raceway, FL 154 **D1**

DeSoto N Mem, FL 154 **B1**

Dessau, 23 **D4**

Destin, FL 122 **B6**

Detroit, MI 103 **B1**, 112 **C6**, 118 **B6**, 125 **F4**, 156 **C6**, 179 **F4**

Detroit City Arpt, MI 156 **E7**

Detroit Civic Ctr, MI 156 **D6**

Detroit Lakes, MN 124 **A7**, 126 **F7**

Detroit Metro Wayne C Arpt, MI 156 **B5**

Detroit Zoo, MI 156 **C8**

Deurne, 31 **G6**

Deurne Arpt, 31 **G5**

Deutch-Wagram, 42 **F8**

Deux Montagnes, 106 **A3**

Deva Temple, AZ 183 **E2**

Devils Lake, ND 126 **D8**

Devils Tower NM, WY 130 **E8**, 178 **C5**

Devon, PA 144 **B4**

Devon Isl, 100 **F7**, 102 **A7**

Devonport, 77 **E3**

Devoo Park, KY 151 **D1**

Devore, CA 171 **G6**

Devoto, 88 **D7**

Dexter, ME 114 **D5**

Dhaka, 58 **E5**

Dhauj, 64 **E5**

Dhrapetsona, 43 A2

Dhulagarh, 65 D2

Di Domitilla Catacombe, 40 C5

Diablo, CA 174 E5

Diadema, 92 B3

Diamond Bar, CA 171 E4

Diamond Creek, 79 D4

Diamond Head SM, HI 177 H1

Diamond Lake, OR 132 B8

Diamond Shoals, NC 187 H1

Diaspora Mus, 50 B6

Dibrugarh, 58 F6

Dickey, ME 114 D8

Dickinson, ND 110 E7, 126 C7

Diego Rivera Mus, 98 B2

Dielsdorf, 37 E2

Diemen, 30 D5

Diepkloof, 51 F2

Dieppe, 19 F1

Diepsloot Nature Reserve, 51 F4

Dietikon, 37 D2

Dietzenbach, 35 C1

Digby, 103 E2

Digul R, 76 B1

Dijon, 16 D5, 20 E6, 23 A1

Dikson, 82 D8

Dili, 61 F1

Dillon, MT 130 B8, 135 F4

Dillon, SC 121 G5

Dimitrovgrad, 25 G5

Dinamo Stad, 56 B4

Dinaric Alps, 24 D5

Dinosaur, CO 130 D5

Dinosaur NM, CO 130 D6, 178 C4

Dinslaken, 34 B8

Diósd, 42 A6

Dire Dawa, 45 H1

Discovery Park, WA 176 A6

Dismal Swamp NWR, VA 121 H6

Disney-MGM Studios Theme Park, FL 153 F2

Disneyland, CA 170 D3

District Hts, MD 148 F6

DC Convention Ctr, DC 149 D4

Ditch Creek, WY 181 G3

Diu, 58 B5

Dixie NF, UT 131 B4

Dixmont, ME 114 D5

Diyarbakir, 49 E6

Djibouti, 45 H2, 49 E1

Djursholm, 36 E7

Dnieper R, 52 A5

Dnipropetrovsk, 53 A4

Dobbins AFB, GA 152 A6

Dobbins Lookout, AZ 168 B2

Döbling, 42 D8

Dobrich, 25 H6

Dobson, NC 118 D1

Dobsonville, 51 E2

Dockton, WA 176 B2

Doctor Phillips, FL 153 F3

Dodecanese, 25 G2

Dodge City, KS 111 F4, 127 D2

Dodge Pt, ME 186 A3

Dodger Stad, CA 170 C5, 172 E7

Dodoma, 47 G5

Dogachia, 65 F4

Doha, 49 G4

Doigoye Ledovo, 56 D5

Dole, 23 B1

Dolgoprudnyy, 56 B6

Dollards-des-Ormeaux, 106 A2

Dolmabahce Palace, 43 E2

Dolni Brezary, 35 E2

Dolphin Research Ctr, FL 188 D2

Dom Pedro II Park, 93 H4

Dome, The, AZ 183 B3

Dominica, 85 E6, 95 H3

Dominican Republic, 95 E4

Dominion Obs, 105 A2

Domjur, 65 D2

Domodedovo, 56 C1

Domodedovo Arpt, 56 D1

Domont, 28 D8

Don Bosco, 88 F6

Don Mills, 104 E7

Don R, 53 B4

Don Torcuato, 88 C8

Donaldsonville, LA 120 A2

Donalsonville, GA 122 D6

Donaustadt, 42 F8

Doncaster, Austral 79 D3

Doncaster, UK 19 E4

Doncaster & Templestowe, 79 D3

Donegal, 19 B4

Donetsk, 45 G6, 53 A4

Dongcaohejing, 74 D5

Dongcheng District, 73 E3

Dongrancun, 73 B3

Dongtangqiaozhen, 74 F6

Dongting Hu, 67 A3

Dongzhimen, 73 E3

Donvale, 79 E3

Doonside, 78 A8

Doordrecht, 30 C1

Doral, The, FL 155 F2

Doraville, GA 152 D6

Dorchester, MA 139 D2

Dorchester, UK 19 D2

Dordogne R, 20 D5

Dorer Mem SF, Richard J, MN 124 B5

Dorking, 26 C5

Dormont, PA 146 B5

Dornach, 42 D7

Dornbirn, 23 D1

Dorris, CA 132 B7

Dorsey, MD 147 B1

Dorseyville, PA 146 D8

Dorstfeld, 34 F7

Dortmund, 23 C4, 34 F7

Dorval, 106 B2

Dorval Intl Arpt, 106 B2

Dothan, AL 113 C3, 120 D2, 122 C6

Douala, 44 D1

Double Bay, 78 F7

Double Oak, TX 164 D6

Douglas, AZ 131 C1

Douglas, GA 121 E3

Douglas, UK 19 C4

Douglas, WY 126 A5, 130 E7

Douglas FP, IL 158 A5

Douglass NHS, Frederick DC 148 E6

Dougting Hu Lake, 60 B6

Dourdan, 28 B5

Dover, DE 112 E5, 119 G3

Dover, MA 139 B2

Dover, NH 115 C3

Dover, NJ 116 A5

Dover, UK 16 C6, 19 F2, 20 D7

Dover-Foxcroft, ME 114 D6

Downers Grove, IL 159 B3

Downey, CA 170 C4

Downsview, 104 D7

Downsview Arpt, 104 D7

Doylestown, PA 119 H5

Dracut, MA 138 A7

Dragor, 36 C5

Drakensberg, 46 F2

Drama, 25 G5

Drammen, 15 E2, 22 C8

Dreieichenhain, 35 B1

Dreileich, 35 B1

Dresden, 17 E6, 23 E3

Dretzka Park, WI 157 A4

Drexel Hill, PA 144 C2

Driggs, ID 135 G3

Drobeta-Turnu Severin, 25 F6

Drogheda, 19 C4

Drottningholm, 36 D6

Drottningholm Palace, 36 E6

Druid Hill Park, MD 147 C3

Druid Hills, GA 152 C4

Drum Barracks Civil War Mus, CA 170 C3

Drummond, MT 135 F5
Drummondville, 114 B6
Drumoyne, 78 E7
Dry Creek Pioneer RP, CA 175 F4
Dry Tortugas NP, FL 179 G1
Dryden, 103 A2, 124 B8
Dubayy, 49 G4
Dubbo, 77 E3
Dubendorf, 37 F2
Dublin, CA 174 E5
Dublin, GA 121 E3
Dublin, Ire 14 B1, 19 C4, 20 B8
Dubois, ID 130 B7, 135 F3
Dubois, WY 135 H3
Dubravka, 57 H2
Dubrovnik, 17 F4, 24 D4
Dubuque, IA 112 B6, 125 C4
Duck, NC 187 G6
Duck Cove, ME 186 A2
Duck Key, FL 188 D2, 135 E2
Duck Valley IR, ID 132 E8, 135 E2
Dudingen, 37 A1
Duero, 21 C3
Duero R, 16 B3
Duffel, 31 H4
Dugway Proving Grounds, UT 130 B5
Duisburg, 23 B4, 34 B7
Dukou, 60 A5
Duluth, MN 103 A1, 112 A7, 124 C7, 179 E5
Dum-Dum, 65 F2
Dum-Dum Intl Arpt, 65 F2
Dumas, AR 120 A4
Dumas, TX 128 D6, 131 F3
Dumfries, 18 D5
Dun Laoghaire, 19 C4
Dunafoldvar, 24 D6
Dunaharaszti, 42 B6
Dunakeszi, 42 B8
Dunaujvaros, 24 D6

Duncan, OK 129 E5
Duncanville, TX 165 E2
Dund-Us, 55 A2
Dundalk, MD 147 E2
Dundalk, UK 19 C4
Dundee, 14 C2, D6
Dunderberg Pk, CA 182 D5
Dunedin, Austral 77 G1
Dunedin, FL 154 A5
Dunfermline, 18 D5
Dunkerque, 23 A3
Dunkirk, NY 116 A2
Dunlap, OH 151 C4
Dunn Loring, VA 148 B6
Dunnellon, FL 123 E5
Dunnville, 116 A3
Dunqian, 74 A8
Dunsmuir, CA 132 B7
Dunwoody, GA 152 C6
Duolun, 66 A6
Dupont, CO 167 H4
Duque de Caxias, 91 C3
Duquesne, PA 146 E5
Durango, CO 111 D4, 131 D4
Durango, Mex 96 C4
Durant, OK 113 A3
Durant Isl, NC 187 F6
Durants Neck, NC 187 E6
Durban, 47 F2
Durham, NC 113 E4, 121 G6
Durham, OR 177 F4
Durham, UK 19 E4
Durrës, 17 G3, 25 E5
Dushanbe, 53 D1, 58 B7
Dusit, 63 F6
Düsseldorf, 20 F7, 23 B3, 34 B5
Düsseldorf Arpt, 34 B6
Duvernay, 106 B4
Duxbury, MA 184 A8
Duxbury Bay, MA 184 A8
Dyer, IN 159 E1
Dyersburg, TN 125 D1, 129 H6
Dzerzhinskiy, 56 D3
Dzhugdzhur Range, 54 E5

E

Eagan, MN 161 D1
Eagle Creek, OR 177 H4
Eagle Lake, CA 132 C7
Eagle Lake, ME 114 E8, 186 D5
Eagle Pass, TX 128 D2
Eagle Pk, CA 182 C6
Eagle Pk, WY 180 D2
Eagle Village, IN 157 D4
Eagleville, PA 144 B6
Eakin Community Park, VA 148 A6
East Aurora, NY 116 B3
East Boston, MA 139 D4
East Brewster, MA 184 E6
East Cape, FL 188 C3
East Carver, MA 184 A7
East Chicago, IN 159 F2
East China Sea, 60 D7, 67 D3
East Cleveland, OH 150 E8
East Dennis, MA 184 E5
East Entrance, WY 180 D3
East Falmouth, MA 185 B4
East Grand Forks, MN 126 E7
East Grinstead, 26 D5
East Hampton, NY 116 D6
East Harwich, MA 184 F5
East Hills, NY 143 H5
East Kew, 79 C3
East Kildonan, 107 G6
East Lake, NC 187 F5
East Lansdowne, PA 144 D2
East London, 47 F2
East Los Angeles, CA 170 C4
East Marion, MA 184 A5
East McKeesport, PA 146 E5
East Meadow, NY 143 H3
East Meredith, NY 117 F2

East New York, NY 143 E3
East Orange, NJ 142 B4
East Orleans, MA 184 F6
East Palo Alto, CA 175 D3
East Patchogue, NY 116 C5
East Point, GA 152 A2
East Potomac Park, DC 149 C1
East Rockaway, NY 143 G2
East Rutherford, NJ 142 C5
East St Louis, IL 125 C2, 162 C1
East San Diego, CA 169 F3
East Sandwich, MA 184 C5
East Siberian Sea, 54 D7, 82 B7
East Tampa, FL 154 D4
East Wareham, MA 184 A5
East York, 104 E6
Eastern Bay, ME 186 C6
Eastern Desert, 48 C4
Eastern Ghats, 59 C4
Eastern Way, ME 186 C3
Eastgate, VA 176 D5
Eastham, MA 115 D2, 184 F6
Eastman, GA 121 E3
Easton, MD 119 G3
Easton, PA 119 G5
Eastpointe, MI 156 E8
Eastport, ME 114 F5
Eastport, NY 116 C5
Eastville, VA 119 G2
Eastwick, PA 144 D1
Eastwood, 78 D8
Eau Claire, WI 112 B6, 124 C5
Ebensburg, PA 119 E5
Ebergassing, 42 F5
Eberswalde-Finow, 23 E4
Ebina, 68 C3
Ebro R, 16 C3, 21 C4
Ebsjerg, 14 D1
Ecatepec, 98 D5
Echo Lake, ME 186 B4
Eckenheim, 35 B4

Eckerd College, FL 154 B3

Ecole Militaire, 29 B1

Ecorse, MI 156 C5

Ecuador, 84 B4

Eddystone, PA 144 C1

Edegem, 31 G5

Eden, ME 186 B6

Eden, NY 116 B2

Eden Park, OH 151 D2

Eden Prairie, MN 161 A1

Edenvale, 51 G3

Edgartown, MA 115 C1, 185 B2

Edgartown Harbor, MA 185 B3

Edgemere, MD 147 F2

Edgemont, PA 144 A3

Edgemont Key NWR, FL 154 A2

Edgewater, CO 167 F3

Edgewater, FL 121 F1

Edgewater Park, NJ 145 H4

Edgewater Park, OH 150 C7

Edgewood, KY 151 D1

Edina, MN 161 B2

Edinburg, TX 129 E1

Edinburgh, 14 C2, 18 D5

Edirne, 25 G5

Edison, NJ 116 A5

Edison NHS, NJ 142 A5

Edisto Isl, SC 121 F3

Edmond, OK 127 E1, 129 E6

Edmonston, MD 148 E7

Edmonton, 101 D3

Edmundston, 103 D2, 114 E8

Edna, TX 129 F2

Edremit, 25 H4

Edward Hatch Mem Shell, MA 140 A3

Edwards Plateau, 111 F3

Edwardsville, KS 162 A5

Eel R, CA 132 A6

Effigy Mounds NM, IA 179 E4

Effinwild, PA 146 C8

Effretikon, 37 F2

Egelsbach, 35 B1

Egersund, 22 B7

Egham, 26 A7

Eglin AFB, FL 120 C2

Eglisau, 37 E3

Egypt, 45 F4, 48 C4

Egyptian Mus, 50 C2

Eichwalde, 32 E5

Eiffel Tower, 29 B2

Eindhoven, 20 E8, 23 B4

Eisenach, 23 D3

Eisenhower Mem Park, NY 143 H4

Eisenhüttenstadt, 23 E4

Ekáli, 43 C4

Ekeren, 31 G6

Ekero, 36 D6

El Aaiún, 44 B4

El Asnam, 21 E1, 44 C5

El Augustino, 87 G5

El Avila NP, 90 C5

El Batán, 39 B2

El Bire, 50 D5

El Bosque, 87 F1

El Cajon, CA 133 E2, 169 H4

El Capitan, CA 182 B3

El Carite, 90 B4

El Castillo, 99 G3

El Centro, CA 133 F2

El Cerrito, CA 171 F3, 174 C6

El Charquito, 90 B1

El Colegio, 90 A1

El Dorado, AR 113 B3, 129 G4

El Dorado, KS 127 F2

El Dorado Intl Arpt, 90 C2

El Fuerte, 128 A1

El Giza, 50 B2

El Granada, CA 175 A3

El Hatillo, 90 D4

El Junquito, 90 A4

El Maadi, 50 C1

El Malpais NM, NM 128 A5, 131 D3

El Matariya, 50 D3

El Molino, 99 E2

El Monte, CA 170 D5

El Noviciado, 87 E3

El Paso, TX 96 C6, 111 D3, 128 B4, 131 E1, 178 C2

El Portal, CA 182 A2

El Portal, FL 155 G2

El Prat de Llobregat, 38 E5

El Pueblo de Los Angeles, CA 172 E6

El Rodeo, 99 H2

El Rosal, 90 B3

El Rosario, 99 G5

El Salto, 99 H3

El Salvador, 81 H5, 84 A6, 97 F2

El Segundo, CA 170 B3

El Sobrante, CA 174 C7

El Sueco, 128 A3

El Tigre, 84 D5

El Vado, 99 H4

El Valle, 90 B4

El Verde, 99 G4

El Zamalik, 50 C2

El Zeitun, 50 D3

Elat, 48 D4

Elba Isl, 17 E3, 24 B4

Elbasan, 25 E4

Elbe R, 17 E6, 23 D4

Elburz Mts, 49 F6

Eldorado, 47 G6

Electric Pk, MT 180 A5

Electric Science Mus, 71 A2

Elefsina, 43 A3

Elephant Butte Lake SP, NM 128 B5

Eleuthera, 94 D6

Elgin, IL 125 D4

Elgin, UK 18 D6

Elizabeth, NJ 116 A5, 119 H5, 142 B2

Elizabethton, TN 118 C1, 121 E6

Elizabethtown, NY 117 G5

Elizabethtown, OH 151 A2

Elk Grove Village, IL 158 B5

Elk Isl, WY 181 G4

Elk SF, PA 119 E6

Elkhovo, 25 H5

Elkins, WV 118 C3

Elkins Park, PA 145 E5

Elko, NV 110 C6, 130 A6, 132 E7, 135 E1

Elkridge, MD 147 B2

Elkton, MD 119 G4

Ellensburg, WA 134 C5

Ellenton, FL 154 C1

Ellenville, NY 117 G1

Ellenwood, GA 152 D1

Ellesmere Isl, 82 D6, 100 F8, 102 A8

Ellicott City, MD 147 B2

Ellinghorst, 34 C8

Ellinikon, 43 B2

Elliniko Intl Arpt, 43 B2

Elliot Lake, 103 B2, 124 F6

Elliott Knob, VA 119 E2

Ellipse, The, DC 149 C3

Ellis Isl, NY 142 C3

Ellis Park Stad, 51 G2

Ellisport, WA 176 B3

Ellisville, MA 184 B6

Ellsworth, ME 114 E5

Ellsworth Land, 83 D4

Ellsworth Mts, 83 D3

Elm Grove, WI 157 A3

Elmali, 43 F3

Elmhurst, IL 159 B4

Elmira, NY 116 D2, 119 F6

Elmont, NY 143 G3

Elmstead, MI 156 F6

Elmwood, PA 144 D2

Elmwood Park, IL 159 C4

Elmwood Park, NJ 142 B6

Elmwood Place, OH 151 D3

Elstal, 32 **A7**
Eltham, 79 **E3**
Elwood, 79 **C2**
Ely, NV 110 **C5**, 130 **A5**, 132 **F6**
Ely, UK 19 **F3**
Elyria, OH 118 **C5**
Elysian Park, CA 172 **E7**
Embarcadero Ctr, CA 173 **E3**
Embrach, 37 **F2**
Embu Guaçu, 92 **A2**
Emden, 22 **B5**
Emerald, 77 **E4**
Emeryville, CA 174 **C6**
Emet, 25 **H3**
Emma Matilda Lake, WY 181 **G4**
Emmett, ID 135 **E3**
Emory U Mus, GA 152 **C4**
Empire State Bldg, NY 141 **E4**
Emporia, KS 112 **A5**, 125 **A2**, 127 **F2**
Emporia, VA 119 **F1**, 121 **G6**
Emporium, PA 119 **F6**
Emsworth, PA 146 **B7**
Encampment, WY 130 **D6**
Encarnación, 86 **C6**
Encinitas, CA 133 **D2**
Ende, 61 **E1**
Enderby Land, 83 **E1**
Endicott, NY 117 **E2**
Endwell, NY 117 **E2**
Enfield, 26 **D8**
Engativá, 90 **C2**
Engelhard, NC 187 **F3**
England, 14 **C1**, 16 **C6**, 19 **E3**, 20 **D8**
Englewood, CO 167 **G2**
Englewood, FL 123 **E3**
Englewood, NJ 142 **D6**
Englewood Cliffs, NJ 142 **D6**
English Chan, 16 **C6**, 19 **E2**, 20 **C7**

English Turn, LA 163 **H4**
Enid, OK 111 **F4**, 127 **E1**, 129 **E6**
Ennepetal, 34 **E6**
Ennerdale, 51 **E1**
Enschede, 20 **F8**, 23 **B4**
Ensenada, 133 **E1**, 96 **A2**
Enskede, 36 **E6**
Ensley, FL 122 **B6**
Enterprise, OR 134 **D4**
Entrevías, 39 **C2**
Enugu, 44 **D1**
Epcot Ctr, FL 153 **F2**
Epernay, 23 **A2**
Ephraim, UT 130 **B5**
Ephrata, WA 134 **C5**
Epinal, 23 **B2**
Eppegem, 31 **G3**
Epping, Austral 78 **D8**
Epping, Austral 79 **C4**
Epping, NH 115 **C3**
Epsom, 26 **C6**
Epworth Hts, OH 151 **F3**
Equatorial Guinea, 46 **C6**
Erasmia, 51 **G6**
Érd, 42 **A6**
Erdőkertes, 42 **C8**
Erembodegem, 31 **E3**
Erenkoy, 43 **E2**
Erfurt, 17 **E6**, 23 **D3**
Erie, CO 167 **F6**
Erie, PA 112 **D6**, 116 **A2**, 118 **D6**
Erie Canal, NY 117 **F3**
Erie NWR, PA 116 **A1**, 118 **D6**
Eritrea, 45 **G2**, 49 **E1**
Erkner, 32 **F6**
Erlangen, KY 151 **C1**
Ermelino Matarazzo, 92 **C5**
Ermington, 78 **D7**
Errol, NH 114 **C5**
Erskine Park, 78 **A7**
Erzurum, 49 **E6**, 53 **A2**
Esbjerg, 22 **C6**
Escanaba, MI 112 **B6**, 124 **E6**

Eschborn, 35 **A3**
Escondido, CA 133 **E2**
Escuintla, 97 **E2**
Esfahan, 49 **F5**
Eshta'ol, 50 **C4**
Eskisehir, 48 **C6**
Esla R, 21 **B4**
Esmeraldas, 84 **B4**
Esperance, 76 **B3**
Esplanade des Invalides, 29 **C2**
Essen, 16 **D6**, 23 **B4**, 34 **C7**
Essendon, 79 **B3**
Essex, MD 147 **E3**
Essex Junction, VT 117 **H5**
Essling, 42 **F7**
Estação Júlio Prestes, 93 **F6**
Esteban Echeverría, 88 **D5**
Estelle, LA 163 **F4**
Estes Park, CO 130 **E5**
Estevan, 101 **E2**, 126 **C8**
Estherville, IA 124 **A5**
Estonia, 15 **G3**, 52 **B6**
Ethiopia, 45 **G1**, 49 **E1**
Ethiopian Highlands, 45 **G2**
Etna, CA 132 **A7**
Etna, Italy 24 **C2**
Etna, PA 146 **C7**
Etobicoke, 104 **C6**
Eton College, 26 **A7**
Etrechy, 28 **C5**
Etropole, 25 **F5**
Euclid, OH 150 **E8**
Euclid Creek Res, OH 150 **E8**
Eufaula, AL 120 **D3**
Eugene, CA 174 **E5**
Eugene, OR 110 **A7**, 134 **B3**, 178 **A5**
Eugenia Pt, 96 **A5**
Euless, TX 164 **D4**
Euphrates R, 45 **G5**, 49 **E5**
E.U.R., 40 **C5**
Eureka, CA 110 **A6**, 132 **A7**, 134 **A1**

Eureka, MT 135 **E6**
Eureka, NV 132 **E6**
Euro Disneyland, 28 **F7**
Europa Ctr, 33 **B2**
Europe, 14 – 17, 22 – 25
European Economic Community Hdqrs, 31 **G2**
Euston Sta, 27 **B4**
Evansburg SP, PA 144 **A6**
Evanston, IL 158 **D5**
Evanston, WY 130 **C6**, 135 **G1**
Evansville, IN 112 **C5**, 125 **E2**
Evendale, OH 151 **E3**
Evere, 31 **G2**
Everett, MA 139 **D4**
Everett, WA 110 **B8**, 134 **B6**
Everglades NP, FL 123 **F2**, 179 **G1**, 188 **E4**
Everglades NP Visitor Ctr, FL 188 **D4**
Evergreen Park, IL 159 **D3**
Evergreen Park, MD 147 **F2**
Everman, TX 164 **C2**
Evesboro, NJ 145 **H2**
Eving, 34 **F8**
Évora, 21 **A2**
Evry, 28 **D5**
Ewa, HI 177 **E2**
Ewa Beach, HI 177 **E2**
Ewell, 26 **C6**
Exchange Square, 75 **C2**
Exeter, NH 115 **C3**
Exeter, UK 19 **D2**, 20 **C7**
Exhibition Park, Can 104 **D6**
Exhibition Park, Can 107 **H2**
Exhibition of Economic Achievements, 56 **C5**
Expo Mem Park, 70 **D6**
Exposition Park, CA 172 **D5**
Eyup, 43 **D3**
Ezeiza Arpt, 88 **C5**
Ezine, 25 **G4**
Ezpeleta, 88 **F6**

F

Fabens, TX 131 E1
Fabreville, 106 A3
Facatativá, 90 A3
Faenza, 24 B5
Fahrland, 32 A6
Fair Park, TX 165 G3
Fairbanks, AK 82 B5,
  100 B6, 136 D7, 178 A2
Fairchild Tropical Gdns,
  FL 155 F1
Fairfax, CA 174 A7
Fairfax, OH 151 E2
Fairfax, VA 119 F3, 148 A6
Fairfield, Austral 78 B7
Fairfield, CA 132 B5
Fairfield, ID 135 E2
Fairfield, NC 187 E3
Fairfield, OH 151 D4
Fairground Park, MO
  162 C2
Fairmont, MN 124 B5,
  126 F5
Fairmont, WV 118 D4
Fairmont City, IL 162 D2
Fairmount, NY 117 E3
Fairmount Hts, MD 148 F6
Fairmount Park, PA 144 D5
Fairview, GA 152 D1
Fairview, NJ 142 D5
Fairview, OR 177 H5
Fairview Hts, IL 162 D1
Fairview Park, OH 150 B6
Fairway, KS 162 C4
Faisalabad, 58 B6
Fajardo, 122 D2
Fakfak, 76 A7
Falcon Hts, MN 161 D3
Falfurrias, TX 129 E1
Falk Park, WI 157 B1
Falkensee, 32 B7
Falkland Islands, 86 B2
Fall River, MA 115 C2
Fallon, NV 132 D6
Fallon NWR, NV 132 D6
Fallon NAS, NV 132 D6

Falls Church, VA 148 B6
Falls City, NE 127 F3
Falls Creek, CA 182 B6
Falls of the Rhine, 37 F4
Falmouth, MA 185 A4
False Cape, 96 A4
Falun, 22 E8
Faneuil Hall, MA 140 C4
Fanhões, 38 B8
Fano, 24 C4
Far Rockaway, NY 143 F2
Farah, 49 H5, 58 A7
Farbach-Werner Nature
  Pres, OH 151 C3
Farghona, 53 E1
Fargo, ND 110 F7, 124 A7,
  126 E7, 179 E5
Faridabad, 64 F5
Farmers Branch, TX 165 F5
Farmer's Market, CA
  172 B7
Farmington, ME 114 D5
Farmington, MI 156 A8
Farmington, MO 125 C2
Farmington, NM 111 D4,
  128 A6, 131 D4
Farmington, OR 177 E5
Farmington, UT 130 B6,
  135 G1
Farmington Hills, MI
  156 A8
Farmville, VA 119 E1
Farnborough, 26 A5
Farnham, 26 A5
Faro, Can 100 B5
Faro, Port 16 A2, 21 A2
Faroe Islands, 14 C3
Farrukhnagar, 64 F8
Farsta, 36 E5
Farum, 36 B7
Favoriten, 42 E7
Fawkner, 79 C4
Faya-Largeau, 45 E3
Fayetteville, AR 113 A4,
  125 B1, 129 F6
Fayetteville, NC 113 D4,
  121 G5

Fayetteville, TN 120 C5,
  125 E1
Fayetteville, WV 118 C2
FBI Bldg, DC 149 D3
Feasterville, PA 145 G6
Fechenhein, 35 C3
Federal, PA 146 A5
Federal Hts, CO 167 G4
Federal Way, WA 176 B2
Feira de Santana, 85 H2
Felix Neck Sanctuary, MA
  185 B3
Fellowship, NJ 145 G2
Felsenthal NWR, AR
  129 G4
Felsöpakony, 42 C5
Fengtai, 73 B1
Fengtai District, 73 C1
Fenino, 56 D4
Fentonville, PA 145 E4
Fenway Park, MA 139 D3
Ferbitz, 32 A7
Ferencváros, 42 B7
Fergus Falls, MN 126 E7
Ferguson, MO 162 B3
Ferihegy Arpt, 42 C6
Fermi Natl Accelerator
  Lab, IL 159 A3
Fernández Blanco Mus,
  89 D4
Fernandina Beach, FL
  123 F6
Ferndale, FL 153 E5
Ferndale, MD 147 C1
Ferndale, MI 156 D8
Fernley, NV 132 C6
Ferntree Gully, 79 F1
Ferrara, 24 B5
Ferraz de Vasconcelos,
  92 D5
Ferris, TX 165 H1
Ferry Bldg, CA 173 F3
Fès, 16 A1, 44 B5
Fianarantsoa, 47 H3
Fidenae, 40 C6
Fiera Campionaria, 40 B2

Fife, WA 176 B1
Figino, 40 B2
Fiji, 80 C3
Filchner Ice Shelf, 83 D3
Fili, 43 B4
Filimonki, 56 A2
Fillmore, UT 130 B5
Fimbul Ice Shelf, 83 E3
Findlay, OH 125 F4, 118 B5
Fine Arts Palace, 98 B3
Finger Lakes NF, NY
  116 D2
Finland, 15 G4, 52 G6,
  82 F7
Finland Sta, 57 G2
Finneytown, OH 151 D3
Fiorito, 88 D6
Fircrest, WA 176 A1
Fire Island NS, NY 116 C5
  179 H4
Fish Camp, CA 182 B1
Fish Creek, WY 181 E1
Fish Lake NF, UT 130 B5
Fish Lake RP, MN 161 A4
Fisherman's Wharf, CA
  173 D4
Fishermens Bend, 79 B2
Fishers, IN 157 F4
Fishguard, 19 C3
Fishing Bridge Visitor Ctr,
  WY 180 C3
Fitchburg, MA 115 B3
Fittja, 36 E6
Fitzgerald, GA 121 E3
Fitzwatertown, PA 145 E6
Fiumicino, 40 A4
Five Dock, 78 E7
Flagg Ranch, WY 181 F6
Flagler Beach, FL 123 F5
Flagstaff, AZ 111 C4,
  131 B3, 178 B3
Flagstaff Lake, ME 114 C6
Flaming Geyser SP, WA
  176 D1
Flaming Gorge NRA, WY
  130 C6, 135 H1
Flamingo, FL 188 D4

Flat Creek, WY 181 **G1**

Flatbush, NY 142 **D2**

Flathead IR, MT 135 **E5**

Flathead NF, MT 135 **F6**

Fleischer Mus, AZ 168 **D5**

Flensburg, 22 **C5**

Flin Flon, 101 **E3**

Flingern, 34 **B5**

Flint, MI 112 **C6**, 124 **F5**

Flint R, GA 120 **D2**

Floral Park, NY 143 **G3**

Florala, AL 122 **C6**

Florence, AL 113 **B4**, 120 **B5**

Florence, AZ 131 **B2**

Florence, CA 170 **C4**

Florence, *Italy* 17 **E4**, 24 **B4**

Florence, KY 151 **C1**

Florence, SC 113 **E4**, 121 **F4**

Florencia, 84 **C4**

Florencio Varela, 88 **F5**

Flores, *Arg* 88 **D6**

Flores, *Indo* 61 **E1**

Floresville, TX 129 **E2**

Floriano, 85 **G3**

Florianópolis, 86 **C6**

Florida, 51 **F3**, 97 **G5**, 113 **D2**, 122, 179 **G2**

Florida Bay, FL 123 **F1**, 188 **B3**

Florida/Intl U, FL 155 **E1**

Florida Keys, 113 **E1**, 188

Florida State Fairgrounds, FL 154 **D5**

Florida Suncoast Dome, FL 154 **B3**

Floridsdorf, 42 **E8**

Florin, CA 132 **B5**

Florissant, MO 162 **B3**

Flourtown, PA 144, **D5**

Flower Mound, TX 164 **D6**

Floyd Bennett Field, NY 143 **E1**

Flushimi-Ku, 71 **E1**

Flushing, NY 143 **F4**

Flushing Meadow Park, NY 143 **E4**

Fly R, 76 **B1**

Foerster Peak, CA 182 **D2**

Foggia, 17 **F3**, 24 **C3**

Foggy Bottom, DC 149 **A4**

Folcroft, PA 144 **C1**

Foligno, 24 **C4**

Folkestone, 19 **F2**

Folkston, GA 123 **E6**

Fomeque, 90 **D1**

Fond du Lac, WI 124 **D5**

Fond du Lac IR, MN 124 **B7**

Fontana, CA 171 **G5**

Fontenay-Trésigny, 28 **F6**

Fontibón, 90 **C2**

Foot Hall IR, ID 130 **B7**

Footscray, 79 **B3**

Ford Estate, Henry, MI 156 **C6**

Ford Isl, HI 177 **F3**

Ford Mus & Greenfield Village, Henry, MI 156 **C6**

Fordham U, NY 143 **E6**

Ford's Theater, DC 149 **D3**

Forest, MS 120 **B3**

Forest City, FL 153 **G5**

Forest Grove, PA 146 **A7**

Forest Hill, *Austral* 79 **E2**

Forest Hill, *Can* 104 **D6**

Forest Hill, TX 164 **C2**

Forest Hills, MA 139 **C3**

Forest Hills, NY 143 **E3**

Forest Park, GA 152 **B2**

Forest Park, MO 162 **B2**

Forest Park, OH 151 **D4**

Forestdale, MA 184 **B5**

Forestville, *Austral* 78 **E8**

Forestville, MD 148 **F6**

Forestville, OH 151 **E1**

Forêt D'Armainvilliers, 28 **E6**

Forêt de Marly, 28 **B7**

Forêt de Notre Dame, 28 **E6**

Forêt de Rambouillet, 28 **A6**

Forêt de Senart, 28 **D6**

Forêt de St Germain, 28 **B7**

Forks NHP, The, 107 **G5**

Forlì, 24 **B5**

Formentera, 21 **E2**

Former Imperial Palace, 71 **E4**

Formosa, 86 **B6**

Forrest City, AR 120 **A5**

Forsyth, MT 130 **D8**

Forsyth Pk, CA 182 **B6**

Forsyth NWR, Edwin B, NJ 119 **H4**

Fort & Portuguese Ruins, 65 **A4**

Fort Apache IR, AZ 131 **C2**

Fort Belknap IR, MT 135 **H6**

Fort Benjamin Harrison, IN 157 **F3**

Fort Benton, MT 135 **G6**

Fort Berthold IR, ND 126 **C7**

Fort Bliss Mil Res, NM 128 **B4**, 131 **E2**

Fort Bragg, CA 132 **A6**

Fort Bridger, WY 130 **C6**

Fort Chaffee Mil Res, AR 129 **F5**

Fort Collins, CO 110 **D5**, 127 **A3**, 130 **E6**

Fort-de-France, 95 **H2**

Fort Desoto, FL 154 **B2**

Fort Desoto Park, FL 154 **B2**

Fort Dodge, IA 112 **A5**, 125 **B4**, 126 **F5**

Fort DuPont Park, DC 148 **E6**

Fort Edward, NY 117 **H4**

Fort Erie, 116 **B3**

Fort Frances, 103 **A2**, 124 **B7**

Fort Franklin, 100 **C5**, 136 **F7**

Fort Garland, CO 131 **E4**

Fort Garry, 107 **G4**

Fort Good Hope, 136 **F7**

Fort Hall IR, ID 130 **B7**

Fort Hamilton, NY 142 **C2**

Fort Hood Mil Res, TX 129 **E3**

Fort Howard, MD 147 **F1**

Fort Irwin Mil Res, CA 133 **E3**

Fort Jones, CA 132 **A7**

Fort Kent, ME 114 **E8**

Fort Landing, NC 187 **F5**

Fort Laramie, WY 130 **E6**

Fort Lauderdale, FL 113 **E2**, 123 **G2**, 155 **G4**

Fort Lauderdale/Hollywood Intl Arpt, FL 155 **G4**

Fort Lauzon, 105 **F3**

Fort Lee, NJ 142 **D5**

Fort McDermitt IR, NV 132 **D7**

Fort McHenry NM & Historic Shrine, MD 147 **D2**, 179 **H4**

Fort McMurray, 101 **E3**

Fort McPherson, *Can* 100 **C6**, 136 **E7**

Fort McPherson, GA 152 **B3**

Fort Mitchell, KY 151 **D1**

Fort Morgan, CO 127 **B3**, 130 **F5**

Fort Myers, FL 94 **B6**, 113 **D2**, 123 **E2**

Fort Myers Beach, FL 123 **E2**

Fort Nelson, 101 **C4**

Fort Peck, MT 126 **A8**

Fort Peck IR, MT 126 **A8**

Fort Peck Lake, MT 126 **A7**, 135 **H6**

Fort Pickett Mil Res, VA 119 **F1**

Fort Pierce, FL 113 **E2**, 123 **F3**

Fort Raleigh NHS, NC 187 **G5**

Fort Robinson, NE 126 **B5**, 130 **F7**

Fort St John, 101 **C4**

Fort Sam Houston, TX 163 **G2**

Fort Scott, KS 125 **A2**, 127 **F2**

Fort Sheridan, IL 158 **C6**

Fort Sill Mil Res, OK 129 **E5**

Fort Simpson, 100 **C5**

Fort Smith, AR 113 **A4**, 125 **A1**, 129 **F6**

Fort Smith, Can 101 **E4**

Fort Snelling SP, MN 161 **D1**

Fort Stockton, TX 111 **E3**, 128 **C3**, 131 **F1**

Fort Sumter NM, SC 179 **G2**

Fort Thomas, KY 151 **E1**

Fort Totten, ND 126 **D7**

Fort Totten IR, ND 126 **D7**

Fort Vancouver NHS, OR 177 **F6**

Fort Walton Beach, FL 120 **C2**, 122 **B6**

Fort Ward SP, WA 176 **A5**

Fort Washakie, WY 135 **H2**

Fort Washington, PA 144 **D6**

Fort Washington SP, PA 144 **D6**

Fort Wayne, IN 112 **C5**, 118 **A5**, 125 **E4**

Fort William, 18 **C6**, 65 **E2**

Fort Worth, TX 96 **D6**, 111 **F3**, 129 **E4**, 164 **C3**, 178 **D2**

Fort Worth Alliance Arpt, TX 164 **B6**

Fort Worth Cultural District, TX 164 **B3**

Fort Worth Nature Ctr & Refuge, TX 164 **A4**

Fort Wright, KY 151 **C1**

Fort Yukon, AK 100 **B6**, 136 **D7**

Fort Zachary Taylor SHS, FL 188 **A1**

Fortaleza, 85 **H3**

Fortuna, CA 132 **A7**

Forum, The, 29 **E2**

Fossil, OR 134 **C4**

Fossil Butte NM, WY 130 **C6**, 178 **C4**

Foster, OH 151 **F4**

Foster City, CA 175 **C3**

Foster Village, HI 177 **F3**

Fót, 42 **B8**

Fountain, CO 130 **E5**

Fountain Valley, CA 170 **D2**

Fox Chapel, PA 146 **D7**

Fox Chase, PA 145 **F5**

Fox Creek, WY 181 **E2**

Fox Lake Hills, IL 158 **A8**

Fox Pt, WI 157 **C4**

Fox River Grove, IL 158 **A6**

Foxe Basin, 102 **B5**

France, 16 **C5**, 19 **F1**, 20 **D6**, 23 **A2**

Franceville, 46 **D6**

Francistown, 47 **F3**

Francisville, KY 151 **B2**

Franco da Rocha, 92 **A6**

Franconia, VA 148 **C5**

Frankford, PA 145 **F4**

Frankfort, IL 159 **C1**

Frankfort, KY 112 **C5**, 118 **A2**, 125 **F2**

Frankfurt, 16 **D6**, 20 **F7**, 23 **C3**, 23 **E4**, 35 **B3**

Frankfurt am Main Intl Arpt, 35 **A2**

Franklin, MI 156 **B8**

Franklin, NH 115 **B4**

Franklin, PA 118 **D6**

Franklin, TN 120 **C6**, 125 **E1**

Franklin, VA 119 **F1**

Franklin Bay, 136 **E8**

Franklin Mts SP, NM 128 **A4**

Franklin Park, DC 149 **C4**

Franklin Park, IL 159 **C4**

Franklin Park, PA 146 **B8**

Franklin Square, NY 143 **G3**

Franz Josef Land, 52 **F7**, 82 **D7**

Frascati, 40 **D4**

Fraser, MI 156 **E8**

Fraser Plateau, 101 **B3**

Fraser R, 101 **C3**

Frattocchie, 40 **D4**

Frazier Park, CA 133 **D3**

Fredensborg, 36 **B8**

Frederick, MD 119 **F4**

Frederick, OK 128 **D5**

Frederick Law Olmsted NHS, MA 139 **C3**

Fredericksburg, TX 129 **E3**

Fredericksburg, VA 119 **F2**

Fredericksburg & Spotsylvania NMP, VA 179 **H4**

Fredericton, 103 **D2**

Frederiksberg, 36 **C6**

Fredonia, NY 116 **B2**

Fredrikstad, 22 **D8**

Freeport, Bah 94 **C6**

Freeport IA, 125 **C4**

Freeport, NY 116 **B5**, 143 **H2**

Freer Gallery of Art, DC 149 **D2**

Freetown, 44 **A1**

Fregene, 40 **A5**

Freiburg, 20 **F6**, 23 **C2**, 24 **A6**

Fremantle, 76 **A3**

Fremont, CA 175 **E3**

Fremont, NE 127 **E4**

Fremont, OH 118 **B5**

Fremont NF, OR 132 **B8**, 134 **C2**

French Guiana, 85 **F5**

French Polynesia, 81 **E3**

French Quarter, LA 163 **G5**

French RP, MN 161 **A3**

Frenchman Bay, ME 186 **D6**

Fresnillo, 96 **C4**

Fresno, CA 110 **A5**, 133 **C4**, 178 **A4**

Fresno, TX 166 **B1**

Frestaby, 36 **E7**

Fribourg, 37 **A1**

Frick Park, PA 146 **D6**

Friday Harbor, WA 134 **B6**

Fridley, MN 161 **C4**

Friedersdorf, 32 **F5**

Friedrichshain, 32 **D7**

Friendswood, TX 166 **D1**

Frimley, 26 **A6**

Frisco, NC 187 **G2**

Frisco, UT 130 **B5**

Front Royal, VA 119 **E3**

Frostproof, FL 123 **F3**

Frosunda, 36 **F8**

Fruit Hill, OH 151 **E1**

Fruitvale, CO 130 **D5**

Fry Canyon, UT 131 **C4**

Frying Pan Landing, NC 187 **F5**

Fuchu, 68 **B7**

Fuencarral-el Pardo, 39 **B4**

Fuji, 66 **F5**

Fujim, 68 **B8**

Fujisawa, 68 **A5**

Fujita Art Mus, 71 **C3**

Fukui, 66 **E5**

Fukuoka, 67 **D4**

Fukushima-Ku, 71 **A4**

Fulda, 23 **C3**

Fullerton, CA 170 **D3**

Fulton, MO 125 **C2**

Fulton, NY 117 **E4**

Funabashi, 68 **D7**

Funafuti, 80 **C4**

Funchal, 44 **A5**

Funza, 90 **B2**

Fushimi-Ku, 70 **F7**, 71 **E1**

Fushun, 55 E2, 60 C8, 66 C6
Futtsu, 68 C5
Fuxin, 66 B6
Fuyang, 67 A4
Fuzhou, 60 D6, 67 B2
Fyn, 22 D6

G

Gabbs, NV 132 D6
Gabon, 46 D6
Gaborone, 47 E3
Gadsden, AL 113 C4, 120 C4
Gaffney, SC 121 F5
Gages Lake, IL 158 B7
Gaggiano, 40 A1
Gagnon, 103 D3
Gainesville, FL 113 D3, 121 E1, 123 E5
Gainesville, GA 121 E4
Gainesville, TX 129 E5
Galapagos Islands, 81 H4, 84 A3
Galátsion, 43 B3
Galati, 17 H5
Galax, VA 121 F6
Galdhøpiggen, 15 E3
Gale Peak, CA 182 D1
Galena Park, TX 166 D3
Galesburg, IL 125 C4
Gallatin, TN 120 C6
Gallatin NF, MT 135 G4, 180 B6
Gallatin Petrified Forest, MT 180 A6
Gallatin Range, 180 A5
Gallatin R, 180 A6
Galle, 59 C3
Gallipolis, OH 118 C3
Galloo Isl, NY 117 E5
Gallup, NM 111 D4, 128 A6, 131 D3
Galveston, TX 113 A2, 129 F2, 179 E1

Galway, 14 B1, 19 A4, 20 A8
Gambia, 44 A2
Gamboa, 91 D2
Gander, 103 F3
Ganea, 53 B2
Ganges R, 58 D5
Ganlose, 36 A7
Ganshoren, 31 F2
Ganzhou, 60 C6, 67 A2
Gao, 44 C2
Garbagnate Milanese, 40 B3
Garbatella, 40 C5
Garden City, Egypt 50 C2
Garden City, KS 127 C2
Garden City, MI 156 B6
Garden City, NY 143 G3
Garden Grove, CA 170 D2
Garden Reach, 65 E2
Gardena, CA 170 B3
Gardendale, TX 163 H2
Gardenstadt, 34 F7
Gardiner, Austral 79 C2
Gardiner, ME 114 D5
Gardiner, MT 180 B5
Gare d'Austerlitz, 29 F1
Gare de l'Est, 29 F4
Gare du Nord, 29 F4
Gare St. Lazare, 29 D4
Garfield, NJ 142 C6
Garfield Hts, OH 150 E6
Garfield Park, IN 157 E2
Garfield Park Res, OH 150 D6
Garges-Les-Gonesse, 28 D8
Gariya, 65 F1
Garland, TX 165 H5
Garment District, CA 172 E6
Garoua, 44 D1
Garrett Park, MD 148 C8
Garrison, MD 147 B4
Garryowen, MT 126 A6, 130 D8
Garulia, 65 F3

Gary, IN 112 C5, 125 D4, 159 F2
Gary Regional Arpt, IN 159 F2
Gaspé, 103 E3
Gaspé Pen, 103 E3
Gastonia, NC 121 E5
Gates of the Arctic NP & Pres, AK 136 C8, 178 B2
Gatesville, NC 119 F1
Gatesville, TX 129 E3
Gateway of India, 65 B1
Gateway NRA, NY 116 B5, 142 C1, 143 E2
Gatineau, 105 A1
Gatineau Prov P, 105 A3
Gatorland, FL 153 G2
Gatow Arpt, 32 B6
Gatwick Arpt, 26 C5
Gauley River NRA, WV 118 C2
Gava, 38 D5
Gåvle, 15 F3, 22 F8
Gaza, 48 D5
Gaziosmanpasa, 43 D3
Gdansk, 15 F1, 22 F5, 52 A6
Gdynia, 22 F5
Geddes, SD 126 E5
Gedera, 50 A4
Gedser, 22 D5
Geelong, 77 E2
Geilo, 22 C8
Gejiu, 60 A5
Gela, 24 C1
Gelsenkirchen, 34 D8
Gem Lake, MN 161 E4
General Mitchell Intl Arpt, WI 157 C1
General San Martín, 88 C7
General San Martín Cultural Centre, 89 C3
General Sarmiento, 88 B7
Genesee R, NY 116 C2
Geneseo, NY 116 C3
Geneva, NY 116 D3

Geneva, Switz 16 D4, 20 F5, 23 B1
Genoa, 17 E4, 24 A5
Gent, 20 E7, 23 A3
Gentilly, 28 D6
Gentofte, 36 C6
George Mason U, VA 148 A6
George Town, 61 A3
George Washington Brdg, NY 142 D5
George Washington NF, OH 119 E3
George Washington U, DC 149 B3
Georges Hall, 78 C6
Georgetown, DE 119 G3
Georgetown, MA 138 E8
Georgetown, SC 121 G4
Georgetown, Guyana 85 E5
Georgia, 97 F6, 113 D3, 121 D2, 179 G2
Georgia, Rus 45 G6
Georgia Dome, GA 152 B3
Georgia Tech, GA 152 B4
Gera, 23 D3
Geraldton, 76 A3, 103 B2
Gerardsville, 51 F5
Gerasdorf, 42 F8
Gering, NE 130 F6
Gerlafingen, 37 C4
Gerli, 88 E6
Germann, TX 165 G1
Germantown, PA 145 E4
Germantown, TN 120 B5, 129 H6
Germany, 17 E6, 20 F8, 23 D4, 24 B6, 44 D6
Germiston, 51 H2
Gerona, 21 E4
Gerthe, 34 E8
Gettysburg, PA 119 F4
Getty Mus, J Paul, CA 170 A5
Gettysburg NMP, PA 179 G4

Gevelsberg, 34 E6

Ghadamis, 44 D4

Ghana, 44 C1

Ghardaïa, 44 C4

Ghatkopar, 65 B2

Ghaziabad, 64 F7

Ghiradelli Square, CA 173 C4

Gianicolense, 40 C5, 41 A1

Gianicolo, 41 B2

Giardini del Quirinale, 41 D3

Gibraltar, 16 A2, 21 B1

Gibson Desert, 76 B4

Gibsonton, FL 154 D4

Giessen, 23 C3

Gifford, FL 123 F3

Gig Harbor, WA 176 B3

Gijón, 16 B4, 21 B4

Gila NF, NM 128 A5, 131 D2

Gila River IR, AZ 131 B2, 168 B1

Gillespie Field, CA 169 H4

Gillette, FL 154 C2

Gillette, WY 126 A5, 130 E7

Gilmore, GA 152 A5

Gilroy, CA 133 B4

Ginkakuji, 71 F3

Ginkaku-ji Temple, 70 F8

Ginnhein, 35 B3

Ginza, 69 D2

Gion, 71 F3

Gisborne, 77 H2

Giv'at Ze'ev, 50 D5

Gjirokastër, 25 E4

Gjøvik, 22 D8

Glacier NP, MT 135 F6, 178 B6

Glacier Bay NP & Pres, AK 136 E6, 178 B1

Glacier Pt, CA 182 B3

Gladbeck, 34 C8

Gladesville, 78 D7

Gladsakse, 36 B6

Gladstone, Austral 77 F4

Gladstone, OR 177 G4

Gladwyne, PA 144 C4

Glama R, 15 E3

Glasgow, KY 120 D6

Glasgow, MT 110 E7, 126 A8

Glasgow, UK 14 C2, 18 C5

Glasgow Village, MO 162 C3

Glattbrugg, 37 D2

Glattfelden, 37 E3

Glen, NH 115 C4

Glen Avon, CA 171 G4

Glen Burnie, MD 147 D1

Glen Canyon NRA, 131 C4, 178 B3

Glen Cove, NY 116 B5, 143 H6

Glen Echo, MD 148 C7

Glen Ellyn, IL 159 A4

Glen Mills, PA 144 A2

Glen Riddle, PA 144 A1

Glen Ridge, NJ 142 B5

Glen Waverly, 79 E2

Glenarden, MD 148 F7

Glencoe, IL 158 D6

Glendale, AZ 131 B2, 168 A4

Glendale, CA 133 D3, 170 C5, 172 E8

Glendale, CO 167 G3

Glendale, MO 162 A1

Glendale, OH 151 D4

Glendale, OR 134 B2

Glendale, VA 148 A7

Glendale, WI 157 B4

Glendale Hts, IL 159 A4

Glendive, MT 126 B7

Glendora, CA 171 E5

Glenfield, 78 B5

Glenolden, PA 144 C1

Glenroy, 79 B4

Glenshaw, PA 146 C7

Glenside, PA 145, E5

Glenview, CA 170 A5

Glenview, IL 158 C5

Glenvista, 51 G2

Glenwillow, OH 150 F5

Glenwood, IL 159 D1

Glenwood Springs, CO 130 D5

Glifada, 43 C1

Globe, AZ 131 C2

Gloria, 91 D2

Glostrup, 36 B6

Gloucester, Can 105 C2

Gloucester, MA 115 C3

Gloucester, UK 19 D3

Gloucester, VA 119 G2

Gloucester City, NJ 145 E1

Gobancho, 69 A4

Gobi Desert, 55 C1, 58 F8, 60 A8, 66 A6

Godalming, 26 B5

Gödöllo, 42 C8

Goethals Brdg, 142 B2

Goiâna, 85 F1

Gokalpur, 64 E8

Gold Beach, OR 132 A8, 134 A2

Gold Mus, 90 C2

Gold Reef City, 51 F2

Golden, CO 130 E5, 167 E3

Golden Beach, FL 155 G3

Golden Gate, FL 123 F2

Golden Gate Brdg, CA 174 A5

Golden Gate NRA, CA 173 B4, 174 A5, 175 A4, 178 A4

Golden Horn, 43 E2

Golden Valley, MN 161 B3

Goldendale, WA 134 C4

Goldenrod, FL 153 H4

Goldfield, NV 132 D5

Goldsboro, NC 121 G5

Goldwater Air Force Range, Barry M, AZ 131 A2

Golf Manor, OH 151 D3

Golfo de Santa Clara, 133 F1

Golmud, 58 F7

Goma, 47 F6

Gomel, 15 H1

Gonaives, 94 D4

Gonder, 45 G2

Gonesse, 28 D8

Gonzales, CA 133 B4

Gonzalez, AL 122 B6

González Catán, 88 C5

Gooding, ID 132 F8, 135 E2

Goodland, KS 127 C3

Goodwell, OK 127 C1

Gooik, 31 E1

Goose Cove, ME 186 A2

Goose Lake, OR 132 C8

Gordon, Austral 78 E8

Gordon, Can 107 F6

Gorelovo, 57 F1

Gorgan, 49 G6

Gorgonzola, 40 D2

Gorham, ME 114 C5

Gorinchem, 30 D1

Gor'ky Park, 56 B4

Gorla, 40 C2

Görlitz, 23 E3

Gorlose, 36 A8

Gorna Oryakhovitsa, 25 G4

Gorontalo, 61 E3

Gorzow Wielkopolski, 23 E4

Goshen, NY 119 H6

Goshute IR, NV 132 F6

Göteborg, 15 E2, 22 D7

Gotland, 15 F2, 22 F7

Gotse Delchev, 25 F5

Göttingen, 23 D4

Gouda, 30 C3

Goupilieres, 28 A7

Goussainville, 28 D8

Gouverneur, NY 117 F5

Governador Valadares, 85 G1

Government Ctr, MA 140 C4

Government Pt, OR 134 A4

Governors Isl, NY 142 D3

Gowanda, NY 116 B2

Grace Cathedral, CA 173 D3

Graceville, FL 122 C6

Gracia, 38 E6

Gradyville, PA 144 A2

Grafton, *Austral* 77 F3

Grafton, ND 126 E8

Grafton, WV 118 D3

Graham, TX 129 E4

Graham Lake, ME 114 E5

Grajaú, 91 F1

Gran Chaco, 86 B6

Granada, *Nic* 90 A1, 97 F1

Granada, *Spain* 16 B2, 21 C2

Granby, 114 A6

Grand Bahama, 94 C6

Grand Canal, 60 C7, 67 B4

Grand Canyon, AZ 111 C4, 131 B3

Grand Canyon Arpt, AZ 183 E1

Grand Canyon Lodge, AZ 183 E2

Grand Canyon NP, AZ 131 B4, 133 F4, 178 B3, 183 D3

Grand Canyon of the Tuolumne R, CA 182 B4

Grand Canyon of the Yellowstone, WY 180 C4

Grand Canyon Village, AZ 183 E2

Grand Central Sta, NY 141 G4

Grand Falls, *Can* 103 D2

Grand Falls, *Can* 103 F3

Grand Falls/Grand Sault, 114 F8

Grand Forks, MN 124 A7

Grand Forks, ND 101 F2, 110 F7, 126 E7, 178 E5

Grand Hotel, 62 C5

Grand Isl, NE 110 F5, 127 D4

Grand Junction, CO 110 D5, 130 C5

Grand-Mère, 114 A7

Grand Palace, 63 F5

Grand Palais, 29 C3

Grand Place Market, 31 F2

Grand Prairie, TX 165 E3

Grand Rapids, *Can* 101 F3

Grand Rapids, MI 112 C6, 124 E5, 179 F5

Grand Rapids, MN 124 B7

Grand R, 116 A3

Grand River NG, SD 126 C6

Grand Terrace, CA 171 H4

Grand Teton, WY 130 C7

Grand Teton NP, WY 130 C7, 135 G3, 178 C5, 180 A1, 181 F5

Grand Trianon, 28 B7

Grand View, ID 135 E2

Grande Pointe, 107 H4

Grande Prairie, 101 D3

Grande R, 85 F1

Grandview Pt, AZ 183 E1

Grangeville, ID 130 A8, 135 E4

Granite City, IL 162 C3

Granite Falls, MN 126 F6

Granite Gorge, AZ 183 D2

Granite Narrows, AZ 183 C3

Granite Pk, MT 135 F4

Granollers, 38 F8

Grant Park, GA 152 C3

Grant Park, IL 160 D6

Grant Park, WI 157 C1

Grant Village Visitor Ctr, WY 180 C3

Grants, NM 128 A6, 131 D3

Grants Pass, OR 132 A8, 134 B2

Granville, NY 115 A4, 117 H4

Granville Isl, *Can* 107 G2

Grapevine, TX 164 D5

Grapevine RA, TX 164 C6

Grasfontein, 51 H6

Grasmere, 51 E1

Grass R, NY 117 F6

Grass-Vadnais RP, MN 161 E4

Grass Valley, CA 132 B6

Grasslands NP, 126 A8

Grassy Key, FL 188 D2

Gravenbruch, 35 C2

Gravesend, NY 142 D1

Gravesend, *UK* 26 F7

Grays, 26 E7

Grayslake, IL 158 B7

Grayson, KY 118 B3

Graz, 17 F5, 23 E1, 24 C6

Grazhdanka, 57 G3

Great Abaco, 94 C6

Great America, CA 175 E2

Great Artesian Basin, 76 D4

Great Australian Bight, 76 C3

Great Barrier Reef, 77 E5

Great Barrington, MA 115 A2, 117 H2

Great Basin, NV 132 E6

Great Basin NP, NV 130 A5, 132 F6, 178 B4

Great Bear Lake, 100 D5

Great Bend, KS 127 E2

Great Brook Farm SF, MA 138 A6

Great Buddha, 68 B5

Great Cranberry Isl, ME 186 C2

Great Dismal Swamp NWR, VA 119 G1

Great Dividing Range, 77 E3, 80 B3

Great Exuma, 94 C5

Great Falls, MT 101 D2, 110 D7, 135 G5, 178 C6

Great Falls, VA 148 A8

Great Falls Park, VA 148 A8

Great Fountain Geyser, WY 180 B3

Great Gott Isl, ME 186 B1

Great Hall of the People, The, 73 D2

Great Inagua, 94 D4

Great Indian Desert, 58 B6

Great Lakes Naval Training Ctr, IL 158 C7

Great Meadows NWR, MA 138 A5

Great Neck, NY 143 G5

Great Neck Plaza, NY 143 G4

Great Notch, NJ 142 B6

Great Plains, 101 D2, 110 E6

Great Pt, MA 185 F2

Great Sacandaga Lake, NY 117 G3

Great Salt Lake, UT 110 C5, 130 B6, 135 F1, 178 B4

Great Sand Dunes NM, CO 127 A2, 131 E4, 178 C3

Great Sandy Desert, 76 B3

Great Slave Lake, 101 D4

Great Smoky Mts NP, 121 E5, 125 F1, 179 F3

Great Thumb Mesa, AZ 183 C3

Great Thumb Pt, AZ 183 C3

Great Victoria Desert, 76 B4

Great Western Forum, CA 170 B4

Great White Heron NWR, FL 123 F1, 188 A2

Great Yarmouth, 19 F3

Greater Cincinnati Intl Arpt, KY 151 B1

Greco, 40 C2

Greece, 17 G2, 25 F3

Greece, NY 116 **C**3

Greeley, CO 110 **E**5, 127 **B**3, 130 **E**6

Green Bay, MI 103 **A**1

Green Bay, WI 112 **B**6, 124 **D**5, 179 **F**5

Green Harbor, MA 184 **A**8

Green Isl, ME 186 **A**5

Green Mountain NF, VT 115 **A**3, 117 **H**5

Green Oaks, IL 158 **C**7

Green Park, 27 **B**2

Green R, KY 125 **E**2

Green R, UT 130 **C**5

Green River, WY 135 **H**1

Green Valley, AZ 131 **B**1

Greenacres, CA 133 **C**3

Greenbelt, MD 148 **F**8

Greenbelt Park, MD 148 **F**7

Greenbrae, CA 174 **A**6

Greendale, WI 157 **B**1

Greenfield, MA 115 **A**3

Greenfield, WI 157 **B**1

Greenfield Park, Can 106 **D**2

Greenfield Park, WI 157 **A**2

Greening Isl, ME 186 **C**3

Greenland Sea, 82 **E**6

Greenock, 18 **C**5

Greenpoint, NY 141 **H**2

Greenport, NY 116 **D**6

Greensboro, AL 120 **C**3

Greensboro, NC 113 **D**4, 121 **F**6

Greensborough, 79 **D**4

Greensburg, IN 118 **A**4

Greensburg, PA 119 **E**4

Greenup, KY 118 **B**3

Greenville, AL 120 **C**3

Greenville, CA 132 **C**6

Greenville, ME 114 **D**6

Greenville, MS 113 **B**3, 120 **A**4, 129 **H**5

Greenville, NC 121 **H**5

Greenville, SC 113 **D**4, 121 **E**5

Greenwich, CT 115 **A**1, 116 **B**6

Greenwich, UK 26 **D**7

Greenwich Village, NY 141 **F**3

Greenwood, SC 121 **E**4

Greenwood Village, CO 167 **G**2

Gregg, PA 146 **A**6

Greifswald, 22 **E**5

Grembergen, 31 **E**4

Grenada, MS 120 **B**4, 129 **H**5

Grenada, WI 85 **E**6, 95 **H**1

Grenchen, 37 **B**4

Grenelle, 29 **A**1

Grenoble, 16 **D**4, 20 **F**5

Gresham, OR 177 **H**5

Gresham Park, GA 152 **D**3

Gretna, LA 163 **G**5

Greve, 36 **A**5

Greve Strand, 36 **B**5

Greymouth, 77 **G**1

Griffin, GA 120 **D**4

Griffith, Austral 77 **E**3

Griffith, IN 159 **F**1

Griffith Obs, CA 172 **D**8

Griffith Park, CA 170 **C**5, 172 **D**8

Grimbergen, 31 **G**3

Grimsby, 19 **E**4

Grimstad, 22 **C**7

Grinter House, KS 162 **A**5

Grise Fiord, 102 **A**7

Grobschmidt Park, WI 157 **B**1

Grodinge, 36 **D**5

Grodno, 15 **G**1

Groenendaal, 31 **G**1

Groesbeck, OH 151 **C**3

Groningen, 14 **D**1, 20 **E**8, 23 **B**4

Gros Ventre R, WY 181 **G**2

Gros Ventre Slide, WY 181 **G**2

Gros Ventre Wilderness Area, WY 181 **H**1

Gross-Enzersdorf, 42 **F**7

Gross Glienicke, 32 **B**6

Grossaffoltern, 37 **B**3

Grossbeeren, 32 **C**5

Grosse Pointe, MI 156 **F**7

Grosse Pointe Farms, MI 156 **F**7

Grosse Pointe Park, MI 156 **F**7

Grosse Pointe Shores, MI 156 **F**7

Grosse Pointe Woods, MI 156 **F**7

Grosser Muggelsee, 32 **E**6

Grosseto, 24 **B**4

Grossjedleresdorf, 42 **E**8

Grossmont College, CA 169 **G**4

Grotta-Ferrata, 40 **D**4

Groveland, MA 138 **D**8

Groveton, NH 114 **B**5

Groznyy, 53 **B**3

Grundy, VA 118 **C**1

Grune Municipal Park, 35 **B**3

Grunewald, 32 **B**6

Guadalajara, Mex 99 **F**5

Guadalajara, Spain 21 **C**3, 96 **C**3

Guadalquivir R, 21 **C**2

Guadalupe, AZ 168 **B**3

Guadalupe, CA 133 **C**3

Guadalupe Mountains NP, TX 128 **B**4, 131 **E**1, 178 **C**2

Guadalupe Pk, TX 131 **E**2

Guadalupe Victoria, 98 **C**5

Guadeloupe, 95 **H**3

Guadiana R, 21 **B**3

Guaianazes, 92 **D**4

Guajará-Mirim, 84 **D**2

Guam, 80 **A**5

Guang'anmen Railway Sta, 73 **C**1

Guangzhou, 60 **C**5, 67 **A**2

Guánica, 122 **A**1

Guantánamo, 94 **D**4

Guaporá R, 84 **D**1

Guaratiba, 91 **A**1

Guarda, 21 **A**3

Guarulhos, 92 **C**5

Guasca, 90 **D**3

Guatemala, 81 **H**5, 84 **A**6, 97 **E**2

Guatemala City, 84 **A**6, 97 **E**2

Guayama, 122 **C**1

Guayaquil, 84 **B**3

Guaymas, 96 **B**5

Guaynabo, 122 **C**2

Guelma, 24 **A**1

Guelph, 116 **A**4

Guernsey, UK 19 **D**1

Guernsey, WY 130 **E**6

Guggenheim Mus, NY 141 **H**6

Guia de Pacobaíba, 91 **D**4

Guiana Highlands, 84 **D**5

Guidonia, 40 **D**6

Guignes, 28 **F**5

Guildford, Austral 78 **C**7

Guildford, UK 19 **E**2, 26 **B**5

Guilford Courthouse NMP, NC 179 **G**3

Guilin, 60 **B**6

Guinea, 44 **A**2

Guinea-Bissau, 44 **A**2

Guiyang, 60 **B**6

Gujranwala, 58 **C**6

Gulf City, FL 154 **C**3

Gulf Coastal Plain, 113 **B**3

Gulf Island NS, FL 120 **C**2, 179 **F**5

Gulf of Aden, 45 **H**2, 49 **F**1

Gulf of Alaska, 82 **A**5, 100 **A**5, 136 **D**5

Gulf of Anadyr, 54 **F**8

Gulf of Aqaba, 48 **D**4

Gulf of Boothia, 15 **F**4, 52 **B**6, 102 **A**6,

Gulf of Cádiz, 21 **A**2

Gulf of California, 96 **A6**, 111 **C2**, 131 **A1**, 133 **F1**
Gulf of Carpentaria, 76 **D6**
Gulf of Finland, 15 **G3**
Gulf of Guinea, 44 **C1**
Gulf of Honduras, 97 **F2**
Gulf of Lion, 21 **E4**
Gulf of Mexico, 81 **H6**, 94 **A6**, 97 **E4**, 113 **C2**, 122 **C4**
Gulf of Oman, 49 **H4**
Gulf of Panama, 97 **H1**
Gulf of Papua, 76 **C1**
Gulf of Riga, 15 **G2**
Gulf of St Lawrence, 103 **E3**
Gulf of St Malo, 19 **E1**, 20 **C6**
Gulf of San Jorge, 86 **B3**
Gulf of Sidra, 45 **E4**, 48 **A5**
Gulf of Suez, 48 **D4**
Gulf of Thailand, 61 **A3**
Gulf of Tonkin, 60 **B5**
Gulf of Valencia, 21 **D3**
Gulf Shores, AL 122 **B6**
Gulfport, FL 154 **B3**
Gulfport, MS 120 **B2**, 122 **A6**, 129 **H3**
Gulfstream Park, FL 155 **G3**
Gulian, 66 **A2**
Gull Rock, NC 187 **F3**
GUM, 57 **F5**
Gum Neck, NC 187 **E4**
Gumet Pt, MA 184 **B8**
Gumpoldskirchen, 42 **D5**
Gumusdere, 43 **E4**
Gunnison, CO 130 **D5**
Gunpowder Falls SP, MD 147 **E4**
Guntersville, AL 120 **C5**
Gunungsindur, 64 **A6**
Gurnee, IL 158 **C7**
Gurupi, 85 **F2**
Gustaf III's Pavilion, 36 **E6**
Gustava A Madero, 98 **B3**
Gustavsberg, 36 **F6**

Güstrow, 22 **D5**
Guterfelde, 32 **C5**
Guthrie, OK 127 **E1**, 129 **E6**
Guttenberg, NY 142 **D5**
Guyana, 85 **E5**
Guymon, OK 127 **C1**, 128 **D6**
Gweru, 47 **F4**
Gwynns Falls Park, MD 147 **C3**
Gyál, 42 **B6**
Gyda Pen, 50 **F5**
Gymea, 78 **D5**
Gympie, 77 **F4**
Gyor, 17 **F5**, 23 **F2**, 24 **D6**

H

Ha Kwai Chung, 75 **B4**
Haacht, 31 **H3**
Haan, 34 **C5**
Haang R, 55 **E1**
Haarlem, 30 **C6**
Habinghorst, 34 **E8**
Habiplet, 43 **D3**
Hachinohe, 66 **F6**
Hachioji, 68 **A7**
Hacienda Hts, CA 170 **D4**
Hackensack, NJ 142 **D4**
Hackensack, NY 119 **H5**
Hackettstown, NJ 116 **A5**
Hackney, 26 **D7**
Haddon Hts, NJ 145 **F1**
Haddonfield, NJ 145 **F1**
Hadfield, 79 **B4**
Hadian District, 73 **A4**
Hadley Pt, ME 186 **B6**
Hagen, 34 **F6**
Hagerstown, MD 112 **E5**, 119 **F4**
Hague, The, 16 **D6**, 20 **E8**, 23 **A4**, 30 **A3**
Hague Central Sta, The, 30 **A3**
Hahn SRA, Kenneth, CA 172 **B5**

Haidian, 73 **C4**
Haifa, 48 **D5**
Haikou, 60 **C5**
Hail, 49 **E4**
Hailar, 55 **D3**, 66 **B2**
Hailey, ID 135 **F2**
Hainan, 60 **B5**
Haines Junction, 136 **E6**
Hainesville, IL 158 **A7**
Haiphong, 60 **B5**
Haiti, 94 **D4**
Hakodate, 66 **F6**
Haldimand, 116 **A3**
Haleakala NP, HI 137 **E2**, 178 **C1**
Haleakala NP Visitor Ctr, HI 137 **E3**
Hales Corners, WI 157 **A1**
Halethope, MD 147 **C2**
Half Dome, CA 182 **C3**
Half Moon Bay, CA 175 **B2**
Halfway, OR 134 **D3**
Halfway House, 51 **G4**
Halifax, Can 103 **E2**
Halifax, NC 119 **F1**
Halim Perdanakusuma Arpt, 64 **C7**
Halisahar, 65 **F4**
Hall Quarry, ME 186 **B4**
Hallandale, FL 155 **G3**
Halmahera, 61 **F3**
Halmstad, 15 **E2**, 22 **D6**
Haltom City, TX 164 **C4**
Halver, 34 **F5**
Hamadan, 49 **F6**
Hamah, 48 **D5**
Hamamatsu, 66 **F5**
Hamborn, 34 **B7**
Hamburg, Ger 15 **E1**, 22 **D5**
Hamburg, NY 116 **B3**
Hamersley Range, 76 **A4**
Hami, 55 **B1**, 58 **E8**
Hamilton, AL 120 **B4**
Hamilton, Austral 77 **H2**

Hamilton, Can 103 **C1**, 112 **D6**, 116 **A4**
Hamilton, MT 135 **F4**
Hamilton, NY 117 **E3**
Hamilton, OH 118 **A4**
Hamilton Pond, ME 186 **C6**
Hamme, 31 **E4**
Hammerfest, 15 **F6**, 82 **E7**
Hammond, IN 159 **E2**
Hammond, LA 120 **A2**
Hammondsport, NY 116 **D2**
Hampstead, 106 **C2**
Hampstead Heath, 26 **C7**
Hampton, Austral 79 **C1**
Hampton, NH 115 **C3**
Hampton, VA 119 **G1**
Hampton Bays, NY 116 **D5**
Hampton Court Palace, 26 **B7**
Hampton NHS, PA 147 **D4**
Hamtramck, MI 156 **E7**
Hanam, 72 **C7**
Hancock, MA 117 **H2**
Hancock Tower, MA 140 **B2**
Handan, 55 **D1**, 60 **B7**, 66 **A5**
Handen, 36 **E5**
Haneda Arpt, 68 **C5**
Hanford, CA 133 **C4**
Hang Hau, 75 **F3**
Hanging Gardens, 65 **A1**
Hangkou District, 74 **E7**
Hangnam, 72 **D6**
Hangpu District, 74 **E6**
Hangzhou, 60 **D7**, 67 **B3**
Hanna, 101 **D2**
Hannibal, MO 112 **B5**
Hannover, 17 **E6**, 20 **F8**, 23 **C4**
Hanoi, 60 **B5**
Hanover, NH 115 **B4**
Hanover Park, IL 159 **A4**
Hansen Park, WI 157 **A3**
Haora, 65 **E2**
Haora Brdg, 65 **E2**
Hapeville, GA 152 **B2**

Happy Valey, 75 **D2**

Happy Valley, OR 177 **G5**

Happy Valley-Goose Bay, 103 **E4**

Harad, 49 **F3**

Harahan, LA 163 **E5**

Harare, 47 **F4**

Harbin, 55 **E2**, 66 **C7**

Harbinger, NC 187 **G6**

Harbord, 78 **F8**

Hardin, MT 135 **H4**

Harer, 45 **H1**

Hareskovby, 36 **B6**

Hargeysa, 45 **H1**

Harlan, IA 125 **A4**, 127 **F4**

Harlan, KY 118 **B1**

Harlem, NY 142 **D5**

Harlowton, MT 135 **G4**

Harmarville, PA 146 **D8**

Harmelen, 30 **D3**

Harney Lake, OR 132 **C8**

Harper Woods, MI 156 **E7**

Harpers Ferry NHP, WV 179 **G4**

Harrisburg, PA 112 **E5**, 119 **F4**

Harrison, AR 125 **B1**

Harrison, NJ 142 **B4**

Harrison, OH 151 **A3**

Harrisonburg, VA 119 **E3**

Harrods, 26 **C7**

Harrodsburg, KY 118 **A2**

Harrogate, 19 **E4**

Harrow, 26 **B8**

Hart Mountain Natl Antelope Refuge, OR 132 **C8**, 134 **C2**

Hartbeespoort, 51 **E6**

Hartford, CT 112 **E6**, 115 **A2**

Hartford, PA 145 **H3**

Hartsfield Atlanta Intl Arpt, GA 152 **B2**

Hartwell, 79 **D2**

Hartwood Acres Park, PA 146 **D8**

Harvard U, MA 139 **C4**

Harvey, IL 159 **D2**

Harvey, LA 163 **F4**

Harvey Point Defense Testing Activity, NC 187 **E6**

Harwich, MA 184 **E5**

Harwich Port, MA 184 **E5**

Harwood Hts, IL 159 **D4**

Haryana, 64 **E6**

Hasbrouck Hts, NJ 142 **C6**

Haslet, TX 164 **B5**

Hässelby, 36 **D6**

Hässleholm, 22 **E6**

Hastings, NE 127 **E3**

Hat Yai, 61 **A3**

Hatboro, PA 145 **F6**

Hatchobori, 69 **E2**

Hatchobori Sta, 69 **F2**

Hatillo, 122 **B2**

Hatogaya, 68 **C8**

Hatteras, NC 187 **G2**

Hatteras Inlet, NC 187 **G1**

Hatteras Isl, NC 187 **H3**

Hattiesburg, MS 113 **B3**, 120 **B2**, 129 **H4**

Hattingen, 34 **D7**

Haugesund, 14 **D2**, 22 **B8**

Hausen, 35 **A3**

Havana, 94 **B5**, 97 **G4**, 113 **D1**

Havasu Canyon, AZ 183 **B3**

Havasu Creek, AZ 183 **B3**

Havasupai IR, AZ 183 **C2**

Havasupai Pt, AZ 183 **D2**

Haverford, PA 144 **C4**

Haverhill, MA 115 **C3**, 138 **D8**

Havering, 26 **E7**

Havertown, PA 144 **C3**

Havre, MT 101 **D2**, 110 **D7**, 135 **G6**

Havre-St Pierre, 103 **D3**

Hawaii, 137, 178 **C1**

Hawaii, HI 137 **F2**

Hawaii, U of, HI 177 **H2**

Hawaii Volcanoes NP, HI 137 **F1**, 178 **D1**

Hawaii Volcanoes NP Visitor Ctr, HI 137 **F1**

Hawaiian Islands, 80 **D6**

Hawawa Hts, HI 177 **F3**

Hawthorne, CA 170 **B3**

Hawthorne, FL 123 **E5**

Hawthorne, NV 110 **B5**, 132 **D5**

Hawthorne Ammunition Depot, NV 132 **D5**

Hay R, 101 **D4**

Hayabusacho, 69 **B3**

Hayden Planetarium, MA 140 **B5**

Hayden Valley, WY 180 **B4**

Haydn Mus, 42 **E7**

Hayfork, CA 132 **A7**

Hays, KS 110 **F5**, 127 **D2**

Hays, MT 135 **H6**

Haystack Peak, CA 182 **B6**

Hayward, CA 132 **B5**, 175 **D4**

Hazard, KY 118 **B1**, 121 **E6**, 125 **F2**

Hazel Park, MI 156 **D8**

Hazelwood, MO 162 **B3**

Headingley, 107 **E5**

Heads, The, OR 134 **A2**

Healdsburg, CA 132 **A5**

Hearst, 103 **B2**

Heart Lake, WY 180 **C2**

Heathrow, FL 153 **G6**

Heathrow Arpt, UK 26 **B7**

Hebgen Lake, MT 180 **A4**

Hebrides, 14 **C2**

Hebron, Can 102 **D5**

Hebron, KY 151 **B1**

Hebron, TX 165 **F6**

Hedehusene, 36 **A5**

Hedingen, 37 **E1**

Hedwig Village, TX 166 **A4**

Heeresgeschichtliches, 42 **E7**

Hefei, 60 **C7**, 67 **B4**

Hegang, 66 **D7**

Heguri, 70 **E5**

Heidelberg, Austral 79 **D3**

Heidelberg, Ger 23 **C2**

Heidelberg West, 79 **C3**

Heilbronn, 23 **C2**

Heiligenhaus, 34 **C6**

Heimberg, 37 **C1**

Heineken Brewery, 30 **D5**

Heinersdorf, 32 **C5**

Heinz NWR, John, PA 144 **C1**

Heisingen, 34 **C7**

Hejaijiao, 74 **C5**

Hekelgem, 31 **E2**

Hekla, 14 **A5**

Helena, AR 120 **A5**

Helena, MT 110 **D7**, 135 **F5**

Helena NF, MT 135 **G5**

Heliopolis, 50 **D3**

Hellersdorf, 32 **F7**

Hellerup, 36 **C6**

Hells Canyon NRA, 130 **A8**, 134 **D4**

Helsingborg, 15 **E1**, 22 **D6**

Helsinki, 15 **G3**, 52 **B6**, 82 **F7**

Hemet, CA 133 **E2**

Hemiksem, 31 **F5**

Hempstead, NY 116 **B5**, 143 **H3**

Henderson, CO 167 **H5**

Henderson, KY 125 **D2**

Henderson, NV 111 **B4**, 133 **F4**

Henderson, NC 119 **F1**, 121 **G6**

Hendersonville, TN 125 **E1**

· Hendon, 26 **C8**

Hengyang, 60 **C6**, 67 **A3**

Henningsdorf, 32 **C8**

Henson Creek Park, MD 148 **E5**

Henzada, 59 **F4**

Hepingli, 73 **E3**

Hepingli Railway Sta, 73 **E4**

Heppner, OR 134 **C4**

Herat, 49 **H6**, 58 **A7**

Hercules, CA 174 **C7**

Hereford, TX 128 **C5**, 131 **F3**

Hereford, UK 19 **D3**

Herkimer, NY 117 **F3**

Herlev, 36 **B6**

Hermitage, The, 57 **F2**

Hermit's Rest, AZ 183 **D2**

Hermosa Beach, CA 170 **B3**

Hermosillo, 96 **B5**, 111 **C3**

Hernals, 42 **D7**

Herne, 31 **E1**, 34 **D8**

Héroes de Padierna, 98 **A1**

Herring Cove Beach, MA 184 **B3**

Herring Run Park, MD 147 **D3**

Herrliberg, 37 **F1**

Herten, 34 **D8**

Hesperia, CA 133 **E3**

Hetch Hetchy Reservoir, CA 182 **A5**

Heusenstamm, 35 **C2**

Hewlett, NY 143 **G2**

HHH Metro Dome, MN 161 **C3**

Hialeah, FL 155 **F2**

Hialeah Gdns, FL 155 **E2**

Hiawatha NF, MI 124 **E6**

Hibbing, MN 112 **A7**

Hibiya Park, 69 **C2**

Hibliya Public Hall, 69 **C2**

Hickory, NC 121 **F5**

Hickory Hills, IL 159 **C3**

Hicksville, NY 116 **B5**

Hidalgo del Parral, 96 **B5**, 128 **B1**

Hidden Falls, WY 181 **B3**

Hie Shrine, 69 **A2**

Hietzing, 42 **D7**

Higashi-Osaka, 70 **D5**

Higashikurume, 68 **B8**

Higashimurayama, 68 **A8**

Higashiyama-Ku, 71 **E3**

Higashiyamato, 68 **A7**

High Level, 101 **D4**

High Pt, FL 154 **B5**

High Pt, NC 121 **F6**

High Point SP, NJ 116 **A6**

High Springs, FL 123 **E5**

High Wycombe, 26 **A8**

Highgrove, CA 171 **H4**

Highland, CA 171 **H5**

Highland, IN 159 **F1**

Highland, NY 117 **G1**

Highland, PA 146 **B8**

Highland Hts, KY 151 **E1**

Highland Hts, OH 150 **F7**

Highland Park, CA 172 **F7**

Highland Park, IL 158 **C6**

Highland Park, MI 156 **D7**

Highland Park, PA 146 **D7**

Highland Park, TX 165 **G4**

Highland Village, TX 164 **D6**

Highlands, NC 121 **E5**

Highlands Ranch, CO 167 **G1**

Highpoint, OH 151 **E4**

Highwood, IL 158 **C6**

Highwoods, IN 157 **D5**

Hilden, 34 **C5**

Hill Air Force Range, UT 130 **B6**, 132 **F7**, 135 **F1**

Hillandale, MD 148 **D8**

Hillcrest Hts, MD 148 **E5**

Hillegon, 30 **B5**

Hillerod, 36 **A8**

Hillingdon, 26 **B7**

Hillsboro, OH 118 **B3**

Hillsboro, OR 134 **B4**, 177 **E5**

Hillsboro, TN 120 **D5**

Hillsboro, TX 129 **E4**

Hillsboro Beach, FL 155 **H6**

Hillsborough, CA 175 **B3**

Hillsborough, NH 115 **B3**

Hillsdale, NY 115 **A2**

Hillside, NJ 142 **B3**

Hilltop, MN 161 **C4**

Hilo, HI 137 **F2**, 178 **D1**

Hilshire Village, TX 166 **A4**

Hilton, NY 116 **C4**

Hilton Head Isl, SC 121 **F3**

Himalayas, 58 **D6**

Himberg, 42 **E6**

Hims, 48 **D6**

Hinakawa, 68 **E5**

Hindar, 64 **F8**

Hindu Amphitheater, AZ 183 **D2**

Hindu Kush, 58 **B7**

Hinesville, GA 121 **F3**

Hingham, MA 139 **F2**

Hino, 68 **A7**

Hinsdale, IL 159 **C3**

Hinterbrühl, 42 **D6**

Hinton, WV 118 **D2**

Hipodromo de las Ameri-cas, 98 **A3**

Hippodrome, 88 **D8**

Hippodrome de la Zaezuela, 39 **B4**

Hirakata, 70 **E6**

Hiroshima, 60 **E8**, 66 **E5**

Hirshhorn Mus, DC 149 **D2**

Hisabpur, 65 **F3**

Hispaniola, 95 **E4**

Historic Richmond Town, NY 142 **B1**

Historical Library, 57 **G5**

Historical Mus, MI 156 **D6**

Ho Chi Minh, 61 **B3**

Ho Chung, 75 **E4**

Ho Man Tin, 75 **D3**

Hobart, Austral 77 **E1**

Hobart, IN 159 **F1**

Hobbs, NM 128 **C4**, 131 **F2**

Hobby Arpt, William P TX 166 **C2**

Hoboken, Bel 31 **G5**

Hoboken, NJ 141 **E4**, 142 **C4**

Hobsons Bay, 79 **B2**

Hochst, 35 **A3**

Hodgdon Pond, ME 186 **A4**

Hodogaya-Ku, 68 **B6**

Hoeilaart, 31 **G1**

Hof, 23 **D3**

Hofburg, 42 **E7**

Hoffman Estates, IL 158 **A5**

Hofgarten, 34 **B5**

Hofstade, 31 **G3**

Hohen Neuendor, 32 **C8**

Hohenlimburg, 34 **F6**

Hohhot, 55 **D1**, 60 **B8**, 66 **A5**

Hokkaido, 66 **F7**

Holbrook, AZ 131 **C3**

Holbrook, MA 139 **E2**

Holbrook, NY 116 **C5**

Holburn, 27 **D3**

Holcomb Botanical Gdns, IN 157 **E3**

Holdrege, NE 127 **D3**

Holesovice, 35 **E3**

Holguín, 94 **D4**

Holliday Park, IN 157 **E3**

Holliday Park, William P, MI 156 **A6**

Hollidaysburg, PA 119 **E4**

Hollister, CA 133 **B4**

Hollow Ground Swamp, NC 187 **E5**

Holly Springs NF, MS 120 **B5**

Hollywood, CA 172 **B8**

Hollywood, FL 123 **G2**, 155 **G3**

Hollywood Bowl, CA 172 **B8**

Holman, 100 **E6**

Holmes Beach, FL 154 **B1**

Holon, 50 **A6**

Holroyd, 78 **C7**

Holstebro, 22 **C6**

Holte, 36 **B7**

Holton SP, Frank, IL 162 **D1**

Holyhead, 19 **C3**

Holyoke, MA 115 **A2**

Homberg, 34 **A7**

Hombruch, 34 **F7**

Home Gdns, CA 171 **G3**

Home Place, IN 157 **E4**

Homecroft, IN 157 **F1**

Homer, NY 117 **E3**

Homerville, GA 123 **E6**

Homestead, FL 123 **F1**

Homestead, PA 146 **D6**

Homestead Canal, FL 188 **D4**

Homestead NM of America, NE 179 **E4**

Homewood, IL 159 **D1**

Homochitto NF, MS 120 **A3**

Homvel, 52 **A5**

Hondo, TX 128 **D2**

Honduras, 81 **H5**, 84 **A6**, 94 **A2**, 97 **F2**

Hønefoss, 22 **D8**

Honesdale, PA 117 **F1**, 119 **G6**

Honeymoon Island SRA, FL 154 **A6**

Hong Kong, 60 **C5**, 75

Hongkou Park and Stad, 74 **E8**

Hongmiao, 73 **F2**

Hongqiao Arpt, 74 **A5**

Honiara, 80 **B4**

Honolulu, HI 81 **E5**, 137 **C3**, 177 **G1**, 178 **C1**

Honolulu Intl Arpt, HI 177 **F2**

Honolulu Obs, HI 177 **E2**

Honolulu Stad, HI 177 **H1**

Honouliuli, HI 177 **E3**

Hönow, 32 **E7**

Honshu, 60 **F8**, 66 **F5**

Hood R, OR 134 **C4**

Hoofddorp, 30 **C5**

Hooghly-Chinsura, 65 **E4**

Hoogvliet, 30 **A2**

Hoomaluhia Botanical Gdns, HI 177 **H3**

Hoopa Valley IR, CA 134 **A1**

Hoosick Falls, NY 117 **H3**

Hoosier Dome, IN 157 **G2**

Hoosier NF, IL 125 **E2**

Hooven, OH 151 **A2**

Hoover Wilderness, CA 182 **C6**

Hope, AR 129 **G5**

Hopewell, VA 119 **F2**

Hopi IR, AZ 131 **C3**

Hopkins, MN 161 **A2**

Hopkinsville, KY 125 **E1**

Horlivka, 53 **B4**

Hormigueros, 122 **B2**

Hornell, NY 116 **C2**

Horní Pocernice, 35 **F3**

Horomerice, 35 **E3**

Horse Ridge, CA 182 **B2**

Horseheads, NY 116 **D2**

Horseshoe Bend NMP, AL 179 **F2**

Horseshoe Lake SP, IL 162 **D2**

Horsholm, 36 **C8**

Horsley Park, 78 **A7**

Horta, 38 **E6**

Hortaleza, 39 **D4**

Hostivar, 35 **F3**

Hot Springs, AR 113 **B4**, 129 **F5**

Hot Springs, SD 126 **B5**, 130 **F7**

Hot Springs NP, AR 179 **E2**

Hotan, 58 **D7**

Hôtel de Ville, 29 **E2**

Hougang, 63 **G2**

Houghs Neck, MA 139 **E2**

Houghton, MI 112 **B7**, 124 **D7**

Houlton, ME 112 **F7**, 114 **E7**

Houma, LA 120 **A1**, 129 **H3**

Houmont Park, TX 166 **D5**

Hounslow, 26 **B7**

House of Seven Gables, MA 138 **F5**

House Rock Buffalo Ranch, AZ 183 **E3**

Houses of Parliament, 27 **C1**

Houston, TX 96 **D5**, 113 **A2**, 129 **F3**, 166 **C4**, 179 **E1**

Houston, U of, TX 166 **C3**

Houston Intl Arpt, TX 166 **C6**

Houston Lake, MO 162 **B6**

Hove, 31 **G5**

Howard Beach, NY 143 **E2**

Howell Park, Elisa, MI 156 **B7**

Howland Isl, 80 **D4**

Howrah, 65 **E2**

Howrah Bridge, 65 **E2**

Hoxton Park, 78 **A6**

Hoya, 68 **B7**

Hradec Králové, 23 **F3**

Hronda, 15 **G1**

Hsichih, 62 **D5**

Hsinchuang, 62 **B5**

Hsintien, 62 **C4**

Huai Khwang, 63 **G6**

Huainan, 67 **B4**

Hualapai Hilltop, AZ 183 **B2**

Hualapai IR, AZ 131 **B3**, 183 **A1**

Huambo, 47 **E4**

Huancayo, 84 **C2**

Huang R, 60 **A7**, 66 **B5**

Huanggenglang, 74 **B5**

Huangshi, 67 **B3**

Huánuco, 84 **C2**

Hubli, 59 **B4**

Huddinge, 36 **E6**

Hudson, NY 117 **H2**, 119 **H6**

Hudson Bay, 103 **A4**

Hudson Falls, NY 117 **H4**

Hudson R, 117 **G4**, 142 **D3**

Hudson Str, 102 **C5**

Hue, 61 **B4**

Huechuraba, 87 **G3**

Huejotitán, 99 **E2**

Huelva, 16 **A2**, 21 **A2**

Huentitán Alto, 99 **G5**

Huentitán Bajo, 99 **G6**

Huesca, 21 **D4**

Hugli-Chunchura, 65 **E4**

Hugo, OK 129 **F5**

Hujialou, 73 **F2**

Huldenberg, 31 **H1**

Hull, Can 103 **C2**

Hull, MA 139 **F3**

Hulls Cove, ME 186 **C6**

Hulls Cove Visitor Ctr, ME 186 **C6**

Hulst, 31 **E6**

Hulun Nur, 66 **B2**

Humacao, 122 **C2**

Humble, TX 166 **C6**

Humboldt NF, NV 132 **E7**, 134 **D1**

Humboldt R, 132 **D7**

Humbolt U, 33 **E3**

Húmera, 39 **A3**

Humphreys Pk, AZ 131 **B3**

Hunewill Peak, CA 182 **C6**

Hung Hom, 75 **D3**

Hung Hom Railway Sta, 75 **D2**

Hungary, 17 **F5**, 23 **F1**, 24 **D6**, 45 **E6**

Hunghnam, 60 **D8**

Hungnam, 55 **F2**, 66 **D5**

Hunjiang, 66 **C6**

Hunter, VA 148 **A7**

Hunters Creek Village, TX 166 **A4**

Hunters Hill, 78 **E7**

Hunters Valley, VA 148 **A7**

Huntingdon, PA 119 **F5**

Huntingdon Valley, PA 145 **F6**

Huntington, VA 148 **C5**

Huntington, WV 112 **D5**, 118 **C3**

Huntington Beach, CA 170 **D2**

Huntington Park, CA 170 **C4**

Huntington Res, OH 150 **B7**

Huntington Sta, NY 116 **B6**

Huntington Woods, MI 156 **C8**

Hunts Point, WA 176 **C5**

Huntsville, AL 113 **C4**, 120 **C5**

Huntsville, TN 118 **A1**

Huntsville, TX 129 **F3**

Hurley, NY 117 **G1**

Hurlingham, 88 **C7**

Huron, SD 126 **E5**

Huron NF, MI 124 **F5**

Hurst, TX 164 **C4**
Hurstville, 78 **D6**
Husinec, 35 **E4**
Hutchins, TX 165 **G2**
Hutchinson, KS 111 **F4**, 127 **E2**
Hutchinson, MN 126 **F6**
Huttenheim, 34 **B6**
Huttonville, 104 **A6**
Huvosvoigy, 42 **A7**
Hvidovre, 36 **B5**
Hwajon, 72 **C7**
Hyannis, MA 115 **D2**, 184 **D5**
Hyannis Port, MA 185 **D4**
Hyattsville, MD 148 **E7**
Hyde Park, MA 139 **C3**
Hyde Park, NY 117 **G1**
Hyde Park, UK 27 **A2**
Hyderabad, 58 **B6**, 59 **C4**
Hyland-Bush-Anderson Lakes RPR, MN 161 **B1**
Hysham, MT 135 **H4**

I

I-n-Amenas, 44 **D4**
I-n-Salah, 44 **C4**
Iahaina, HI 137 **D3**
Iao Valley SP, HI 137 **D3**
Iasi, 17 **H5**
Ibadan, 44 **C1**
Ibagué, 84 **C5**
Ibaraki, 70 **D6**
Iberian Mts, 21 **C4**
Iberian Pen, 16 **B3**
Ibiza, 16 **C3**, 21 **E2**
Ibri, 49 **H3**
Ica, 84 **C2**
Ice Stad, 37 **B2**
Iceland, 14 **A5**, 82 **F6**
Ichibancho, 69 **A4**
Ichigaya Sta, 69 **A4**
Ichihara, 68 **E6**
Ichikawa, 68 **C7**
Ichinomiya, 68 **F5**
Idabel, OK 129 **F5**

Idaho, 101 **C1**, 110 **C7**, 130 **A7**, 135 **F2**, 178 **B5**
Idaho City, ID 130 **A7**, 135 **E3**
Idaho Falls, ID 110 **C6**, 130 **B7**, 135 **F2**, 178 **B5**
Idaho Natl Engineering Lab, ID 130 **B7**
Idar-Oberstein, 23 **C3**
Ide, 70 **F6**
Idemitsu Art Mus, 69 **D2**
Idledale, CO 167 **E2**
Idlewild, KY 151 **A1**
Igarka, 54 **A5**
Iglesias, 24 **A2**
Ignacio, CA 174 **A7**
Igreja Dos Enforcadas, 93 **G2**
Igreja NS Achiropita, 93 **E1**
Iguaçua, 91 **B4**
Iguala, 96 **D3**
Ihsaniye, 43 **D4**
Iiortaleza, 39 **D4**
Ijmuiden, 30 **B6**
Ikeda, 70 **C6**
Ikoma, 70 **E5**
Ilebo, 47 **E6**
Ile-Perrot, 106 **A1**
Ilerin, 44 **C1**
Îles-de-Boucherville Prov P, 106 **A4**
Ilford, 26 **D7**
Ilha, 91 **A1**
Ilhéus, 85 **H2**
Iliamna Lake, AK 136 **C6**
Ililoueete Creek, CA 182 **C2**
I'linskoye, 56 **A4**
Ilion, NY 117 **F3**
Ilioúpolis, 43 **C2**
Illahee SP, WA 176 **A5**
Illinois, 112 **B5**, 125 **D4**, 179 **F4**
Illinois Beach SP, IL 158 **C8**
Illinois Ctr, IL 160 **D6**
Illinois Institute of Technology, IL 159 **E3**

Illinois R, IL 125 **C3**
Iloilo, 61 **E4**
Ilsan, 72 **B8**
Imax, 30 **B2**
Imba, 68 **F8**
Imbabah, 50 **C2**
Imbariê, 91 **D4**
Imola, 24 **B5**
Imperatriz, 85 **G3**
Imperial Beach, CA 169 **F1**
Imperial Palace, 68 **C7**, 69 **B3**
Imperial Palace East Gdn, 69 **C3**
Imperial Palace Mus & Forbidden City, 73 **E2**
Imperial Palace Outer Gdn, 69 **C3**
Imperial Theater, 69 **D2**
Imperial War Mus, 27 **D1**
Imphal, 58 **F5**
Imuris, 131 **C1**
Imus, 62 **B1**
Inagawa, 70 **B7**
Inagi, 68 **A7**
Inárcs, 42 **C5**
Inari, 71 **E2**
Inchon, 55 **F1**, 72 **A6**
Incline Village, NV 132 **C6**
Independence, CA 133 **D4**
Independence, KS 125 **A2**
Independence, MO 125 **B3**, 162 **D5**
Independence, OH 150 **D5**
Independence, VA 118 **D1**
Independence NHP, PA 145 **E2**, 179 **H4**
Independencia, 87 **F6**
India, 58 **C5**
Indian Hills, CO 167 **E2**
Indian Key, FL 188 **E3**
Indian Lake, NY 117 **G4**
Indian Mounds Park, MN 161 **E2**
Indian Ocean, 59 **C2**
Indian Pt, ME 186 **A5**

Indian Rocks Beach, FL 154 **A4**
Indian Shores, FL 123 **E3**
Indiana, 112 **C5**, 125 **E3**, 179 **F4**
Indiana, PA 119 **E5**
Indiana Conv Ctr & Hoosier Dome, IN 157 **E2**
Indiana Dunes NL, IN 159 **F2**, 179 **F4**
Indianapolis, IN 112 **C5**, 125 **E3**, 157 **D2**, 179 **F4**
Indianapolis, U of, IN 157 **E1**
Indianapolis Intl Arpt, IN 157 **D1**
Indianapolis Speedway, IN 157 **D2**
Indianola, PA 146 **D8**
Indianola, WA 176 **A6**
Indianópolis, 92 **B4**
Indiantown, FL 123 **F3**
Indigirka R, 54 **D6**
Indio, CA 133 **E2**
Indira Gandhi Intl. Arpt, 64 **D6**
Indonesia, 59 **F2**, 61 **D1**, 76 **A6**, 80 **A4**
Indonesia, U of, 64 **B7**
Indore, 58 **C5**
Indus R, 58 **B6**
Industrial Exh Hall, 74 **D6**
Ingleburn, 78 **A5**
Inglewood, CA 133 **D3**, 170 **B4**
Inglewood, WA 176 **D5**
Ingolstadt, 23 **D2**
Ingraham Pt, ME 186 **D3**
Inhambane, 47 **G3**
Inhaúma, 91 **C3**
Inkster, MI 156 **B6**
Inner Harbor, MD 147 **D2**
Innisbrook, FL 154 **B6**
Innoko NWR, AK 136 **C7**
Innsbruck, 17 **E5**, 23 **D1**, 24 **B6**
Inoã, 91 **F2**

Inspiration Pt, WY 181 F3
Inta, 52 E5
Intercession City, FL 153 F1
International Conference Ctr, 70 A5
International Court of Justice (World Court), 30 A3
International Expo Ctr, OH 150 B6
International Falls, MN 112 A7, 124 B7
International Swimming Hall of Fame, FL 155 G4
International Trade Fair Exh Hall, 70 C5
Intracoastal Waterway, FL 188 D2
Inukjuak, 103 B4
Inuvik, 82 B5, 100 C6, 136 E8
Invalides, Hôtel des, 29 C2
Invercargill, 77 G1
Inverness, FL 121 E1, 123 E4
Inverness, IL 158 A5
Inverness, UK 14 C2, 18 D6
Inwood, NY 143 G2
Inyo NF, CA 132 D5, 182 D5
Inzai, 68 E8
Ioánnina, 17 G3, 25 E4
Ione, CA 132 B5
Ionian Islands, 25 E3
Ionian Sea, 17 G2, 25 E2
Iowa, 103 A1, 112 A5, 124 B4, 179 E4
Iowa City, IA 125 C4
Ipanema, 91 D1
Ipiíba, 91 F2
Ipiranga, 92 B4
Ipiranga Mus, 92 B4
Ipoh, 61 A2
Ipswich, MA 138 F7
Ipswich, UK 19 F3, 20 D8

Iqaluit, 102 C5
Iquique, 84 D1
Iquitos, 84 C3
Iráklion, 17 H2, 25 G1, 48 B6
Iran, 45 H5, 49 G5, 58 A7
Iranshahr, 49 H4
Irapuato, 96 C3
Iraq, 45 G4, 49 E5
Irbil, 49 E6
Ireland, 14 B1, 19 B4, 20 A8
Irifune, 69 F2
Iringa, 47 G5
Irish Sea, 19 C4, 20 B8
Irkutsk, 55 B3
Iron Mt, MI 124 D6
Irondequoit, NY 116 D3
Ironton, OH 118 C3
Iroquois Falls, 103 B2
Iroquois NWR, NY 116 C3
Iroquois Pt, HI 177 F2
Irrawaddy R, 58 F5
Iruma, 68 A8
Irvine, CA 171 E1
Irving, TX 129 E4, 165 E4
Irvington, NJ 142 A3
Isabela, 122 B2
Ísafjördhur, 14 A5
Ishim, 53 E3
Ishøj, 36 B5
Isidro Casanova, 88 C6
Isiro, 45 F1
Isis Temple, AZ 183 E2
Isla de Culebra, 122 D2
Isla de Pascua, 81 G3
Isla de Vieques, 122 D1
Islamabad, 58 C7
Islamorada, FL 123 F1, 188 B3
Island Lake, IL 158 A7
Island Park, ID 135 G3
Island Pond, VT 114 B5
Islay, 18 C5
Isle au Haut, ME 115 E4
Isle of Wight, 20 C7
Isle of Youth, 94 A5

Isle Royale NP, MI 124 D7, 179 F6
Islesford, ME 186 C2
Isleta IR, NM 128 A5
Islington, MA 139 C2
Islington, UK 27 D4
Israel, 45 F4, 48 D5
Issaquah, WA 176 D4
Istana, 63 F1
Istanbul, 17 H4, 25 H5, 43 D2, 45 E6
Isthmus of Kra, 61 A3
Isthmus of Panama, 97 H1
Isthmus of Tehuantepec, 97 E3
Itabuna, 85 H2
Itaipu, 91 E1
Ital Park, 89 C4
Italy, 17 E3, 20 F5, 23 D1, 24 C4, 44 D6
Itambi, 91 F4
Itami, 70 C6
Itaquaquecetuba, 92 D5
Itaquera, 92 C4
Itasca, IL 159 B4
Ithaca, NY 112 E6, 117 E2
Ittingen, 37 B2
Iturup, 66 F7
Itzehoe, 22 C5
Iupeba, 92 D3
Ivalo, 15 F5
Ivanhoe, 79 D3
Ivanovo, 52 C5
Ivanteyevka, 56 D6
Ivry-sur-Seine, 28 D7
Iwaki, 66 F5
Ixtlahuacán de los Membrillos, 99 H2
Izembek NWR, AK 136 A5
Izhevsk, 53 C4
Izmaylovo, 56 C4
Izmir, 17 H3, 25 G3, 45 F5, 48 C6
Iztacalco, 98 C3
Iztapalapa, 98 C2

J

Jabal Tuwayq, 49 E3
Jabalpur, 58 C5
Jabaquara, 92 B4
Jabavu, 51 E2
Jacarepaguá, 91 C2
Jacinto City, TX 166 D3
Jack Murphy Stad, CA 169 F4
Jackman, ME 114 C6
Jackson, AL 120 B3
Jackson, CA 132 C5
Jackson, KY 118 B2
Jackson, MI 118 A6, 125 F4
Jackson, MS 97 E6, 113 B3, 120 A3, 129 H4, 179 F2
Jackson, OH 118 C3
Jackson, TN 113 B4, 120 B5, 125 D1, 129 H6
Jackson, WY 110 D6, 130 C7, 135 G2, 181 F1
Jackson Heights, NY 143 E4
Jackson Hole, WY 181 F2
Jackson Hole Arpt, WY 181 F2
Jackson Lake, WY 180 A1, 181 G5
Jackson Lake Lodge, WY 181 G4
Jackson Natl Fish Hatchery, WY 181 F1
Jackson Park, IL 159 E3
Jackson Park, WI 157 B2
Jacksonville, AR 129 G5
Jacksonville, FL 113 D3, 121 F2, 123 E6, 179 G2
Jacksonville, NC 121 H5
Jacksonville Beach, FL 121 F2, 123 F6
Jacob Javits Conv Ctr, NY 141 F4
Jacobs Field, OH 150 D7
Jadabpur, 65 F1
Jade Buddha Temple, 74 C7
Jaffna, 59 C3

Jagatpur, 64 E8
Jaipur, 58 C6
Jakarta, 61 B1, 64 B7
Jakobsberg, 36 D7
Jalan Kayu, 63 G3
Jalazun, 50 D5
Jamaica, NY 143 F3
Jamaica, WI 94 C3, 97 H3
Jamaica Bay WR, NY 143 E2
Jamaliya, 50 C2
Jambi, 61 B2
James Bay, 103 B3
James R, SD 126 E6
Jamestown, NY 112 D6, 116 B2, 119 E6
Jamestown, ND 110 F7, 126 D7
Jammu, 58 C6
Jampur, 65 D4
Jamshedpur, 58 D5
Jamul, CA 169 H3
Janai, 65 E3
Janalli, 78 D5
Janesville, WI 125 C4
Janos, 128 A3, 131 D1
Japan, 60 E8, 66 E5, 80 A6
Jaraguá, 92 A5
Jardim Da Luz, 93 G6
Jardim Paulista, 92 B4
Jardim Vera Cruz, 92 C4
Jardim Zoo, 38 B7
Jardin des Plantes, 29 F1
Jardin des Tuileries, 29 D2
Jardin du Carroussel, 29 D2
Jardine, MT 180 B6
Jardines de Morelos, 98 D5
Jarfalla, 36 D7
Jarvis Isl, 80 D4
Jask, 49 H4
Jasper, AL 120 C4
Jasper, TX 129 G3
Jataí, 85 F1
Java, 61 C1
Java Sea, 61 C1
Jayapura, 76 B2, 80 A4

Jayuya, 122 B2
Jean Lesage Intl Arpt, 105 D3
Jedediah, WY 181 E5
Jefferson, LA 163 F5
Jefferson, WI 124 D5
Jefferson City, MO 112 B5, 125 B2
Jefferson Mem, Thomas, DC 149 C1
Jefferson Natl Expansion Mem, MO 162 C2
Jefferson NF, VA 118 B1, 121 E6
Jefferson Square, CA 173 C1
Jeffersonville, VT 114 A5
Jegenstorf, 37 C3
Jejur, 65 D4
Jelenia Gora, 23 F3
Jena, 23 D3
Jenec, 35 D3
Jenkintown, PA 145 E5
Jennings, MO 162 B3
Jenny Lake, WY 181 F3
Jenny Lake Lodge, WY 181 F3
Jerada, 21 D1
Jeremy Pt, MA 184 E6
Jericho, 48 D5
Jerome, ID 130 A7, 132 F8, 135 E2
Jersey, 19 D1
Jersey City, NJ 119 H5, 142 C3
Jersey Village, TX 166 A5
Jerseyville, IL 125 C3
Jerusalem, 45 G4, 48 D5, 50 D4
Jerusalem Arpt, 50 D5
Jesenice, 35 F2
Jestetten, 37 E4
Jesup, GA 121 E3
Jesus María, 87 F5
Jiading County, 74 B7
Jiamusi, 66 C7
Jian, 67 A3
Jiangjiaqiao, 74 E7

Jiaozuo, 67 A4
Jicarilla Apache IR, 128 B6, 131 D4
Jiddah, 45 G3, E2
Jihlava, 23 E3
Jinsha R, 58 F6
Jijel, 21 F2
Jilin, 55 F2, 66 C6
Jílové u Prahy, 35 F1
Jílovíštié, 35 E1
Jim Thompson's House, 63 G5
Jim Thorpe, PA 119 G5
Jima, 45 G1
Jinan, 55 E1, 60 C7, 66 B5
Jingan District, 74 C6
Jinganzhuang, 73 E3
Jingdezhen, 60 C6, 67 B3
Jingshan Park, 73 E3
Jining, 67 B4
Jinja, 47 G6
Jinocany, 35 D2
Jinzhou, 55 E2, 60 C8, 66 B6
Jixi, 55 F3, 66 D7
João Pessoa, 85 H3
Jocotepec, 99 F1
Jodhpur, 58 B6
Joe Robbie Stad, FL 155 G3
Joensuu, 15 G4
Johannesburg, 47 F3, 51 F3
Johannesburg Arpt, 51 H3
Johannesburg Zoological Gdn, 51 F3
Johns Hopkins U, MD 147 D3
Johnson, VT 114 A5
Johnson City, NY 117 E2
Johnson City, OR 177 G4
Johnson City, TN 113 D4, 121 E6
Johnson Mem, Lyndon B, DC 149 A1
Johnston Key, FL 188 A2
Johnstown, NY 117 G3
Johnstown, PA 119 E4
Joinville, 86 C6

Joka, 65 E1, 125 D4
Joliet, IL 112 B5, 125 D4, 159 A1
Jones Beach SP, NY 143 H1
Jonesboro, AR 113 B4, 120 A6, 125 C1, 129 H6
Jönköping, 15 E2, 22 E7
Joplin, MO 113 A4, 125 A2, 129 F6
Jordan, 45 G4, 48 D5
Jordan Pond, ME 186 C4
Jordan Valley, OR 134 D2
Jordbro, 36 E5
Jorge Chávez Intl Arpt, 87 F5
Joshua Tree NP, CA 133 F3, 178 B3
José C Paz, 88 B8
Joyo, 70 F7
Joyous Pavilion Park, 73 D1
Juan Fernández Islands, 81 H2
Juana Díaz, 122 B1
Juanacatlán, 99 H3
Juàzeiro do Norte, 85 G3
Juba, 45 F1
Júcar, 21 C3
Juhu Beach, 65 A2
Juiz de Fora, 85 G1
Juliaca, 84 C2
Jumpup Canyon, AZ 183 C4
Jumpup Pt, AZ 183 C4
Junction City, KS 127 E3
Junction City, OR 134 B3
Juneau, AK 82 A5, 101 B4, 136 E6 178 B1
Juneau Park, WI 157 C3
Junín, 86 B5
Jupiter, FL 123 G3
Jurong East, 63 E2
Juruá R, 84 D3
Justice, IL 159 C3
Jutland, 15 E2, 22 C6
Jyväskylä, 15 F4

K

K Wilhelm Gedachtnis-
kirche, 33 **B2**
K2 Mt, 58 **C7**
Ka Lae, HI 137 **E1**
Kaarst, 34 **A5**
Kabinda, 47 **F5**
Kabukiza Theater, 69 **E1**
Kabul, 58 **B7**
Kabwe, 47 **F4**
Kadirkoy, 43 **E2**
Kadoma, 70 **D6**
Kaena Pt, HI 137 **B3**
Kaesong, 66 **C5**
Kafr Hakim, 50 **A2**
Kagiso, 51 **E3**
Kagithane, 43 **E3**
Kagoshima, 60 **E7**, 67 **D4**
Kagran, 42 **E8**
Kahnawake, 106 **B1**
Kahoolawe, HI 137 **D2**
Kahuku Pt, HI 137 **C4**
Kahului, HI 137 **D3**
Kai Tak Arpt, 75 **D3**
Kaibab NF, AZ 183 **D4**
Kaibab Plateau, AZ 183 **D4**
Kaifeng, 67 **A4**
Kailu, HI 137 **C3**
Kailua-Kona, HI 137 **E2**
Kaisarianí Monasterý,
43 **C2**
Kaiser dom Cathedral,
35 **B3**
Kaiserebersdorf, 42 **E7**
Kaiserstuhl, 37 **E3**
Kaiwi Channel, HI 137 **C3**
Kaktovik, AK 136 **D8**
Kalahari Desert, 47 **E3**
Kalámai, 17 **G2**, 25 **E2**
Kalamakion, 43 **B2**
Kalamazoo, MI 112 **C6**,
118 **A6**, 125 **E4**
Kalaupapa NHP, HI 137 **D3**
Kalemie, 47 **F5**

Kalgoorlie, 76 **B3**
Kaliningrad, 15 **F1**, 52 **A6**,
56 **D6**
Kalispell, MT 110 **C7**,
135 **F6**
Kallhall, 36 **D7**
Kallithea, 43 **B2**
Kallnach, 37 **A3**
Kalmar, 15 **F2**, 22 **E6**
Kalundborg, 22 **D6**
Kalwa, 65 **C3**
Kam Shan CP, 75 **B4**
Kama R, 53 **D4**
Kamagaya, 68 **D8**
Kamakura, 68 **B5**
Kaman, 65 **B4**
Kamarhati, 65 **F2**
Kamat Gan, 50 **B6**
Kamaterón, 43 **B3**
Kamchatka Pen, 54 **B7**,
82 **A8**
Kamenice, 35 **F1**
Kameoka, 70 **D8**
Kamiak Mt, WA 135 **D5**
Kamigyo-Ku, 71 **E3**
Kamina, 47 **F5**
Kamloops, 101 **C2**
Kampala, 47 **F6**
Kampong Cham, 61 **B4**
Kampong Saom, 61 **A3**
Kanab Canyon, AZ 183 **C3**
Kanab Creek, AZ 183 **C4**
Kanab Creek Wilderness,
AZ 183 **C4**
Kanab Plateau, AZ 183 **B4**
Kananga, 47 **E5**
Kanazawa, 66 **E5**
Kanazawa-Ku, 68 **B5**
Kanchrapara, 65 **F4**
Kanda-Nishikicho, 69 **D4**
Kandy, 59 **C3**
Kaneohe, HI 137 **C3**,
177 **H3**
Kaneohe FP, HI 177 **H3**
Kangaroo Isl, 76 **D2**
Kangdong, 72 **E7**
Kangnam, 72 **D6**

Kangso, 72 **C7**
Kanheri Caves, 65 **B3**
Kankan, 44 **B2**
Kannapolis, NC 121 **F5**
Kano, 44 **D2**
Kanpur, 58 **C5**
Kansaripara, 65 **D4**
Kansas, 110 **F5**, 127 **E2**,
178 **D3**
Kansas City, KS 112 **A5**,
125 **A3**, 127 **F3**, 162 **B6**
Kansas City, MO 112 **A5**,
125 **A3**, 162 **C5**, 179 **E3**
Kansas City Downtown
Arpt, MO 162 **B6**
Kansas City Mus, MO 162 **C5**
Kansas City Zoo, MO 162 **C4**
Kansk, 55 **B3**
Kanuti NWR, AK 136 **C5**
Kaohsiung, 60 **D6**, 67 **B2**
Kaolack, 44 **A2**
Kapaa, HI 137 **B4**
Kapenhout, 31 **H3**
Kaposvar, 24 **D6**
Kapuskasing, 103 **B2**,
124 **F8**
Kara Kum, 53 **C1**
Kara Sea, 52 **E6**, 82 **D8**
Karachi, 58 **A6**
Karamay, 53 **F2**, 58 **D8**
Karawang Pt, 64 **C8**
Karbala, 49 **E5**
Karkuk, 49 **E6**, 53 **A1**
Karlebo, 36 **B8**
Karlovac, 23 **F1**, 24 **D5**
Karlshamn, 22 **E6**
Karlskrona, 22 **F6**
Karlslunde, 36 **A5**
Karlslunde Strand, 36 **A5**
Karlsruhe, 20 **F7**, 23 **C2**
Karlstad, 15 **E2**, 22 **E8**
Kartal, 43 **F1**
Kasai R, 47 **E5**
Kashan, 49 **F5**
Kashi, 53 **E1**, 58 **C7**
Kashiwa, 68 **D8**
Kasinathpur, 65 **F2**

Kassala, 45 **G2**, 48 **D1**
Kassel, 17 **E6**, 23 **C3**
Kastoría, 25 **E4**
Kastrup, 36 **C5**
Kasumigaseki, 69 **B2**
Katama, MA 185 **B2**
Katanga Plateau, 47 **F5**
Katano, 70 **E6**
Kateríni, 25 **F4**
Katherine, 76 **C6**
Kathmandu, 58 **D6**
Katlehong, 51 **G1**
Katmai NP & Pres, AK
136 **C6** , 178 **A1**
Katowice, 17 **F6**
Katsina, 44 **D2**
Katsura, 71 **D2**
Kattegat, 15 **E2**, 22 **D7**
Katwijk aan Zee, 30 **B4**
Kauai, HI 137 **B4**
Kauai Chan, HI 137 **B4**
Kaulakahi Chan, HI
137 **A4**
Kauna Pt, HI 137 **E1**
Kaunas, 15 **G1**, 52 **A5**
Kaválä, 17 **H3**, 25 **G4**
Kawaguchi, 68 **C8**
Kawaiahao Church, HI
177 **G2**
Kawaihoa Pt, HI 137 **A3**
Kawanishi, 70 **C6**
Kawasaki, 66 **F5**, 68 **C6**
Kayenta, AZ 131 **C4**
Kayes, 44 **B2**
Kayseri, 48 **D6**
Kazakhstan, 45 **H6**, 58 **C8**
Kazan, 53 **C4**
Kazan Cathedral, 57 **G2**
Kazanluk, 25 **G5**
Kbely, 35 **F3**
Keahole Pt, HI 137 **E2**
Keaiwa Heiau SRA, HI
177 **G3**
Kearney, NE 110 **F5**, 127 **D3**
Kearny, NJ 142 **B4**
Kecskemet, 17 **F5**
Kedawung, 64 **C8**

Keene, NH 115 **B3**

Keerbergen, 31 **H4**

Keetmanshoop, 47 **E3**

Keflavík, 14 **A5**

Keilor, 79 **A4**

Keilor East, 79 **A3**

Kelafo, 45 **H1**

Kelang, 61 **A2**

Kelenfold, 42 **A6**

Keller, TX 164 **C5**

Kelleys Isl, OH 118 **C6**

Kelly, WY 181 **G2**

Kelly AFB, TX 163 **F2**

Kelly Park, Dr Howard A
FL 153 **F6**

Kelowna, 101 **C2**

Kelso, OR 177 **H4**

Kelso, WA 134 **B4**

Kelsterbach, 35 **A2**

Kemerburgaz, 43 **D3**

Kemi, 15 **F5**

Kemmerer, WY 130 **C6**,
135 **G1**

Kempten, 23 **D2**, 24 **B6**

Kempton Park, 51 **H3**

Ken Caryl Ranch, CO
167 **F1**

Kenai, AK 100 **A6**,
136 **C6**

Kenai Fjords NP, AK
136 **C6**, 178 **B1**

Kenburma, MA 139 **F2**

Kendal, 19 **D4**

Kendall, FL 155 **F1**

Kendari, 61 **E2**

Keng Hau, 75 **C4**

Kennebeck R, ME 114 **D6**

Kennebunk, ME 115 **C4**

Kennedy Ctr For the Per-
forming Arts, DC 149 **A3**

Kennedy Intl Arpt, NY
143 **F2**

Kennedy Library & Mus, MA
139 **D3**

Kennedy NHS, MA 139 **C3**

Kennedy Space Ctr, FL
121 **F1**, 123 **F4**

Kennedy Stad, Robert F, DC
148 **E6**

Kenner, LA 163 **E6**

Kennesaw, GA 120 **D4**

Kenneth City, FL 154 **B4**

Kennett, MO 120 **B6**,
125 **C1**

Kennewick, WA 110 **B7**

Kenora, 103 **A2**, 124 **B8**,
126 **F8**

Kenosha, WI 125 **D4**

Kensington, CA 174 **C6**

Kensington, MD 148 **D8**

Kensington, PA 145 **E3**

Kensington, 26 **C7**

Kent, WA 176 **C3**

Kentfield, CA 174 **A6**

Kentland, MD 148 **F7**

Kenton, OH 118 **B5**

Kentucky, 113 **C4**, 118 **B2**,
179 **F3**

Kentucky R, KY 118 **B2**

Kenwood, MD 147 **E3**

Kenwood, OH 151 **E3**

Kenya, 45 **G1**, 47 **G6**

Keokuk, IA 125 **C3**

Keratsinion, 43 **A2**

Kerby, OR 132 **A8**

Kerepestarcsa, 42 **C6**

Kérkira, 25 **E4**

Kermadec Isl, 80 **D2**

Kerman, 49 **G5**

Kermit, TX 128 **C4**

Kern Park, WI 157 **C3**

Kernville, CA 133 **D4**

Kerr Reservoir, John H, VA
121 **G6**

Kerrville, TX 128 **D3**

Kerzers, 37 **A2**

Kessariani Monastery,
43 **C2**

Ketchikan, AK 101 **B4**,
136 **E5**

Ketchum, ID 130 **A7**,
135 **F3**

Kettwig, 34 **C6**

Keuka Lake, NY 116 **D2**

Kew, *Austral* 79 **C2**

Kew, S *Afr* 51 **G3**

Kew Gardens, NY 143 **F3**

Kew Gardens, *UK* 26 **C7**

Keweenaw Pen, MI 124 **D7**

Key Biscayne, FL 155 **G1**

Key Colony Beach, FL
188 **D2**

Key Deer NWR, FL 188 **B2**

Key Largo, FL 123 **G1**,
188 **F3**

Key Largo Natl Marine
Sanctuary, FL 188 **F3**

Key West, FL 94 **B6**,
113 **D1**, 123 **E1**, 188 **A1**

Key West Intl Arpt, FL
188 **A1**

Key West NAS, FL 188 **A1**

Keybayoran Baru, 64 **B7**

Keyser, WV 119 **E4**

Khabarovsk, 55 **F3**, 66 **E7**

Khalándrion, 43 **C3**

Khalkís, 25 **F1**

Khaniá, 17 **H2**, 25 **F1**

Khanty-Mansiysk, 53 **E4**

Kharkiv, 53 **A4**

Khartoum, 45 **F2**, 48 **C1**

Khimki, 56 **B5**

Khíos, 25 **G3**

Khlong Toey, 63 **G5**

Kholargós, 43 **C3**

Khon Kaen, 61 **A4**

Khorramabad, 49 **F5**

Khovrino, 56 **B5**

Khulna, 58 **E5**

Khuralji Khas, 64 **E7**

Kicevo, 25 **E5**

Kidderville, NH 114 **C5**

Kiel, 15 **E1**, 22 **D5**

Kieldrecht, 31 **F6**

Kielce, 17 **G6**

Kiesen, 37 **C1**

Kiev, 17 **H6**, 53 **A4**

Kifisia, 43 **C4**

Kigali, 47 **F6**

Kihei, HI 137 **D3**

Kikwit, 47 **E5**

Kilchberg, 37 **E1**

Kilimanjaro, 47 **G6**

Kilkenny, NC 187 **E4**

Kill Devil Hills, NC 187 **G6**

Killara, 78 **E8**

Killarney, *Can* 107 **G1**

Killarney, *Ire* 19 **A3**

Killeen, TX 111 **F3**, 129 **E3**

Killington Pk, VT 117 **H4**

Kilmarnock, 18 **C5**

Kilsyth, 79 **F3**

Kilyos, 43 **E4**

Kimball, NE 127 **B4**

Kimberley, 47 **E2**

Kimberley Plateau, 76 **B5**

Kimchaek, 66 **D6**

Kimitsu, 68 **D5**

Kimp'o, 72 **A7**

Kimp'o Intl Arpt, 72 **B7**

Kinali, 43 **E1**

Kinderhook, NY 117 **H2**

Kindu, 47 **F6**

King City, CA 133 **B4**

King City, OR 177 **F4**

King Contrivance, MD
147 **A1**

King of Prussia, PA 144 **B5**

Kingdome, The, WA
176 **B5**

Kingman, AZ 111 **B4**,
131 **A3**, 133 **F3**

Kings Canyon NP, CA
133 **D4**, 178 **A4**

King's Cross Sta, 27 **C4**

Kings Landing, 114 **F7**

King's Lynn, 19 **F3**

Kings Mountain NMP, SC
179 **G3**

Kings Park, MD 147 **A4**

Kings Park, VA 148 **B5**

Kings Point, NY 143 **G5**

Kingsbury Reservoir, 79 **C4**

Kingsford, 78 **F6**

Kingsgrove, 78 **D6**

Kingsport, TN 118 **B1**,
121 **E6**

Kingston, Can 103 D1, 117 E5

Kingston, Jam 94 C3, 97 H3

Kingston, MA 184 A7

Kingston, NY 117 G1, 119 H6

Kingston upon Hull, 14 C1, 19 E4, 20 D8

Kingston upon Thames, 26 C6

Kingstown, 95 H2

Kingsville, TX 129 E1

Kinshasa, 47 E6

Kinston, NC 121 H5

Kioicho, 69 A3

Kiowa NG, NM 128 C6

Kirby, TX 163 H2

Kirchberg, 37 C3

Kirdasah, 50 A2

Kirensk, 55 C3

Kiribati, 80 D4

Kiribati Isl, 80 C4

Kiritimati, 81 E4

Kirkland, Can 106 A2

Kirkland, WA 176 C6

Kirkland Lake, 103 B2

Kirklareli, 25 H5

Kirksville, MO 125 B3

Kirkwall, 18 D7

Kirkwood, MO 125 C2, 162 A1

Kirov, 53 D4

Kirov Stad, 57 F3

Kirsirmandira, 43 D4

Kiruna, 15 F5

Kisangani, 47 F6

Kisarazu, 68 D5

Kishinev, 17 H5

Kisirkaya, 43 E4

Kismaayo, 47 H6

Kispest, 42 B6

Kisshoin, 71 D2

Kissimmee, FL 123 F4, 153 F2

Kissimmee Park, FL 153 G1

Kisumu, 47 G6

Kita-Ku, 71 B4

Kita-mido Temple, 71 B3

Kitakyushu, 60 E8, 67 E4

Kitanomaru Park, 69 B4

Kitchener, 103 C1

Kitimat, 101 B3, 136 F5

Kitsilano, 107 F2

Kittanning, PA 119 E5

Kittery, ME 115 C3

Kitty Hawk, NC 187 G6

Kitwe, 47 F4

Kitzbühel, 23 D2

Kiyose, 68 B8

Kizu, 70 F6

Kladow, 32 B6

Klagenfurt, 17 F5, 23 E1, 24 C6

Klaipeda, 15 F1

Klamath, CA 132 A7, 134 A1

Klamath Falls, CA 134 B2

Klamath Falls, OR 110 B6, 132 B8

Klamath NF, CA 132 A7, 134 A2

Klamath R, CA 132 A7

Kleinburg, 104 C8

Kleinmachnow, 32 C6

Klerksdorp, 47 F3

Klettgau, 37 D4

Kliprivier, 51 G1

Kliprivierberg Nature Reserve, 51 F2

Klodzko, 23 F3

Klosterneuburg, 42 D8

Kloten, 37 F2

Kluane NP, 136 E6

Klyaz'ma, 56 D6

Knesset, 50 D4

Knin, 24 D5

Knole Park, 26 E5

Knollwood, MD 148 E8

Knotts Berry Farm, CA 170 D3

Knox, 79 F2

Knoxville, TN 113 C4, 121 E6, 125 F1

Köbánya, 42 B7

Kobe, 60 E8, 66 E5, 70 A5

Kobe U, 70 A6

Koblenz, 23 C3

Kobuk R, AK 136 C7

Kobuk Valley NP, AK 136 C8, 178 A2

Kochi, 60 E8, 67 E4

Kodaira, 68 A7

Kodiak, AK 136 C5

Kodiak Isl, AK 82 A5, 136 C5

Kodiak NWR, AK 136 C5

Koganei, 68 B7

Kogarah, 78 E6

Køge, 22 D6

Kojimachi, 69 A3

Kokkola, 15 F4

Kokomo, IN 125 E3

Kokshetau, 53 E3

Kokubunji, 68 A7

Kola Pen, 15 G5, 52 D6, 82 E8

Kolding, 22 C6

Kolobrzeg, 22 E5

Kolpashevo, 53 F3

Kolpino, 57 H1

Kolsher, 65 C3

Koltushi, 57 H2

Kolwezi, 47 E5

Kolyma, 82 B7

Kolyma Mts, 82 A7

Kolyma Range, 54 F6

Kolyma R, 54 E6

Kolyuchin Bay, 136 A8

Komae, 68 B7

Komatke, AZ 168 B1

Komorany, 35 E2

Komotiní, 25 G4

Komsomolsk na Amure, 55 F4, 66 D8

Konduz, 58 B7

Kongresshalle, 33 C3

Kongsvinger, 22 D8

König-Wusterhausen, 32 E5

Königsallee, 34 B5

Koniz, 37 B2

Konnagar, 65 E2

Konolfingen, 37 C2

Konstantinovo, 56 D1

Konstantinovskiy, 56 C1

Konstanz, 23 C2, 24 A6

Kontich, 31 G5

Konya, 48 D6

Kootenai NF, MT 135 E6

Kopenick, 32 E6

Korce, 25 E4

Korea Bay, 66 C5

Korea Exhib Ctr, 72 D6

Korea Stock Exchange, 72 C6

Korea Str, 60 E8, 66 D5

Korhogo, 44 B1

Koridhallós, 43 B3

Korla, 53 F1, E8

Koropion, 43 C2

Koror, 80 A5

Korsør, 22 D5

Koryak Range, 54 F7

Kosciusko, MS 129 H5

Koshien Baseball Stad, 70 B5

Kosice, 17 G5

Kosino, 56 D4

Kostelec, 35 F4

Koszalin, 22 F5

Kota, 58 C5

Kota Baharu, 61 A3

Kota Kinabalu, 61 D3

Kotel'niki, 56 D3

Kotka, 15 G3

Kotlas, 52 D5

Koto-Ku, 68 C7

Kotzebue, AK 100 A7, 136 B7

Kourou, 85 F5

Kovalevo, 57 G3

Kowloon, 67 A2, 75 D3

Kowloon Park, 75 C3

Kowloon Tong, 75 D4

Koyomizu Palace, 71 F3

Koyukuk NWR, AK 136 C7

Kozáni, 25 E4

Kozu Shrine, 71 B1

Kozugi Shrine, 71 C2
Kragujevac, 25 E6
Krakow, 17 F6
Kralupy, 35 D4
Krasnodar, 53 A3
Krasnogorsk, 56 A5
Krasnowodsk, 53 B2
Krasnoye Selo, 57 F1
Krefeld, 34 A6
Kremlin, 56 C4, 57 F5
Kreuzberg, 32 D7, 33 D1, 33 E1
Krimpen ann de Ijssel, 30 B2
Krionérion, 43 B4
Kristiansand, 14 D2, 22 C7
Kristianstad, 22 E6
Kristinehamn, 22 E8
Kroger Hills Park, OH 151 F2
Kronstadt, 57 E3
Krotoszyn, 23 F4
Krugersdorp, 51 E3
Kruibeke, 31 F5
Krusevac, 25 E6
Kryvyy Rih, 53 A4
Kuala Lumpur, 61 A2
Kuching, 61 C2
Kudan-Minami, 69 A4
Kulturforum, 33 D3
Kumamoto, 60 E7, 67 E4
Kumanovo, 25 F5
Kumasi, 44 C1
Kumch'on, 72 B8
Kumiyama, 70 E7
Kumla, 36 F5
Kummelnäs, 36 F6
Kumo, 44 D2
Kuna Peak, CA 182 D3
Kunashir, 66 F7
Kungsangen, 36 D7
Kunlun Mts, 58 D7
Kunming, 60 A5
Kunp'o, 72 C5
Kunsthaus, 37 E1
Kunsthistorisches Mus, 42 E7

Kuopio, 15 G4
Kupang, 61 F1
Kupchino, 57 G2
Kuraymah, 45 G3
Kurdzhali, 25 G5
Kurgar, 53 D3
Kuri, 72 D7
Kurla, 65 B2
Kurnell, 78 F5
Kuro, 72 C6
Kursk, 53 A4
Kursk Sta, 57 H5
Kushiro, 66 F7
Kuskokwim Bay, AK 136 B6
Kuskokwim Mts, AK 136 B6
Kuskokwin R, 100 A6
Kusnacht, 37 F1
Kusti, 45.F2
Kuujjuaq, 103 C4
Kuwait, 45 H4, 49 F4
Kwach'on, 72 D5
Kwagunt Butte, AZ 183 F2
Kwai Chung, 75 B4
Kwanak, 72 C6
Kwangju, 60 C5, 72 E5
Kwangming, 72 C6
Kwun Tong, 75 E3
Kyobashi, 69 E2
Kyoto, 60 E8, 66 E5, 70 E8, 71 F3
Kyoto Intl Conference Ctr, 70 F8
Kyoto U, 71 F4
Kyrgyzstan, 58 C8
Kyushu, 60 E7, E5
Kyustendil, 25 F5
Kyzyl, 55 H2
Kyzyl Kum, 53 D2
Kzyl-Orda, 58 B8

La Belle, FL 123 F3
La Boca Stad, 88 E7
La Brea Tar Pits, CA 172 B6
La Calera, 90 D2
La Cañada, 99 G2

La Ceiba, 97 F2
La Cisterna, 87 F2
La Colmena, 98 A5
La Concepción, 39 D3
La Coruña, 16 A4, 21 A4
La Crosse, KS 127 D2
La Crosse, WI 112 B6, 124 C5
La Defense, 28 C7
La Fayette, GA 120 D5
La Florida, 90 A3
La Giustiniana, 40 B6
La Grande, OR 134 D4
La Grange, GA 120 D4
La Grange, IL 159 C3
La Grange, KY 118 A3
La Granja, 87 G2
La Guaira, 90 B6
La Guardia Arpt, NY 143 E4
La-Guepiere, 28 A5
La Habra, CA 170 D4
La Honda, CA 175 C1
La Jolla, CA 169 E5
La Junta, CO 111 E4, 127 B2, 131 F4
La Llagosta, 38 E7
La Loche, 101 D2
La Matanza, 88 C6
La Mesa, CA 169 G4
La Mesa, Col 90 A2
La Mirada, CA 170 D3
La Molina, 87 H5
La Montaña, 84 C3
La Paz, 84 D1, 96 B4
La Perouse, 78 F5
La Perouse Str, 66 F7
La Pintana, 87 F1
La Plaine, 106 B6
La Plata, 86 B5
La Prairie, 106 D1
La Puente, CA 170 D4
La Punta, 99 H4
La Quebrada, 98 A5
La Reina, 87 G3
La Reja, 88 A7
La Rinconada, 90 B4

La Rioja, 86 B5
La Rochelle, 16 C5, 20 D5
La Ronge, 101 E3
La Salle, 106 C2, 156 D5
La Scala, 40 C1
La Serena, 86 A5
La Spezia, 24 B5
La Tuque, 114 A8
La Unión del Cuatro, 99 F4
La Ventra del Astillero, 99 E5
La Verne, CA 171 E5
Laau Pt, HI 137 C3
Labé, 44 A2
Labrador, 103 D4
Labrador City, 103 D3
Labrador Sea, 102 E5
Lac Courte Oreilles IR, WI 124 C6
Lac Du Flambeau IR, WI 124 C6
Lac-Mégantic, 114 C6
Lac St Pierre, 114 A7
Lachenaie, 106 C5
Lachine, 106 B2
Lackland AFB, TX 163 E1
Laconia, NH 115 B4
Ladera, CA 174 C2
Ladue, MO 162 A2
Lae, 76 C1, 80 B4
Lafayette, CA 174 C6
Lafayette, CO 167 F6
Lafayette, IN 112 C5, 125 E3
Lafayette, LA 113 B3, 129 G3
Lafayette Hill, PA 144 D5
Lafayette Park, CA 173 C2
Lafayette Square, DC 149 C4
Laferrere, 88 C6
Lagny-sur-Marne, 28 E7
Lagos, 44 C1
Laguna Beach, CA 171 F1
Laguna Hills, CA 171 F1
Laguna IR, NM 131 D3
Laguna Niguel, CA 171 F1

Lahat, 61 **B1**
Lahore, 58 **C6**
Lahti, 15 **G3**
Lai Chi Kok, 75 **B3**
Lainate, 40 **A3**
Lainyungang, 55 **E1**
Lairg, 18 **C7**
Lajpat Nagar, 64 **E6**
Lake Accotink Park, VA 148 **A5**
Lake Albert, 47 **F6**
Lake Athabasca, 101 **E4**
Lake Baikal, 55 **C3**
Lake Balkhash, 53 **E2**, 58 **C8**
Lake Barcroft, VA 148 **C6**
Lake Bluff, IL 158 **C7**
Lake Buena Vista, FL 123 **E4**, 153 **F3**
Lake Butler, FL 123 **E5**
Lake Chad, 44 **D2**
Lake Champlain, 114 **A5**, 117 **H5**
Lake Chapala, 96 **C3**
Lake Charles, LA 113 **B2**, 129 **G3**
Lake City, FL 121 **E2**
Lake City, GA 152 **C1**
Lake City, SC 121 **G4**
Lake Clark NP & Pres, AK 136 **C6**, 178 **A1**
Lake Eleanor Reservoir, CA 182 **A5**
Lake Elsinore, CA 171 **H2**
Lake Erie, 103 **C1**, 112 **D6**, 116 **A2**, 118 **C6**,125 **F4**, 179 **G4**
Lake Eyre, 76 **D4**
Lake Fairfax Park, VA 148 **A7**
Lake Forest, CA 171 **F1**
Lake Forest, IL 158 **C7**
Lake George, NY 117 **G4**,
Lake Havasu City, AZ 131 **A3**, 133 **F3**

Lake Huron, 103 **B1**, 112 **C6**, 124 **F5**, 179 **F5**
Lake Isabella, CA 133 **D4**
Lake Jem, FL 153 **E6**
Lake Kariba, 47 **F4**
Lake Key, FL 188 **F4**
Lake Khanka, 66 **D7**
Lake Ladoga, 15 **G3**, 52 **C5**
Lake Landing, NC 187 **F3**
Lake Malawi, 47 **G4**
Lake Managua, 97 **F1**
Lake Manatee SRA, FL 154 **D1**
Lake Manitoba, 101 **F2**, 110 **F8**
Lake Maracaibo, 84 **C5**, 95 **H1**
Lake Mary, FL 153 **G6**
Lake Mattamuskeet, NC 187 **E3**
Lake Mead NRA, AZ 131 **A3**, 133 **F4**, 178, **B3**, 183 **A3**
Lake Meredith NRA, TX 128 **D6**
Lake Michigan, 103 **B1**, 112 **C6**, 124 **E5**, 179 **F5**
Lake Monroe, FL 153 **G6**
Lake Mweru, 47 **F5**
Lake Nasser, 45 **F3**, 48 **C3**
Lake Nicaragua, 97 **G1**
Lake Nipigon, 103 **A2**, 112 **B7**, 124 **C8**
Lake of the Woods, 101 **F2**, 112 **A7** , 124 **A8**, 126 **F8**, 179 **E6**, 181 **F6**
Lake Okeechobee, FL 113 **E2**, 123 **F3**, 179 **G1**
Lake Onega, 15 **H4**, 52 **C5**
Lake Ontario, 103 **C1**, 112 **D6**, 116 **C4**, 179 **G5**
Lake Oswego, OR 177 **F4**
Lake Park, FL 154 **C6**
Lake Park, WI 157 **C3**
Lake Peipus, 15 **G2**
Lake Placid, FL 123 **F3**
Lake Placid, NY 117 **G5**

Lake Pontchartrain, LA 120 **A2**
Lake Poopó, 84 **D1**
Lake Powell, AZ 131 **B4**
Lake Providence, LA 120 **A4**
Lake Quannapowitt, 138 **D5**
Lake Quivira, KS 162 **A5**
Lake Region, 15 **G3**
Lake St Clair, MI 118 **C6**
Lake St-Francois, 114 **C6**
Lake Sammamish SP, WA 176 **D5**
Lake Superior, 112 **B7**, 124 **D7**, 179 **F5**
Lake Superior Prov P, 124 **F7**
Lake Tahoe, CA 132 **C6**
Lake Tana, 45 **G2**
Lake Tanganyika, 47 **F5**
Lake Titicaca, 84 **D2**
Lake Turkana, 45 **G1**
Lake Urmia, 49 **F6**
Lake Van, 49 **E6**
Lake Victoria, 47 **G6**
Lake Volta, 44 **C1**
Lake Wales, FL 123 **E3**
Lake Winnipeg, 101 **F3**, 110 **F8**, 124 **A8**
Lake Winnipesaukee, NH 115 **C4**
Lake Worth, TX 164 **A3**
Lake Zurich, IL 158 **B6**
Lakefront Arpt LA, 163 **G6**
Lakeland, FL 123 **E4**
Lakeland Village, CA 171 **H1**
Lakemba, 78 **D6**
Lakeport, CA 132 **A6**
Lakeside, CA 133 **E2**, 169 **H5**
Lakeside, CO 167 **F4**
Lakeside, TX 164 **A4**
Lakeview, NY 143 **H3**
Lakeview, OR 132 **C8**, 134 **C2**

Lakeview, TX 164 **A5**
Lakewood, CA 170 **C3**
Lakewood, CO 167 **F2**
Lakewood, NY 116 **A2**
Lakewood, OH 150 **C7**
Lakewood FP, IL 158 **A6**
Lakewood Park, GA 152 **B3**
Lakshadweep, 59 **B3**
Lale, HI 137 **C3**
Lalor Park, 78 **B8**
Lamar, CO 131 **F4**
Lamar R, WY 180 **C5**
Lambaréné, 46 **D6**
Lambert-St. Louis Intl Arpt, MO 162 **B3**
Lambeth, 27 **D1**
Lambeth Bridge, 27 **C1**
Lambrate, 40 **C2**
Lamesa, TX 128 **C4**
Lamma Island, 75 **B1**
Lampagnano, 40 **B2**
Lampasas, TX 129 **E3**
Lanai, HI 137 **D3**
Lancaster, CA 133 **D3**
Lancaster, OH 118 **F4**
Lancaster, PA 119 **F4**
Lancaster, SC 121 **F5**
Lancaster, TX 165 **G1**
Lancaster, UK 19 **D4**
Lancaster Sound, 102 **A7**
L'Ancienne-Lorette, 105 **D3**
Land Between the Lakes, KY 120 **C6**
Lander, WY 110 **D6**, 130 **C7**, 135 **H2**
Landfall, MN 161 **F2**
Landmark Ctr, MN 161 **E2**
Landover, MD 148 **F7**
Land's End, 16 **B6**, 19 **C2**
Landsdowne, 78 **C6**
Landshut, 23 **D2**
Landskrona, 22 **E6**
Landsmeer, 30 **D6**
Landstrasse, 42 **E7**
Lane Cove, 78 **E7**
Langen, 35 **B1**
Langenberg, 34 **D6**

Langenzersdorf, 42 E5

Langley, VA 148 B7

Langley Park, MD 148 E8

Langnau, 37 E1

Langsa, 61 A2

Laugstaff, 104 E8

Lank-Latum, 34 A6

Lansdowne, MD 147 C2

Lansdowne, PA 144 C2

L'anse IR, MI 124 D6

Lansing, IL 159 E1

Lansing, MI 112 C6, 125 E4

Lanús, 88 E6

Lanzhanchang, 73 B3

Lanzhou, 60 A7

Laoag, 60 D5, 67 C1

Laobaiduzhen, 74 E6

Laon, 20 E7, 23 A3

Laos, 61 A4

Lapa, 91 D2, 92 A5

Lapakahi SHP, HI 137 E2

Lapland, 15 F5, 82 E7

Laptev Sea, 54 B6, 82 C7

L'Aquila, 24 C4

Laramie, WY 110 D5, 127 A4, 130 E6

Laredo, TX 96 D5, 111 F2, 128 D1, 178 D1

Lares, 122 B2

Largo, FL 154 A4

Lárisa, 17 G3, 25 F4

Larkspur, CA 174 A6

Larnia, 25 F3

Larsen Ice Shelf, 83 E4

Las Adjuntas, 90 B4

Las Condes, 87 H3

Las Cruces, NM 111 D3, 128 B4, 131 E2

Las Fuentes, 99 F4

Las Juntas, 99 F4

Las Palmas, 44 A4

Las Piedras, 122 C2

Las Pinas, 62 B1

Las Pintas de Arriba, 99 G4

Las Trampas Regional Wilderness, CA 174 D5

Las Tunitas, 90 A6

Las Vegas, NV 111 B4, 131 A4, 133 F4, 178 B3

Las Vegas, NM 111 E4, 127 A1, 128 B6, 131 E3

Lasalle U, PA 145 E4

Lassen NF, CA 132 B7, 134 B1

Lassen Pk, CA 132 B7

Lassen Volcanic NP, CA 132 B7, 178 A4

L'Assomption, 106 D6

Lat Phrao, 63 G6

Latakia, 48 D6

Lathrup Village, MI 156 C8

Latin Quarter, 29 E1

Latina, Italy 24 B3

Latina, Spain 39 B2

Latino, 40 C5

Latvia, 15 G2, 52 B6

Lauderdale, MN 161 D3

Lauderdale-by-the-Sea, FL 155 G5

Lauderdale Lakes, FL 155 G5

Lauderhill Sunrise, FL 155 F5

Launceston, 77 E2

Laurel, MS 120 B3, 129 H4

Laurel, MT 130 C8

Laurel, OR 177 E4

Laurentides, 106 B6

Lausanne, 20 F6, 23 B1, 24 A6

Lausannem, 16 D5

Lava Beds NM, CA 132 B7, 178 A5

Lava Creek, WY 181 H4

Lava Hot Springs, ID 130 B7

Laval, 106 B3

Laval-Ouest, 106 A3

Lavallol, 88 D5

Lavras, 92 D6

Lavriki, 57 G3

Lawndale, CA 170 B3

Lawndale, PA 145 F4

Lawnside, NJ 145 F1

Lawrence, IN 156 F3

Lawrence, KS 112 A5, 127 F3

Lawrence, MA 115 C3, 138 C8

Lawrence, NY 143 G1

Lawrenceburg, KY 118 A2

Lawrenceburg, TN 120 C5

Lawrenceville, VA 119 E1

Lawton, OK 111 F4, 129 E5

Laxenburg, 42 E6

Layton, IL 188 D2

Layton, UT 135 G1

Laytonville, CA 132 A6

Lázaro Cárdenas, 96 C3

Le Bourget Arpt, 28 D8

Le Creusot, 20 E6

Le Gardeur, 106 D5

Le Havre, 16 C6, 19 E1, 20 D7

Le Kremlin, 28 D6

Le Mans, 16 C5, 20 D6

Le Mars, IA 126 E5

Le Perray-en-Yvelines, 28 A6

Le Plessis-Belleville, 28 F8

Le Puy, 20 E5

Le Roy, NY 116 C3

Le Val-Saint-Germain, 28 B5

Lead, SD 126 B5

Leadore, ID 135 F3

Leadville, CO 127 A3, 130 D5

Leaside, 104 E6

Leatherhead, 26 C6

Leavenworth, KS 125 A3, 127 F3

Leavenworth, WA 134 C5

Lebanon, 45 G5, 48 D5

Lebanon, KY 118 A2

Lebanon, MO 125 D4

Lebanon, NH 115 B4

Lebanon, OH 118 B4

Lebanon, PA 119 C4

Lebanon, TN 120 C6

Lebanon, VA 118 C1

Lebanon SF, NJ 119 H4

Lebbeke, 31 E3

Leblon, 91 D1

Lecce, 24 D3

Leech Lake IR, MN 124 B7, 126 F7

Leeds, 14 C1, 19 E4, 20 C8

Leerbeek, 31 E1

Leesburg, VA 119 F3

Leesville, LA 129 G3

Leeward Islands, 95 G3

Leganés, 39 A1

Legazpi, 61 D5

Legler Barn Museum, Adam, KS 162 A4

Legok, 64 A7

Lehi, UT 130 B6

Leicester, 19 E3

Leichhardt, 78 E7

Leiden, 30 B4

Leidschendam, 30 B3

Leigh Lake, WY 181 F4

Leimuiden, 30 C4

Leipzig, 17 E6, 23 D4

Leitrim, 105 C1

Lemay, MO 162 B1

Leme, 91 D2

Lemon, SD 126 C6

Lemon Grove, CA 169 G3

Lemont, IL 159 B2

Lemoore, CA 133 C4

Lena R, 54 C5, 82 B8

Lenasia, 51 E1

L'Enfant Plaza, DC 149 D2

Lengnau, 37 D3

Lenin Stad, 56 B4

Lenino, 56 C3

Leninsk, 53 D2

Lenox, MA 115 A2

Lens, 23 A3

Lensk, 55 C4

Leominster, MA 115 B3

León, Mex 96 C3, 97 F1

León, Spain 16 B4, 21 B4

Leon Valley, TX 163 E3

Leonardo Da Vinci Intl Arpt, 40 A4

Leonardtown, MD 119 G2

Leonia, NJ 142 D6

L'Epiphanie, 106 D6

Leppington, 78 A6

Lérida, 16 C3, 21 D4

Lerma R, 96 C3

Lerwick, 18 E8

Les Eboulements, 114 C8

Les Halles, 29 E2

Les Mureaux, 28 B8

Les Ulis, 28 C6

Leskovac, 25 E6

Lesosibirsk, 55 A3

Lesotho, 47 F2

Lesser Antilles, 95 G2

Lésvos, 25 G3

Leszno, 23 F4

Letchworth SP, NY 116 C3

Lethbridge, 101 D2, 110 D8

Letmathe, 34 F6

Leuwiliang, 64 A5

Levallois-Perret, 28 C7

Level Green, PA 146 F6

Levelland, TX 128 C5, 131 F2

Levendas Park, 87 F5

Levin RP, Ed, CA 175 F3

Lévis, 105 F3, 114 C7

Levittown, NY 116 B5

Lewis, 18 C7

Lewis & Clark NF, MT 135 G5

Lewis Lake, WY 180 B2

Lewis R, WY 180 B2

Lewis Smith Lake, AL 120 C4

Lewisburg, PA 119 F5

Lewisburg, TN 120 C5

Lewisburg, WV 118 D2

Lewisdale, MD 148 E7

Lewiston, ID 110 C7, 134 D4

Lewiston, ME 112 F7, 115 D4

Lewistown, MT 135 H5

Lewistown, PA 119 F5

Lewisville, TX 165 E6

Lexington, KY 112 C5, 118 A2, 125 F2, 179 F3

Lexington, MA 139 B4

Lexington, NE 127 D4

Lexington, VA 119 E2

Leyden, CO 167 E4

Leyte, 61 E4

Lhasa, 58 E6

L'Hospitalet de Llobregat, 38 E6

Lianxian, 67 A2

Lianyungang, 60 C7, 67 B4

Liaoyuan, 66 C3

Liard R, 136 F6

Libby, MT 135 E6

Libcice nad Vltavou, 35 E4

Liben, 35 E3

Liberal, KS 127 C1, 128 D6

Liberdade, 93 H2

Liberec, 17 F6, 23 E3

Liberia, 44 B1

Libertad, 88 B6

Liberty, NY 117 F1

Liberty Plain, MA 139 F1

Libertyville, IL 158 B7

Libeznice, 35 E4

Liboc, 35 D3

Library of Congress, DC 149 F2

Libreville, 46 D6

Libya, 17 G1, 45 E4, 48 A4

Libyan Desert, 45 F3, 48 B3

Lichtenberg, 32 E6

Lichtenrade, 32 D5

Lidingo, 36 E6

Lido Beach, NY 143 H1

Lido di Faro, 40 A4

Lido di Ostia, 40 A4

Liechtenstein, 17 E5, 23 C1, 24 B6

Liège, 16 D6, 20 E7, 23 B3

Liepaja, 15 F2

Lier, 31 H5

Liesing, 42 D6

Lighthouse Park, 107 F3

Lighthouse Pt, FL 155 G6

Lignumvitae Key, FL 188 E3

Lignumvitae Key St Botanical Site, FL 188 E3

Ligurian Sea, 24 A4

Lihue, HI 137 B4

Likasi, 47 F5

Lille, 16 D6, 20 E7, 23 A3

Lillehammer, 15 E3, 22 D8

Lillerod, 36 A7

Lilongwe, 47 G4

Lilydale, Austral 79 F3

Lilydale, MN 161 D2

Lilymoor, IL 158 A7

Lima, OH 118 A5, 125 F3

Lima, PA 144 A2

Lima, Peru 84 C2, 87 G6

Limaburg, KY 151 B1

Limassol, 48 D5

Limbour, 28 B5

Limito, 40 D2

Limoges, 16 C4, 20 D5

Limours, 105 A4

Limpopo R, 47 F3

Linate Arpt, 40 C1

Lince, 87 F5

Lincoln, CA 132 B6

Lincoln, ME 114 E6

Lincoln, MA 139 A4

Lincoln, NE 112 A5, 127 F4, 178 D4, 179 E4

Lincoln, NM 131 E2

Lincoln, UK 19 E4

Lincoln Ctr, NY 141 G5

Lincoln Hts, OH 151 D3

Lincoln Mem, DC 149 A2

Lincoln Mon, IL 160 D5

Lincoln NF, NM 128 B5

Lincoln Park, IL 159 D4

Lincoln Park, MI 156 C5

Lincoln Park, WI 157 C3

Lincolnia, VA 148 B5

Lincolnwood, IL 158 D5

Linden, NJ 142 A2

Lindenberg, 32 E8

Lindenhurst, IL 158 B8

Lindenhurst, NY 116 C5

Lindesberg, 22 E8

Lindfield, 78 E8

Lindholmen, 36 E8

Line Islands, 81 E4

Liniers, 88 D7

Linköping, 15 F2, 22 E7

Linkou, 62 B5

Linndale, OH 150 C6

Lint, 31 H5

Linthicum, MD 147 C1

Lintorf, 34 B6

Linz, 17 E5, 23 E2

Lion Park, 51 F4

Lion Rock CP, 75 D4

Lipetsk, 53 B4

Lisbon, OH 118 D5

Lisbon, Port 16 A3, 21 A2, 38 B7, 44 B5

Lisiy Nos, 57 F3

Lisle, IL 159 A3

L'Isle-Adam, 28 C8

Lismore, 77 F4

Lisse, 30 B5

Lissone, 40 C3

Litchfield, MN 126 F6

Lithuania, 15 G1, 52 B5

Little Bighorn Battlefield NM, MT 178 C5

Little Canada, MN 161 E3

Little Colorado R, AZ 183 F2

Little Cranberry Isl, ME 186 D2

Little Falls, MN 124 B6, 126 F6

Little Falls, NJ 142 A6

Little Falls, NY 117 F3

Little Ferry, NJ 142 C5

Little Gott Isl, ME 186 B1

Little Italy, NY 141 F2

Little Kinnakeet US Lifesaving Svc Sta, NC 187 H3

Little Manatee River SRA, FL 154 **D3**

Little Mermaid, The, 36 **C6**

Little Missouri NG, ND 126 **B7**

Little Missouri R, MT 126 **B6**

Little Neck, NY 143 **F4**

Little Rock, AR 113 **B4**, 129 **G5**, 179 **E2**

Little Tokyo, CA 172 **E6**

Littlefield, TX 128 **C5**, 131 **F2**

Littleton, CO 167 **G2**

Littleton, NH 114 **B5**

Liulitun, 73 **F3**

Liupukeng, 73 **E3**

Liuzhou, 60 **B5**

Live Oak, FL 121 **E2**, 123 **E5**

Live Oak, TX 163 **H3**

Livermore, CA 175 **F4**

Livermore, ME 114 **C5**

Liverpool, *Austral* 78 **B6**

Liverpool, *UK* 14 **C1**, 19 **D4**, 20 **C8**

Liverpool Bay, 136 **E8**

Liverpool Street Sta, 27 **F3**

Livingston, MT 130 **C8**, 135 **G4**

Livingston, TX 129 **F3**

Livingstone, 47 **F4**

Livonia, MI 156 **A7**

Livorno, 24 **B4**

Livry-Gargan, 28 **E7**

Ljubljana, 17 **F4**, 23 **E1**, 24 **C6**

Ljungby, 22 **E6**

Llanos, 84 **C5**

Llissá de Munt, 38 **E8**

Lloydminster, 101 **E3**

Lo Espejo, 87 **F2**

Lo Prado, 87 **F3**

Lobito, 46 **D5**

Loch Ness, 18 **C6**

Loch Raven, MD 147 **D4**

Lochearn, MD 147 **C3**

Lock Haven, PA 119 **F5**

Lockport, IL 159 **B2**

Lockport, NY 116 **B3**

Locust Valley, NY 143 **H6**

Lod, 50 **B6**

Lodge Grass, MT 135 **H4**

Lodi, CA 132 **B5**

Lodi, NJ 142 **C6**

Lodz, 17 **F6**

Logan, OH 118 **C4**

Logan, PA 145 **E4**

Logan, UT 110 **C6**, 130 **B6**, 135 **G1**

Logan Hts, CA 169 **F3**

Logan Intl Arpt, MA 139 **E3**, 140 **D5**

Logroño, 21 **C4**

Loia, 84 **B3**

Loire R, 16 **C5**, 20 **D6**

Lolo, MT 135 **F5**

Lolo Pk, MT 135 **E5**

Loma Linda, CA 171 **H4**

Loma Mar, CA 175 **C1**

Lomas de Zamora, 88 **E6**

Lomas Verdes, 98 **A4**

Lombard, IL 159 **B4**

Lomé, 44 **C1**

Lomita, CA 170 **B3**

Lomonosov, 57 **E2**

Lompoc, CA 133 **C3**

Londerzeel, 31 **F3**

London, *Can.* 103 **C1**, 112 **D6**

London, KY 118 **B1**, 120 **D6**

London, *UK* 16 **C6**, 19 **E2**, 20 **D7**, 26 **D7**, 27

London Arena, 26 **C7**

London Bridge Sta, 27 **F2**

London City Arpt, 26 **D7**

London Zoo, 27 **A4**

Londonderry, 14 **B1**, 18 **B5**

Londrina, 86 **C6**

Lone Star Geyser, WY 180 **B3**

Lonerock, OR 134 **C4**

Long Beach, CA 111 **A4**, 133 **D2**, 170 **C3**

Long Beach, NY 116 **B5**, 143 **G1**

Long Branch, Can 104 **C5**

Long Branch, NJ 119 **E4**

Long Island, 94 **D5**, 112 **F6**

Long Island City, NY 142 **D7**

Long Island Sd, 115 **B1**, 116 **C6**

Long Key SRA, FL 188 **E2**

Long Lake, NY 117 **G5**

Long Lake RP, MN 161 **D4**

Long Pt, 78 **B5**

Long Pt, MA 184 **E8**

Long Pond, ME 186 **B4**

Long Pond, MA 184 **B6**

Long Porcupine Isl, ME 186 **D6**

Long Shoal R, NC 187 **F4**

Longboat Key, FL 123 **E3**

Longchamp Hippodrome, 28 **C7**

Longdaocun, 73 **E4**

Longhua Park, 74 **C5**

Longhuazui, 74 **E5**

Longlac, 124 **E8**

Longmont, CO 130 **E5**

Longreach, 77 **E4**

Longueuil, 106 **D3**, 114 **A6**

Longview, TX 113 **A3**, 129 **F4**

Longwood, FL 153 **G5**

Lonholt, 36 **B8**

Loni, 64 **E8**

Looe Key Nat Marine Sanctuary, FL 188 **B2**

Lookout Canyon, AZ 183 **D4**

Lookout Pt, ME 186 **C6**

Lookout Pts, WY 180 **C4**

Loop, The, IL 160 **C6**

Lopaus Pt, ME 186 **B2**

Lords Cricket Ground, 26 **C7**

Lordsburg, NM 131 **D2**

Loreto, 96 **A5**

Loretteville, 105 **D3**

Lorient, 20 **C6**

Lorraine, 106 **B4**

Los Alamos, NM 127 **A1**, 128 **B6**, 131 **D3**

Los Altos, CA 175 **D2**

Los Altos Hills, CA 175 **D2**

Los Angeles, CA 81 **G6**, 111 **A4**, 133 **D3**, 170 **C5**, 172, 178 **A3**

Los Angeles Civic Ctr, CA 172 **E6**

Los Angeles Conv Ctr, CA 172 **C4**

Los Angeles County Mus of Art, CA 172 **B6**

Los Angeles Intl Arpt, CA 170 **B4**

Los Angeles Mem Coliseum, CA 172 **D5**

Los Banos, CA 133 **C4**

Los Beleres, 99 **F6**

Los Gatos, CA 175 **E1**

Los Gavilares, 99 **F4**

Los Lunas, NM 128 **B5**, 131 **E3**

Los Mohis, 96 **B5**

Los Molinos, CA 132 **B6**

Los Padres NF, CA 133 **B4**, 133 **C3**

Los Penasquitos Canyon Pres, CA 169 **F6**

Los Pínamos P, 98 **A1**

Los Reyes, 98 **D2**

Lostwood NWR, ND 126 **C8**

Lot R, 20 **D5**

Louangphrabang, 60 **A5**

Loudixia, 74 **E5**

Loughman, FL 153 **F1**

Louisa, KY 118 **B2**

Louisa, VA 119 **F2**

Louiseville, 114 **A7**

Louisiana, 97 **E6**, 113 **A3**, 129 **H3**, 179 **E2**

Louisiana Superdome, LA 163 **F5**

Louisville, CO 167 **F6**

Louisville, KY 112 **C5**, 125 **E2**, 179 **F3**

Louisville, MS 120 **B4**

Loures, 38 **B8**

Lousa, 38 **A8**

Louvre, The, 29 **E2**

Louvres, 28 **E8**

Lovech, 25 **G6**

Loveland, OH 151 **E4**

Loveland Park, OH 151 **F4**

Lovelock, NV 132 **D6**

Lovington, NM 128 **C4**, 131 **F2**

Lowe Art Mus, FL 155 **F1**

Lowell, MA 138 **A7**

Lowell NHP, MA 138 **A7**

Lower Brule IR, SD 126 **D5**

Lower Geyser Basin, WY 180 **A3**

Lower Hadlock Pond, ME 186 **C3**

Lower Matecumbe Key, FL 188 **E2**

Lower Mills, 139 **D2**

Lower Red Lake, MN 124 **A7**

Lower Slide Lake, WY 181 **G2**

Lower Suwannee NWR, FL 121 **E1**

Lower Templestowne, 79 **D3**

Lower Tunguska R, 55 **A4**

Lowestoft, 19 **F3**

Lowry Park, FL 154 **C5**

Lowville, NY 117 **F4**

Loyalton, CA 132 **C6**

Loyola U, IL 158 **D5**

Luanda, 46 **D5**

Luanshya, 47 **F4**

Lubango, 46 **D4**

Lubbock, TX 96 **C6**, 111 **E3**, 128 **D5**, 178 **D2**

Lübeck, 15 **E1**, 22 **D5**

Lubin, 23 **F4**

Lublin, 17 **G6**

Lubumbashi, 47 **F5**

Lucena, 61 **E4**

Luchou, 62 **B5**

Luchu, 62 **A5**

Lucknow, 58 **D5**

Lüderitz, 46 **D3**

Ludiana, 58 **C6**

Ludlow, VT 115 **A4**

Ludvika, 22 **E8**

Ludwigsfelde, 32 **C5**

Luena, 47 **E5**

Lugo, 21 **A4**

Lugu, 73 **A2**

Lugouqiao, 73 **A1**

Luhansk, 53 **B4**

Lujiazui, 74 **E7**

Luleå, 15 **F4**

Lumpkin, GA 120 **D3**

Lund, 22 **E6**

Lunda, 36 **E8**

Lunen, 34 **F8**

Lung Shan Temple, 62 **B5**

Lunghezza, 40 **D6**

Luoyang, 60 **B7**, 67 **A4**

Luray, VA 119 **E3**

Lusaka, 47 **F4**

Lutherville, MD 147 **D4**

Luton, 19 **E3**

Lutz, FL 154 **C6**

Luwan District, 74 **D6**

Luxembourg, 16 **D6**, 20 **F7**, 23 **B3**

Luxembourg City, 20 **F7**

Luxembourg Gdns, 29 **D1**

Luxembourg Palace, 29 **D1**

Luxmanor, MD 148 **C8**

Luxor, 45 **F4**, 48 **D3**

Luzern, 23 **C1**, 24 **A6**

Luzon, 60 **D5**

Luzon Str, 60 **D5**, 67 **C1**

Lvov, 17 **G6**

Lyell Canyon, CA 182 **D3**

Lynbrook, NY 143 **G2**

Lynchburg, VA 119 **E2**

Lyndhurst, NJ 142 **B5**

Lyndhurst, OH 150 **F7**

Lyngby, 36 **C7**

Lynge, 36 **A7**

Lynn, MA 115 **C3**, 138 **E5**

Lynn Canyon Park, 107 **H3**

Lynn Haven, FL 122 **C6**

Lynn Lake, 101 **F3**

Lynnfield, MA 138 **D6**

Lynnhurst, MA 138 **E5**

Lynwood, CA 170 **C3**

Lynwood, IL 159 **E1**

Lyon, 16 **D4**, 20 **E5**, 23 **A1**, 44 **D6**

Lyon Arboretum, HI 177 **H2**

Lyons, IL 159 **C3**

Lyons, NY 116 **D3**

Lyss, 37 **A3**

Lysterfield, 79 **F1**

Lytkarino, 56 **D2**

Lytle Creek, CA 171 **G6**

Lyttelton, 51 **H6**

Lyubertsy, 56 **D3**

Lyublino, 56 **C3**

M

Ma On Shan CP, 75 **E4**

Ma'ale Adummim, 50 **D4**

Maan, 48 **D4**

Maasdam, 30 **B1**

Maassluis, 30 **A2**

Maastricht, 23 **B3**

Mac Robertson Land, 83 **D1**

Macapá, 85 **F4**

Macarao NP, 90 **A4**

Macau, 60 **C5**, 67 **A2**

Maccarese, 40 **A5**

Macclenny, FL 123 **E6**

Macdona, TX 163 **E1**

Macdonnell Ranges, 76 **C4**

Macedonia, 17 **G3**, 25 **F5**, 45 **E6**

Macedonia, OH 150 **F5**

Maceió, 85 **H2**

Machakos, 47 **G6**

Machala, 84 **B3**

Machias, ME 114 **F5**

Machida, 68 **A6**

Mack, OH 151 **B2**

Mackay, 77 **E5**

Mackay Island NWR, NC 119 **G1**

Mackenzie, 101 **C3**

Mackenzie Mts, 100 **C5**, 136 **F7**

Mackenzie R, 82 **B5**, 100 **C6**

Mackerel Cove, ME 186 **A1**

Mâcon, Fr 20 **E6**, 23 **A1**

Macon, GA 113 **D3**, 121 **E3**

Macon, MO 125 **B3**

Macquarie Fields, 78 **B5**

Macquarie Isl, 83 **A2**

Macuto, 90 **C6**

Macwahoc, ME 114 **F4**

Macy's, NY 141 **E4**

Madagascar, 47 **H3**

Madaket, MA 185 **H4**

Madama Palace, 41 **C3**

Madang, 76 **C2**, 80 **B4**

Madawaska, ME 114 **E8**

Madeira, OH 151 **E3**

Madeira Beach, FL 154 **A4**

Madeira Islands, 44 **B5**

Madeira R, 84 **D3**

Madeleine, 29 **D2**

Madera, CA 133 **C4**

Madgeburg, 17 **E6**

Madira Bickel Mound HS, FL 154 **B2**

Madison, FL 122 **D6**

Madison, IL 162 **C2**

Madison, IN 118 **A3**, 125 **E2**

Madison, SD 126 **E5**

Madison, WV 118 **C2**

Madison, WI 112 **B6**, 124 **C5**, 179 **F4**

Madison Hts, MI 156 **D8**

Madison IR, WA 176 A6
Madison Plateau, WY 180 A3
Madison R, WY 180 A4
Madison Square Gdn, NY 141 E4
Madison Valley, WY 180 A4
Madisonville, KY 125 E2
Madras, India 59 C4
Madras, OR 134 C3
Madrid, Col 90 B2
Madrid, Spain 16 B3, 21 C3, 39 D3, 44 C6
Madrid City U, 39 B3
Madrid Geographical & Cadestral Inst, 39 C4
Madurai, 59 C3
Madureira, 91 C2
Magadan, 54 A7, 54 F5
Magaliesberg Natural Area, 51 E6
Magdagachi, 55 E3
Magdalena Contreras, 98 A2
Magdalena R, 84 C5
Magdeburg, 23 D4
Magdalena del Mar, 87 F5
Magic Kingdom Park, FL 153 F3
Magic Land, 63 G6
Magnitogorsk, 53 D3
Magog, 114 B6
Magoúla, 43 A4
Mahajanga, 47 H4
Mahlow, 32 D5
Mahmut Sevket Pasa, 43 F3
Mahmutbey, 43 D2
Mahogany Hammock, FL 188 B4
Mahrauli, 64 E6
Mahtomedi, MN 161 F4
Maidan, 77 B3
Maidenhead, 26 A7
Maidstone, Can. 156 F5
Maidstone, UK 19 F2, 26 F6

Maiduguri, 44 D2
Main RR Sta, 35 B3
Maine, 103 D2, 112 F7, 114 E5, 179 H6
Mainz, 20 F7, 23 C3
Maipú, 87 F2
Maiquetía, 90 B6
Mairiporã, 92 B6
Maisons-Laffitte, 28 C7
Maitland, FL 123 F4, 153 G5
Majé, 91 F4
Majorca, 16 C3, 21 E3
Majors House, Alexander, MO 162 B4
Majoshaza, 42 A5
Majuro, 80 C5
Makapuu Pt., HI 137 D3
Makassar Strait, 61 E2
Makati, 62 C2
Makhachkala, 53 B2
Makoti, ND 126 C7
Makurdi, 44 D1
Malabo, 44 D1
Malabon, 62 B3
Malacanang Palace, 62 C2
Malad, 65 B3
Malad City, ID 135 F2
Málaga, 16 B2, 21 B2
Malagrotta, 40 B5
Malakal, 45 G1
Malang, 61 D1
Malanje, 47 E5
Malawi, 47 G5
Malaysia, 61 A2, 61 D2
Malden, MA 139, D4
Maldives, 59 B2
Male, 59 B2
Malheur OR, 134 C2
Malheur NF, OR 134 D3
Malheur NWR, OR 132 D8
Mali, 44 B2
Mall, The, DC 149 D2
Mall of America, MN 161 C1
Malmo, 15 E1, 22 E6
Malone, NY 117 G6

Måløv, 36 A6
Malta, 17 F1, 24 C1, 44 D5 , 48 A6
Malta, MT 135 H6
Maltepe, 43 F1
Malton, 104 B7
Malvern, Can 104 A5
Malvern, AR 129 G5
Malvern, Austral 79 C2
Malverne, NY 143 G3
Mamelodi, 51 H6
Mamie, NC 187 F6
Mammoth Cave NP, KY 120 D6, 125 E2, 179 F3
Mammoth Hot Springs, WY 180 B5
Mammoth Lakes, CA 132 C5
Mammoth Pk, CA 182 D4
Mamo, 90 A6
Mamontovka, 56 D6
Manado, 61 F3
Managua, 84 A6, 94 A1, 97 F1
Manama, 49 F4
Manassas, VA 119 F3
Manati, 122 B2
Manaus, 85 E4
Manchester, CT 115 B2
Manchester, NH 112 F6, 115 B3
Manchester, TN 120 D5
Manchester, UK 14 C1, 19 D4, 20 C8
Manchester, VT 117 H3
Manchester, WA 176 A4
Manchester SF, SC 121 F4
Manchester SP, WA 176 A5
Manchurian Plain, 66 C3
Mandal, 22 C7
Mandalay, 58 F5
Mandaluyong, 62 C2
Mandan, ND 126 C7
Mandaoli, 64 F7
Mandaula, 64 E8
Mandi, 64 D5

Mandra, 43 A3
Mandurah, 76 A3
Manfredonia, 24 D3
Mangalia, 25 H6
Mangalore, 59 B4
Mangus Corner, TX 163 E1
Manhasset, NY 143 G5
Manhattan, KS 110 F5, 127 E3
Manhattan, NY 116 B5, 141 E4, 142 D4
Manhattan Beach, CA 170 B3
Manila, Phil 61 D4, 62 C4
Manila, UT 135 H1
Manila Intl Arpt, 62 C1
Manisa, 25 H3
Manistee NF, MI 124 E5
Manitoba, 101 F3
Manitoulin Isl, 124 F6
Manitowoc, WI 124 D5
Manitsoq, 102 D6
Manizales, 84 C5
Mankato, MN 112 A6, 124 A5, 126 F5
Manlius, NY 117 E3
Manly, 78 F8
Mannheim, 16 D6, 20 F7, 23 C3
Mann's Chinese Theater, CA 172 B8
Manns Harbor, NC 187 G5
Manoa Falls, HI 177 H2
Manokwari, 76 A2
Manomet Pt, MA 184 B2
Manorhaven, NY 143 G5
Mansel Isl, 103 B4
Manset, ME 186 B2
Mansfield, LA 129 G4
Mansfield, OH 112 C5, 118 C5
Mansfield, TX 164 D1
Mansfield, WA 134 C5
Manteca, CA 132 C5
Manteo, NC 187 G5
Mantes-la-Jolie, 28 A8
Mantova, 24 B5

Mantua, VA 148 **A6**

Manvel, TX 166 **C1**

Manzanillo, 94 **C4**

Manzhouli, 66 **A7**

Maoming, 67 **A1**

Maple, 104 **C8**

Maple Grove, MN 124 **B6**

Maple Hts, OH 150 **E6**

Maple Leaf Gdns, 104 **E6**

Maple Shade, NJ 145 **G3**

Maple Valley, WA 176 **D4**

Maplewood, MN 161 **E3**

Maplewood, MO 162 **B1**

Map'o, 72 **C7**

Maputo, 47 **G3**

Mar del Plata, 86 **B4**

Maracaibo, 84 **C6**, 95 **E1**

Maracana Stad, 91 **D2**

Maracay, 84 **D5**, 95 **F1**

Maradi, 44 **D2**

Marais, 29 **F2**

Maraisburg, 51 **F3**

Marajó Isl, 85 **F4**

Marathon, *Can* 103 **B2**, 124 **E7**

Marathon, FL 123 **F1**, 188 **C2**

Marayong, 78 **B8**

Marble Arch, 27 **A3**

Marble Canyon, AZ 183 **F4**

Marblehead, MA 138 **F5**

Marbleton, WY 135 **G2**

Marco, FL 123 **E2**

Marcos Paz, 88 **A6**

Margarita Isl, 95 **G1**

Margate, FL 155 **G5**

Mari Girgis Sta, 50 **C1**

Maria Lanzendorf, 42 **E6**

Marianna, AR 120 **A5**

Marianna, FL 120 **D2**, 122 **C6**

Mariano Acosta, 88 **A6**

Marias Islands, 96 **B4**

Maribor, 23 **F1**, 24 **C6**

Maricopa, AZ 168 **A2**

Maricopa, CA 133 **C3**

Marie Byrd Land, 83 **C3**

Mariemont, OH 151 **E2**

Marienfelde, 32 **D6**

Mariestad, 22 **E7**

Marietta, GA 113 **C4**, 120 **D4**

Marietta, OH 118 **C4**

Marikina, 62 **D3**

Marin City, CA 174 **A6**

Marina, CA 133 **B4**

Marina District, CA 173 **B3**

Marina del Rey, CA 170 **A4**

Marinette, WI 124 **D6**

Marino, 40 **D4**

Mar'ino, 56 **C3**

Marinwood, CA 174 **A7**

Marion, IN 118 **A5**, 125 **E3**

Marion, OH 118 **B5**, 125 **F3**

Marion, SC 121 **G4**

Marion, VA 118 **C1**

Marion NF, Francis, SC 121 **F4**

Mariposa, CA 132 **C5**

Mariposa Grove, CA 182 **B1**

Maritime Mus & Planetarium, 107 **G2**

Mariupol, 53 **A4**

Mark Twain NF, MO 120 **A6**, 125 **B2**

Markham, *Can* 104 **F8**

Markham, IL 159 **D2**

Markleeville, CA 132 **C5**

Marksville, LA 129 **G3**

Marlboro, MA 138 **E8**

Marley, IL 159 **B1**

Marlin, TX 129 **E3**

Marlton, NJ 145 **H1**

Marmot Pk, MT 135 **E5**

Marne R, 20 **E6**

Marona, 44 **D2**

Maronouchi, 69 **D3**

Maroubra, 78 **E6**

Marquesas Islands, 81 **G5**

Marquette, MI 112 **B7**, 124 **D6**

Marra Mts, 45 **E2**

Marrakech, 44 **B4**

Marrero, LA 163 **F4**

Marrickville, 78 **E6**

Marrot Park, IN 157 **E3**

Mars Hill, ME 114 **E7**

Marsa al Burayqah, 48 **B5**

Marsa Matruh, 48 **C5**

Marsabit, 47 **G6**

Marsala, 24 **C2**

Marseille, 16 **D4**, 21 **E4**, 44 **D6**

Marsfield, 78 **D8**

Marshall, CO 167 **E5**

Marshall, MN 124 **A5**, 126 **F6**

Marshall Creek, TX 164 **C6**

Marshall Fields, IL 160 **C6**

Marshall Islands, 80 **C5**

Marshall Loxahatchee NWR, Arthur R, FL 155 **F6**

Marshalltown, IA 125 **B4**

Marshfield, MA 184 **A8**

Marsta, 36 **D8**

Marstons Mills, MA 184 **C5**

Martha's Vineyard, MA 115 **H3**, 185 **G1**

Martha's Vineyard SF, MA 185 **G1**

Marthalen, 37 **F4**

Martin Luther King Jr Mem Library, DC 149 **D3**

Martin Luther King Jr NHS, GA 152 **C3**

Martin Luther King Jr Park, TX 163 **G2**

Martínez, *Arg* 88 **D8**

Martinez, CA 174 **D7**

Martinez, TX 163 **H2**

Martinique, 95 **H2**

Martinsburg, WV 119 **F4**

Martinsville, VA 118 **D1**, 121 **F6**

Martorell, 122 **C1**

Mary, 53 **C1**

Maryborough, 77 **F4**

Maryland, 112 **E5**, 119 **F3**, 179 **G4**

Maryland, U of, MD 148 **E7**

Maryland Hts, MO 162 **A3**

Marylebone Sta, 27 **A3**

Marystown, 103 **F3**

Marysville, CA 132 **B6**

Marysville, OH 118 **B4**

Maryville, MO 125 **A3**, 127 **F3**

Marzahn, 32 **E7**

Masan, 66 **D5**

Mascot, 78 **E6**

Mascouche, 106 **C5**

Mascuala, 99 **H6**

Maseru, 47 **F2**

Masha, 50 **C6**

Mashhad, 49 **H6**, 58 **A7**

Mashoes, NC 187 **G5**

Mashpee, MA 184 **B5**

Masirah, 49 **H3**

Mason City, IA 112 **A6**, 124 **B5**

Maspeth, NY 143 **E3**

Massa, 24 **B5**

Massachusetts, 103 **D1**, 112 **E6**, 115 **B2**, 179 **H5**

Massachusetts Inst of Technology, MA 139 **D3**

Massawa, 45 **G2**, 49 **E1**

Massena, NY 117 **F6**

Masset, AK 101 **B3**

Massif Central, 20 **E5**

Massimina, 40 **B5**

Massy, 28 **C6**

Mastic, NY 116 **C5**

Matadepera, 38 **D8**

Matadi, 46 **D5**

Matagami, 103 **C2**

Matamoros, 96 **D4**, 129 **E1**

Matane, 103 **D3**

Matanzas, 94 **B5**

Mataram, 61 **D1**

Matatlán, 99 **H5**

Matera, 24 **D3**

Mather, CA 182 **A4**

Mathias Church, 42 **A7**

Mato Grosso Plateau, 85 **E2**

Matsudo, 68 **D8**

Matsue, 66 **E5**

Matsuyama, 67 **E4**

Mattamuskeet NWR, NC 187 **E3**

Matterhorn, 16 **D4**, 23 **C1**, 24 **A6**

Matterhorn Canyon, CA 182 **C5**

Matterhorn Pk, CA 182 **D6**

Matteson, IL 159 **D1**

Mattituck, NY 116 **C6**

Matunga, 65 **B2**

Maturín, 84 **D5**, 95 **G1**

Mauá, 92 **C4**

Maubeuge, 23 **A3**

Maui, HI 137 **E3**

Mauna Kea, HI 137 **F2**

Mauna Loa, HI 137 **E1**

Maunawili, HI 177 **H3**

Maupin, OR 134 **C4**

Maurepas, 28 **B6**

Maurice NP, 114 **A7**

Mauritania, 44 **B3**

Mausoleum of Augustus, 41 **C4**

Mayaguana, 94 **D5**

Mayagüez, 95 **F3**, 122 **B2**

Mayfair, PA 145 **F4**

Mayfair, UK 27 **B2**

Mayfield, KY 120 **B6**

Mayfield, OH 150 **F8**

Mayfield Hts, OH 150 **F7**

Maymanah, 58 **A7**

Mayo, Can 100 **B5**

Mayo, FL 122 **D5**

Mays Landing, NJ 119 **H4**

Maysville, KY 118 **B3**

Maywood, CA 170 **C4**

Maywood, IL 159 **C4**

Maywood, NJ 142 **C6**

Maywood Park, OR 177 **G6**

Mazar-e Sharif, 58 **B7**

Mazatlán, 96 **B4**

Mbabane, 47 **F3**

Mbala, 47 **F5**

Mbandaka, 47 **E6**

Mbanza-Ngungu, 46 **D5**

Mbeya, 47 **G5**

M'boi Mirim, 92 **A3**

Mbuji-Mayi, 47 **F5**

McAlester, OK 113 **A4**, 129 **F5**

McAllen, TX 111 **F2**, 129 **E1**

McCall, ID 130 **A8**

McCandless, PA 146 **B8**

McClintock Chan, 100 **F6**

McCloud, CA 132 **B7**

McComb, MS 120 **A2**

McConnellsburg, PA 119 **E4**

McCook, NE 127 **D3**

McDermitt, NV 132 **D7**, 134 **D1**

McFarland, CA 133 **D4**

McKees Rocks, PA 146 **B7**

McKeesport, PA 146 **E5**

McKelvie NF, Samuel R, NE 126 **C5**

McKinleyville, CA 132 **A7**

McLean, VA 148 **B7**

McLoughlin House, OR 177 **G4**

McMichael Canadian Collection, 104 **B8**

McMinnville, OR 134 **B4**

McMurdo Sd, 83 **B2**

McPherson, KS 127 **E2**

Meadow Brook Park, MN 161 **B2**

Meadowlands, Can 105 **A1**

Meadowlands, S Afr 51 **F2**

Meadowlands Sports Complex, NJ 142 **C5**

Meadows, The, TX 166 **A3**

Meadowvale, 104 **A5**

Meadowvale Village, 104 **A5**

Meadville, PA 116 **A1**, 118 **D6**

Meazza Stad, 40 **B1**

Mecca, CA 133 **E2**

Mecca, Saudi Arabia 45 **G3**, 49 **E2**

Mechelen, 31 **G4**

Mechigmen, 136 **A7**

Medan, 61 **A2**

Medellin, 84 **C5**

Medfield, MA 139 **A1**

Medfield Junction, MA 139 **A1**

Medford, MA 139 **C4**

Medford, OR 110 **A6**, 132 **B8**, 134 **B2**

Media, PA 144 **B2**

Medicine Bow NF, WY 127 **A4**, 130 **E7**

Medicine Hat, 101 **D2**

Medicine Lake, MN 161 **A3**

Medicine Lodge, KS 127 **D2**

Medina, NY 116 **B3**

Medina, OH 118 **C5**

Medina, Saudi Arabia 49 **E3**

Medina, WA 176 **C5**

Mediodia, 39 **C2**

Mediterranean Sea, 16 **C2** 21 **F2**, 24 **A2**, 25 **E1**, 45 **E5**, 48 **B5**

Medley, FL 155 **F2**

Meerbusch, 34 **B5**

Meeteese, WY 135 **H3**

Meiderich, 34 **B7**

Meidling, 42 **D7**

Méier, 91 **C2**

Meikirch, 37 **B3**

Meilen, 37 **F1**

Meir, 31 **G6**

Mekele, 45 **G2**

Mekinac Lake, 114 **A8**

Mekong R, 60 **A5**, 61 **B4**

Melbourne, Austral 77 **E2**, 79 **C3**, 80 **B2**

Melbourne, FL 113 **E2**, 123 **F4**

Melbourne, KY 151 **E1**

Melbourne Cricket Grounds, 79 **C2**

Melbourne Royal Exh Bldg, 79 **C2**

Melilla, 16 **B1**, 21 **C1**, 44 **C5**

Melíssia, 43 **C3**

Melo, 86 **C5**

Melrose, MA 138, **D5**

Melrose Park, PA 145 **E5**

Melun, 28 **E5**

Melville Isl, Austral 76 **C6**, 80 **A3**

Melville Isl, Can 100 **E7**

Melville Pen, 102 **A5**

Melvindale, MI 156 **C6**

Melzo, 40 **D2**

Memorial Park, TX 166 **B4**

Memphis, FL 154 **C1**

Memphis, TN 113 **B4**, 120 **B5**, 125 **D1**, 129 **H6**, 179 **E3**

Menai, 78 **C5**

Mende, 20 **E5**

Mendota, CA 133 **C4**

Mendota, MN 161 **D1**

Mendota Hts, MN 161 **E1**

Mendoza, 86 **A5**

Mengede, 34 **E8**

Menguiafen, 73 **B2**

Menlo Park, CA 175 **D3**

Mennecy, 28 **D5**

Menominee, WI 124 **D6**

Menongue, 47 **E4**

Menor's Ferry, WY 181 **F2**

Menzel Bourguiba, 24 **A1**

Merano, 23 **D1**

Merauke, 76 **B1**, 80 **A4**

Meraux, LA 163 **H5**

Mercado, 93 **G4**

Merced, CA 132 **C5**

Merced Pk, CA 182 **C2**

Merced R, CA 182 **C3**

Merchandise Mart, IL 160 **B7**

Merchantville, NJ 145 **E2**

Merchtem, 31 **F3**

Mergui, 61 **A3**

Mérida, Mex 97 **F3**

Mérida, *Spain* 21 **B2**
Mérida, *Ven* 84 **C5**
Meridan, CT 115 **A1**
Meridian, MS 113 **B3**, 120 **B3**, 129 **H4**
Meridian Hills, IN 157 **E4**
Merion, PA 144 **D4**
Merksem, 31 **G6**
Merlo, 88 **B6**
Merredin, 76 **B3**
Merriam, KS 162 **B4**
Merrifield, VA 148 **B6**
Merrill, OR 132 **B8**
Merrillville, IN 159 **F1**
Merrimack R, NH 115 **C3**
Merritt Isl, FL 123 **F4**
Merriweather Post Pavilion, MD 147 **A1**
Merrylands, 78 **C7**
Mersin, 48 **D6**
Merthyr Tydfil, 19 **D3**
Merton, 26 **C6**
Meru, 47 **G6**
Mesa, AZ 131 **B2**, 168 **D3**
Mesa, WA 134 **D5**
Mesa College, CA 169 **F4**
Mesa Verde NP, CO 131 **D4**, 178 **C3**
Mescalero Apache IR, NM 128 **B4**, 131 **E2**
Mesolóngion, 25 **E3**
Mesquita, 91 **B3**
Mesquite, NV 133 **F4**
Mesquite, TX 165 **H3**
Messina, 17 **F2** , 24 **C2**, 47 **F3**
Metairie, LA 129 **H3**, 163 **F5**
Methuen, MA 138 **C8**
Metropolitan Mus of Art, NY 141 **H6**
Metropolitan Oakland Intl Arpt, CA 174 **C5**
Metropolitan Park, 87 **G3**
Metropolitan Stad, MN 161 **C1**
Mettmann, 34 **C5**

Metz, 20 **F7**, 23 **B2**
Metzger, OR 177 **F5**
Meudon, 28 **C6**
Meulan, 28 **A8**
Meuse R, 20 **E7**
Mexicali, 96 **A6**, 111 **B4**, 133 **F2**
Mexican Customs, 169 **G1**
Mexican Hat, UT 131 **C4**
Mexico, 81 **H5**, 94 **A4**, 96 **C4**
Mexico, MO 125 **C3**
Mexico Bay, NY 117 **E4**
Mexico City, 96 **D3**, 98 **C2**
Mezieres-sur-Siene 28 **A7**
Miami, FL 94 **C6**, 97 **G5**, 113 **E2**, 123 **F2**, 155 **G2**, 179 **G1**
Miami, OK 127 **F1**
Miami, U/of, FL 155 **F1**
Miami Beach, FL 123 **G2**, 155 **G2**
Miami Hts, OH 151 **B2**
Miami Intl Arpt, FL 155 **F1**
Miami Lakes, FL 155 **F3**
Miami Shores, FL 155 **G2**
Miami Springs, FL 155 **F2**
Miami Whitewater Forest, OH 151 **B3**
Miamitown, OH 151 **B3**
Miamiville, OH 151 **F3**
Michigan, 103 **B1**, 112 **C6**, 124 **D5**, 179 **F5**
Michigan City, IN 125 **E4**
Michipicoten Isl, 124 **E7**
Michurinets, 56 **A3**
Micronesia, Federated States of, 80 **B4**
Middelburg, 23 **A4**, 47 **E2**
Middle Cape, FL 188 **C4**
Middle Church, 107 **G6**
Middle East, 45, 49
Middle Fork Tuolumne R, CA 182 **A4**
Middle Granite Gorge, AZ 183 **C3**

Middle R, MD 147 **F3**
Middle Village, NY 143 **E3**
Middleburg, FL 123 **F5**
Middleburg Hts, OH 150 **C5**
Middlebury, VT 115 **A4**, 117 **H5**
Middlesboro, KY 120 **D6**
Middlesbrough, 19 **E4**
Middleton, MA 138 **D6**
Middletown, CT 115 **B2**
Middletown, NY 117 **G1**
Middletown, NC 187 **F3**
Midland, MI 124 **E5**
Midland, TX 111 **E3**, 128 **C4**, 178 **D2**
Midlothian, IL 159 **D2**
Midrand, 51 **G4**
Midway, FL 153 **H6**
Midway, OR 177 **E4**
Midway Geyser Basin, WY 180 **A3**
Midway Islands, 80 **C6**
Midwest City, OK 129 **E6**
Midwest Stock Exchange, IL 160 **C5**
Mifflintown, PA 119 **F5**
Miguel Hidalgo, 98 **A3**
Miguel Hidalgo Intl Arpt, 99 **G3**
Migum, 72 **E7**
Mijdrecht, 30 **D4**
Mikhaylovgrad, 25 **F6**
Milan, 17 **E4**, 23 **C1**, 24 **B5**, 40 **B2**
Milbank, SD 126 **E6**
Milbridge, ME 114 **F5**
Mildura, 76 **D3**
Mile High Stad, CO 167 **G3**
Miles City, MT 110 **E7**, 126 **A8**, 130 **E8**
Miles Standish Mon, MA 184 **A8**
Milford, CT 116 **C6**
Milford, NH 115 **B3**
Milford, NJ 116 **A6**
Milford, OH 151 **F3**
Milford, PA 119 **H5**

Military Academy of Colombia, 90 **C2**
Military Hospital, 93 **H6**
Military Mus, 35 **E3**
Military Reserve, 78 **B5**
Mill Grove, PA 144 **A6**
Mill Stream Run Res, OH 150 **C5**
Mill Valley, CA 174 **A6**
Millbrae, CA 175 **B4**
Mille Lacs Lake, MN 124 **B6**
Milledgeville, GA 121 **E4**
Millersburg, OH 118 **C5**
Milliken, 104 **F8**
Millinocket, ME 114 **E6**
Millis, MA 139 **A1**
Milltail Creek, NC 187 **F5**
Millvale, PA 146 **C7**
Mílos, 25 **G2**
Milpitas, CA 132 **B5**, 175 **F2**
Milton, FL 120 **C2**, 122 **B6**
Milton, MA 139 **D2**
Milton, WA 176 **C1**
Milwaukee, WI 103 **A1**, 112 **B6**, 124 **D5**, 157 **C2**, 179 **F4**
Milwaukee County Stad, WI 157 **B2**
Milwaukie, OR 177 **G5**
Mimico, 104 **C5**
Minami Mido Temple, 71 **A2**
Minami-Ku, *Kyoto* 71 **E2**
Minami-Ku, *Osaka* 71 **B2**
Minas, 86 **C5**
Minato, 69 **F2**
Minato Machi Sta, 71 **A1**
Minato-Ku, 68 **C7**, 69 **A1**
Mindanao, 61 **F4**
Minden, LA 129 **G4**
Minden, NE 127 **D3**
Minden, NV 132 **C6**
Mindoro, 61 **D4**
Mineola, NY 143 **H4**
Mingo NWR, MO 120 **B6**
Minna, 44 **C1**

Minneapolis, MN 103 **A1**, 112 **A6**, 124 **B6**, 161 **C2**, 179 **E5**

Minneapolis Chain of Lakes RP, MN 161 **C2**

Minneapolis Planetarium, MN 161 **C3**

Minneapolis-St. Paul Intl Arpt, MN 161 **C1**

Minnehaha, WA 177 **G6**

Minnehaha RP, MN 161 **D2**

Minnesota, 103 **A2**, 112 **A8**, 124 **B6**, 179 **E5**

Minnesota R, 124 **A6**, 126 **F6**

Minnesota U, MN 161 **C3**

Minnetonka, MN 161 **A2**

Mino, 70 **C6**

Minorca, 16 **D3**, 21 **F3**

Minot, ND 110 **F7**, 126 **C8**

Minshat al-Bakkari, 50 **B2**

Minsk, 15 **G1**, 52 **A5**

Minto, 78 **A5**

Minute Man NHP, MA 138 **A5**, 179 **H5**

Miquon, PA 144 **D5**

Mira Loma, CA 171 **F4**

Mirador, 99 **G3**

Miraflores, 87 **F4**

Miramar, FL 155 **E3**

Miramar College, CA 169 **F5**

Miramar NAS, CA 169 **G5**

Mirasierra, 39 **B4**

Miri, 61 **D3**

Mirnyy, 55 **C4**

Mirror Plateau, WY 180 **C4**

Misato, 68 **D8**

Miskolc, 17 **F5**

Misratah, 44 **D4**, 48 **A5**

Missinaibi R, 124 **F8**

Mission, KS 162 **B4**

Mission Bay Park, CA 169 **E4**

Mission Hills, KS 162 **B4**

Mission Pk R Pres, CA 175 **E3**

Mission Trails RP, CA 169 **G5**

Mission Viejo, CA 171 **F1**

Missisquoi NWR, VT 117 **H6**

Mississauga, 104 **C5**, 116 **B4**

Mississippi, 97 **E6**, 113 **B3**, 120 **A3**, 179 **F2**

Mississippi R, 97 **E6**, 112 **A6**, 113 **B4**, 120 **A4**, 124 **B6**, 125 **C3**, 129 **H5**, 179 **E4**

Missoula, MT 110 **C7**, 135 **F5**, 178 **B6**

Missouri, 113 **A4**, 125 **C2**, 179 **E3**

Missouri City, TX 129 **F2**, 166 **A2**

Missouri R, 101 **D2**, 110 **E7**, 112 **A5**, 125 **B3**, 126 **C8**, 127 **F4**, 135 **H5**, 178 **C6**, 179 **E4**

Mistassini, 103 **C2**

Misty Fiords NM, AK 136 **F5**, 178 **B1**

Mitaka, 68 **B7**

Mitchell, IL 162 **D3**

Mitchell, SD 126 **E5**

Mitchell Mem Forest, OH 151 **B3**

Mitilíni, 25 **G3**

Mitry-Mory, 28 **E8**

Mitte, 33 **E4**

Miyakojima-Ku, 71 **C4**

Miyazaki, 67 **E4**

Mmabatho, 47 **E3**

Mníšek pod Brdy, 35 **D1**

Mo-i-Rana, 15 **E4**

Moab, UT 110 **D5**, 130 **C5**

Moapa, NV 133 **F4**

Mobara, 68 **F5**

Mobile, AL 97 **F6**, 113 **B3**, 120 **B2**, 122 **A6**, 179 **F2**

Mobridge, SD 110 **F6**, 126 **D6**

Moca, 122 **A2**

Modderfontein, 51 **G3**

Modena, *Italy* 24 **B5**

Modena, UT 132 **F5**

Modesto, CA 132 **C5**

Modica, 24 **C1**

Mödling, 42 **D6**

Modoc NF, CA 132 **C7**, 134 **C1**

Modrany, 35 **E2**

Moers, 34 **A7**

Mofolo, ʼ **E2**

Mogadishu, 47 **H6**

Mogilev, 15 **H1**

Mogocha, 55 **D3**

Mogyoród, 42 **C8**

Mohawk Canyon, AZ 183 **A2**

Mohawk R, NY 117 **G3**

Mojave Desert, CA 111 **B4**, 133 **E3**

Mojave NP, CA 133 **F3**, 178 **A3**

Mokena, IL 159 **C1**

Mokpo, 67 **C4**

Molde, 14 **D4**

Moldova, 17 **H5**, 45 **F6**

Molino, FL 122 **B6**

Molíns de Rey, 38 **D6**

Mollet del Valles, 38 **F7**

Molokai, HI 137 **D3**

Molokovo, 56 **D2**

Moluccas, 61 **F2**

Mombasa, 47 **G6**

Mona Passage, 95 **F3**, 122 **A1**

Monaco, 16 **D4**, 20 **F5**, 24 **A4**

Monahans, TX 128 **C4**

Monavoni, 51 **G5**

Mönchaltorf, 37 **F1**

Moncloa-Aravaca, 39 **B3**

Monclova, 96 **C5**, 128 **C1**

Moncton, 103 **E2**

Moncucco, 40 **B1**

Monfort Hts, OH 151 **C3**

Mongolia, 58 **F8**, 60 **A8**, 66 **A7**

Mongolian Plateau, 55 **C2**, 60 **A8**

Monjolo, 91 **F3**

Monmorency, 79 **D3**

Mono Lake, CA 132 **D5**

Monomoy Isl, MA 115 **D2**, 185 **E6**

Monomoy NWR, MA 185 **E6**

Monomoy Pt, MA 185 **E6**

Monongahela NF, WV 118 **D3**

Monroe, LA 113 **B3**, 129 **G4**

Monroe, MI 118 **B6**

Monroe, NY 116 **A6**

Monroe, NC 121 **F5**

Monroeville, AL 120 **C3**

Monroeville, PA 146 **E6**

Monrovia, Afr 44 **B1**

Monrovia, CA 170 **D5**

Monserrat, 89 **D2**

Monster, 30 **A3**

Mont Blanc, 20 **F5**

Mont Clare, PA 144 **A6**

Mont-Laurier, 103 **C2**

Mont-Royal, 106 **C2**

Montana, 101 **D2**, 110 **D7**, 126 **A7**, 135 **F6**, 178 **C5**

Montara, CA 175 **A3**

Montauk, NY 115 **B1**, 116 **D6**

Montauk Pt, NY 115 **B1**

Montbéliard, 23 **B2**

Montcada i Reixac, 38 **E7**

Montclair, CA 171 **F5**

Montclair, NJ 142 **A5**

Monte Alto, 90 **B5**

Monte Grande, 88 **D5**

Monte Sacro, 40 **C6**

Monte Sereno, CA 175 **E1**

Monte Spaccato, 40 **B5**

Montebello, CA 170 **D4**

Montego Bay, 94 **C4**

Montenegro, 17 F4, 25 E6
Monterey, CA 110 A5, 133 B4
Monterey Park, CA 170 C5
Monteria, 84 C5
Monterrey, 96 D4, 111 F1, 128 D1
Montes Claros, 85 G1
Montesano, WA 134 B5
Montevideo, MN 124 B6
Montevideo, Uru 86 C5
Montezuma NWR, NY 116 D3
Montfoort, 30 D3
Montfort-l'Amaury, 28 A6
Montgat, 38 F7
Montge, 28 F8
Montgomery, AL 113 C4, 120 C3, 179 F2
Montgomery, OH 151 F3
Monticello, FL 122 D6
Monticello, KY 118 A1
Monticello, ME 114 E7
Monticello, NY 117 G1, 119 H6
Montjuïc Castle, 38 E6
Montmagny, 114 C7
Montmartre, 29 D4
Montmelo, 38 F7
Montparnasse, 29 C1
Montparnasse Cemetery, 29 C1
Montpelier, ID 135 G2
Montpelier, VT 112 F7, 114 A5
Montpellier, 16 D4, 21 E4
Montréal, 103 D2, 106 D3, 112 E7
Montréal Botanical Gdns, 106 C3
Montréal Conv Ctr, 106 C3
Montréal-Est, 106 D4
Montréal Forum, 106 C2
Montréal Nord, 106 C4
Montréal Olympic Stad, 106 D3

Montréal Zoological Gdns, 106 C2
Montreuil, 28 D7
Montrose, CO 110 D5, 130 D5
Montross, VA 119 F2
Montrouge, 28 D6
Montry, 28 F7
Montserrat, 95 H3
Montverde, FL 153 E4
Monumental Bullring, 99 G5
Monywa, 58 F5
Monza, 40 C3
Moon Run, PA 146 A6
Moonee Ponds, 79 B3
Moorabbin, 79 D1
Moorebank, 78 B6
Moorestown, NJ 145 H3
Moorhead, MN 124 A7, 126 E7
Moose, WY 181 F2
Moose Basin, WY 181 F5
Moose Creek, WY 181 F5
Moose Jaw, 101 E2
Moose Mt Pres P, 126 C8
Moose Village Visitor Ctr, WY 181 F2
Moosehead Lake, ME 114 D6
Mooselookmeguntic Lake, ME 114 C5
Moosonee, 103 B3, 112 C8
Mopti, 44 B2
Moraga, CA 174 D6
Moran, WY 181 H4
Moran Creek, WY 181 F4
Moran Entrance Sta, WY 181 H4
Moran Pt, AZ 183 F1
Moratalaz, 39 D2
Morden, 101 F2, 126 D8
Moreau R, SD 126 C6
Moree, 77 E4
Morehead, KY 118 B2
Morehead City, NC 121 H5
Moreland, Austral 79 B3

Moreland Hills, OH 150 F6
Morelia, 96 C3
Morena, 40 D4
Moreno, 88 A7
Moreno Valley, CA 171 H3
Mörfelden, 35 A1
Morgan City, LA 113 B2
Morgan Pierpont Library, NY 141 G4
Morgan Terr R Pres, CA 174 F6
Morgan, UT 135 G1
Morgantown, WV 112 D5, 118 F4
Moriguchi, 70 D6
Morioka, 66 F6
Morningside, MD 148 F5
Morocco, 16 A1, 21 B1, 44 B4
Morogoro, 47 G5
Morón, Arg 88 C7
Moron, Mong 55 B2
Moroni, 47 G5
Morris, MN 124 A6, 126 F6
Morris Isl, MA 184 F5
Morrison, CO 167 E2
Morristown, NJ 116 A5
Morrisville, NY 117 F3
Morro Bay, CA 133 B3
Morrow, GA 152 C1
Morton, PA 144 C2
Morton Grove, IL 158 D5
Mortsel, 31 G5
Morumbi, 92 A4
Morumbi Stad, 92 A4
Moscavide, 38 C7
Moscone Conv Ctr, CA 173 E1
Moscoviskiy, 56 A2
Moscow, ID 134 D5
Moscow, Rus 15 H2, 52 B5, 56 C4, 57 F5, 82 F8
Moscow R, 56 B3
Moselle R, 20 F6
Moshannon SF, PA 119 E5
Moskhaton, 43 B2
Mosman, 78 F7

Mosquera, 90 B2
Mosquito Coast, 97 G2
Moss, 22 D8
Moss Beach, CA 175 A3
Moss Park, FL 153 H2
Moss Park, Henry S, TX 165 G4
Mostar, 24 D4
Mosul, 49 E6, 53 A2
Motala, 22 E7
Motown Mus, MI 156 D6
Moulin Rouge, 29 D4
Moulineaux, 28 C7
Moulins, 23 A1
Moulmein, 59 F4
Moultrie, GA 121 E2, 122 D6
Moundon, 45 E1
Mounds View, MN 161 C4
Moundsville, OH 118 D4
Mount Airy, NC 121 F6
Mount Airy Forest, OH 151 C2
Mount Angel, OR 134 B4
Mount Ararat, 49 E6
Mount Blanc, 16 D4, 24 A6
Mount Carmel, OH 151 F2
Mount Clark, CA 182 C2
Mount Conness, CA 182 D5
Mount Cook, 77 G1
Mount Dana, CA 182 D4
Mount Davis, PA 119 E4
Mount Demavend, 49 F6
Mount Desert, ME 186 B6
Mount Desert Isl, ME 114 F5, 186 B4
Mount Diablo SP & Game Rfg, CA 174 E6
Mount Doane, WY 180 C3
Mount Dora, FL 153 E6
Mount Druitt, 78 A8
Mount Echo Park, OH 151 C2
Mount Elbert, CO 110 D5, 130 E5

Mount Etna, 17 **F2**

Mount Evans, CO 130 **E5**

Mount Everest, 58 **E5**

Mount Florence, CA 182 **D3**

Mount Gambier, 76 **D2**

Mount Greylock, MA 117 **H2**

Mount Hagen, 76 **C1**

Mount Hancock, WY 180 **C2**

Mount Hayden, AZ 183 **E3**

Mount Healthy, OH 151 **D3**

Mount Hebron, MD 147 **A3**

Mount Hoffman, CA 182 **C4**

Mount Holmes, WY 180 **A5**

Mount Hood, OR 134 **B4**, 178 **A5**

Mount Houston, TX 166 **C5**

Mount Isa, 76 **D5**

Mount Jefferson, NV 132 **E6**

Mount Jefferson, OR 134 **B3**

Mount Kenya, 76 **D5**

Mount Kirkpatrick, 83 **C3**

Mount Kisco, NY 116 **B6**

Mount Kosciusko, 77 **E2**

Mount Langford, WY 180 **D3**

Mount Laurel, PA 145 **H2**

Mount Lebanon, PA 146 **C5**

Mount Logan, 100 **B5**

Mount Mansfield, VT 117 **H6**

Mount Marcy, NY 117 **G5**

Mount McKinley, AK 82 **A5**, 100 **A6**

Mount McLoughlin, OR 134 **B2**

Mount Mitchell, NC 113 **D4**

Mount Moriah, NV 132 **F6**

Mount Morris, NY 116 **C3**

Mount Nebo, PA 146 **B8**

Mount of Olives, 50 **D4**

Mount Oliver, PA 146 **C6**

Mount Olympus, *Greece* 17 **G3**, 25 **F4**

Mount Olympus, WA 110 **A8**

Mount Pleasant, MI 112 **C6**

Mount Pleasant, TX 129 **F4**

Mount Plymouth, FL 153 **F6**

Mount Prospect, IL 158 **C5**

Mount Rainier, MD 148 **E7**

Mount Rainer, WA 110 **B7**, 134 **B5**

Mount Rainer NP, WA 134 **B5**

Mount Robson, 101 **C3**

Mount Rogers NRA, VA 118 **C1**

Mount Rushmore NM, SD 178 **D5**

Mount Schurz, WY 180 **D2**

Mount Shasta, CA 132 **B7**, 134 **B1**

Mount Sheridan, WY 180 **B2**

Mount Sterling, KY 118 **B2**

Mount Stimson, MT 135 **F6**

Mount Thielsen, OR 134 **B2**

Mount Trumbull, AZ 183 **A3**

Mount Vernon, IL 125 **D2**

Mount Vernon, NY 116 **B6**, 143 **F6**

Mount Vernon, OH 118 **C5**

Mount Vernon, WA 134 **B6**

Mount Vernon Square, DC 149 **D4**

Mount Vesuvius, 17 **F3**

Mount Waddington, 101 **B3**

Mount Warren, CA 182 **D5**

Mount Washburn, WY 180 **C5**

Mount Washington, NH 179 **H5**

Mount Washington Inclines, PA 146 **B6**

Mount Waverley, 79 **D2**

Mount Whitney, CA 110 **A5**, 133 **D4**

Mount Wilhelm, 76 **C2**

Mount Wilson Obs, CA 170 **C6**

Mount Zimmer, MT 180 **D6**

Mount Zion, 50 **D4**

Mountain Creek Lake Park, TX 165 **E2**

Mountain High, 142 **A9**

Mountain Home, AR 34 **G6**

Mountain Home, ID 130 **A7**, 132 **E8**, 135 **E2**

Mountain View, CA 175 **D2**

Mountain View, CO 167 **F3**

Mozambique, 47 **G4**

Mozambique Channel, 47 **G3**

Mratin, 35 **F4**

Mtwara, 47 **G5**

Muckleshoot IR, WA 176 **D1**

Mud Lake, MN 126 **F7**

Mudaniiang, 55 **E3**

Mudanjiang, 66 **C3**

Mugla, 25 **H2**

Mühleberg, 37 **A2**

Muhlenbeck, 32 **D8**

Mühlhausen, 23 **C3**

Mülheim an der Ruhr, 34 **C7**

Muir Beach, CA 174 **A6**

Muir NHS, John, CA 174 **D7**

Muir Woods NM, CA 174 **A6**, 178 **A4**

Muko, 70 **E7**, 71 **D1**

Mulhouse, 20 **F6**, 23 **B2**, 24 **A6**

Mullingar, 19 **B4**

Multan, 58 **B6**

Mulund, 65 **C3**

Mumbra, 65 **C3**

Munchenbuchsee, 37 **B3**

Munchendorf, 42 **E5**

Muncie, IN 112 **C5**, 118 **A4**, 125 **E3**

Mundelein, IL 158 **B7**

Munhall, PA 146 **D6**

Munich, 17 **E5**, 23 **D2**, 24 **B6**, 44 **D6**

Municipal Ferry Bldg, NY 141 **E1**

Municipal Gallery of Art & Culture & Modern Art Center, 99 **F5**

Municipal Market, 93 **H4**

Municipal Park, MN 161 **B1**

Munsingen, 37 **C1**

Münster, *Ger* 23 **C4**

Munster, IN 159 **E1**

Münster Cathedral, 34 **C7**

Murcia 16 **B2**, 21 **C2**

Murdo, SD 126 **C5**

Murfreesboro, TN 120 **D5**, 125 **E1**

Muri, 37 **C2**, 37 **D1**

Murino, 57 **G3**

Murmansk, 15 **G6**, 52 **D6**, 82 **E7**

Muroran, 66 **F6**

Murphy, ID 132 **E8**, 135 **E2**

Murphy, TX 165 **H6**

Murphy Candler Park, GA 152 **C6**

Murray R, 76 **D3**

Murrieta, CA 171 **H1**

Murrumbeena, 79 **D1**

Musashimurayama, 68 **A8**

Musashino, 68 **A8**

Muscat, 49 **H3**

Muscoy, CA 171 **G5**

Musé D'Orsay, 29 **D2**

Museo do Bellas Artes, 90 **C5**

Museu Memorias do Bixiga, 93 **E1**

Museum, WY 180 **A4**

Museum Folkwang, 34 **C7**

Museum of Art & Fort Lauderdale Hist Mus, FL 155 **G4**

Museum of Chinese History, 73 E2

Museum of Contemporary Art, *Chile* 87 F3

Museum of Contemporary Art, IL 160 D7

Museum of Fine Arts, TX 166 B3

Museum of Flight, WA 176 D4

Museum of German History, 33 E3

Museum of Modern Art, Mex 98 B3

Museum of Modern Art, NY 141 G5

Museum of Oriental Art, 57 H5

Museum of Oriental Ceramics, 71 B3

Museum of Sacred Art, 93 H6

Museum of Science, MA 140 B5

Museum of Science & Industry, FL 154 D6

Museum of Science & Industry, IL 159 E3

Museum of Stone Age Antiquities, ME 186 D5

Museum of the Battle of Borodino, 56 B4

Museum of Transportation, 33 D2

Museuminsel, 33 E4

Muskeget Chan, MA 185 G3

Muskeget Isl, MA 185 G4

Muskegon, MI 112 C6, 124 E5

Muskogee, OK 113 A4, 125 A1, 127 F1, 129 F6

Musocco, 40 B2

Mustang Pt Park, TX 164 A1

Mutare, 47 F4

Mwanza, 47 G6

Mwene Ditu, 47 F5

Myingyan, 58 F5

Myitkyina, 58 F5

Myles Standish SF, MA 184 A6

Myrtle Beach, SC 113 E4, 121 G4

Myrtle Creek, OR 132 A8, 134 B2

Myrtle Pt, OR 132 A8, 134 A2

Mys Schmidta, 136 A8

Mysore, 59 C4

Mystery Castle, AZ 168 B2

Mytishchi, 56 C6

N

Naaldwijk, 30 A3

Naberezhnyye Chelny, 53 D4

Nacala, 47 G4

Nacka, 36 F6

Nacogdoches, TX 129 F4

Naestved, 22 D5

Naga, 61 E4

Nagano, 66 F5

Nagaokakyo, 70 E7, 71 D1

Nagareyama, 68 D8

Nagasaki, 60 E7, 67 D3

Nagatacho, 69 B2

Nagatino, 56 C3

Nagoya, 60 F8, 66 E5

Nagpur, 58 C5

Nags Head, NC 187 G5

Nags Head Wood Pres, NC 187 G5

Nagykanizsa, 23 F1, 24 D6

Nagytarcsa, 42 C7

Nagytétény, 42 A6

Naha, 60 E6, 67 D3

Nahanni NP, 136 F7

Nahant, MA 139 F4

Nahunta, GA 123 E6

Nahya, 50 B2

Naiguatá, 90 D6

Naihati, 65 F4

Nain, 103 D4

Nairobi, 47 G6

Naka-Ku, 68 B5

Nakagyo-Ku, 71 E3

Nakano-Ku, 68 B8

Nakanoshima Park, 71 B3

Nakhodka, 55 F2, 66 C6

Nakhon Ratchasima, 61 A4

Nakhon Sawan, 61 A4

Nakhon Si Thammarat, 61 A3

Nakurú, 47 G6

Naledi, 51 E2

Nalikul, 65 D3

Nam, 72 A6

Namangan, 53 D1, 58 C8

Namdong, 72 A5

Namhansan Prov P, 72 E6

Namib Desert, 46 E3

Namibe, 46 D4

Namibia, 47 E3

Nampo, 66 C5

Nampula, 47 G4

Namsos, 15 E4

Nanaimo, 101 B2, 134 B6

Nanakuli, HI 137 C3

Nanha Baseball Stad, 71 B1

Nanba Sta, 71 B1

Nanchang, 60 C6, 67 B3

Nancy, 16 D5, 20 F6, 23 B2

Nangi, 65 E1

Nangloi Jat, 64 D7

Naniwa-Ku, 71 A1

Nanjing, 60 C7, 67 B4

Nanning, 60 B5

Nanole, 65 B2

Nanpin, 67 B3

Nanshi District, 74 E6

Nantahala NF, NC 125 F1

Nantasket Beach, MA 139 F2

Nantes, 16 C5, 20 C6

Nanticoke, 116 A3

Nantong, 67 C4

Nantucket, MA 115 D1, 185 H5

Nantucket Harbor, MA 185 G6

Nantucket Isl, MA 115 D1, 185 H5

Nantucket NWR, MA 185 G6

Nantucket Sd, MA 115 D2, 185 F4

Nantucket SF, MA 185 H5

Nanyang, 60 B7, 67 A4

Napa, CA 132 B5

Naperville, IL 159 A3

Napier, 77 H1

Naples, FL 113 D2, 123 E2

Naples, *Italy* 17 E3, 24 C3, 44 D5

Naples Park, FL 123 E2

Napoleon, OH 118 A6

Napoleonic Mus, 41 C3

Nara, 66 E5, 70 F5

Nara Dreamland, 70 F5

Nara Park, 70 F5

Narashino, 68 E7

Narcoossee, FL 153 H2

Nari, 71 C2

Naricalps Mts, 17 F4

Narita, 68 F8

Narrogin, 76 B3

Narrows, The, ME 186 B3

Narvik, 15 E5

Naryan-Mar, 52 E5, 82 D8

Nashua, NH 115 B3

Nashville, GA 122 D6

Nashville, TN 113 C4, 120 C6, 125 E1, 179 F3

Nasik, 58 B5

Nasr City, 50 D2

Nassau, 94 C6, 97 H5, 113 F2

Natal, 85 H3

Natchez, MS 113 B3, 129 H4

Natchez Trace SP & Forest, TN 120 B6

Natchitoches, LA 129 G4

Natick, MA 139 A2

NASA Michoud Assembly Facility, LA 163 **H6**

National Agricultural Exh Ctr, 73 **F3**

National Air & Space Mus, DC 149 **E2**

National Aquarium, DC 149 **C3**

National Aquarium, MD 147 **D2**

National Arboretum, DC 148 **E6**

National Archives, DC 149 **D3**

National Art Mus, 98 **B3**

National Bunraku Theater, 71 **B1**

National Canyon, AZ 183 **B1**

National City, CA 169 **F2**

National Congress, IL 162 **C2**

National Congress, 89 **C2**

National Diet Bldg, 69 **B2**

National Elk Rfg, WY 181 **G1**

National Gallery Ger, 33 **D2**

National Gallery, UK 27 **C2**

National Gallery of Art, DC 149 **E3**

National Gallery of Art, East Wing, DC 149 **E2**

National Institutes of Health, MD 148 **C8**

National Library & Archives, 105 **A3**

National Maritime Mus, CA 17 **E3**

National Mem Cemetery of the Pacific, HI 177 **G2**

National Mus of American Art, DC 149 **D3**

National Mus of American History, DC 149 **C3**

National Mus of Anthropology, 98 **B3**

National Mus of Fine Arts, 89 **C4**

National Mus of Modern Art, Kyoto 71 **F3**

National Mus of Modern Art, Tokyo 69 **C4**

National Mus of Natural History, DC 149 **C3**

National Mus of Oriental Art, 41 **E3**

National Mus of Science & Technology, 105 **C2**

National Palace, 98 **B3**

National Palace Mus, 62 **C5**

National Park, NJ 145 **E1**

National Postal Mus, DC 149 **F3**

National Railways Mus, 89 **D4**

National Roman Mus, 41 **D4**

National Stad, India 64 **E7**

National Stad, Japan 68 **C7**

National Stad, Peru 87 **F5**

National Stad, Port 38 **A6**

National Tennis Ctr, NY 143 **F4**

National Theater, Japan 69 **B3**

National Theatre, UK 27 **D2**

National U of Colombia, 90 **C2**

Natuna Islands, 61 **B2**

Natural Bridge, WY 180 **B3**

Natural Bridges NM, UT 131 **C4**, 178 **C3**

Nature Reserve, 63 **E3**

Naucalpan de Juárez, 98 **A4**

Nauen, 32 **A8**

Nauru, 80 **C4**

Naushon Isl, MA 185 **F1**

Navajo IR, AZ 128 **A6**, 131 **C4**, 183 **F4**

Naval Air Sta, CA 169 **E3**

Naval Amphibious Base, CA 169 **F2**

Naval Avionics Ctr, IN 157 **F2**

Naval Comm Sta, Imperial Beach, CA 169 **F2**

Naval Landing Field, CA 169 **F1**

Naval Reserve, CA 169 **E3**

Naval Space Surv Sta, CA 169 **H1**

Naval Sta, CA 169 **F3**

Navojoa, 96 **B5**

Navotas, 62 **B3**

Navy Pier, IL 160 **F7**

Navy Pier Park, IL 160 **E7**

Naze, 67 **D3**

Nazilli, 25 **H3**

Nazlat as-Samman, 50 **B1**

Nazret, 45 **G1**

N'Djamena, 44 **D2**

Ndola, 47 **F4**

Nea Erithraia, 43 **C4**

Néa Ionía, 43 **C3**

Nea Liosia, 43 **B3**

Neah Bay, WA 134 **A6**

Nebitdag, 53 **B2**

Nebraska, 110 **F6**, 178 **D4**,

Nebraska, NC 187 **F3**

Nebraska City, NE 125 **A3**, 127 **F3**

Nebraska NF, NE 127 **D4**

Necochea, 86 **B4**

Necropolis of the Port of Rome, 40 **A4**

Ned Brown FP, IL 158 **B5**

Nee Soon, 63 **F3**

Needham, MA 139 **B2**

Needles, CA 131 **A3**, 133 **F3**

Neffenbach, 37 **F3**

Negotin, 25 **F6**

Negro R, 84 **D4**

Negros, 61 **E4**

Neiderursel, 35 **B4**

Neihart, MT 135 **G5**

Neiva, 84 **C4**

Nellis Air Force Range, NV 131 **A4**, 132 **E5**

Nelson, AZ 131 **B3**

Nelson, New Zealand 77 **H1**

Nelson R, 101 **F3**

Nemchinovka, 56 **A4**

Neosho, MO 125 **A1**

Nepal, 58 **D6**

Nepean, 105 **A1**

Nepean City Hall, 105 **A1**

Neratovice, 35 **F4**

Nes Ziyyona, 50 **A5**

Neshaminy SP, PA 145 **H5**

Nespelem, WA 134 **D6**

Netherlands, 16 **D6**, 20 **E8**, 23 **B4**

Netherlands Antilles, 95 **F2**

Neu Zittau, 32 **F5**

Neubrandenburg, 22 **E5**

Neuces R, TX 129 **E2**

Neuenegg, 37 **A2**

Neuenhagen, 32 **F7**

Neuhausen, 37 **F4**

Neu-Isenburg, 35 **B2**

Neukölln, 32 **D6**

Neunkirch, 37 **F5**

Neuquén, 86 **A4**

Neuss, 34 **A5**

Neustrelitz, 22 **E5**

Neusussenbrunn, 42 **F8**

Nevada, 110 **B5**, 132, 134 **D1**, 178 **B4**

Nevada, MO 125 **A2**

Nevada Great Basin, 110 **B5**

Nevada Test Site, NV 132 **C4**

Nevado de Colima, 96 **C3**

Nevers, 23 **A1**

Neves, 91 **E2**

New Albany, IN 125 **E2**

New Albany, MS 120 **B5**

New Amsterdam, 85 **E5**

New Baltimore, OH 151 **B4**

New Bedford, MA 112 **F6**, 115 **C2**

New Bern, NC 113 E4, 121 H5

New Braunfels, TX 129 E2

New Brighton, MN 161 C4

New Britain, CT 115 A2

New Britain, PNG 76 D2, 80 B4

New Brunswick, Can 114 F7

New Brunswick, NJ 119 H5

New Caledonia, 80 B3

New Carrollton, MD 148 F7

New Castle, PA 118 D5

New Chicago, 88 D6

New City, NY 116 B6, 119 H6

New Cumberland, OH 118 D5

New Delhi, 58 C6, 64 E7

New Dorp, NY 142 C1

New Eden, IL 153 H1

New England Aquarium, MA 140 D4

New Glasgow, 103 F2

New Guinea, 76 B2, 80 A4

New Hampshire, 103 D1, 112 E6, 115 C3, 179 H5

New Haven, CT 112 E6, 115 A1, 116 C6

New Haven, OH 151 E6

New Holland, NC 187 E3

New Hope, MN 161 B3

New Hyde Park, NY 143 G4

New Iberia, LA 129 G3

New Ireland, 76 D2, 80 B4

New Jersey, 103 D1, 112 E6, 116 A5, 119 H5, 179 H4

New Kensington, PA 146 F8

New Kowloon, 75 C4

New Lenox, IL 159 B1

New Lexington, OH 118 C4

New Liskeard, 103 C2

New London, CT 115 B1

New Martinsville, OH 118 C4

New Meadows, ID 135 E3

New Mexico, 111 D4, 128 B5, 131 E3, 178 C3

New Milford, CT 117 H1

New Orleans, LA 97 E5, 113 B2, 120 A1, 129 H3, 163 G5, 179 F1

New Orleans, U of, LA 163 G6

New Orleans Intl Arpt, LA 163 E6

New Palace, 37 C2

New Palace Bldg, 69 C3

New Paltz, NY 117 G1

New Philadelphia, OH 118 C5

New Plymouth, 77 H2

New Providence, 94 C6

New River Gorge Natl R, WV 118 D2

New Roads, LA 129 G3

New Sharon, ME 114 D5

New Siberian Isl, 54 C7, 82 C7

New Smyrna Beach, FL 123 F4

New South Wales, 77 E3

New Springville, NY 142 B1

New Ulm, MN 124 A5, 126 F6

New York, 103 D1, 112 E6, 116, 119 H6, 179 G5

New York, NY 103 D1, 112 F6, 116 B5, 119 H5, 141, 142 D4, 179 H4

New York Aquarium for Wildlife Conservation, NY 142 D1

New York Botanical Gdns, NY 143 E6

New York Public Library, NY 141 G4

New York Stock Exchange, NY 141 E1

New York U, NY 141 F3

New Zealand, 77 G2, 80 C2

Newark, CA 175 E3

Newark, DE 119 G4

Newark, NJ 112 F6, 116 A5, 119 H5, 142 B3

Newark, NY 116 D3

Newark, OH 118 C4

Newark, TX 164 A6

Newark Intl Arpt, NJ 142 B3

Newberry, SC 121 F4

Newberry Wildlife Sanctuary, OH 151 B3

Newburgh, NY 117 G1

Newburgh Hts, OH 150 D6

Newburyport, MA 115 C3

Newcastle, Afr 47 E5

Newcastle, Austral 77 E3

Newcastle, Can 103 E2

Newcastle, UK 14 C1, 18 E5

Newcastle, WY 126 B5, 130 E7

Newfane, NY 116 B4

Newfoundland, NC 187 E6

Newham, 26 D7

Newman, 76 B4

Newmarket, 79 B3

Newnan, GA 120 D4

Newport, AR 120 A5, 129 G6

Newport, Austral 79 B2

Newport, KY 151 D2

Newport, MN 161 F1

Newport, OR 134 A3

Newport, RI 115 C2

Newport, UK 19 D2

Newport, WA 134 D6

Newport Beach, CA 133 D2, 170 D1

Newport Hills, WA 176 C4

Newport News, VA 112 E5, 119 G1

Newry, 19 C4

Newton, IA 125 B4

Newton, KS 127 E2

Newton, MA 139 C3

Newton, NJ 116 A6, 119 H5

Newton Highlands, MA 139 B3

Newtown, Austral 78 E6

Newtown, OH 151 F2

Newtown Square, PA 144 B3

Neyagawa, 70 D6

Nez Perce, ID 135 E4

Nez Perce IR, ID 130 A8, 135 E4

Nez Perce NHP, ID 178 B6

Nezahualcóyotl, 98 D3

Ngau Chi Wan, 75 D4

Nha Trang, 61 C4

Niagara Falls, 116 B3

Niagara-on-the-Lake, 116 B4

Niamey, 44 C2

Nicaragua, 81 H5, 84 A6, 94 A2 , 97 G2

Nice, CA 132 B6

Nice, Fr 16 D4, 20 F5, 24 A4

Niceville, FL 122 B6

Nicholasville, KY 118 A2

Nickerson SP, MA 184 F5

Nicobar Islands, 59 F3

Nicolás R Casillas, 99 E4

Nicolet, 114 A7

Nicolet NF, WI 124 D6

Nicosia, 48 D5

Nictau, 114 F8

Nied, 35 A2

Nieder-Neuendorf, 32 C8

Niederrad, 35 B2

Niel, 31 F5

Niemeyer, 91 D1

Nienburg, 23 C4

Nieuw Vennep, 30 C5

Nieuwerkerk aan de IJssel, 30 C2

Nieuwkerken Waas, 31 F5

Niger, 44 D3

Niger R, 44 C2

Nigeria, 44 D1

Niguarda, 40 C2

Nihonbashi, 69 E3

281

Nihonbashi-Ningyocho, 69 F4

Niigata, 66 F6

Niihau, HI 137 A4

Niiza, 68 B8

Nijo Castle, 71 E3

Nikaia, 43 B2

Nikolayevsk-na-Amure, 55 F4

Niland, CA 133 F2

Nile R, 45 F4, 48 C4

Niles, IL 158 C5

Nilópolis, 91 B3

Nimes, 21 E4

Ningbo, 60 D7, 67 C3

Ninove, 31 E2

Ninoy Aquino Intl Arpt, 62 C1

Niobrara R, NE 127 C4

Nipigon, 103 A2, 124 D8

Nipomo, CA 133 C3

Nis, 17 G4, 25 F6

Nishi-Ku, 71 A2

Nishi-Kyogoku, 71 E2

Nishikyo-Ku, 71 D2

Nishijin Textile Ctr, 71 E4

Nishinomiya, 70 B6

Nishishinbashi, 69 C1

Niterói, 86 D6, 91 E2

Niue, 80 D3

Niva, 36 C8

Nizhnevartovsk, 53 F4

Nizhniy Novgorod, 53 B4

Nizhniy Tagil, 53 D4

No Man's Land, 50 C5

Noatak N Pres, AK 136 C8, 178 A2

Nob Hill, CA 173 D2

Nobska Pt, MA 185 F1

Nodebo, 36 A8

Nogales, AZ 111 C3, 131 B1

Nogales, Mex 96 B6, 131 B1

Nohili Pt, HI 137 A4

Noisy-le-Grand, 28 E7

Nokomis-Hiawatha RP, MN 161 C2

Nome, AK 82 A6, 136 B7

Nonantum, MA 139 B3

Noord, 30 D6

Noordwijk aan Zee, 30 B5

Noordwijkerhout, 30 B5

Norco, CA 171 F4

Norcross, GA 152 D6

Nordvik, 54 B6, 82 C8

Nordwest-stadt, 35 A3

Norfolk, NE 126 E4

Norfolk, VA 112 E5, 119 G1, 121 H6, 179 H3

Norfolk Isl, 77 G3, 80 C2

Norilsk, 54 A5, 82 C8

Normal, IL 125 D3

Norman, OK 129 E5

Norman Wells, 136 F7

Normandy Park, WA 176 B3

Nørre Herlev, 36 A8

Norridge, IL 159 C4

Norridgewock, ME 114 D5

Norris Geyser Basin, WY 180 B4

Norris Lake, TN 120 D6

Norristown, PA 119 G4, 144 C6

Norrköping, 15 F2, 22 F7

Norrsunda, 36 E8

North Absaroka Wilderness, WY 180 D4

North Adams, MA 115 A3, 117 H3

North Andover, MA 138 C8

North Arlington, NJ 142 C4

North Barrackpore, 65 F3

North Battleford, 101 E3

North Bay, Can 103 C2

North Bay Village, FL 155 G2

North Beach, CA 173 D4

North Bend, OH 151 B2

North Bergen, NJ 142 C5

North Caldwell, NJ 142 A6

North Canadian R, OK 127 D1

North Cape, 15 F6, 82 E7

North Carolina, 113 E4, 121 F5, 179 G3

North Cascades NP, WA 134 C6, 178 B6

North Chagrin Res, OH 150 F8

North Channel, Can 124 F6

North Chan, UK 18 C5

North Chatham, MA 184 F5

North Chevy Chase, MD 148 D8

North Chicago, IL 158 C7

North China Plain, 66 A5

North College Hill, OH 151 B3

North Creek, NY 117 G4

North Crows Nest, IN 157 F3

North Dakota, 101 F2, 110 F7, 126 E7, 178 D6

North Decatur, GA 152 C4

North Druid Hills, GA 152 C4

North Dupo, IL 162 C1

North Eastham, MA 184 F6

North End, MA 140 B4

North Fair Oaks, CA 175 C3

North Harbor, 62 B2

North Houston, TX 166 B5

North Isl, 77 H2, 80 C2

North Kansas City, MO 162 C6

North Korea, 60 D8, 66 C3

North Lake Park, TX 165 E5

North Lauderdale, FL 155 G5

North Miami, FL 155 G3

North Miami Beach, FL 155 G3

North Mountain RA, AZ 168 B5

North Myrtle Beach, SC 121 G4

North New Hyde Park, NY 143 G4

North Oaks, MN 161 E4

North Olmsted, OH 150 B6

North Park, PA 146 C4

North Parramatta, 78 C8

North Plains, OR 177 E6

North Platte, NE 110 F5, 127 C4

North Platte R, NE 127 B4, 130 F6

North Pt, Hong Kong 75 D2

North Pt, ME 186 A5

North Point SP, MD 147 F1

North Pole, 82 C7

North Port, PA 123 E3

North Powder, OR 134 D4

North Randall, OH 150 E6

North Randolph, MA 139 D1

North Reading, MA 138 D6

North Richland Hills, TX 164 C4

North Richmond, CA 174 B6

North Rim, AZ 183 E2

North Rocks, 78 D8

North Royalton, OH 150 C5

North Ryde, 78 D8

North St Paul, MN 161 F3

North Sea, 14 D1, 18 F5, 20 D8, 22 A6, 82 F7

North Siberian Lowland, 54 B6

North Springfield, VA 148 B5

North Sta & Fleet Ctr, MA 140 C4

North Stratford, NH 114 B5

North Sydney, 78 E7

North Tisbury, MA 185 G1

North Tonawanda, NY 116 **B3**

North Truro, MA 184 **E8**

North Valley Stream, NY 143 **G3**

North Vancouver, 107 **G3**

North Wellington, 77 **H1**

North West Cape, 76 **A4**

North Woburn, MA 138 **C5**

North York, 104 **D7**

Northbridge, 78 **E8**

Northbrook, IL 158 **C6**

Northbrook, OH 151 **C3**

Northcliff, 51 **F3**

Northcote, 79 **C3**

Northeast Creek, ME 186 **B6**

Northeast Entrance, MT 180 **D5**

Northeast Harbor, ME 186 **C3**

Northeast Philadelphia Arpt, PA 145 **G5**

Northern Cheyenne IR, MT 126 **A6**, 130 **D8**

Northern Dvina R, 52 **C5**

Northern European Plain, 15 **G1**, 52 **B5**

Northern Mariana Islands, 80 **B5**

Northern Terr, 76 **C5**

Northern Yukon NP, 136 **E8**

Northfield, IL 158 **C5**

Northfield, OH 150 **E5**

Northfield Ctr, OH 150 **E5**

Northglenn, CO 167 **G5**

Northlake, IL 159 **C4**

Northmead, 78 **C8**

Northport, WA 134 **D6**

Northwest Cape, FL 188 **C4**

Northwest Pk, MT 135 **E6**

Northwest Terr, Can 100 **E5**

Northwestern U, IL 158 **D5**

Northwestway Park, IN 157 **D3**

Northwoods, MO 162 **B2**

Norton Sd, AK 136 **B7**

Norwalk, CA 170 **D3**

Norwalk, CT 115 **A1**, 116 **B6**

Norway, 22 **C8**

Norway, ME 114 **C5**

Norwegian Sea, 14 **D4**, 52 **C7**, 82 **E7**

Norwich, CT 115 **B2**

Norwich, NY 117 **E2**

Norwich, UK 19 **F3**, 20 **D8**

Norwood, MA 139 **B1**

Norwood, OH 151 **E2**

Norwood, PA 144 **C1**

Nose, 70 **C8**

Notre Dame, 29 **E1**

Notre-Dame Basilica, 106 **C2**

Notting Hill, 79 **D1**

Nottingham, 14 **C1**, 19 **E3**, 20 **C8**

Nou Camp Stad, 38 **E6**

Nouadhibou, 44 **A3**

Nouakchott, 44 **A3**

Nouméa, 80 **C3**

Nova U, FL 155 **F4**

Novara, 20 **F5**, 24 **A5**

Novate Milanese, 40 **B2**

Novato, CA 174 **A7**

Novaya Zemlya, 52 **E6**, 82 **D7**

Novgorod, 15 **G3**, 52 **B5**

Novi Pazar, 25 **E6**

Novi Sad, 17 **G4**

Novo Iguaçu, 91 **B3**

Novonikol'skoye, 56 **C2**

Novokuznetsk, 55 **A3**

Novosaratovka, 57 **H2**

Novosel'tsevo, 56 **B6**

Novosibirsk, 53 **F3**

Nowitna NWR, AK 136 **C7**

Nowon, 72 **D8**

Noxubee NWR, MS 120 **B4**

Nuannuan, 62 **D6**

Nubian Desert, 45 **G3**, 48 **D2**

Nueva Casas Grandes, 96 **B6**, 131 **D1**

Nueva Gerona, 94 **B5**

Nueva Rosita, 128 **C2**

Nuevo España, 99 **F4**

Nuevo Laredo, 96 **D5**, 128 **D1**

Nuevo México, 99 **F6**

Nukualofa, 80 **D3**

Nukus, 53 **C2**, 58 **A8**

Nullarbor Plain, 76 **C3**

Nunavut, 100 **F6**

Nunawading, 79 **E2**

Nuñez, 88 **D7**

Nunivak Isl, AK 82 **A6**, 136 **A6**

Nunyagmo, 136 **A7**

Nürnberg, 17 **E5**, 23 **D3**

Nutley, NJ 142 **B5**

Nutter Pt, ME 186 **A2**

Nutting Lake, MA 138 **B5**

Nuuk, 82 **E5**, 102 **D6**

Nyack, NY 116 **B6**

Nyala, 45 **F2**

Nyssa, OR 134 **D3**

O

Oahu, HI 81 **E5**, 137 **C4**

Oak Bluff, 107 **F4**

Oak Bluffs, MA 115 **D2**, 185 **G2**

Oak Brook, IL 159 **B3**

Oak Forest, IL 159 **C2**

Oak Grove, OR 177 **G4**

Oak Hill, MA 139 **C2**

Oak Lane, PA 145 **E4**

Oak Lawn, IL 159 **C3**

Oak Park, Austral 79 **B4**

Oak Park, IL 159 **C4**

Oak Park, MI 156 **C8**

Oak Ridge, TN 120 **D6**, 125 **F1**

Oakdale, GA 152 **A4**

Oakdale, MN 161 **F3**

Oakhurst, CA 132 **C5**

Oakland, CA 110 **A5**, 132 **B5**, 174 **C5**

Oakland, FL 153 **E4**

Oakland, MD 119 **E4**

Oakland Mus, CA 174 **C5**

Oakland Park, FL 155 **G5**

Oakland Park, TX 165 **E6**

Oakland-Alameda County Coliseum, CA 174 **C5**

Oakleigh, 79 **D1**

Oakley, ID 135 **F2**

Oakley, KS 127 **C3**

Oaklyn, NJ 145 **F2**

Oakmont, PA 146 **E7**

Oakridge, Can 107 **G1**

Oakridge, OR 134 **B3**

Oaks, MO 162 **C6**

Oakton, VA 148 **A6**

Oakview, MD 148 **E8**

Oakville, CT 117 **H1**

Oakwood, OH 150 **F5**

Oamishirasato, 68 **F6**

Oaxaca, 96 **D2**

Ob R, 53 **E4**, 82 **D8**

Oban, 18 **C6**

Obatange PP, 124 **E7**

Obelisk, 89 **D3**

Oberbilk, 34 **B5**

Oberhausen, 34 **B7**

Oberlaa, 42 **E6**

Oberlin, KS 127 **D3**

Oberursel, 35 **A4**

Oboldino, 56 **D5**

Observatory Hill, 78 **E7**

Obsidian Cliff, WY 180 **B5**

Óbuda, 42 **A7**

Ocala, FL 113 **D2**, 121 **E1**, 123 **E5**

Ocala NF, FL 121 **F1**

Ocean Bluff, MA 184 **A8**

Ocean Falls, 101 **B3**

Ocean Park, *Hong Kong* 75 C1

Ocean Park, WA 134 A5

Oceanside, CA 133 D2

Oceanside, NY 143 H2

Ochakovo, 56 B3

Ochoco NF, OR 134 C3

Ocoee, FL 153 F4

Oconee NF, GA 121 E4

Ocracoke, NC 187 F1

Ocracoke Inlet, NC 187 F1

Ocracoke Isl, NC 187 F1

Ocracoke Isl Visitor Ctr, NC 187 F1

Ocracoke Lighthouse, NC 187 F1

Ócsa, 42 C5

October Stad, 56 B4

Odemis, 25 H3

Odense, 15 E1, 22 D6

Oder R, 17 F6, 23 E4

Odesa, 45 F6, 17 H5

Odessa, TX 111 E3, 128 C4, 131 F1

Odintsovo, 56 A3

Odivelas, 38 B7

Odolena Voda, 35 E4

Oeiras, 38 A6

Oeuzzane, 21 B1

O'Fallon Park, MO 162 C2

Offenbach, *Ger* 35 C3

Offenbach, *Switz* 37 D1

Offenburg, 23 C2

Offentahl, 35 C1

Ogallala, NE 127 C4, 130 F6

Ogbomosho, 44 C1

Ogden, UT 110 C6, 130 B6, 135 G3

Ogdensburg, NY 117 F6

Ogimachi Park, 71 B4

Ogo, 70 A6

Ogoki R, 124 D8

Ohatsu Tenjin Shrine, 71 A4

O'Higgins Park, 87 F2

Ohio, 103 C1, 112 C5, 118 A5, 179 G4

Ohio R, 112 C5, 118 B3, 125 E2, 179 F4

Ohiopyle SP, PA 119 E4

Ohrid, 25 E4

Oinville-sur-Montcient, 28 A8

Oita, 67 E4

Oji Park, 70 A5

Ojibway Prov P, 156 D5

Ojinaga, 128 B2

Okamedari, 71 F1

Okanogan, WA 134 C6

Okanogan NF, WA 134 C6

Okayama, 66 E5

Okeana, OH 151 A4

Okeechobee, FL 123 F3

Okefenokee NWR, GA 121 E2, 123 E6

Okha, 55 F4

Okhla, 64 E6

Okhotsk, 54 E5

Okinawa, 60 E6, 67 D3

Oklahoma, 96 D6, 111 F4, 129 E6, 178 D3

Oklahoma City, OK 111 F4, 127 E1, 129 E5, 178 D3

Okmulgee, OK 127 F1

Olalla, WA 176 A3

Öland, 15 F2, 22 F6

Olbia, 24 A3

Old Cairo, 50 C2

Old Crow, 136 D7

Old Faithful, WY 180 B3

Old Faithful Visitor Ctr, WY 180 B3

Old Man House SP, WA 176 A6

Old Mill Creek, IL 158 B8

Old North Church, MA 140 D5

Old Opera House, 35 B3

Old Orchard Beach, ME 115 D4

Old Saybrook, CT 116 D6

Old Shawnee Town, KS 162 A4

Old South Meeting House, MA 140 C3

Old Statehouse & Boston Massacre Site, MA 140 C3

Old Tampa Bay Park, FL 154 B5

Old Town, ME 114 E5

Old US Mint, CA 173 E1

Old Yafo, 50 A6

Oldcastle, 156 E5

Oldenburg, 23 C4

Oldsmar, FL 154 B5

Olean, NY 116 C2, 119 E6

Olenek R, 54 C5

Ol'gino, 57 F3

Olinda, 91 B3

Olivais, 38 C7

Olivar de los Padres, 98 A2

Olive Park, IL 160 E8

Oliver, 156 E5

Olivette, MO 162 B2

Olivon, 43 A4

Olivos, 88 D8

Olmos Park, TX 163 G3

Olmsted Falls, OH 150 B5

Olney, IL 125 D2

Olney, PA 145 E4

Olstykke, 36 A7

Olympia, WA 110 A7, 134 B5

Olympia Hts, FL 155 F1

Olympia Stad, 43 C3

Olympiastadion, 32 C7

Olympic NP, WA 134 B6, 178 A6

Olympic Sports Ctr, 73 D3

Olympic Stad, *Indo* 64 B7

Olympic Stad, *Mex* 98 B2

Olympic Stad, *Spain* 38 E6

Omagh, 19 B4

Omaha, NE 112 A5, 125 A4, 127 F4, 179 E4

Oman, 49 H3

Omdurman, 45 F2, 48 C1

Omiya Sento Palace, 71 B3

Omni, The, GA 152 B4

Oneco, FL 154 C1

Oneida, NY 117 F3

Oneida Lake, NY 117 F3

O'Neill, NE 127 E4

O'Neill NHS, CA 174 E5

O'Neill RP, CA 171 F1

Oneonta, NY 117 F2

Omsk, 53 E3

Once Train Sta, 89 B2

Onitsha, 44 D1

Onset, MA 184 E5

Ontario, CA 171 F4

Ontario Intl Arpt, CA 171 F4

Ontario Science Ctr, 104 E6

Oost, 30 D6

Oostende, 20 E7, 23 A4

Opa Locka, FL 155 F3

Opalikha, 56 A5

Opava, 23 F3

Opéra Bastille, 29 F1

Opera House, WA 176 A5

Opp, AL 120 C2

Opwijk, 31 F3

Oradea, 17 G5

Oral, 53 C3

Oran, 16 B1, 21 D1, 44 C5

Orange, *Austral* 77 E3

Orange, CA 171 E3

Orange, NJ 142 A4

Orange, OH 150 F6

Orange, VA 119 E2

Orange Bowl, FL 155 F2

Orange Park, FL 123 F5

Orange R, 47 E2

Orangeburg, SC 121 F4

Oranienburg, 23 D4

Oranjestad, 95 E1

Orbottyán, 42 C8

Orcasitas, 39 B1

Orchard Beach, MD 147 E1

Orchards, WA 177 G6

Orchestra Hall, IL 160 C6

Örebro, 15 F2, 22 E8

Oregon, 101 B1, 110 A7, 134 B4, 178 A5

Oregon City, OR 134 **B4**, 177 **G4**

Oregon Conv Ctr, OR 177 **G5**

Oregon Hist Ctr, OR 177 **G5**

Oregon Inlet, NC 187 **H5**

Oreland, PA 145 **E6**

Orem, UT 130 **B6**

Orenburg, 53 **C3**

Orense, 21 **A4**

Orford, NH 115 **B4**

Organ Pipe Cactus NM, AZ 131 **B2**, 178 **B2**

Orient, NY 116 **D3**

Orient, OR 177 **H5**

Orient Park, FL 154 **D5**

Oriental Plaza, 51 **F2**

Orinda, CA 174 **D6**

Orinoco R, 84 **D5**

Oriole Park at Camden Yards, MD 147 **D2**

Oriskany, NY 117 **F3**

Oristano, 24 **A3**

Orizaba, 96 **D3**

Orkney Islands, 14 **C2**

Orland, CA 132 **B6**

Orland Hills, IL 159 **C2**

Orland Park, IL 159 **C2**

Orlando, Afr 51 **F2**

Orlando, FL 113 **D2**, 121 **F1**, 123 **E4**, 153 **G4**, 179 **G1**

Orlando Arena, FL 153 **G4**

Orlando Intl Arpt, FL 153 **G3**

Orléans, Fr 16 **C5**, 20 **D6**

Orleans, MA 184 **F6**

Orlovista, FL 153 **F4**

Orly Arpt, 28 **D6**

Ormond Beach, FL 123 **F5**

Orofino, ID 135 **E4**

Orono, ME 114 **E5**

Oroville, CA 132 **B6**

Oroville, WA 134 **C6**

Orpington, 26 **D6**

Orsay, 28 **C6**

Orsk, 53 **D3**

Orszaghez, 42 **B7**

Orumiyeh, 49 **E6**

Oruro, 84 **D1**

Orwell, VT 115 **A4**

Osa, 40 **D5**

Osage IR, OK 127 **F1**, 129 **E6**

Osage R, MO 125 **B2**

Osaka, 60 **E8**, 66 **E5**, 70 **D5**, 71 **B2**

Osaka Castle, 70 **D5**, 71 **C3**

Osaka Chamber of Industry & Commerce, 71 **C3**

Osaka Festival Bldg, 71 **A3**

Osaka Intl Arpt, 70 **C6**

Osaka Mint & Mus, 70 **D5**, 71 **C3**

Osaka Scientific Tech Ctr, 71 **A3**

Osaka Sta, 71 **A4**

Osaka Stock Exchange, 71 **B3**

Osaka U, 70 **C5**, 71 **A3**

Osakajo Park, 71 **C3**

Osark NF, AR 129 **F6**

Osasco, 92 **A5**

Osceola NF, 121 **E2**

Oshawa, 103 **C1**, 116 **B3**

Oshkosh, WI 124 **D5**

Oshogbo, 44 **C1**

Osijek, 24 **D5**

Oskarshamn, 22 **F7**

Oskemen, 53 **F2**

Oslo, 15 **E3**, 22 **D8**, 82 **F7**

Osnabrück, 20 **F8**, 23 **C4**

Osorno, 86 **A4**

Osteen, FL 153 **H6**

Osteraker, 36 **F7**

Osterang, 36 **F5**

Osterath, 34 **A6**

Osterfeld, 34 **B7**

Osterhaninge, 36 **F5**

Osteria dell' Osa, 40 **D5**

Ostermundigen, 37 **C2**

Östersund, 15 **E4**

Osterville, MA 185 **E3**

Ostiense, 40 **C5**

Ostrava, 17 **F6**

Ostrov, 56 **D2**

Ostrup, 36 **A6**

Oswego, NY 117 **E4**

Otaki, 68 **F5**

Ota-Ku, 68 **C6**

Otaru, 66 **E7**

Otemachi, 69 **D4**

Othello, WA 134 **C5**

.is, MA 115 **A2**

Otis AFB, MA 184 **B5**

Otradnoye, 57 **H1**

Otsu, 70 **F8**

Ottakring, 42 **D7**

Ottavia, 40 **B6**

Ottawa, Can 103 **C2**, 105 **B3**, 112 **E7**

Ottawa, KS 125 **A2**, 127 **F2**

Ottawa Civic Ctr, 105 **B2**

Ottawa Intl Arpt, 105 **B1**

Ottawa NF, MI 124 **D6**

Ottawa NWR, OH 118 **B6**

Otter Cove, ME 186 **D3**

Otter Creek, ME 186 **D4**

Otter Creek, VT 117 **H5**

Otter Pt, ME 186 **D3**

Ottumwa, IA 112 **A5**, 125 **B4**

Ouachita NF, AR 129 **F5**

Ouagadougou, 44 **C1**

Oud-Beijerland, 30 **B1**

Oud-Zuid, 30 **D5**

Oudewater, 30 **D3**

Oudja, 21 **C1**, 44 **C5**

Oulo, 15 **G4**

Oulu, 52 **C6**

Our Lady of Guadalupe Basilica, 98 **B4**

Our Lady of Lourdes Shrine, OH 150 **E8**

Outfall Canal, NC 187 **B3**

Outremont, 106 **C3**

Oveido, FL 153 **H5**

Overbrook, PA 144 **D3**

Overijse, 31 **H1**

Overland, MO 162 **B2**

Overland Park, MO 162 **B4**

Overlea, MD 147 **E3**

Overlook Mt, WY 180 **D2**

Overton, NV 133 **F4**

Overtoomse, 30 **D6**

Oviedo, 21 **B4**

Ovilla, TX 165 **F1**

Owasco Lake, NY 117 **E3**

Owatonna, MN 124 **B5**

Owego, NY 119 **F6**

Owen Sd, 103 **C1**

Owensboro, KY 113 **C4**, 125 **E2**

Owings Mills, MD 147 **B4**

Owyhee, NV 132 **E8**, 135 **E1**

Oxford, MS 120 **B4**

Oxford, NC 119 **E1**, 121 **G6**

Oxford, UK 19 **E3**

Oxnard, CA 133 **C3**

Oxon Hill, MD 148 **E5**

Oxon Hill Farm, MD 148 **D5**

Oyamazaki, 70 **E7**

Ozark, AL 120 **D3**

Ozark NF, AK 125 **B1**

Ozark Natl Scenic Riverways, MO 125 **C2**

Ozark Plateau, 113 **A4**

Ozoir-a-Ferriere, 28 **E6**

Ozona, FL 154 **A6**

Ozone Park, NY 143 **E3**

P

Pablo Iglesias, 39 **F1**

Pabst Brewery, WI 157 **C3**

Pacaembú Stad, 92 **B5**

Pace, FL 122 **B6**

Pace Railway Sta, 62 **C2**

Pacheco, CA 174 **D7**

Pachena Pt, 134 **A6**

Pachuca, 96 **D3**

Pacific, WA 176 **C1**

Pacific Beach, CA 169 **E4**

Pacific Coast Stock Exchange, CA 173 **E2**

Pacific Hts, CA 173 **B3**

Pacific Ocean, 80 – 81,
84 **A4**, 96 **C2**, 101 **A3**,
136 **D5**

Pacific Spirit RP, 107 **F2**

Pacifica, CA 175 **A4**

Padang, 61 **A2**

Paddington, 78 **F7**

Paderno Dugnano, 40 **B3**

Padova, 23 **E1**, 24 **B5**

Padre Hurlado, 87 **E1**

Padre Island NS, TX
178 **D1**

Padstow, 78 **C6**

Paducah, KY 113 **B4**,
120 **B6**, 125 **D2**

Page, AZ 131 **B4**

Pago Pago, 80 **D3**

Pahaska, WY 180 **D3**

Pahokee, FL 123 **F3**

Paianía, 43 **C2**

Painesville, OH 118 **C6**

Painted Desert, AZ 183 **F3**

Paintsville, KY 118 **B2**

Paio Pires, 38 **C5**

Paisley, OR 134 **C2**

Pakistan, 49 **H5**, 58 **A6**

Pakxe, 61 **B4**

Palace of Congresses, 57 **E5**

Palace of Fine Arts, CA
173 **A3**

Palace of Justice, 41 **C4**

Palace of Natl Assembly,
38 **B6**

Palace of the Arts, 40 **B2**

Palace of Versailles, 28 **C6**

Palaion Faliron, 43 **B2**

Palais de Chaillot, 29 **A2**

Palais du Justice, 29 **E2**

Palais Royal, 29 **D2**

Palais Unter den Linden,
33 **E3**

Palaiseau, 28 **C6**

Palam, 64 **D7**

Palana, 54 **B8**, 54 **F6**

Palapye, 47 **F3**

Palatine, IL 158 **B6**

Palatino Hill, 41 **D2**

Palatka, FL 121 **F1**, 123 **F5**

Palau, 80 **A5**

Palau-Solità, 38 **E8**

Palawan, 61 **D4**

Palazzo del Quirinale,
41 **D3**

Palazzo Venezia, 41 **D3**

Palembang, 61 **B1**

Palermo, Arg 88 **D7**,
89 **A4**

Palermo, CA 132 **B6**

Palermo, Italy 17 **E2**,
24 **C2**, 48 **A6**

Palhais, 38 **C5**

Pali, 62 **B6**, 64 **E5**

Palidoro, 40 **A6**

Palikir, 80 **B4**

Palisades Park, NJ 142 **D5**

Palm Bay, FL 123 **F4**

Palm Beach, FL 123 **G3**

Palm Coast, FL 123 **F5**

Palm Harbor, FL 154 **A6**

Palm Key, FL 188 **E3**

Palm R, FL 154 **D5**

Palm Springs, CA 133 **E3**

Palma, 16 **C3**, 21 **E3**

Palma Sola, FL 154 **B1**

Palmdale, CA 133 **D3**

Palmer Park, MD 148 **F7**

Palmetto, FL 154 **B1**

Palmira, 84 **C4**

Palmyra, NJ 145 **G3**

Palmyra, NY 116 **D3**

Palmyra Atoll, 80 **D5**

Palo Alto, CA 175 **D2**

Palomeras, 39 **D2**

Palopo, 61 **E2**

Palos FP, IL 159 **C3**

Palos Hts, IL 159 **C2**

Palos Hills, IL 159 **C2**

Palos Verdes Estates, CA
170 **B3**

Palu, 61 **E2**

Pamirs, 53 **E1**, 58 **C7**

Pamlico Sd, NC 121 **H5**,
187 **F2**

Pampa, TX 128 **D6**

Pampas, 86 **B5**

Pamplona, 16 **B4**, 21 **C4**

Panaca, NV 131 **A4**, 132 **F5**

Panaji, 59 **B4**

Panama, 81 **H5**, 84 **B5**,
97 **H1**

Panama Canal, 97 **H1**

Panama City, Pan 84 **B5**,
97 **H1**

Panama City, FL 113 **C3**,
120 **C2**, 122 **C5**

Panania, 78 **C6**

Panay, 61 **E4**

Panchiao, 62 **B5**

Pangkalpinang, 61 **B2**

Pangnirtung, 102 **C6**

Panhandle Key, FL 188 **E3**

Panihati, 65 **F2**

Pankow, 32 **D7**

Pantego, TX 164 **C3**

Pantelleria, 24 **B1**

Panthéon, Fr 29 **E1**

Pantheon, Italy 40 **C5**,
41 **C3**

Panthersville, GA 152 **D3**

Pantigliate, 40 **D1**

Pantitlán, 98 **C3**

Paoli, PA 144 **A4**

Paomachang, 73 **C2**

Papago Park, AZ 168 **C3**

Papeeté, 81 **E3**

Papendrecht, 30 **C1**

Papua New Guinea, 76 **C1**,
80 **B4**

Parabiago, 40 **A3**

Paradise, CA 132 **B6**

Paradise, NV 131 **A4**

Paradise Hills, CA 169 **G3**

Paradise Valley, AZ 168 **C4**

Paragould, AR 120 **A6**,
125 **C1**, 129 **H6**

Paraguay, 85 **E1**, 86 **B6**

Paraguay R, 85 **E1**, 86 **B6**

Paramaribo, 85 **F5**

Paramount Studios, CA
170 **C3**, 172 **C7**

Paraná, 86 **B5**

Paraná R, 86 **B5**, 86 **C6**

Paranapiacaba, 92 **D3**

Paranaque, 62 **B1**

Parasnath Jain Temple,
65 **E2**

Parc des Princes Stad,
28 **C7**

Parc Monceau, 29 **C4**

Parc Naturel Regional de
la Haute Vallee de
Chevreuse, 28 **B5**

Parco Traianeo, 41 **E2**

Parel, 65 **B2**

Parelheiros, 92 **A2**

Parent Naval Orange Tree,
CA 171 **G4**

Parepare, 61 **E2**

Parets del Vallès, 38 **F8**

Pargolovo, 57 **F3**

Parioli, 40 **C6**

Paris, Fr 16 **C5**, 20 **E6**,
23 **A2**, 28 **D7**, 29, 44 **D6**

Paris, ID 135 **G2**

Paris, IL 125 **D3**

Paris, KY 118 **B2**

Paris, TN 120 **B6**, 125 **D1**,
129 **H6**

Paris, TX 113 **A3**, 129 **F5**

Park City, IL 158 **C7**

Park City, UT 130 **C6**

Park Hills, KY 151 **D1**

Park Orchards, 79 **E3**

Park Ridge, IL 158 **C5**

Parker, TX 165 **H6**

Parker Ranch, HI 137 **E2**

Parker River NWR, MA
138 **F8**

Parker SF, Harold, MA
138 **D7**

Parkersburg, WV 112 **D5**,
118 **C3**

Parkland, FL 155 **F6**

Parkville, MD 147 **E4**

Parkville, MO 162 **B6**

Parliament, Aus 42 **E7**

Parliament, India 64 **E7**

Parliament Bldg, 64 **B7**

Parma, *Italy* 24 **B5**
Parma, OH 150 **D6**
Parma Hts, OH 150 **C6**
Parnaíba, 85 **G3**
Pärnu, 15 **G2**
Parque Almirante Guillermo Brown, 88 **D6**
Parque Ameghino, 89 **C1**
Parque Mus, NJ 142 **B6**
Parque Chacabuco, 89 **A1**
Parque Colón, 89 **E3**
Parque del Centenario, 89 **A2**
Parque Do Estado, 92 **B4**
Parque Lezama, 89 **E2**
Parque Nacional da Tujica, 91 **D2**
Parque Natural Costanera Sur, 89 **F3**
Parque Paricios, 89 **C1**
Parque Rivadavia, 89 **A2**
Parramatta, 78 **C7**
Parrish, FL 154 **D2**
Parry Sound, 103 **C1**
Parsons, KS 127 **F2**
Parsons Pk, CA 182 **D3**
Parung, 64 **A6**
Pas, The, 101 **F3**
Pasadena, CA 133 **D3**, 170 **C4**
Pasadena, TX 129 **F3**, 166 **D3**
Pasarét, 42 **A7**
Pasaunda, 64 **F7**
Pasay, 62 **C2**
Pascagoula, MS 122 **A6**
Pasco, WA 134 **D4**
Pascoe Vale, 79 **B3**
Pasig, 62 **C2**
Pasir Panjang, 63 **E1**
Pasir Ris, 63 **G3**
Paso del Rey, 88 **B6**
Passage Key NWR, FL 154 **B2**
Passaic, NJ 116 **B5**, 142 **B6**
Passau, 23 **E2**
Passo Fundo, 86 **C6**
Passy, 29 **A2**
Pasteros, 62 **C2**

Pasto, 84 **B4**
Patagonia, 86 **A3**
Patapsco Valley SP, MD 147 **B2**
Pate, 62 **A4**
Paterson, NJ 112 **E6**, 116 **A6**, 119 **H5**
Pathumwan, 63 **G5**
Patna, 58 **D5**, 65 **E4**
Pátrai, 17 **G2**, 25 **E3**
Patten, ME 114 **E7**
Patterson, NJ 142 **B9**
Patuxent River Park, MD 147 **A1**
Pau, 21 **D4**
Paul Revere House, MA 140 **D4**
Paulatuk, 136 **F8**
Paullo, 40 **D1**
Pauls Valley, OK 129 **E5**
Paurotis Pond, FL 188 **D4**
Pavia, 24 **A5**
Pavillion, WY 135 **H2**
Pavlodar, 53 **F3**
Pawnee, OK 127 **F1**
Pawnee NG, CO 127 **B4**, 130 **E6**
Pawtucket, RI 115 **C2**
Paya Ledar, 63 **G2**
Paye, 65 **C4**
Payette, ID 134 **D3**
Payette NF, ID 130 **A8**, 135 **E4**
Paysandú, 86 **B5**
Payson, AZ 131 **B3**
Payson, UT 130 **B5**
Pazardzhik, 25 **G5**
Pea Island, NC 187 **H4**
Pea Island NWR, NC 187 **H4**
Pea Ridge NMP, AR 179 **E3**
Peabody, MA 138 **E5**
Peabody Institute, MD 147 **D2**
Peace R, *Can* 101 **D3**
Peace R, FL 123 **E3**

Peakhurst, 78 **C6**
Peania, 43 **C2**
Pearl City, HI 137 **C3**, 177 **F3**
Pearl Harbor, HI 137 **C3**
Pearl Harbor NWR, HI 177 **E2**
Pearl R, MS 129 **H4**
Pearland, TX 166 **C2**
Pearsall, TX 128 **D2**
Pearson Int'l Arpt, 104 **B6**
Pec, 25 **E5**
Pecan Valley Park, TX 164 **A2**
Pecel, 42 **C7**
Peche Island Prov P, 156 **F6**
Pechora, 52 **D5**
Pechora R, 52 **D5**
Peco de Aneto, 21 **D4**
Pecos, TX 128 **C3**, 131 **F1**
Pecos R, NM 128 **B4**, 131 **E3**
Pecs, 17 **F5**, 24 **D6**
Pecs, 17 **F5**, 24 **D6**
Pedley, CA 171 **G4**
Pedro García, 90 **B5**
Peekskill, NY 116 **B6**
Peel R, 136 **E7**
Pegu, 59 **F4**
Pekanbaru, 61 **A2**
Pelee Isl, 118 **C6**
Pelham, NH 138 **A8**
Pelham, NY 143 **F6**
Pelham Bay Park, NY 143 **F6**
Pelham Manor, NY 143 **F6**
Pell City, AL 120 **C4**
Pelly Crossing, 136 **E7**
Pelly R, 136 **E6**
Peloponnesus, 17 **G2**, 25 **F3**
Pelotas, 86 **C5**
Pematangsiantar, 61 **A2**
Pemba Isl, 47 **G5**
Pembina, ND 126 **E8**
Pembroke, *Can* 103 **C2**
Pembroke, UK 19 **C2**

Pembroke Park, FL 155 **G3**
Pembroke Pines, FL 155 **E3**
Peña Grande, 39 **B4**
Penaflor, 87 **E1**
Peñalolén, 87 **G1**
Pendleton, OR 110 **B7**, 134 **D4**
Pengpu, 74 **D8**
Penha, 91 **C3**, 92 **C4**
Peniche, 21 **A3**
Penn Hills, PA 144 **E7**
Penn Square, PA 144 **C6**
Penn Wynne, PA 144 **C3**
Penn Yan, NY 116 **D2**
Penndel, PA 145 **H6**
Pennekamp Coral Reef SP, John, FL 188 **F3**
Pennsauken, NJ 145 **F3**
Pennsuco, FL 155 **F2**
Pennsylvania, 103 **C1**, 112 **D5**, 119 **F5**, 179 **G4**
Pennsylvania, U of, PA 144 **F2**
Pennsylvania Sta, NY 141 **E4**
Pennypack Park, PA 145 **G5**
Penobscot Bay, ME 114 **E6**
Penobscot R, ME 114 **E6**
Pensacola, FL 113 **C3**, 120 **C2**, 122 **B6**
Pensacola Mts, 83 **D3**
Pentagon, VA 148 **D6**
Penza, 53 **C4**
Penzance, 19 **C2**
Penzing, 42 **D7**
Peoria, AZ 168 **A5**
Peoria, IL 112 **B5**, 125 **D3**
Pepacton Reservoir, NY 117 **F2**
Pepper Pike, OH 150 **F7**
Perama, 43 **A2**
Perchtoldsdorf, 42 **D6**
Perdizes, 92 **A5**
Pereira, 84 **C5**
Périgueux, 20 **D5**
Peristerion, 43 **B3**
Perm, 53 **D4**

Pernik, 25 **F5**
Pero, 40 **B2**
Perovo, 56 **C4**
Perpignan, 16 **C3**, 21 **E4**
Perrine, FL 123 **G2**
Perry, FL 121 **E2**, 122 **D5**
Perry, GA 121 **D3**
Perry, NY 116 **C3**
Perry, OK 127 **E1**
Perry Hall, MD 147 **E4**
Perry Park, IN 157 **E1**
Perrysville, PA 146 **B8**
Perryton, TX 127 **D1**,
  128 **D6**
Perryville, MO 125 **C2**
Persian Gulf, 45 **H4**, 49 **F4**
Perth, *Austral* 76 **A3**
Perth, *Can* 117 **E6**
Perth, *UK* 18 **D6**
Perth Road, 117 **E5**
Peru, 84 **C3**
Perugia, 24 **B4**
Perus, 92 **A6**
Pesaro, 24 **C4**
Pescadero, CA 175 **B1**
Pescadero Creek CP, CA
  175 **C1**
Pescara, 24 **C4**
Peshawar, 58 **B7**
Pesthidegkút, 42 **A7**
Pestimre, 42 **B6**
Pestszenterzsébet, 42 **A7**
Pestszentimre, 42 **B6**
Petah Tiqwa, 50 **B6**
Petare, 90 **D4**
Peter & Paul Fortress, 57 **E2**
Peterborough, *Can* 103 **C1**
Peterborough, *UK* 19 **F3**
Peter's Palace, 56 **B4**
Petersburg, AK 101 **B4**
Petersburg, VA 112 **E5**,
  119 **F1**, 121 **D6**
Petershagen, 32 **F7**
Petersham, 78 **E6**
Petinesca Castle, 37 **A3**
Petit Palais, 29 **C3**

Petoskey, MI 124 **E6**
Petrified Forest NP, AZ
  131 **C3**, 178 **C3**
Petrified Tree, WY 180 **B5**
Petro-Slavyanka, 57 **H1**
Petrodvorets, 57 **E2**
Petrolina, 85 **G2**
Petropavl, 53 **E3**
Petropavlovsk-Kamchatskiy,
  54 **C7**
Petroúpolis, 43 **B3**
Petrozavodsk, 15 **H4**, 52 **C5**
Pettit Pk, MS 182 **C5**
Pevek, 54 **E7**
Pfeiffers Corners, MD
  147 **B1**
Pferderennbahn, 34 **F8**
Phalen-Keller RP, MN
  161 **E3**
Phantom Ranch, AZ 183 **E2**
Phasi Charoen, 63 **E5**
Phelps Lake, WY 181 **F2**
Philadelphia, MS 120 **B3**
Philadelphia, PA 103 **D1**,
  112 **E5**, 119 **H4**, 145 **E4**,
  179 **H4**
Philadelphia College of
  Textile & Science, PA
  144 **D4**
Philadelphia Intl Arpt, PA
  144 **D1**
Philadelphia Mus of Art,
  PA 145 **E3**
Philadelphia Naval
  Shipyard, PA 145 **E1**
Philharmonic Hall, 33 **D3**
Philippi, WV 118 **D3**
Philippine Sea, 60 **F5**
Philippines, 65 **H5**, 67 **C1**
Philippines, U of, 62 **C3**
Philipsburg, MT 135 **F4**
Phillipsburg, KS 127 **D3**
Phipps Conservatory, PA
  146 **C6**
Phitsanulok, 61 **A4**
Phnom Penh, 61 **B3**

Phoenix, AZ 96 **B6**, 111 **C4**,
  131 **B2**, 168 **B4**, 178 **B3**
Phoenix Isl, 80 **D4**
Phongsali, 60 **A5**
Phra Khanong, 63 **H5**
Phra Nakhon, 63 **F5**
Phra Pradeng, 63 **F4**
Phuket, 61 **A3**
Piacenza, 24 **B5**
Piana del Sole, 40 **B5**
Picasso Mus, *Fr* 29 **F2**
Picasso Mus, *Spain* 38 **E6**
Picayune, MS 120 **B2**
Piccadilly Circus, 27 **B2**
Pickering, 116 **B4**
Pico de Aneto, 16 **C4**
Pico de Bandeira, 85 **G1**
Pico de Orizaba, 96 **D3**
Pico Duarte, 95 **E4**
Pico Rivera, CA 170 **D4**
Pictured Rocks NL, MI
  124 **D6**, 179 **F5**
Piedmont, CA 174 **C5**
Piedmont Park, CA 152 **C4**
Piedras Negras, 128 **D2**
Pierre, SD 110 **F6**, 126 **D5**,
  178 **D5**
Pierrefonds, 106 **A3**
Pietermaritzburg, 47 **F2**
Pietralata, 40 **C6**
Piety Corner, MA 139 **B4**
Pijnacker, 30 **B3**
Pike NF, CO 127 **A3**
Pikes Pk, CO 110 **E5**,
  127 **A3**, 130 **E5**
Pikesville, MD 147 **C4**
Pikeville, KY 118 **B2**
Pila, 22 **F5**
Pilcomayo R, 84 **D1**, 86 **B6**
Pilgram Creek, WY 181 **G5**
Pilgrim Mem SP, MA
  184 **A7**
Pilisvörösvár, 42 **A8**
Pilot Pk, NV 135 **F1**
Pilot Rock, OR 134 **D4**
Pima Pt, AZ 183 **D2**

Pimlico Race Course, MD
  147 **C3**
Pimmit Hills, VA 148 **B7**
Pinar del Rio, 94 **A5**
Pinchot NF, Gifford, WA
  177 **H6**
Pindus Mts, 25 **E4**
Pine Bluff, AR 113 **A4**,
  129 **G5**
Pine Grove, FL 153 **H1**
Pine Hills, FL 153 **F4**
Pine Island SF, MN 126 **F8**
Pine Lake, GA 152 **D4**
Pine Lawn, MO 162 **B2**
Pine Orchard, MD 147 **A2**
Pine Ridge, SD 126 **C5**
Pine Ridge IR, SD 126 **C5**,
  130 **F7**
Pine Springs, MN 161 **F3**
Pine Springs, TX 131 **E1**
Pinedale, WY 135 **G2**
Pinehurst, MA 138 **B6**
Pinellas NWR, FL 154 **B3**
Pinellas Park, FL 154 **B4**
Pinerolo, 24 **A5**
Pineville, KY 118 **B1**
Piney Pt, FL 122 **D5**
Piney Pt Village, TX 166 **A4**
Pingdingshan, 67 **A4**
Pinghsi, 62 **D5**
Pinglin, 62 **D4**
Pingxiang, 67 **A3**
Pinnacles NM, CA 178 **A4**
Pinole, CA 174 **C7**
Pintendre, 105 **F2**
Pioche, NV 131 **A4**, 132 **F5**
Pioneer Village, 104 **D7**
Piraiévs, 25 **F3**
Piratininga, 91 **E2**
Pireas, 43 **B2**
Pírgos, 25 **E3**
Piriniccikoy, 43 **D3**
Pirituba, 92 **A5**
Pirogovo, 56 **C6**
Pirque, 87 **G1**
Pisa, 17 **E4**, 24 **B4**
Pisgah, OH 151 **E4**

Pisgah NF, NC 121 **E5**

Pismo Beach, CA 133 **B3**

Pistakee Highlands, IL 158 **A8**

Pitcairn, 81 **F3**

Pitchstone Plateau, WY 180 **B2**

Pitlochry, 18 **D6**

Pittsburg, CA 174 **E7**

Pittsburgh, PA 112 **D5**, 118 **D5**, 146 **D7**, 179 **G4**

Pittsburgh, U of, PA 146 **C6**

Pittsburgh Civic Area, PA 146 **C6**

Pittsburgh Zoo, PA 146 **D7**

Pittsfield, ME 114 **D5**

Pittsfield, MA 115 **A3**, 117 **H2**

Pittsfield, NH 115 **C3**

Piura, 84 **B3**

Piute Mt, CA 182 **B5**

Place Charles de Gaulle, 29 **B3**

Place de la Bastille, 29 **F2**

Place de la Concorde, 29 **D3**

Place de la République, 29 **F3**

Place des Ternes, 29 **B4**

Place du Tertre, 29 **E4**

Place Pigalle, 29 **D4**

Place Royale, 105 **F3**

Placentia, CA 171 **E3**

Placentia Isl, ME 186 **B1**

Plainfield, IL 159 **A2**

Plainfield, NJ 116 **A5**

Plains of Abraham, 105 **E3**

Plainview, TX 111 **E4**, 128 **D5**

Planetarium & Jan Smut House, 51 **G3**

Plano, TX 129 **F4**, 165 **G6**

Plantation, FL 155 **F4**, 188 **F3**

Plantation Key, FL 188 **E3**

Plaster Rock, 114 **F8**

Plateau of Tibet, 58 **E6**

Platte R, 110 **F5**, 127 **D4**, 178 **D4**

Plattsburgh, NY 114 **A5**, 117 **H6**

Plattsmouth, NE 125 **A4**

Plaza de Armeria, 39 **B3**

Plaza de la Constitución, 89 **D1**

Plaza de Mayo, 88 **E7**, 89 **D3**

Plaza de Miserere, 89 **B2**

Plaza de Toros, 39 **C3**

Plaza de Toros Mon, 38 **E6**

Plaza del Congreso, 89 **C2**

Plaza Dorrego, 89 **D2**

Plaza General Lavalle, 89 **C3**

Plaza Libertad San Martin, 89 **D3**

Plaza Mexico, 98 **A3**

Plaza San Martín, 88 **E7**

Plaza V López, 89 **C4**

Pleasant Bay, MA 184 **F5**

Pleasant Hill, CA 174 **D6**

Pleasant Hills, PA 146 **C5**

Pleasant Lake, MA 184 **E5**

Pleasant Run, OH 151 **C4**

Pleasant View, CO 167 **F3**

Pleasanton, CA 175 **F4**

Pleasanton Ridge RP, CA 175 **E4**

Plessisville, 114 **B7**

Pleven, 17 **H4**, 25 **G6**

Pljevlja, 25 **E6**

Ploiesti, 17 **H4**

Plovdiv, 17 **H4**, 25 **G5**

Plum, PA 146 **F7**

Plumas NF, CA 132 **C6**

Plumpton, 78 **A8**

Plymouth, CA 132 **C5**

Plymouth, FL 153 **F5**

Plymouth, MA 115 **C2**, 184 **A7**

Plymouth, MN 161 **A3**

Plymouth, NH 115 **B4**

Plymouth, UK 16 **B6**, 19 **D2**, 20 **C7**

Plymouth Bay, MA 184 **A7**

Plymouth Meeting, PA 144 **C5**

Plymouth Plantation, MA 184 **A7**

Plzen, 17 **E6**, 23 **E3**

Po R, 16 **D4**, 24 **B5**

Poá, 92 **D5**

Pocahontas, AR 120 **A6**, 125 **C1**, 129 **H6**

Pocasset, MA 184 **A5**

Pocatello, ID 110 **C6**, 130 **B7**, 135 **F2**

Pocosin Lakes NWR, NC 187 **E4**

Podgorica, 17 **G3**, 25 **E5**

Podol'sk, 56 **B1**

Poeldijk, 30 **A3**

Pogliano, 40 **A2**

Pohang, 66 **D5**

Point Arena, CA 132 **A6**

Point Barrow, AK 82 **B6**, 100 **B7**, 136 **C8**

Point Brown, WA 134 **A5**

Point Defiance Park, WA 176 **A2**

Point Gammon, MA 185 **E4**

Point Harbor, NC 187 **G6**

Point Hope, AK 100 **A8**, 136 **B8**

Point Imperial, AZ 183 **E3**

Point Judith, RI 115 **C1**

Point Loma, CA 169 **E4**

Point Lookout, NY 143 **H1**

Point Pelee, 118 **C6**

Point Petre, 116 **D4**

Point Pleasant, OH 118 **C3**

Point Reyes NS, CA 178 **A4**

Point SP, PA 146 **B6**

Point Sublime, AZ 183 **D2**

Pointe-à-Pitre, 95 **H3**

Pointe aux Pins, 118 **C6**

Pointe aux Trembles, 106 **D4**

Pointe-Claire, 106 **B2**

Pointe Gatineau, 105 **B4**

Pointe-Noire, 46 **D6**

Poissy, 28 **B7**

Poitiers, 20 **D5**

Pok Fu Lam, 75 **B2**

Pok Fu Lam CP, 75 **B2**

Pokhara, 58 **D6**

Poland, 15 **E1**, 17 **F6**, 23 **F4**

Polar Plateau, 83 **D3**

Polba, 65 **E4**

Police, 22 **E5**

Pollux Pk, WY 180 **D4**

Polonez, 43 **F3**

Polpis, MA 185 **G6**

Polynesian Cultural Ctr, HI 137 **D3**

Polytechnical Mus, *Russia* 57 **F6**

Pomáz, 42 **A8**

Pomeroy, OH 118 **C3**

Pomona, CA 171 **E4**

Pompano Beach, FL 123 **G2**, 155 **G5**

Pompeys Pillar, MT 130 **D8**

Ponca City, OK 127 **E1**, 129 **E6**

Ponce, 95 **F3**, 122 **B1**

Ponce de Leon Bay, FL 123 **F1**, 188 **C4**

Pond Inlet, 102 **A7**

Pondicherry, 59 **C3**

Ponferrada, 21 **B4**

Ponkapoag, MA 139 **C1**

Ponta Grossa, 86 **C6**

Pontchartrain, 28 **A6**

Ponte Galeria, 40 **B4**

Pontiac, IL 125 **D4**

Pontiac, MI 125 **D4**

Pontianak, 61 **C2**

Pontoise, 28 **B8**

Pontonnyy, 57 **H1**

Pontoon Beach, IL 162 **D3**

Pont-Viau, 106 **B3**

Poopenaut Valley, CA 182 **A4**

Popayan, 84 **B4**

Poplar Bluff, MO 113 **B4**, 120 **A6**, 125 **C1**, 129 **H6**

Poplar Creek FP, IL 158 **A5**

Popponesset Beach, MA 185 E3

Porcupine R, AK 136 D7

Pordenone, 23 D1, 24 C5

Pori, 15 F3

Port Angeles, WA 134 B6

Port Arthur, TX 129 G3

Port-au-Prince, 94 D3

Port Augusta, 76 D3

Port-Cartier, 103 D3

Port Charlotte, FL 123 E3

Port Clinton, OH 118 B6

Port Colborne, 116 B3

Port Costa, CA 174 C7

Port Credit, 104 C5

Port Elizabeth, 47 F2

Port-Gentil, 46 D6

Port Harcourt, 44 C1

Port Hardy, 101 B3

Port Hedland, 76 A5

Port Huron, MI 124 F5

Port Jackson, 78 F7

Port Jefferson, NY 116 C6

Port Johnson, NY 115 A1

Port Lavaca, TX 129 F2

Port Lincoln, 76 C3

Port Macquarie, 77 F3

Port Madison, WA 176 A6

Port Madison IR, WA 176 A6

Port Melbourne, 79 B2

Port Moresby, 76 C1, 80 B4

Port Orange, FL 123 F5

Port Orchard, WA 134 B5

Port Orford, OR 132 A8, 134 A2

Port Phillip Bay, 79 B1

Port Pirie, 76 D3

Port Richmond, NY 142 B2

Port Said, 45 F4, 48 C5

Port St Joe, FL 122 C5

Port St Lucie, FL 123 F3

Port Salerno, FL 123 F3

Port Sudan, 45 G3, 48 D2

Port Townsend, WA 134 B6

Port Union, OH 151 D4

Port-Villa, 80 C3

Port Washington, NY 143 G5

Portadown, 19 B4

Portage, IL 125 E4

Portage, ME 114 E7

Portage, WA 176 B3

Portage la Prairie, 101 F2

Portales, NM 131 F3

Porterville, CA 133 D4

Portland, IN 118 A5

Portland, ME 103 E1, 112 F7, 115 D4, 179 H5

Portland, OR 101 B1, 110 A7, 134 B4, 177 G5, 178 A6

Portland Intl Arpt, OR 177 G6

Portland Mem Coliseum, OR 177 G5

Portland SU, OR 177 G5

Porto, 16 A3, 21 A3, 44 B6

Porto Alegre, 86 C5

Porto Salvo, 38 A6

Pôrto Velho, 84 D3

Portola, CA 132 C6

Portola SP, CA 175 C1

Portola Valley, CA 175 C2

Portoviejo, 84 B4

Portree, 18 C6

Portsmouth, NH 112 F6, 115 C3

Portsmouth, OH 118 B3, 125 F3

Portsmouth, UK 16 C6, 19 E2, 20 D7

Portsmouth, VA 112 E5, 119 G1

Portsmouth Isl, NC 187 E1

Portsmouth Village, NC 187 F1

Portuense, 40 B5

Portugal, 16 A3, 21 A3, 44 B5

Posadas, 86 C6

Postholes, The, WY 181 G4

Poteau, OK 129 F5

Potenza, 24 D3

Potomac, MD 148 B8

Potomac R, MD 148 D5

Potosí, 84 D1

Potsdam, Ger 23 E4, 32 B6

Potsdam, NY 117 F6

Potsdamerplatz, 33 D3

Potters Bar, 26 C8

Pottstown, PA 119 G4

Pottsville, PA 119 G5

Poughkeepsie, NY 117 H1, 119 H6

Poultney, VT 115 A4

Povoa de Santa Iria, 38 C8

Povungnituk, 103 B4

Poway, CA 133 E2, 169 H6

Powder Horn Park, MN 161 C2

Powell, WY 130 D8

Powellhurst, OR 177 G5

Powells Pt, NC 187 F6

Poyang Hu, 67 B3

Poyang Hu Lake, 60 C6

Poydras, LA 163 H4

Poza Rica, 96 D3

Poznan, 17 F6, 23 F4

Pozuelo de Alarcon, 39 A3

Praça da Liberdade, 93 G2

Praça Da Republica, 93 F4

Prado Mus, 39 C2

Prados de Ecatepec, 98 C6

Praga, 17 E6, 23 E3, 35 E3

Praia Grande, 92 C1

Prairie Village, KS 162 B4

Prairie du Chien, WI 124 C5

Prater Mus, 42 E7

Prato, 24 B4

Pratt, KS 127 E2

Prawet, 63 H5

Precolumbian Mus, 87 G3

Pregnana, 40 A2

Prenestino, 40 C5

Prenzlauer Berg, 32 D7

Prescott, AZ 111 C4, 131 B3

Presidente Prudente, 85 F1

Presidential Palace, 87 G5

Presidential Palace & Natl Mon, 64 B7

Presido,The CA 173 A3

Presque Isle, ME 112 F7, 114 E7

Presque Isle, PA 118 D6

Preston, Austral 79 C3

Preston, ID 135 G1

Preston, UK 19 D4

Prestonsburg, KY 118 B2

Pretoria, 47 F3, 51 H6

Pretoria Church Square, 51 G6

Pretoria Natl Zoological Gdn, 51 G6

Pretty Marsh, ME 186 A4

Pretty Marsh Harbor, ME 186 A4

Préveza, 25 E3

Pribilof Islands, AK 136 A6

Price, UT 130 E8

Price Pk, CA 182 C6

Prilep, 25 F5

Primavalle, 40 B6

Prince Albert, 101 E3

Prince Charles Isl, 102 B6

Prince Edward Pt, 116 D4

Prince Frederick, MD 119 G3

Prince George, 101 C3

Prince Patrick Isl, 100 E7

Prince Rupert, 101 B3, 136 F5

Prince of Wales Isl, 100 F6

Prince of Wales Mus, 65 B1

Princeton, IL 125 D4

Princeton, IN 125 D2

Princeton, KY 120 C6

Princeton, WV 118 D2

Principe, 46 C6

Prineville, OR 134 C3

Prins Hendrick Maritime Mus, 30 B2

Pristina, 25 **E5**
Progress Village, FL 154 **D4**
Prome, 59 **F4**
Promontory, UT 130 **B6**
Promontory, WY 180 **C2**
Prospect Creek, AZ 183 **A2**
Prospect Hts, IL 158 **B5**
Prospect Park, PA 144 **C1**
Prosser, WA 134 **C4**
Prostejov, 23 **F3**
Providence, RI 112 **F6**, 115 **C2**
Providencia, 87 **G3**
Provideniya, 54 **F8**
Providenya, 136 **A7**
Province Lands Visitor Ctr, MA 184 **D8**
Provincetown, MA 115 **D2**, 184 **D8**
Provincetown Harbor, MA 184 **E8**
Provo, UT 110 **C5**, 130 **B5**
Prudential Ctr, MA 140 **A2**
Prudhoe Bay, AK 136 **D8**
Pruhonice, 35 **F2**
Prut R, 17 **H5**
Pskov, 15 **G2**, 52 **B5**
Pucallpa, 84 **C3**
Puch'on, 72 **B6**
Pudahuel, 87 **E3**
Puebla, 96 **D3**
Pueblo, CO 110 **E5**, 127 **B2**, 131 **E4**
Pueblo Libre, 87 **F5**
Puente Alto, 87 **G1**
Puente de Vallecas, 39 **D2**
Puente Grande, 99 **H4**
Puerto Ayacucho, 84 **D5**
Puerto Barrios, 97 **F2**
Puerto Escondido, 96 **D2**
Puerto Limon, 97 **G1**
Puerto Maldonado, 84 **D2**
Puerto Montt, 86 **A4**
Puerto Peñasco, 96 **A6**, 131 **A1**
Puerto Princesa, 61 **D4**

Puerto Rico, 95 **F4**
Puget Sound Naval Shipyard, WA 176 **A5**
Puiseux-Pontoise, 28 **B8**
Puk, 72 **A6**
Pukalani, HI 137 **E3**
Puk'ansan NP, 72 **C8**
Pukaskwa NP, 124 **E7**
Pula, 24 **C5**
Pulaski, NY 117 **E4**
Pulaski, VA 118 **D1**
Pulau Ubin, 63 **H3**
Pulkovo, 57 **G1**
Pulkovo Arpt, 57 **F1**
Pune, 59 **B4**
Punggol, 63 **G3**
Punjabi Bagh, 64 **D7**
Puno, 84 **D1**
Punta Alta, 86 **B6**
Punta Arenas, 86 **A2**
Punta Brea, 122 **B1**
Punta Gorda, FL 123 **E3**
Punta Santiago, 122 **C2**
Punta Yeguas, 122 **C1**
Puntarenas, 97 **G1**
Puras R, 84 **D3**
Pusan, 55 **F1**, 60 **D8**, 66 **D5**
Pushkin Mus of Fine Arts, 57 **E4**
Pushkino, 56 **D6**
Puskin, 57 **G1**
Putnam, CT 115 **B2**
Putte, 31 **H4**
Puttgarden, 22 **D5**
Putumayo R, 84 **C4**
Putuo District, 74 **B7**
Puuhonuao Honaunau NHP, HI 137 **E1**
Puurs, 31 **F4**
Puyallup IR, WA 176 **B1**
Pymble, 78 **D8**
Pyokche, 72 **C8**
Pyongyang, 55 **F2**, 60 **D8**, 66 **C5**
Pyramid Lake, NV 132 **C6**

Pyramid Lake IR, NV 132 **C7**
Pyramid Pk, WY 180 **D4**
Pyramids of Giza, 50 **B1**
Pyrenees Mts, 16 **C4**, 21 **D4**

Q

Qaanaaq, 82 **D6**, 102 **A8**
Qandahar, 58 **A7**
Qaqortok, 102 **E6**
Qaraghandy, 53 **E2**
Qarshi, 53 **D1**
Qatar, 45 **H4**, 49 **G3**
Qattara Depression, 45 **F4**, 48 **C4**
Qazvin, 49 **F6**
Qeqertarsuaq, 102 **C7**
Qibya, 50 **C5**
Qingdao, 55 **E1**, 60 **C7**, 66 **C5**
Qinghai Hu Lake, 58 **F7**
Qinghuayuan, 73 **D4**
Qinhuangdao, 66 **B5**
Qiqian, 66 **B8**
Qiqihar, 55 **E3**, 66 **C7**
Qom, 49 **F6**
Quail Valley, CA 171 **H2**
Quantico US Marine Corps Reserve, VA 119 **F3**
Quanzhou, 67 **B2**
Quartzsite, AZ 133 **F3**
Québec, 103 **D2**, 105 **E3**, 112 **E7**, 114 **B8**
Québec Aquarium, 105 **E2**
Québec City, 114 **B7**
Queen Charlotte Isl, 101 **A3**, 136 **F5**
Queen Elizabeth Isl, 82 **C5**
Queen Emma Summer Palace, HI 177 **H2**
Queen Mary, CA 170 **C2**
Queen Maud Land, 83 **E2**
Queen Maud Mts, 83 **C3**
Queens, NY 116 **B5**, 141 **H4**, 143 **E3**
Queensland, 77 **E4**

Queenstown, 63 **F1**, 77 **E2**
Queimados, 91 **A4**
Quelimane, 47 **G4**
Queluz, 38 **A7**
Querétaro, 96 **D3**
Quetico PP, 124 **C7**
Quetta, 58 **B6**
Quezaltenango, 97 **E2**
Quezon City, 62 **C3**
Qui Nhon, 61 **C4**
Quiapo Church, 62 **C2**
Quidnet, MA 185 **G6**
Quilicura, 87 **F3**
Quilmes, 88 **F6**
Quincy, CA 132 **B6**
Quincy, FL 122 **D6**
Quincy, IL 112 **B5**, 125 **C3**
Quincy, MA 115 **C2**, 139 **E2**
Quincy Market, MA 140 **D4**
Quinta Normal, 87 **F3**
Quinto Romano, 40 **B1**
Quiryat Mal'akhi, 50 **A5**
Quiryat 'Eqron, 50 **B5**
Quitman, GA 121 **E2**, 122 **D6**
Quito, 84 **B4**
Qujialang, 74 **C6**
Qustanay, 53 **D3**
Qyzylorda, 53 **D2**, 58 **B8**

R

Raasdorf, 42 **F8**
Raba, 61 **E1**
Rabat, 16 **A1**, 44 **B5**
Rabaul, 76 **D2**, 80 **B4**
Raccoon Key, FL 188 **B2**
Race Pt, MA 184 **D8**
Racine, WI 112 **B6**, 125 **D4**
Radevormwald, 34 **E5**
Radisson, 103 **C3**
Radnor, PA 144 **C1**
Radom, 17 **G6**
Radotín, 35 **D2**
Rafferty Pk, CA 182 **D3**

Rafael Castillo, 88 C6

Raffles Park, 63 E2

Rafz, 37 E3

Ragged Pk, CA 182 D4

Raging Waters Theme
Park, CA 171 E5

Ragusa, 24 C1

Rahkot, 58 B5

Rahway, NJ 142 A2

Railway Sta, 63 F5

Rainy Lake, 124 B8

Raipur, 58 D5

Raj Ghat, 64 E7

Rajpur, 65 E1

Rajshahi, 58 E5

Rákoscsaba, 42 C7

Rákoshegy, 42 C7

Rákoskert, 42 C7

Rákospalota, 42 B8

Raleigh, NC 113 E4, 121 G6

Ramallah, 50 D5

Ramanbati, 65 D3

Ramblewood, NJ 145 H2

Rambouillet, 28 A5

Ramla, 50 B6

Ramos, 91 D2

Ramrod Key, FL 188 B2

Rancagua, 86 A5

Ranchi, 58 D5

Rancho Cucamonga, CA
171 F5

Rancho Grande, 92 C3

Rancho Palos Verdes CA,
170 B2

Rancho Rinconada, CA
175 E1

Rancho Santa Margarita,
CA 171 G1

Rand Arpt, 51 G2

Randallstown, MD 147 B4

Randburg, 51 F3

Randolph, MA 139 D1

Randolph, MO 162 D6

Randolph, UT 135 G1

Randolph AFB, TX 163 H3

Randwick, 78 F6

Rangeley, ME 114 C5

Rangoon, 59 F4

Rangsdorf, 32 D5

Rankin Inlet, 100 F5

Ranst, 31 H6

Rapid City, SD 110 E6,
126 B5, 130 F7, 178 D5

Raquette Lake, NY 117 F4

Rasht, 49 F6

Rat Burana, 63 F4

Ratak Chain, 80 C5

Ratcha Thewi, 63 G6

Rath, 34 B5

Ratingen, 34 B6

Raton, NM 127 B1,
128 C6, 131 E4

Ravena, NY 117 G2

Ravenna, 24 C5

Ravenswood, IN 157 E3

Rawalpindi, 58 B7

Rawhide, AZ 168 C6

Rawlins, WY 130 D6

Rawson, 86 B4

Raytown, MO 162 D4

Razmetelovo, 57 H2

Reach RA, AZ 168 C5

Reading, MA 138 D5

Reading, OH 151 E3

Reading, PA 112 E6, 119 G5

Reading, UK 19 E2

Real del Castillo, 133 E1

Real Felipe Castle & Mus,
87 E5

Recife, 85 H2

Recklinghausen, 34 D8

Recoleta, Arg 89 B4

Recoleta, Chile 87 G3

Recoleta Cemetery, 89 C4

Reconquista, 86 B6

Red Bluff CA, 132 B6

Red Deer, 101 D3

Red Fort, 64 E7

Red Lake IR, MN 124 A7

Red Lodge, MT 135 H4

Red Oak, GA 152 A1

Red Oak, IA 127 F4

Red R, 101 F1

Red R, 111 F4, 113 A3,
129 G4, 179 E2

Red River, NM 127 A1,
131 E4

Red River of the North,
MN 124 A7

Red Sea, 45 G3, 48 D3

Red Square, 57 F5

Red Wing, MN 124 B5

Redbridge, 26 D7

Redding, CA 110 A6,
132 B7, 134 B1

Redfield, SD 126 D6

Redhill, 26 C5

Redington Beach, FL 154 A4

Redington Shores, FL 154 A4

Redlands, CA 171 H4

Redlands Bowl, CA 171 H5

Redmond, WA 176 D6

Redondo Beach, CA 170 B3

Redway, CA 132 A6

Redwood City, CA 132 B5,
175 C3

Redwood NP, CA 132 A7,
134 A1, 178 A5

Redwood RP, CA 174 D5

Reedley, CA 133 C4

Reedsport, OR 134 A3

Reerslev, 36 A5

Reese R, NV 132 D6

Refuge Hdqrs, WY 181 F1

Regattastrecke, 32 E6

Regensburg, 17 E5, 23 D2

Regensdorf, 37 E2

Regent's Park, 27 A4

Reggio di Calabria, 17 F2,
24 D2

Regina, 101 E2, 110 E8

Rehovot, 50 A5

Reichstag, 33 D3

Reigate, 26 C5

Reims, 20 E7, 23 A3

Reinckendorf, 32 C7

Reindeer Lake, 101 E3

Reisenberg, 42 F5

Rembrandt House, 30 D6

Remington, OH 151 F3

Remscheid, 34 D5

Renaissance Ctr, MI 156 D6

Renca, 87 F3

Rendezvous Mts, WY 181 E2

Rendon, TX 164 C1

Renfrew, 107 G2

Renmin Park, 74 D6

Rennes, 16 C5, 20 C6

Reno, NV 110 B5, 132 C6,
178 A4

Rensselaer, IN 125 E4

Renton, WA 176 D4

Repentigny, 106 D5

Repulse Bay, Can 102 A5

Repulse Bay, Hong Kong
75 D1

Resaró, 36 F7

Reservation Pk, WY
180 D3

Reservoir, 79 C3

Resistencia, 86 B6

Resolute, 82 C5, 100 F7

Retiro, Arg 89 D4

Retiro, Spain 99 C3

Retiro Sta, 88 E7, 89 D4

Retta, TX 164 C1

Reutov, 56 D4

Revelstoke, 101 C2

Revere, MA 139 E4

Revesby, 78 C6

Revnice, 35 D1

Rexburg, ID 130 B7, 135 G3

Rexdale, 104 C7

Rexhame, MA 184 A8

Reykjavik, 14 A5, 82 F6

Reynosa, 96 D4, 128 D1

Rhawnhurst, PA 145 F5

Rheinberg, 34 A8

Rheinhaussen, 34 A7

Rheinkamp, 34 A7

Rhine, 16 D5

Rhine R, 20 F6, 23 D3

Rhinebeck, NY 117 G1

Rhinelander, WI 124 D6

Rho, 40 A2

Rhode Island, 103 **D1**, 112 **E6**, 115 **C2**, 179 **H5**

Rhodes, 17 **H2**, 25 **H2**, 48 **C5**

Rhodope Mts, 25 **F5**

Rhome, TX 164 **A6**

Rhône R, 16 **D4**, 20 **E5**

Rialto, CA 171 **G5**

Rialto, OH 151 **D4**

Ribas de Jarama, 39 **F2**

Ribbon Falls, CA 182 **B3**

Ribeirão Pires, 92 **C3**

Ribeirão Prêto, 85 **F1**

Riberalta, 84 **D2**

Riccar Art Mus, 69 **D2**

Rice U, TX 166 **B3**

Richardson, TX 165 **G5**

Richardson FP, OH 151 **C4**

Richardson Mts, 136 **E8**

Richelieu R, 114 **A6**

Richfield, ID 135 **F2**

Richfield, MN 161 **C1**

Richfield, UT 110 **C5**, 130 **B5**

Richland Ctr, WI 124 **C5**

Richland Hills, TX 164 **C4**

Richmond, CA 174 **B6**

Richmond, Can 107 **G1**

Richmond, IN 118 **A4**, 125 **E3**

Richmond, KY 118 **A2**, 125 **F2**

Richmond, VA 112 **E5**, 119 **F2**

Richmond Hts, OH 150 **F8**

Richmond Hts, MO 162 **B2**

Richmond Hill, Can, 104 **D8**

Richmond Hill, NY 143 **F3**

Richmond upon Thames, 26 **C7**

Richton Park, IL 159 **C1**

Rickmansworth, 26 **B8**

Ridderkerk, 30 **C2**

Rideau Hall, 105 **B3**

Rideau R, 117 **E6**

Ridgecrest, CA 133 **E4**

Ridgefield, NJ 142 **D5**

Ridgefield Park, NJ 142 **C6**

Ridgewood, NY 143 **E3**

Ridley Creek SP, PA 144 **A2**

Ridley Park, PA 144 **C1**

Rift Valley, 45 **G1**, 47 **F5**

Riga, 15 **G2**, 52 **B5**

Rigby, ID 135 **G3**

Riggins, ID 135 **E4**

Riggisberg, 37 **B1**

Riiser-Larsen Ice Shelf, 83 **E3**

Riiser-Larsen Pen, 83 **E2**

Rijeka, 17 **F4**, 24 **C5**

Rijnsburg, 30 **B4**

Rijokri, 64 **D6**

Rijswijk, 30 **A3**

Riksten, 36 **E5**

Rímac, 87 **F5**

Rimforest, CA 171 **H6**

Rimini, 24 **C5**

Rimouski, 103 **D2**

Ringwood, Austral 79 **F2**

Ringwood, NJ 116 **A6**

Rio Branco, 84 **D2**

Rio Comprido, 91 **D2**

Rio Conchos R, 128 **B2**

Río Cuarto, 86 **B5**

Rio de Janeiro, 86 **D6**, 91 **C2**

Rio de Janeiro Intl Arpt, 91 **D3**

Río de la Plata, 86 **B5**, 89 **F4**

Rio Dell, CA 132 **A7**, 134 **A1**

Río Gallegos, 86 **A2**

Rio Grande, 96 **D5**, 111 **E2**

Rio Grande City, TX 129 **E1**

Rio Grande da Serra, 92 **C3**

Rio Grande NF, CO 131 **D4**

Rio Grande R, 128 **B6**, 131 **E1**, 178 **C2**

Rio Rancho, NM 128 **B6**, 131 **D3**

Rio Salado R, 128 **D1**

Rio Vista, MA 138 **A5**

Ripley, MS 129 **H5**

Ripley, WV 118 **C3**

Ri'ppollet, 38 **E7**

Rishon Leziyyon, 50 **A5**

Rishra, 65 **E3**

Risør, 22 **C7**

Rita Blanca NG, TX 127 **C1**

Ritchie, MD 148 **F6**

Ritzville, WA 134 **D5**

River Hills, WI 157 **B4**

River Neck, NC 187 **E6**

River North, IL 160 **B8**

River Oaks, TX 164 **B3**

River Pines, MA 138 **B6**

River Ridge, LA 163 **E5**

River Rouge, MI 156 **D5**

River Rouge Park, MI 156 **B6**

Rivera, 86 **C5**

Riverbend Nature Ctr, VA 148 **A8**

Riverdale, IL 159 **D2**

Riverdale, MD 148 **E7**

Riverfront Stad, OH 151 **D2**

Rivergrove, OR 177 **F4**

Riverhead, NY 115 **B1**, 116 **C4**

Riverside, CA 111 **B4**, 133 **E3**, 171 **H4**

Riverside, MO 162 **C6**

Riverside, NJ 145 **G4**

Riverside Church, NY 142 **D5**

Riverside Park, IN 157 **E3**

Riverside Park, NY 141 **F6**

Riverton, NJ 145 **G4**

Riverton, WY 130 **D7**

Riverview, FL 154 **D4**

Riverview, PA 146 **B7**

Riverwoods, IL 158 **B6**

Riviera Beach, FL 123 **D3**

Rivière-à-Pierre, 114 **B8**

Rivière-aux-Rats, 114 **A8**

Rivière-du-Loup, 103 **D2**

Rivière-Matawin, 114 **A7**

Riyadh, 45 **H4**, 49 **F3**

Rizal Mem Coliseum, 62 **C2**

Roanoke, TX 164 **C6**

Roanoke, VA 112 **D5**, 118 **D1**, 121 **G6**

Roanoke Isl, NC 187 **G5**

Roanoke Rapids, NC 121 **H6**

Roanoke Sd, NC 187 **G5**

Robbinsdale, MN 161 **B3**

Robertsdale, AL 122 **A6**

Robinson Mt, MT 135 **E6**

Rochelle Park, NJ 142 **C6**

Rochester, MN 112 **A6**, 124 **B5**

Rochester, NH 115 **C4**

Rochester, NY 112 **E6**, 116 **D3**

Rochester Park, TX 165 **G3**

Rock Creek Farm CP, CO 167 **F5**

Rock Creek Park, DC 148 **D7**

Rock Hill, MO 162 **B1**

Rock Hill, SC 121 **F5**

Rock Isl, IL 112 **B5**, 125 **C4**

Rock Springs, WY 110 **D6**, 130 **C6**

Rockaway Beach, NY 143 **E1**

Rockburn Branch Park, MD 147 **B1**

Rockcliffe Park, 105 **B3**

Rockdale, Austral 78 **E6**

Rockdale, MD 147 **B3**

Rockefeller Ctr, NY 141 **G5**

Rockefeller Mem Parkway, John D Jr, WY 180 **B1**

Rockefeller Park, OH 150 **E7**

Rockford, IL 112 **B6**, 125 **D4**

Rockhampton, 77 **F4**

Rockingham, NC 121 **G5**

Rockland, ME 114 **E5**

Rockledge, PA 145 **F5**

Rockville, MD 119 **F3**

Rockville Ctr, NY 143 **H2**

Rockwood, ME 114 **D6**

Rocky Mount, NC 121 **G6**

Rocky Mount, VA 118 **D1**

Rocky Mountain NP, CO 127 **A3**, 130 **E6**, 178 **C4**

Rocky Mts, 81 **G6**, 101 **C4**, 110 **D6**, 130 **C7**, 135 **E6**

Rocky Pt, MA 184 **B2**

Rocky Pt, NY 116 **C6**

Rocky Pt Park, MD 147 **F2**

Rocky Ripple, IN 157 **E3**

Rocky River, OH 150 **B7**

Rocky River Res, OH 150 **B6**

Rodanthe, NC 187 **H4**

Rodbyhavn, 22 **D5**

Rodelheim, 35 **A3**

Rodeo, CA 174 **C7**

Rodermark, 35 **C1**

Rodin Mus, 29 **C2**

Rodovre, 36 **B6**

Roeland Park, KS 162 **B5**

Rogersville, TN 118 **B1**

Rogue R, 132 **A8**

Rokko Mts, 70 **A6**

Rokubancho, 69 **A4**

Rolla, MO 113 **A4**, 125 **B2**

Rolling Meadows, IL 158 **B5**

Rollins Savanna FP, IL 158 **B8**

Roma, 77 **E4**

Rómaifürdo, 42 **B8**

Roman Forum, 41 **D2**

Romania, 17 **G5**, 25 **G6**, 45 **E6**

Romashkovo, 56 **A4**

Rome, GA 120 **D4**

Rome, *Italy* 17 **E3**, 24 **C4**, 40 **C5**, 41, 44 **D6**

Rome, NY 117 **F3**

Rome, U of, 40 **C5**

Romeoville, IL 159 **B2**

Romney, WV 119 **E3**

Romohr Acres, OH 151 **F2**

Romoland, CA 171 **H2**

Romulus, MI 156 **A5**

Rønne, 22 **E5**

Ronne Ice Shelf, 83 **D3**

Rönninge, 36 **D5**

Roodepoort, 51 **E3**

Roosevelt Isl, 83 **B3**

Roosevelt Mem, Franklin D, DC 149 **B2**

Rooty Hill, 78 **A8**

Rosamond, CA 133 **D3**

Rosario, 86 **B5**

Rosarito, 96 **A6**, 133 **E2**

Roscommon, 19 **B4**

Rose Ball, CA 170 **C5**

Rose Valley, PA 144 **B1**

Roseau, 95 **H2**

Rosebank, NY 142 **C2**

Rosebud IR, SD 126 **D5**

Roseburg, OR 132 **A8**, 134 **B2**

Rosedale, MD 147 **E3**

Rosedale, NY 143 **G2**

Roselle, IL 159 **A4**

Roselle, NJ 142 **A2**

Roselle Park, NJ 142 **A3**

Rosemead, CA 170 **C5**

Rosemére, 106 **B4**

Rosemont Horizon, IL 158 **B5**

Rosenheim, 23 **D2**, 24 **B6**

Rosersberg, 36 **D8**

Rosetown, 101 **E2**

Roseville, CA 132 **C6**

Roseville, MI 156 **F8**

Roseville, MN 161 **D4**

Rosh Ha'Ayin, 50 **B6**

Rosicrucian Egyptian Mus & Planetarium, CA 175 **E2**

Roskilde, 22 **D6**

Roslags-Näsby, 36 **E7**

Roslyn, PA 145 **E6**

Roslyn Hts, NY 143 **H5**

Ross, OH 151 **B4**

Ross Ice Shelf, 83 **C3**

Ross Isl, 83 **B2**

Ross Sea, 83 **B3**

Rossmore, 78 **A6**

Rossville, MD 147 **E3**

Rostock, 15 **E1**, 22 **D5**

Rostorguyevo, 56 **C2**

Rostov, 53 **A3**

Roswell, NM 111 **E3**, 128 **B5**, 131 **F2**

Rotebro, 36 **D7**

Rotorua, 77 **H2**

Rotterdam, 16 **D6**, 20 **E8**, 23 **A4**, 30 **B2**

Rotterdam Arpt, 30 **B2**

Rouen, 16 **C6**, 19 **F1**, 20 **D7**

Round Lake Beach, IL 158 **B7**

Round Rock, TX 129 **E3**

Roundup, MT 135 **H5**

Rouyn-Noranda, 103 **C2**, 112 **D7**

Rovaniemi, 15 **G5**

Rovereto, 23 **D1**

Rovigo, 24 **B5**

Rowland Hts, CA 171 **E4**

Rowlett, TX 165 **H5**

Rowley, MA 138 **F8**

Rowville, 79 **E1**

Roxboro, NC 119 **E1**

Roxborough, PA 144 **D4**

Roxbury, MA 139 **D3**

Royal Botanic Gdns, 79 **C2**

Royal Canadian Mint, 107 **H5**

Royal Festival Hall, 27 **C2**

Royal Oak, MI 156 **C8**

Royal Observatory, 26 **D7**

Royal Palace, *Bel* 31 **G2**

Royal Palace, *Swe* 36 **E6**

Royal Park, 79 **C3**

Roztoky, 35 **E3**

Rub al Khali, 45 **H3**, 49 **G2**

Rubí, 38 **D7**

Rubidoux, CA 171 **G4**

Rubonia, FL 154 **C2**

Rubtsovsk, 53 **F2**

Ruby Lake Natl Wildlife Rfg, NV 132 **F6**

Rudersdorf, 32 **F6**

Rudná, 35 **D2**

Rudow, 32 **E6**

Rugby, ND 126 **D8**

Ruidoso, NM 131 **E2**

Ruins of Naniwa Palace, 71 **C2**

Ruins of Yuanmingyuan, 73 **C4**

Ruisbroek, 31 **F1**

Rum Cove, ME 186 **B1**

Rumbek, 45 **F1**

Rumeli Hisari, 43 **E3**

Rumelifeneri, 43 **F4**

Rumford, ME 114 **C5**

Rumlang, 37 **E2**

Rumpin, 64 **A6**

Rungsted, 36 **C8**

Rupelmonde, 31 **F5**

Rupert, ID 130 **B7**, 132 **F8**, 135 **F2**

Rural Ridge, PA 146 **E8**

Ruse, 17 **H4**, 25 **G6**

Rushville, IN 118 **A4**

Ruskin, FL 154 **C3**

Russell, IL 158 **B8**

Russell Key, FL 188 **E3**

Russell NWR, Charles M, MT 135 **H5**

Russellville, AL 120 **B5**

Russellville, KY 120 **C6**

Russia, 45 **G6**, 52 **B5**, 55 **B3**, 66 **C8**

Russian Hill, CA 173 **D3**

Russian Mus, 57 **G2**

Rustenfeld, 42 **E6**

Ruston, WA 176 **A2**

Rutherford, NJ 142 **C5**

Rutland, VT 112 **E6**, 115 **A4**, 117 **H4**

Ruttenscheid, 34 **C7**

Ruzyne Arpt, 35 **D3**

Rwanda, 47 **F6**

Ryazan, 53 **B4**

Rybatskoye, 57 **G1**

Rydbo, 36 **F7**

Ryde, 78 **D7**

Rye, FL 154 **D1**

Ryegate, MT 135 **H4**

Ryukyu Isl, 60 **E6**, 67 **D3**

Rzhevka, 57 **G2**

S

Saarbrücken, 16 **D5**, 20 **F7**, 23 **C2**
Saarmund, 32 **C5**
Sabac, 25 **E6**
Sabadell, 38 **E7**
Sabha, 48 **A4**
Sabinas, 128 **D2**
Sabinas Hidalgo, 128 **D1**
Sabine NWR, LA 129 **G3**
Sacajawea Pk, OR 134 **D4**
Sacavém, 38 **B7**
Sachs Harbour, 100 **D7**
Sachse, TX 165 **H5**
Sackler Gallery & Natl Mus of African Art, DC 149 **D2**
Saco, ME 115 **C4**
Saco, MT 135 **H6**
Sacramento, CA 110 **A5**, 132 **C5**, 178 **A4**
Sacré Coeur, 29 **D4**
Saddle Brook, NJ 142 **C6**
Saddle Mountain, WY 130 **C8**, 135 **G3**, 180 **D4**
Saddle Mountain Wilderness, AZ 183 **E3**
Saddlebag Lake, CA 182 **D5**
Sadler Pk, CA 182 **D2**
Sado, 66 **E6**
Safety Harbor, FL 154 **B5**
Säffle, 22 **D7**
Safford, AZ 131 **C2**
Safi, 44 **B5**
Sag Harbor, NY 115 **B1**, 116 **D6**
Sagamihara, 68 **A6**
Sagamore, MA 184 **B6**
Sagamore Beach, MA 184 **B6**
Sagamore Hills, OH 150 **E5**
Saginaw, MI 112 **C6**, 124 **F5**
Saginaw, TX 164 **B4**
Saguaro NM, AZ 131 **B2**, 178 **B2**
Sahara, 44 **C3**

Sahel, 44 **C2**
Sai Ying Pun, 75 **B2**
Saida, 21 **D1**
Saidpur, 58 **E5**
St Adriá de Besós, 38 **F6**
St Albans, Austral 79 **A3**
St Albans, NY 143 **F3**
St Albans, VT 114 **A5**, 117 **H6**
St Andrews, Can 114 **F6**
St Andrews, UK 18 **D5**
St Ann, MO 162 **A3**
St Anthony, Can 101 **F4**
St Anthony, ID 135 **G3**
St Anthony, MN 161 **C3**
St Apolinaris Church, 35 **E3**
St-Arnoult-en-Yvelines, 28 **B5**
St-Athanase, 114 **D8**
St Augustine, FL 113 **E3**, 121 **F1**, 123 **F5**
St Austell, 19 **C2**
St Barthelemy, 95 **G3**
St-Basile, 114 **E8**
St Basil's Cathedral, 57 **F5**
St Bernard, OH 151 **D2**
St Bernard SP, LA 163 **H4**
St Boniface, 107 **H5**
St Catharines, 103 **C1**
St Catherines, 116 **B3**
St Charles, MD 119 **F3**
St Clair Beach, 156 **F6**
St Clair Shores, MI 156 **F8**
St Clairsville, OH 118 **D4**
St Cloud, FL 153 **H1**
St Cloud, MN 112 **A6**, 124 **A6**, 126 **F6**
St-Constant, 106 **C1**
St Croix, 95 **G3**
St Croix R, 114 **F6**
St Cyr l'Ecole, 28 **B6**
St David's, PA 144 **B4**
St-Denis, 28 **D7**
St-Dizier, 20 **E6**, 23 **B2**
St Edward SP, WA 176 **C6**
St-Emile, 105 **D4**
St-Etienne, 20 **E5**

St-Eustache, 106 **A3**
St Francis, SD 126 **C5**
St Francis, WI 157 **C2**
St François, 106 **C4**
St-Francois R, 114
St George, NY 142 **C2**
St George, UT 110 **C5**, 131 **A4**
St George Isl, AK 136 **A5**
St Georges, Can 103 **D2**, 114 **C7**
St George's, Grenada 95 **H1**
St George's Castle, 38 **B6**
St George's Chan, 19 **C3**
St Germain, 29 **C2**
St-Germain-en-Laye, 28 **B7**
St-Germain-Laxis, 28 **F5**
St Helena, UK 46 **B4**
St Helens, OR 134 **B4**
St-Hubert, 106 **D3**
St-Hyacinthe, 114 **A6**
St Ignatius, MT 135 **F5**
St James' Park, 27 **C1**
St-Janvier, 106 **A5**
St Jean-Chryosostome, 105 **F2**
St-Jean-de-Boischatel, 105 **F4**
St-Jean-sur-Richelieu, 114 **A6**
St Joe NF, ID 135 **E5**
St John, Can 103 **E2**, 112 **F7**
St John, MO 162 **B3**
St Johns, WI 95 **H3**
St Johns Park, 78 **B7**
St Johns R, 114 **F7**
St John's, Can 103 **F3**
St John's U, NY 143 **F4**
St Johnsbury, VT 114 **B5**
St Joseph, MO 112 **A5**, 125 **A3**, 127 **F3**
St Joseph Sd, FL 154 **A5**
St Katelijne Waver, 31 **H4**
St Kilda, 79 **C2**
St Kitts & Nevis, 95 **G3**
St-Lambert, 106 **D2**

St Laurent, 106 **B3**
St Lawrence Isl, AK 54 **F8**, 82 **A6**, 136 **A7**
St Lawrence R, 103 **D2**, 112 **E7**, 114 **C8**, 179 **H6**
St Léonard, 106 **C4**
St-Léonard, 114 **E8**
St-Louis, Afr 44 **A2**
St Louis, MO 112 **B5**, 125 **C2**, 162 **B2**, 179 **E3**
St Louis Park, MN 161 **B2**
St Louis Zoo, MO 162 **B2**
St Lucia, 85 **E6**, 95 **H2**
St Malo, 20 **C3**
St-Marcel, 114 **D8**
St Maries, ID 135 **E5**
St Marks NWR, FL 120 **D1**
St Martin, 95 **G3**
St Marylebone, 27 **A3**
St Marys, GA 121 **F2**, 123 **F6**
St Marys, PA 119 **E5**
St Mary's Cathedral, Austral 78 **F7**
St Mary's Cathedral, CA 173 **C2**
St Mary's U, TX 163 **F2**
St-Maur-des-Fosses, 28 **D6**
St-Nazaire, 20 **C6**
St-Ouen-l'Aumone, 28 **C8**
St-Pacôme, 114 **D8**
St Pancras Sta, 27 **C4**
St Patrick's Cathedral, NY 141 **G4**
St Paul, MN 112 **A6**, 124 **B6**, 161 **D2**, 179 **E5**
St Paul, TX 165 **H6**
St Paul Downtown Arpt, MN 161 **E2**
St Paul Isl, AK 136 **A6**
St Paul's Cathedral, 27 **E2**
St Pete Beach, FL 154 **A3**
St Peter, MN 124 **B5**
St Peter's Basilica, 41 **A3**
St Petersburg, FL 97 **G5**, 113 **D2**, 123 **E3**, 154 **C4**
St Petersburg, Rus 15 **H3**, 52 **B5**, 57 **F2**, 82 **F7**

St Petersburg/Clearwater Intl Arpt, FL 154 **B5**

St Petersburg Mus of Fine Arts, FL 154 **B3**

St-Philippe, 106 **D1**

St Pierre & Miquelon, 103 **F3**

St Redempteur, 105 **E2**

St Roch-de-l'Achigan, 106 **C6**

St-Romauld, 105 **E2**

St-Soupplets, 28 **F8**

St Stephen, 114 **F6**

St Stephens, WY 130 **C7**

St Stephen's Cathedral, 42 **E7**

St-Tite, 114 **A7**

St-Tite-des-Caps, 114 **C8**

St Vincent & the Grenadines, 85 **E6**, 95 **H2**

St Vincent NWR, FL 120 **D1**

St Vital, 107 **G4**

Ste Anne-des-Plaines, 106 **B5**

Ste Catherine, 106 **C1**

Ste Etienne, 16 **D4**

Ste-Foy, 105 **E2**

Ste-Geneviéve, 106 **A2**

Ste-Genevieve des-Bois, 28 **D5**

Ste Maria at Aracoeli, 41 **D2**

Ste Maria at Cosmedin, 41 **D2**

Ste Maria Maggiore Basilica, 41 **E3**

Ste-Perpérue, 114 **D8**

Ste-Petronille, 105 **F3**

Ste-Rose, 106 **B4**

Ste-Therése, 106 **A4**

Sakae, 68 **F8**

Sakhalin, 55 **F4**, 66 **F8**

Sakura, 68 **F7**

Sakuranomiya Park, 71 **C4**

Sakyo-Ku, 71 **F3**

Sala Y Gomez, 81 **G3**

Salalah, 49 **G2**

Salamanca, NY 116 **B2**

Salamanca, Spain 16 **B3**, 21 **B3**, 39 **C3**

Salario, 41 **E4**

Salekhard, 52 **F5**

Salem, India 59 **C3**

Salem, MA 115 **C3**, 138 **F5**

Salem, NJ 119 **G4**

Salem, NY 115 **A3**

Salem, OR 110 **A7**, 134 **B4**, 178 **A6**

Salem, Swe 36 **D5**

Salem, VA 118 **D1**

Salem Maritime NHS, MA 138 **F6**

Salerno, 17 **F3**, 24 **C3**

Salina, KS 110 **F5**, 127 **E2**

Salina Cruz, 96 **D2**

Salinas, CA 133 **B4**

Salinas, PR 122 **C1**

Salisbury, MD 112 **E5**, 119 **G3**

Salisbury, UK 19 **E2**

Salisbury Cove, ME 186 **C6**

Salmon, ID 110 **C7**, 130 **A8**, 135 **F4**

Salmon NF, ID 135 **E4**

Salmon River, ID 135 **E3**

Salmon River Reservoir, NY 117 **E4**

Salt Lake, HI 177 **F2**

Salt Lake City, UT 110 **C5**, 130 **B6**, 135 **G1**, 178 **B4**

Salt Plains NWR, OK 127 **E1**

Salt Pond Visitor Ctr, MA 184 **F6**

Salt River IR, AZ 168 **D4**

Salta, 86 **A6**

Saltillo, 96 **C4**

Salto, 86 **B5**

Salton Sea, CA 133 **F2**

Saltsjobaden, 36 **F6**

Saltwater SP, WA 176 **B2**

Salvador, 85 **H2**

Salvador Dali Mus, FL 154 **B3**

Salvo, NC 187 **H3**

Salyer NWR, J Clark, ND 126 **C8**

Salzburg, 17 **E5**, 23 **E2**, 24 **C6**

Sam Houston NF, TX 129 **F3**

Sam Rayburn Reservoir, TX 129 **F3**

Samalga Pass, AK 136 **A5**

Samandia, 43 **F2**

Samar, 61 **E4**

Samara, 53 **C4**

Samarinda, 61 **D2**

Samarkand, 58 **B8**

Samarqand, 53 **D1**

Samoset, FL 154 **C1**

Sampeng Market, 63 **F5**

Sampit, 61 **C2**

Samukawa, 68 **A5**

San Andres Atenco, 98 **A5**

San Andrés Totoltepec, 98 **B1**

San Angelo, TX 111 **E3**, 128 **D3**

San Anselmo, CA 174 **A7**

San Antonio, TX 96 **D5**, 111 **F2**, 129 **E2**, 163 **F1**, 178 **D1**

San Antonio Coliseum, TX 163 **G2**

San Antonio Conv Ctr, TX 163 **G2**

San Antonio Intl Arpt, LA 163 **G3**

San Antonio Missions NHP, TX 178 **D1**

San Antonio de Tequendama, 90 **A2**

San Antonio Tlayacapan, 99 **H1**

San Augustín, 99 **E4**

San Basilio, 40 **D6**

San Bernabe Ocotepec, 98 **A2**

San Bernardino, CA 111 **B4**, 133 **E3**, 171 **H5**

San Bernardino NF, CA 171 **F6**

San Bernardo, 86 **A5**, 87 **F1**

San Blás, 39 **D3**

San Boi de Llobregat, 38 **D6**

San Borja, 87 **G5**

San Bovio, 40 **D1**

San Bruno, CA 175 **B4**

San Bruno Mountain State & CP, CA 175 **B4**

San Carlos, CA 169 **G4**, 175 **C3**

San Carlos de Bariloche, 86 **A4**

San Carlos IR, AZ 131 **C2**

San Clemente, CA 133 **D2**

San Clemente de Llobregat, Spain 38 **D5**

San Cristobal, 84 **C5**, 89 **C2**

San Cristóbal Ecatepec, 98 **C5**

San Diego, CA 111 **A4**, 133 **D2**, 169 **F4**, 178 **A3**

San Diego, U of, CA 169 **F4**

San Diego Intl Arpt, CA 169 **F3**

San Diego SU, CA 169 **G4**

San Diego Zoo, CA 169 **F3**

San Dimas, CA 171 **G6**

San Donato Milanese, 40 **C1**

San Felípe, 131 **A1**, 133 **F1**

San Felipe de Jesús, 98 **C4**

San Fernando, Arg 88 **C8**

San Fernando, CA 170 **B6**

San Fernando de Apure, 84 **D5**

San Fernando de Henares, 39 **F3**

San Francisco, CA 81 **F6**, 110 **A5**, 132 **A5**, 173, 174 **B5**, 178 **A4**

San Francisco, U of, CA 173 **A1**

San Francisco Bay, 173 **F3**, 175 **C4**

San Francisco Bay NWR, CA 175 **D3**

San Francisco Intl Aprt, CA 175 **B4**

San Francisco Mus of Modern Art, CA 173 **C1**

San Francisco State Fish & Game Rfg, CA 175 **B3**

San Francisco Tesistán, 99 **E6**

San Francisco Visitor Info Ctr, CA 173 **D2**

San Gabriel, CA 170 **D5**

San Gabriel Wilderness, CA 170 **D6**

San Gaspar de las Flores, 99 **G5**

San German, 122 **B1**

San Giovanni in Laterano Basilica, 41 **F2**

San Gregorio, CA 175 **B2**

San Gregorio Atlapulco, 98 **D1**

San Ignacio de Loyola, 39 **A2**

San Isabel NF, CO 127 **A2**

San Isidro, PR 75, 88 **D8**

San Jose, CA 94 **A1**, 97 **G1**, 110 **A5**, 132 **B5**, 175 **F1**

San José, CR 84 **A5**

San Jose Arena, CA 175 **F2**

San Jose Intl Arpt, CA 175 **E2**

San Jose SU, CA 175 **F2**

San Juan, Arg 86 **A5**

San Juan, Mex 99 **G2**

San Juan, Phil 62 **C2**

San Juan, PR 95 **F3**, 122 **C2**

San Juan Capistrano, CA 133 **D2**

San Juan Cosalá, 99 **G1**

San Juan de Lurigancho, 87 **G6**

San Juan de Miraflores, 87 **G4**

San Juan de Ocotán, 99 **F5**

San Juan NF, CO 131 **D4**

San Justo, 88 **C6**

San Leandro, CA 174 **D5**

San Lorenzo, CA 175 **D4**

San Lorenzo, PR 122 **C2**

San Lorenzo Tezonco, 98 **C2**

San Lucas, 96 **B4**

San Luis, 87 **G5**

San Luis Obispo, CA 133 **C3**

San Luis Potosi, 96 **C4**

San Luis Río Colorado, 131 **A2**, 133 **F2**

San Marcos, Mex 99 **E1**

San Marcos, TX 129 **E3**

San Marino, 17 **E4**, 24 **B4**

San Martín de las Flores, 99 **G4**

San Martín de Porras, 87 **F5**

San Martín Sq, 87 **F5**

San Mateo, CA 132 **B5**, 175 **C3**

San Mateo, Phil 62 **D3**

San Mateo Canyon Wilderness, CA 171 **G1**

Sān Mateus, 91 **C3**

San Matías Gulf, 86 **B4**

San Miguel, Arg 88 **B7**

San Miguel, CA 133 **C4**

San Miguel, Chile 87 **F2**

San Miguel, El Sal 97 **F2**

San Miguel, Peru 87 **F5**

San Miguel Cuyutlán, 99 **F2**

San Miguel de Tucumán, 86 **B6**

San Miguel Tatepozco, 99 **F6**

San Nicolas, 89 **D3**

San Nicolás de Ibarra, 99 **H1**

San Nicolas Isl, CA 133 **C2**

San Pablo, CA 174 **B7**

San Pablo Bay NWR, CA 174 **B8**

San Pedrito, 99 **F4**

San Pedro, CA 170 **B2**

San Pedro de Macorís, 95 **F4**

San Pedro Sula, 97 **F2**

San Pedro Xalostoc, 98 **C4**

San Po Kong, 75 **D3**

San Quentin, CA 174 **A6**

San Rafael, Arg 86 **A5**

San Rafael, CA 132 **A5**, 174 **A7**

San Ramon, CA 174 **E5**

San Remo, 24 **A5**

San Sabastián, 21 **C4**

San Salvador, 84 **A6**, 94 **D5**, 97 **F2**

San Salvador de Jujuy, 86 **B6**

San Sebastián, PR 122 **A2**

San Sebastián, Spain 16 **C4**

San Sebastián el Grande, 99 **F4**

San Severo, 24 **C3**

San Telmo, 89 **E2**

San Ysidro, CA 169 **G1**

Sanaa, 45 **H2**, 49 **F1**

Sanbancho, 69 **A4**

Sanborn Skyline CP, CA 175 **D1**

Sanchez Adobe HS, CA 175 **A4**

Sanchung, 62 **B5**

Sand Beach, ME 186 **D4**

Sand Point, ME 186 **C6**

Sanda, 70 **A7**

Sandakan, 61 **D3**

Sandberg, CA 133 **D3**

Sandpoint, ID 135 **E6**

Sandringham, 79 **C1**

Sands Point, NY 143 **G6**

Sandton, 51 **F3**

Sandusky, OH 118 **C6**

Sandwich, MA 184 **B5**

Sandy Lake, 103 **A3**

Sandy Neck, MA 184 **D5**

Sandy Springs, GA 152 **B6**

Sanford, FL 123 **F4**, 153 **H6**

Sanford, ME 115 **C4**

Sanga, 36 **D6**

Sangazi, 43 **F2**

Sangerhausen, 23 **D3**

Sanhsia, 62 **B4**

Sanibel, FL 123 **E2**

Sankaty Head, MA 185 **H6**

Sankt-Gallen, 23 **C1**, 24 **A6**

Sanlihe, 73 **C2**

Sanliurfa, 48 **D6**

Sans Souci, 78 **E5**

Sansom Park, TX 164 **B4**

Sant Andreu del la Barca, 38 **D7**

Sant Cugat del-Valles, 38 **E7**

Sant Feliu de Llobregat, 38 **D6**

Santa Ana, CA 171 **E2**

Santa Ana, El Sal 97 **F2**

Santa Ana, Mex 131 **C1**

Santa Ana River RP, CA 171 **G4**

Santa Ana Tepetitlán, 99 **F4**

Santa Anita, 99 **F4**

Santa Barbara, CA 111 **A4**, 133 **C3**

Santa Cecília, 93 **E5**

Santa Clara, CA 175 **E2**

Santa Clara, Cuba 94 **C5**

Santa Clara, Mex 98 **C5**

Santa Clarita, CA 133 **D3**

Santa Coloma de Gramanet, 38 **F6**

Santa Cruz, AZ 168 **B1**

Santa Cruz, Bol 84 **D1**

Santa Cruz, CA 133 **B4**

Santa Cruz, India 65 **B2**

Santa Cruz, Spain 44 **A4**

Santa Cruz de las Flores, 99 **E3**

Santa Cruz de la Soledad, 99 **H1**

Santa Cruz del Valle, 99 **G4**

Santa Cruz Isl, CA 133 **C2**

Santa Cruz Meyehualco, 98 **C2**

Santa Fe, Arg 86 **B5**

Santa Fe, NM 111 **D4**, 127 **A1**, 128 **B6**, 131 **E3**, 178 **C3**

Santa Fe NF, NM 127 **A1**, 128 **B6**, 131 **D4**

Santa Ifigênia, 93 **F5**

Santa Isabel, 122 **B1**

Santa Maria, *Arg* 86 **C5**

Santa Maria, AZ 168 **A3**

Santa Maria, CA 133 **C3**

Santa María Chiconautla, 98 **D6**

Santa María Chimalhuacán, 98 **D3**

Santa Maria in Trastevere, 41 **C2**

Santa Maria Tequepexpan, 99 **F4**

Santa Marta, 84 **C6**, 94 **D1**

Santa Monica, CA 170 **A4**

Santa Monica Mountains NRA, CA 170 **A5**, 172 **A8**, 178 **A3**

Santa Paula, CA 133 **D3**

Santa Rosa, *Arg* 86 **B4**

Santa Rosa, CA 110 **A5**, 132 **B5**

Santa Rosa, *Mex* 99 **H2**

Santa Rosa, NM 131 **E3**

Santa Rosa Isl, CA 133 **C2**

Santa Venetia, CA 174 **A7**

Santana, 92 **B5**

Santander, 16 **B4**, 21 **C4**

Santandercito, 90 **B1**

Santarém, 85 **F4**

Santee, CA 169 **H5**

Santee R, SC 121 **G4**

Santiago, *Chile* 86 **A5**, 87 **G2**

Santiago, *Dom Rep* 95 **E4**

Santiago, *Spain* 21 **A4**

Santiago de Cuba, 94 **D4**, 97 **H4**

Santiago del Estero, 86 **B6**

Santo Amaro, 92 **A4**

Santo André, 92 **C4**

Santo Domingo, 95 **E3**

Santo Domingo's Church, 89 **D2**

Santo Tomé, 86 **C6**

Santos, 86 **C6**, 92 **D1**

Santos Dumont Arpt, 91 **D2**

Santpoort, 30 **C6**

Santuit, MA 185 **E3**

São Bernardo do Campo, 92 **C3**

São Caetano do Sul, 92 **C4**

São Francisco, 85 **G2**

São Gonçalo, 91 **F3**

São João de Meriti, 91 **C3**

São José do Rio Prêto, 85 **F1**

São Julião do Tojal, 38 **B8**

São Luís, 85 **G4**

São Mateus, 91 **B3**

São Miguel Paulista, 92 **C5**

São Paulo, 86 **C6**, 92 **B5**

São Paulo/Guarulhos Intl Arpt, 92 **C6**

São Tome and Principe, 46 **C6**

São Vicente, 92 **D1**

Saône R, 20 **E6**

Sappington, MO 162 **A1**

Sapporo, 66 **F7**

Sarajevo, 17 **F4**, 24 **D4**

Saransk, 53 **C4**

Sarasota, FL 113 **D2**, 123 **E3**

Saratoga, CA 175 **D1**

Saratoga Lake, NY 117 **H3**

Saratoga Springs, NY 117 **G3**

Saratov, 53 **C4**

Sarcelles, 28 **D8**

Sardinia, 17 **E3**, 24 **A3**, 44 **D5**

Sarh, 45 **E1**

Sari, 49 **G6**

Sariyer, 43 **E3**

Sarmiento Frigate & Naval Mus, 89 **E3**

Sarnia, 103 **B1**

Saronno, 40 **A3**

Sarrià, 38 **E6**

Sasad, 42 **A7**

Saskatchewan, 101 **E3**

Saskatoon, 101 **E2**, 110 **E8**

Sassari, 16 **D3**, 24 **A3**

Sassenheim, 30 **B4**

Sassnitz, 22 **E5**

Sassuolo, 24 **B5**

Sathorn, 63 **G5**

Satilla R, GA 123 **E6**

Sattahip, 61 **A3**

Sattra, 36 **F8**

Saúde, 92 **B4**

Saudi Arabia, 45 **H3**, 49 **E3**

Saugerties, NY 117 **G2**

Sauget, IL 162 **C1**

Saugus, MA 138 **E5**

Saugus Iron Works NHS, MA 138, **E5**

Sauk Ctr, MN 126 **F6**

Sauk Village, IL 159 **E1**

Sault Ste Marie, *Canada* 103 **B1**, 112 **C7**, 124 **F6**

Sault Ste Marie, MI 112 **C7**, 124 **E6**

Sausalito, CA 174 **A6**

Sava R, 24 **D5**

Savannah, GA 113 **D3**, 121 **F3**, 179 **G2**

Savannah, TN 120 **C5**, 125 **D1**

Savannah R, GA 121 **E4**

Savannakhet, 61 **A4**

Savigny-sur-Orpe, 28 **D6**

Savona, 24 **A5**

Sawtooth NF, ID 132 **F8**, 135 **F1**

Sawtooth NRA, ID 130 **A7**, 135 **E3**

Sayama, 68 **A8**

Sayan Mts, 55 **B3**

Sayhut, 49 **G1**

Sayre, PA 117 **E1**

Sayville, NY 116 **C5**

Saywun, 49 **F1**

SB Canyon, AZ 183 **B3**

SB Point, AZ 183 **B3**

Scarborough, 104 **F7**

Scarface Pk, MT 135 **F5**

Scarsdale, LA 163 **H4**

Sceaux, 28 **C6**

Schaerbeek, 31 **G2**

Schaffhausen, 23 **C2**, 37 **F4**

Schalksmühle, 34 **F5**

Scharnhorst, 34 **F8**

Schaumburg, IL 158 **A5**

Schauspielhaus, 33 **E3**

Schefferville, 103 **D4**

Schenectady, NY 117 **G3**

Schenley Park, PA 146 **D6**

Schererville, IN 159 **F1**

Schiedam, 30 **B2**

Schilde, 31 **H6**

Schildow, 32 **D8**

Schiller Park, IL 159 **C4**

Schipol Arpt, 30 **C5**

Schleswig, 22 **C5**

Schlieren, 37 **E2**

Schlitz Audubon Ctr, WI 157 **C4**

Schloss Charlottenburg, 32 **C7**

Schoemansville, 51 **E6**

Schoenfeld, 32 **D5**

Scholls, OR 177 **E4**

Schonebeck, 34 **C7**

Schoneberg, 32 **C6**, 33 **B1**

Schonefeld Arpt, 32 **E5**

Schonwalde, 32 **D8**

School of Engineering, 89 **E2**

Schoonbrunn Palace, 42 **D7**

Schoonhoven, 30 **D2**

Schoten, 31 **G6**

Schroon Lake, NY 117 **H4**

Schupfen, 37 **B3**

Schurz, NV 132 **D6**

Schwanebeck, 32 **E8**

Schwanheim, 35 **A2**

Schwarzenburg, 37 **B1**

Schwechat, 42 **F6**

Schwedt, 23 **E4**

Schwelm, 34 **E6**

Schwerin, 22 **D5**

Schwerte, 34 **F7**

Scioto R, OH 118 **B5**

Scoresby, 79 **E2**

Scotia, NY 117 **G3**

Scotia Sea, 83 **F4**

Scotland, 14 **B2**, 18 **D6**

Scott City, KS 127 **C2**

Scott Isl, 83 **A3**

Scott Pk, ID 135 **F3**

Scottdale, GA 152 **D4**

Scotts Bluff NM, NE 178 **D4**

Scotts Run Nature Pres, VA 148 **B7**

Scottsbluff, NE 110 **E5**, 127 **B4**, 130 **F6**

Scottsboro, AL 120 **D5**

Scottsdale, AZ 131 **B2**, 168 **D6**

Scottsdale Ctr for the Arts & Dwtn Shopping District, AZ 168 **C4**

Scottsdale Municipal Arpt, AZ 168 **C5**

Scranton, PA 112 **E6**, 119 **G3**

Scripps Inst, CA 169 **E5**

Scunthorpe, 19 **E4**

Scuppernong, NC 187 **B6**

Scusset Beach SR, MA 184 **B6**

Sé, 93 **G3**

Sea Cliff, NY 143 **H5**

Sea of Azov, 53 **A3**

Sea of Crete, 17 **H2**, 25 **G2**

Sea of Japan, 55 **F2**, 60 **E8**, 66 **E6**

Sea of Marmara, 25 **H4**

Sea of Okhotsk, 54 **B7**, 82 **A8**

Sea Ranch Lakes, FL 155 **G5**

Sea World, CA 169 **E4**

Sea World of Texas, TX 163 **E2**

Seabrook, MD 148 **F7**

Seagoville, TX 165 **H2**

Seal Beach, CA 170 **C2**

Seal Beach NWR, CA 170 **D2**

Seal Cove, ME 186 **A3**

Seal Cove Pond, ME 186 **A3**

Seal Harbor, ME 186 **C3**

Searingtown, NY 143 **G4**

Sears Tower, IL 160 **C6**

Seat Pleasant, MD 148 **F6**

Sea Tac, WA 176 **C3**

Seattle, WA 101 **C2**, 110 **B8**, 134 **B5**, 176 **A5**, 178 **A6**

Seattle Ctr & Space Needle, WA 176 **B5**

Seattle-Tacoma Intl Arpt, WA 176 **C3**

Seawall, ME 186 **C2**

Seaworld, FL 153 **F3**

Sebago Lake, ME 115 **C4**

Sebastian, FL 123 **F3**

Sebastopol, CA 132 **A5**

Sebring, FL 123 **F3**

Secaucus, NJ 142 **C4**

Sedalia, MO 125 **B2**

Sedco Hills, CA 171 **H1**

Sedona, AZ 131 **B3**

Seeberg, 32 **F7**

Seefeld, 32 **E8**

Seeley, CA 133 **E2**

Ségou, 44 **B2**

Segura R, 21 **C2**

Seika, 70 **F6**

Seine R, 16 **C5**, 20 **E6**, 23 **A2**

Seixal, 38 **C6**

Selawik NWR, AK 136 **C7**

Selinia, 43 **A2**

Selkirk, 124 **A8**

Selma, AL 113 **C3**, 120 **C3**

Selma, CA 133 **C4**

Selvas, 84 **D3**

Selwyn Mts, 136 **F6**

Semarang, 61 **C1**

Semey, 53 **F2**

Seminole, FL 154 **A4**

Seminole, TX 128 **C4**

Seminole Indian Village, FL 155 **G4**

Seminole Park, FL 154 **A4**

Senago, 40 **B3**

Senaoane, 51 **E2**

Sendai, 66 **F6**

Seneca Falls, NY 116 **D3**

Seneca Lake, NY 116 **D3**

Sènègal, 44 **A2**

Sènègal R, 44 **A2**

Sengelose, 36 **A6**

Sensa, 63 **F1**

Seoul, 55 **F1**, 60 **D8**, 66 **D4**, 72 **D7**

Seoul Grand Park, 72 **D6**

Seoul Natl Assembly Bldg, 72 **C6**

Seoul Olympic Stad, 72 **D6**

Seoul Stn, 72 **C7**

Seoul Tower, 72 **D7**

Sepik R, 76 **B2**

Sept-Iles, 103 **D3**

Sequoia NP, CA 133 **D4**

Serampore, 65 **E3**

Serangoon, 63 **F3**

Serengeti Plain, 47 **G6**

Serbia, 17 **G4**, 25 **E6**

Serdo, 47 **F3**

Serowe, 47 **F3**

Serpong, 64 **A6**

Serra Da Cantareira, 92 **B6**

Serra Mesa, CA 169 **F3**

Sérrai, 25 **F4**

Sesto S. Giovanni, 40 **C2**

Sestoresk, 57 **E3**

Setagaya-Ku, 68 **B7**

Sete Pontes, 91 **E3**

Sétif, 21 **F1**

Seton Hall U, NJ 142 **A4**

Settala, 40 **D1**

Settecamini, 40 **D6**

Settimo Milanese, 40 **A1**

Settler's Cabin Park, PA 146 **A6**

Settsu, 70 **D6**

Setúbal, 16 **A3**, 21 **A2**

Seuzach, 37 **F3**

Seven Corners, VA 148 **B6**

Seven Hills, OH 150 **D5**, 151 **D4**

Seven Mile Brdg, FL 188 **C2**

Sevenoaks, 26 **E6**

Severn R, 19 **E3**

Severnaya Zemlya, 54 **A6**, 82 **C7**

Sevilla, 16 **A2**, 21 **B2**, 44 **C5**

Sevilleta NWR, NM 128 **B5**

Sevran, 28 **E7**

Seward, AK 100 **A5**

Seward, NE 127 **E4**

Seward Park, IL 160 **B8**

Seward Pen, AK 100 **A7**, 136 **B7**

Sewickley, PA 146 **A8**

Sewickley Hts, PA 146 **A8**

Sewri, 65 **B2**

Seydhisfjördhur, 14 **B5**

Sfax, 17 **E1**, 44 **D5**

Sforza Castle, 40 **B2**

Shabramant, 50 **B1**

Shache, 58 **C7**

Shackleton Ice Shelf, 83 **C1**

Shady Cove, OR 134 **B2**

Shahdara, 64 **E7**

Shaker Hts, OH 150 **E7**

Shaker Historic Mus, OH 150 **E7**

Sham Shui Po, 75 **C3**

Shandon, OH 151 **B4**

Shandong Pen, 66 **B5**

Shanghai, 60 **D7**, 67 **C4**, 74 **D7**

Shanghai County, 74 **B5**

Shanghai Exh Ctr, 74 **D6**

Shanghai Indoor Stad, 74 **C5**

Shanghai Mansions, 74 **E7**

Shanghai Stn, 74 **D7**

Shannon R, 19 **B3**

Shantou, 60 **C5**, 67 **B2**

Shaoguan, 67 **A2**

Shaoxing, 67 **A3**

Shaoyang, 60 **B6**, 67 **A3**

Sharon, PA 118 **D5**

Sharon Hill, PA 144 **D2**

Sharon Woods, OH 151 **E4**

Sharonville, OH 151 **E4**

Shashi, 67 **A3**

Shasta NF, CA 134 **B1**

Shawano, WI 124 **D5**

Shawinigan, 103 **D2**, 114 **A7**

Shawnee, KS 162 **A4**

Shawnee, OK 129 **E5**

Shawnee Crowell SF, MA 184 **B6**

Shawnee Lookout Park, OH 151 **A2**

Shawnee NF, IL 125 **D2**

Shawnee NF, KY 120 **B6**

Shawseen Village, MA 138 **C7**

Shchelkovo, 56 **D6**

Shcherbinka, 56 **B1**

Shea Stad, NY 143 **F4**

Sheboygan, WI 112 **B6**, 124 **D5**

Sheep Mts, WY 181 **G1**

Sheep Mountain Wilderness, CA 171 **E6**

Sheep Porcupine Isl, ME 186 **D5**

Sheepshead Bay, NY 142 **D1**

Sheffield, 14 **C1**, 19 **E4**, 20 **C8**

Shek Kip Mei, 75 **C3**

Shek O, 75 **F1**

Shek O Country Park, 75 **E1**

Shelburne, 103 **E2**

Shelby, MT 135 **G6**

Shelbyville, KY 118 **A3**

Sheldon Antelope Range, Charles, NV 132 **C7**, 134 **C1**

Shelikhov Gulf, 54 **A8**, 54 **F6**

Shell Key, FL 188 **F4**

Shelton, CT 116 **C6**

Shelton, WA 134 **B5**

Shenandoah Mts, 119 **E3**

Shenandoah NP, VA 119 **E2**, 179 **G4**

Sheng-Li Feng, 53 **F1**, 58 **D8**

Shenguasi, 73 **F2**

Shenkeng, 62 **C5**

Shenyang, 55 **E2**, 60 **C8**, 66 **B6**

Sherborn, MA 139 **A2**

Sherbrooke, 103 **D2**, 114 **B6**

Sheremet'yevo Arpt, 56 **A6**

Sheridan, CO 167 **F2**

Sheridan, WY 110 **E6**, 126 **A6**, 130 **D8**

Sheridan Park, WI 157 **C2**

Sherman, TX 129 **F5**

Sherwood, OR 177 **F4**

Shetland Isl, 14 **C3**

Sheung Wan, 75 **C2**

Sheva Nhava, 65 **C1**

Shibuya-Ku, 68 **B7**

Shihting, 62 **D4**

Shihung, 72 **B6**

Shijazhuang, 55 **E1**, 60 **B7**, 66 **A5**

Shijingshan District, 73 **B2**

Shijo-omiya, 71 **D3**

Shijonawate, 70 **E6**

Shiki, 68 **B8**

Shikoku, 60 **E8**, 67 **E4**

Shikote Alin Range, 66 **E7**

Shiloh NMP, TN 179 **F3**

Shilong, 58 **E5**

Shimamoto, 70 **E7**

Shimogamo, 71 **E4**

Shimogyo, 71 **E3**

Shin-Kabuki-za Theater, 71 **B1**

Shinagawa-Ku, 68 **C7**

Shinbashi, 69 **C1**

Shinbashi Sta, 69 **C1**

Shindo, 72 **D7**

Shinkawa, 69 **F2**

Shintomi, 69 **E2**

Ship Harbor, ME 186 **B2**

Shiprock, NM 131 **D4**

Shipwreck Beach, HI 137 **D3**

Shiraz, 49 **G4**

Shiroi, 68 **E8**

Shisui, 68 **F7**

Shiziguan, 73 **E1**

Shizuoka, 66 **F5**

Shkodër, 17 **G3**, 25 **E5**

Sholapur, 59 **C4**

Shonan, 68 **D8**

Shore Acres, CA 174 **E7**

Shore Acres, IN 157 **E3**

Shoreditch, 27 **E4**

Shoreview, MN 161 **D4**

Shorewood, IL 159 **A1**

Shorewood, WI 157 **C3**

Shorts Corner, TX 163 **G3**

Shoshone, ID 135 **E2**

Shoshone Lake, WY 180 **B3**

Shoshone NF, WY 135 **H3**, 180 **D5**

Shoshoni, WY 135 **H2**

Show Low, AZ 131 **C3**

Shreveport, LA 97 **E6**, 113 **A3**, 129 **G4**, 179 **E2**

Shrewsbury, MO 162 **B1**

Shrewsbury, UK 19 **D3**, 20 **C8**

Shrirampore, 65 **E3**

Shuangyashan, 55 **F3**, 66 **B4**

Shuangyushu, 73 **C3**

Shubra, 50 **C3**

Shubra El-Kheim, 50 **C3**

Shulin, 62 **B4**

Shumen, 25 **H6**

Shushary, 57 **G1**

Shymkent, 53 **D1**

Siasconset, MA 185 **H6**

Sibaté, 90 **B1**

Sibenik, 24 **D4**

Siberia, 82 **B8**

Sibolga, 61 **A2**

Sibu, 61 **C2**

Sicily, 17 **F2** , 24 **C1**, 44 **D5**, 48 **A6**

Sid Key, FL 188 **E3**

Sidi Bel Abbas, 21 **D1**

Sidney, Can 134 **B6**

Sidney, MT 126 **B8**

Sidney, NE 127 **C4**, 130 **F6**

Sidney, NY 117 **F2**

Sidney, OH 118 **A4**

Siegen, 23 **C3**

Siegessaule, 33 **B3**

Siegfried Pyre, AZ 183 **F2**

Siena, 24 **B4**

Sierra Blanca, TX 131 **E1**

Sierra Leone, 44 **A1**

Sierra Madre Del Sur, 96 **C3**

Sierra Madre Occidental, 96 **B5**, 111 **D2**

Sierra Madre Oriental, 96 **C5**, 111 **E2**

Sierra Morena, 21 **B2**

Sierra NF, CA 182 **A1**, 182 **B2**

Sierra Nevada, CA 110 **A5**, 132 **C5**

Sierra Vista, AZ 131 **C1**

Signal Hill, IL 162 **D1**

Signal Mt Lodge, WY 181 **C4**

Sigtuna, 36 **D8**

Sikasso, 44 **B2**

Sikeston, MO 120 **B6**

Sikhote Alin Range, 55 **F3**

Silistra, 25 **H6**

Sillery, 105 **E2**

Silver Beach, MA 185 **E1**

Silver City, ID 132 **E8**

Silver City, NM 111 **D3**, 128 **A4**, 131 **D2**

Silver Creek, NY 116 **B2**

Silver Gate, MT 180 **D5**

Silver Hill, MD 148 **E5**

Silver Hill, MA 139 **A4**

Silver Lake, CA 172 **D7**

Silver Lake, MA 138 **C6**

Silver Spring, MD 148 **D8**

Silver Springs, FL 121 **F1**, 123 **E5**

Silver Springs, NV 132 **D6**

Silverton, OH 151 **E3**

Simmering, 42 **E7**

Simmons Park, E G, FL 154 **C3**

Simón Bolívar Intl Arpt, 90 **B6**

Simón Bolívar Plaza, 90 B5, 90 C1

Simón Bolívar Villa, 90 D2

Simpson Desert, 76 D4

Sinai, 48 D4

Sincelejo, 84 C5

Sing Pk, CA 182 D1

Singapore, 61 A2, 63 G1

Singapore Botanic Gdns, 63 F1

Singapore City, 61 B2

Singapore Natl Mus, 63 F1

Singapore Natl Stad, 63 G1

Singapore Railway Sta, 63 F1

Singapore, U of, 63 F2

Singapore War Mem, 63 E3

Singapore Zoological Gdns, 63 F3

Singawang, 61 C2

Singur, 65 D3

Sinjil, 50 D6

Sint Amands, 31 F4

Sint-Gensius-Rode, 31 G1

Sint-Gillis-Waas, 31 E6

Sint-Niklaas, 31 E5

Sinton, TX 129 E2

Sinuiju, 66 C5

Sioux Center, IA 126 F5

Sioux City, IA 125 A4, 126 F5

Sioux Falls, SD 110 F6, 124 A5, 126 E5, 179 E4

Sipe Island, 83 B4

Siping, 66 C3

Sippewisset, MA 185 E1

Siracusa, 24 D1

Sisimiut, 102 C6

Siskiyou NF, OR 134 A2

Sisseton Wahpeton IR, SD 126 E6

Sisters, OR 134 B3

Sitka, AK 101 B4, 136 E5

Sittwe, 58 E5

Siuslaw NF, OR 134 A3

Siwah, 45 F4, 48 B4

Six Flags Over Texas, TX 164 D3

Sixteen Mile Stand, OH 151 F4

Skaevinge, 36 A8

Skagerrak, 15 E2, 22 C7

Skagway, AK 100 B5

Skaneateles, NY 117 E3

Skaneateles Lake, NY 117 E3

Skånela, 36 E8

Skellefteå, 15 F4

Skhodnya, 56 A6

Skien, 15 E2, 22 C8

Skikda, 44 D5

Skodsborg, 36 C7

Skokie, IL 158 D5

Skopje, 17 G3, 25 E5

Skövde, 22 E7

Skovorodino, 55 D3

Skowhegan, ME 114 D5

Sky Harbor Intl Arpt, AZ 168 C3

Sky Lake, FL 153 G3

Skydome, 104 D6

Skye, 18 C5

Skyland, GA 152 C5

Skyway, WA 176 C4

Slangerup, 36 A7

Slavonski Brod, 24 D5

Sleeping Bear Dunes NL, MI 124 E6, 179 F5

Sleigh Ride Visitors Ctr, WY 181 F1

Slide Mt, NY 117 G1, 119 H6

Slidell, LA 120 A2

Sliedrecht, 30 C1

Sligo, 19 B4

Sliven, 25 G5

Slobozia, 25 G6

Slocomb, AL 122 C6

Slough, 26 A7

Slovakia, 17 F5, 45 E6

Slove, 45 E6

Slovenia, 17 F4, 23 E1, 24 C6

Smallwood Reservoir, 103 D4

Smethport, PA 119 E6

Smíchov, 35 E3

Smith Wilderness Area, WY 181 E4

Smithfield, Austral 78 C7

Smithfield, NC 121 G5

Smiths Falls, 117 E6

Smithsonian Inst, DC 149 D2

Smoky Dome, ID 135 E3

Smoky Hill R, KS 127 D2

Smolensk, 15 H2, 52 B5

Smolyan, 25 G5

Smyrna, GA 152 A6

Smyrna, TN 120 C6

Snake R, 110 C7, 130 A7, 132 E8, 134 D3, 178 B5, 180 C2, 181 G4

Snelgrove, 104 A7

Snug Harbor, FL 154 B4

Snyder, TX 128 D4

So, 72 A6

So Kon Po, 75 D2

Soacha, 90 B1

Soborg, 36 B6

Sochi, 53 A3

Soch'o, 72 D6

Socialville, OH 151 F4

Society Isl, 81 E3

Socorro, NM 111 D4, 128

Socorro Isl, 96 A3

Socotra, 45 H2, 49 G1

Soda Springs, ID 135 G2

Sodaemun, 72 C7

Sodegaura, 68 D6

Soekarno-Hatta Intl Arpt, 64 A8

Sofia, 17 G4, 25 F5

Soho, NY 141 F2

Soho, UK 27 B2

Soignolles-en-Brie, 28 E5

Soissons, 23 A3

Soka, 68 C8

Söke, 25 H3

Sokol'niki, 56 C4

Sokoto, 44 C2

Soldier Field, IL 159 E4

Soldiers Delight Natural Environ Area, MD 147 A4

Soledad, CA 133 B4

Solingen, 34 C5

Sollentuna, 36 E7

Sollerod, 36 B7

Solley, MD 147 D1

Solna, 36 E6

Solntsevo, 56 A3

Solomon, 80 B4

Solomon Isl, 77 G6

Solomon R, KS 127 E3

Solomon Sea, 76 C1

Solon, OH 150 F6

Solothurn, 37 C4

Solymár, 42 A8

Somali Pen, 45 H1

Somalia, 45 H1, 47 H6

Somerset, KY 118 A1, 120 D6, 125 F2

Somerset, MD 148 C7

Somerset, PA 119 E4

Somerset Isl, 100 C7

Somerton, AZ 131 A2, 133 F2

Somerton, PA 145 G6

Somerville, MA 139 C4, 140 A6

Somerville, NJ 116 A5, 119 H5

Somes Pond, ME 186 B5

Somes Sd, ME 186 B4

Somesville, ME 186 B5

Sonarpur, 65 F1

Sonda de Vieques, 122 D2

Sønderborg, 22 D5

Songbuk, 72 D7

Songdong, 72 D7

Songea, 47 G5

Songhua R, 55 F3, 66 B3

Songnam, 72 E6

Songp'a, 72 E6

Sonora, CA 132 C5

Sonoran Desert, 96 B6

Sonoyta, 131 A1

Sopron, 23 F2, 24 D6

Sorae, 72 B6

Sorbonne, 29 E1

Sorel, 114 **A6**

Soria, 21 **C4**

Sorocaba, 86 **C6**

Soroksár, 42 **B6**

Sorong, 76 **A2**

Sorrento, FL 153 **F6**

Sossenheim, 35 **A3**

Souk Ahras, 24 **A1**

Sousse, 24 **B1**

South Africa, 47 **E2**

South African Broadcasting Corp, 51 **F3**

South Apopka, FL 153 **F5**

South Australia, 76 **C3**

South Badger Creek, WY 181 **E4**

South Bend, IN 112 **C5**, 125 **E4**

South Bend, WA 134 **B5**

South Bitch Creek, WY 181 **E5**

South Boston, MA 139 **D3**, 140 **D2**

South Boston, VA 119 **E1**

South Byfield, MA 138 **F8**

South Canal, 88 **E7**

South Cape Beach SP, MA 185 **E2**

South Carolina, 113 **D4**, 121 **F4**, 179 **G3**

South Carver, MA 184 **A6**

South Chatham, MA 184 **D6**

South Chicago Hts, IL 159 **D1**

South China Sea, 61 **C3**, 67 **A1**

South Dakota, 101 **F1**, 110 **F6**, 126 **D6**, 178 **D5**

South Dennis, MA 184 **E5**

South Dum-Dum, 65 **F2**

South Duxbury, MA 184 **A8**

South Entrance, WY 180 **B1**

South Euclid, OH 150 **F7**

South Fork Merced R, CA 182 **B1**

South Gate, CA 170 **C4**

South Georgetown, MA 138 **E8**

South Georgia, 83 **F4**, 87 **G2**

South Groveland, MA 138 **D8**

South Hamilton, MA 138 **F7**

South Harbor, 62 **B2**

South Holland, IL 159 **E2**

South Houston, TX 166 **C3**

South Isl, 77 **H1**, 80 **C1**

South Korea, 60 **D8**, 66 **D5**

South Lake Tahoe, CA 132 **C6**

South Lawrence, MA 138 **C8**

South Lehigh Creek, WY 181 **E4**

South Lincoln, MA 139 **A4**

South Lynnfield, MA 138 **D9**

South Mashpee, MA 185 **E2**

South Melbourne, 79 **B2**

South Miami, FL 155 **F1**

South Milwaukee, WI 157 **C1**

South Mtn Park, AZ 168 **B2**

South Natich, MA 139 **A2**

South Nation R, 117 **F6**

South Orange, NJ 142 **A4**

South Orkney Isl, 83 **E4**

South Orleans, MA 184 **F5**

South Park, PA 146 **C5**

South Pasadena, FL 154 **A3**

South Pass City, WY 130 **C6**

South Philadelphia, PA 145 **E2**

South Platte R, CO 127 **B3**

South St Paul, MN 161 **E1**

South San Francisco, CA 175 **B4**

South Sandwich Isl, 83 **F4**

South Shore Park, WI 157 **C2**

South Sioux City, IA 127 **E4**

South Sister, OR 134 **B3**

South Sta, MA 140 **D2**

South Street Seaport, NY 141 **F1**

South Truro, MA 184 **E7**

South Tucson, AZ 131 **C2**

South Valley Stream, NY 143 **G2**

South Wellfleet, MA 184 **F7**

South Weymouth, MA 139 **E1**

South Whittier, CA 170 **D4**

Southampton, NY 115 **B1**, 116 **D6**

Southampton, UK 19 **E2**, 20 **C7**

Southampton Isl, 102 **A5**

Southern Alps, 77 **G1**

Southern California, U of, CA 172 **D5**

Southern Methodist U, TX 165 **F4**

Southern Shores, NC 187 **C6**

Southern U at New Orleans, LA 163 **G6**

Southern Ute IR, CO 131 **D4**

Southfield, MI 156 **B8**

Southfork Ranch, TX 165 **H6**

Southgate, KY 151 **D1**

Southgate, MI 156 **C5**

Southlake, TX 164 **D5**

Southold, NY 116 **C6**

Southport, Austral 77 **F4**

Southport, IN 157 **E1**

Southport, NY 116 **D2**

Southside Place, TX 166 **B3**

Southwark, 26 **D7**, 27 **E2**

Southwest Harbor, ME 186 **B3**

Southwest Mus, CA 172 **F7**

Southwest Research Inst, TX 163 **E2**

Southwestern College, CA 169 **G2**

Southworth, WA 176 **A4**

Sovetskaya Gavan, 55 **F4**, 66 **E8**

Soviet Victory Mem, 33 **C3**

Sovong, 36 **C5**

Soweto, 51 **E2**

Spain, 16 **B3**, 21 **B3**, 44 **C5**

Spandau, 32 **B7**

Spanish Steps, 41 **D4**

Sparks, NV 132 **C6**

Sparrows Pt, MD 147 **E1**

Sparta, Greece 17 **G2**, 25 **F2**

Sparta, NJ 116 **A6**

Spartanburg, SC 113 **D4**, 121 **E5**

Spatsizi Plateau Wilderness Prov P, 136 **F6**

Spearfish, SD 126 **B6**, 130 **F8**

Specimen Ridge, WY 180 **C5**

Spectrum, PA 145 **E1**

Speedway, IN 157 **D2**

Spencer, ID 130 **B7**, 135 **F3**

Spencer, IA 124 **A5**

Spencer, MA 115 **B2**

Spencer, WV 118 **C3**

Spencer Gulf, Austral 76 **D3**

Spencerport, NY 116 **C3**

Sphinx, 50 **B1**

Spijkenisse, 30 **A1**

Spinaceto, 40 **C4**

Spitalfields, 27 **F3**

Split, 17 **F4**, 24 **D4**

Spokane, WA 101 **C2**, 110 **B7**, 134 **D5**,178 **B6**

Spongeorama Exh Ctr, FL 154 **B6**

Sports Arena, 42 **B7**

Sportsforum Berlin, 32 **D7**

Spot, NC 187 **G6**

Spotsylvania, VA 119 **F2**

Spratly Isl, 61 **D3**

Spread Creek, WY 181 **H3**

Sprecher Brewery, WI 157 **C2**

Spreitenbach, 37 **D2**

Sprendlingen, 35 B1

Spring Creek, NV 130 A6, 132 E7

Spring Hill, FL 123 E4

Spring Hill, VA 148 B7

Spring Hills, IN 157 D3

Spring Lake, NC 121 G5

Spring Lake FP, IL 158 A6

Spring Valley, CA 169 G3

Spring Valley, TX 166 A4

Springbok, 47 E2

Springdale, AR 125 B1, 129 F6

Springdale, OH 151 D4

Springdale, OR 177 H5

Springdale, PA 146 E8

Springfield, FL 122 C5

Springfield, IL 112 B5, 125 C3, 179 E4

Springfield, ME 114 E6

Springfield, MA 112 E6, 115 B2

Springfield, MO 113 A4, 125 B2

Springfield, OH 118 B4, 125 F3

Springfield, PA 144 C2

Springfield, TN 120 C6

Springfield, VT 115 A3

Springfield, VA 148 B5

Springvale, 79 D1

Springville, NY 116 B2

Sprockhövel, 34 D6

Sproul SF, PA 119 F5

Spruce Knob, WV 118 D3

Spruce Woods Prov P, 126 D8

Squantum, MA 139 D3

Squaw Peak RA, AZ 168 C4

Sri Lanka, 59 C3

Srinagar, 58 C7

Staatsburg, NY 117 G1

Stadion Rote-erde, 34 F7

Stafford, TX 166 A2

Staines, 26 B7

Stamford, CT 115 A1, 116 B6

Stammersdorf, 42 E8

Standing Rock IR, SD 126 C6, 130 F8

Stanford, CA 175 D2

Stanford, KY 118 A2

Stanford, MT 135 G5

Stanford le Hope, 26 F7

Stanford U, CA 175 C2

Stanislaus NF, CA 182 A6

Stanley, Falk Isl, 86 B2

Stanley, ID 130 A7, 135 E3

Stanley Park, 107 F3

Stanovoy Range, 55 D4

Stanton, CA 170 D3

Stanton, KY 118 B2

Star Ferry Pier, 75 C2

Stara Zagora, 17 H4, 25 G5

Staraya, 57 H2

Starbeyevo, 56 B6

Starke, FL 121 E1, 123 E5

Starkville, MS 120 B4

Starlight Theatre, MO 162 C4

State Administration Bldg, 99 F5

State Agricultural Park, 87 F2

State Capitol, IN 156 E2

State Fairgrounds, MI 156 D7

State Fairgrounds, WI 157 A2

State House, MA 140 C3

State Library & Mus of Victoria, 79 C3

Staten Isl, NY 116 B5, 142 B1

Staten Isl Zoo, NY 142 C2

Statenville, GA 123 E6

Statesboro, GA 121 F3

Statue of Liberty NM, NY 142 C3, 179 H4

Staunton, VA 119 E2

Stavanger, 14 D2, 22 B7

Stavropol, 53 A3

Steamboat Mt, AZ 183 D3

Steamboat Springs, CO 127 A3, 130 D6

Steele, 34 C7

Steffisburg, 37 C1

Steglitz, 32 C6

Steinbach, Can 126 E8

Steinbach, Ger 35 A4

Steinberg, 35 C1

Stekene, 31 E6

Stendal, 23 D4

Stenhamra, 36 D6

Stenlose, 36 A7

Stephenville, TX 129 E4

Steppes, The, 53 D3

Sterling, CO 110 E5, 127 B3, 130 F6

Steuben, NY 117 F4

Steubenville, OH 118 D4

Stevens Pk, ID 135 E5

Stevens Pt, WI 124 D5

Stevenson Pt, NC 187 A6

Stewart Crossing, 136 E7

Stewart Isl, 77 G1, 80 C1

Stewart R, 136 E7

Stillwater, OK 127 E1, 129 E6

Stillwater Reservoir, NY 117 F4

Stinson Arpt, TX 163 G1

Stip, 25 F5

Stirling, 18 C5

Stock Isl, FL 188 A1

Stockbridge, MA 117 H2

Stockholm, 15 F2, 22 F8, 36 F6, 52 A6, 82 F7

Stockholm Train Sta, 36 E6

Stocksund, 36 E7

Stockton, CA 110 A5, 132 C5

Stockyards Natl Hist District, TX 164 B3

Stodulky, 35 D2

Stoke-on-Trent, 19 E3, 20 C8

Stoneham, MA 138 D5

Stony Brook, NY 116 C6

Stony Isl, NY 117 E4

Stoppenberg, 34 C7

Storm Lake, IA 125 A4, 126 F5

Stornoway, 18 C7

Stowe, VT 114 A5

Strafford, PA 144 B4

Strahov Stad, 35 E3

Strait of Dover, 19 F2, 20 D7

Strait of Gibraltar, 16 A2, 21 B1, 44 B5

Strait of Hormuz, 49 G4

Strait of Juan de Fuca, WA 134 A6

Strait of Magellan, 86 B2

Strait of Malacca, 61 A2

Strait of Sicily, 17 E2, 24 B1

Straits of Florida, 94 B5 113 E1, 188 E1

Straits Pond, MA 139 F2

Stralsund, 22 E5

Strasbourg, 16 D5, 20 F6, 23 B2

Strasburg, CO 130 E5

Strasnice, 35 F3

Stratford, 26 D7

Stratford-upon-Avon, 19 E3

Strathfield, 78 D7

Streamwood, IL 158 A5

Streatham, 26 C7

Streetsville, 104 B5

Strel'na, 57 E1

Stresovice, 35 E3

String Lake, WY 181 F3

Stringtown, KY 151 B2

Strongsville, OH 150 B5

Stroudsburg, PA 119 G5

Strumica, 25 F5

Stuart, FL 123 B3

Stuart, VA 118 D1

Stubblefield Canyon, CA 182 B6

Stumpy Pt, NC 187 G4

Stumpy Pt Bay, NC 187 G4

Stupsk, 22 F5

Sturgeon Bay, WI 124 E5

Sturgis, SD 126 **B6**, 130 **F7**

Stuttgart, *Ger* 17 **E5**, 23 **C2**

Stuttgart, AR 120 **A5**

Suba, 90 **C2**

Subia, 90 **A1**

Sucre, 84 **D1**

Sudan, 45 **F2**, 48 **C2**

Sudbury, 103 **B2**, 112 **D7**

Suez, 48 **D4**

Suez Canal, 45 **F4**, 48 **D4**

Suffolk, VA 119 **G1**, 121 **H6**

Suffolk Downs Race Track, MA 139 **E4**

Sugandha, 65 **E4**

Sugar Creek, MO 162 **D5**

Sugarloaf, FL 188 **B2**

Sugarloaf Mt, 91 **E2**

Suhar, 49 **H3**

Suita, 70 **C6**

Suitland, MD 148 **E6**

Sukkur, 58 **B6**

Sullana, 84 **B3**

Sulu Sea, 61 **D3**

Sumatra, 59 **F2**, 61 **A2**

Sumba, 61 **E1**

Summer Palace, 57 **G2**, 73 **B4**

Summerland Key, FL 188 **B6**

Summerside, OH 151 **F2**

Summersville, WV 118 **D2**

Summerville, GA 120 **D4**

Summerville, SC 121 **F4**

Summit, CA 171 **G6**

Summit, IL 159 **C3**

Summit Lake IR, NV 132 **C7**

Summit, TX 166 **B3**

Sumner, WA 176 **C1**

Sumter, SC 121 **F4**

Sumter NF, SC 121 **E4**

Sun City, AZ 168 **A5**

Sun City, CA 171 **H2**

Sun City, FL 154 **C2**

Sun City Ctr, FL 154 **D3**

Sun Lakes, AZ 168 **D1**

Sun Valley, ID 135 **F3**

Sunbeam, ID 130 **A7**

Sunburst, MT 135 **F6**

Sunbury, PA 119 **F5**

Sundbyberg, 36 **E7**

Sundbyrester, 36 **C5**

Sunderland, 18 **E5**

Sundsvall, 15 **E3**

Sunfish Lake, MN 161 **E1**

Sunflower R, MS 120 **A4**

Sunken Gdns, FL 154 **B3**

Sunnyside, CA 169 **G2**

Sunnyvale, CA 132 **B5**, 175 **D2**

Sunnyvale, TX 165 **H3**

Sunol, CA 175 **F4**

Sunol Reg Wilderness, CA 175 **F3**

Sunset Beach, CA 170 **C2**

Sunshine, 79 **A3**

Sunshine West, 79 **A3**

Supai, AZ 183 **B2**

Superior, CO 167 **F5**

Superior, MI 112 **B7**

Superior, MT 135 **E5**

Superior, WI 124 **C6**

Superior NF, MN 124 **C7**

Supreme Court, 69 **B3**

Suquamish, WA 176 **A6**

Sur, 49 **H3**

Surabaya, 61 **D1**

Surakarta, 61 **C1**

Surat, 58 **B5**

Surco, 87 **G4**

Surfside, FL 155 **G2**

Surfside, MA 185 **H5**

Surgut, 53 **E4**

Suriname, 85 **E5**

Surquillo, 87 **G4**

Surry, VA 121 **H6**

Surrey Hills, 26 **B5**

Suruf, 91 **E4**

Susanville, CA 132 **C7**

Susquehanna R, PA 117 **E1**, 119 **G6**

Susquehannock SF, PA 119 **E6**

Süssenbrunn, 42 **F8**

Sussex, NJ 116 **A6**

Susuman, 54 **E6**

Sutherland, 78 **D5**

Sutton, UK 26 **C6**

Sutton, WV 118 **D3**

Sutton Isl, ME 186 **C3**

Suva, 80 **C3**

Suwannee R, FL 121 **E2**

Suzano, 92 **D5**

Suzhou, 60 **D7**, 67 **C3**

Svalbard, 52 **E7**, 82 **E7**

Svinninge, 36 **F7**

Svishtov, 25 **G6**

Svobodnyy, 55 **E3**

Swainsboro, GA 121 **E3**

Swanley, 26 **E6**

Swampscott, MA 138 **E5**

Swan R, 101 **E2**

Swanquarter, NC 187 **E3**

Swanquarter NWR, NC 187 **E2**

Swans Isl, ME 186 **A1**

Swansea, 16 **B6**, 19 **C2**, 20 **C7**

Swanton, VT 114 **A5**

Swarthmore, PA 144 **B1**

Swarthmore College, PA 144 **C2**

Swaziland, 47 **G3**

Sweden, 22 **E7**

Sweeney Ridge, CA 175 **A4**

Sweetwater, FL 123 **F2**, 155 **F1**

Sweetwater, TX 128 **D4**

Sweetwine, OH 151 **E1**

Swift Current, 101 **D2**

Swindon, 19 **E2**

Swinoujscie, 22 **E5**

Swiss Natl Mus, 37 **E1**

Swissvale, PA 146 **D6**

Switzerland, 16 **D5**, 20 **F6**, 23 **C1**, 24 **A6**, 44 **D6**

Sydney, *Can* 103 **F3**

Sydney, *Austral* 77 **E3**, 78 **E7**, 80 **B2**

Sydney Centennial Park, 78 **F6**

Sydney Cricket Ground, 78 **E7**

Sydney Intl Arpt, 78 **E6**

Sydney Opera House, 78 **F7**

Syktyvkar, 52 **D5**

Sylacauga, AL 120 **C4**

Sylhet, 58 **E5**

Symphony Hall, CA 173 **C1**

Symphony Hall, MA 140 **A1**

Syracuse, NY 103 **D1**, 112 **E6**, 117 **E3**

Syria, 45 **G5**, 48 **D5**

Syrian Desert, 49 **E5**

Százhalombatta, 42 **A5**

Szczecin, 15 **F1**, 22 **E5**

Szczecinek, 22 **F5**

Szeged, 17 **F5**

Szekesfehervar, 24 **D6**

Szentendre, 42 **B8**

Szigetcsép, 42 **A5**

Szigetszentmiklós, 42 **B6**

Szigethalom, 42 **A5**

Szombathely, 23 **F2**, 24 **D6**

T

Tablada, 88 **D6**

Table Mt, WY 180 **D2**

Taboão da Serra, 92 **A4**

Tabora, 47 **F5**

Tabriz, 49 **F6**, 53 **A2**

Tabuk, 48 **D4**

Täby, 36 **E7**

Tachikawa, 68 **A7**

Tacloban, 61 **E4**

Tacna, 84 **C1**

Tacoma, WA 110 **B7**, 134 **B5**, 176 **B1**

Tacoma Dome, WA 176 **B1**

Tacony, PA 145 **F4**

Tadmur, 48 **D5**

Taegu, 55 **F1**, 60 **D8**, 66 **D5**

Taejon, 66 **C5**

Tafers, 37 **A1**

Taft, CA 133 **C3**

Taft, FL 153 G3
Taguig, 62 C2
Taguao, 90 A6
Tagus R, 16 A3, 21 B3
Tahiti, 81 E3
Tahlequah, WA 176 A2
Tahoe City, CA 132 C6
Taholah, WA 134 A5
Tai Hang, 75 D2
Tai Hu, 67 B4
Tai Kok Tsui, 75 C3
Tai Po Tsai, 75 F4
Tai Tam Country Park, 75 D2
Taichung, 60 D6, 67 C2
Tainan, 67 C2
Taipei, 60 D6, 62 C5, 67 G3
Taipei Sung Shan Arpt, 62 C5
Taishan, 62 B5
Taitao Pen, 86 A3
Taiwan, 60 D6, 67 C2
Taiwan Str, 60 D6, 67 B2
Taiyuan, 55 D1, 60 B7, 66 A5
Taizz, 49 F1
Tajikistan, 58 B7
Takamatsu, 66 E5
Takarazuka, 70 B6
Takarazuka Theater, 69 D2
Takatsuki, 70 D7
Takeda, 71 E2
Takla Makan Desert, 53 F1, 58 D7
Takoma Park, MD 148 D8
Takoradi, 44 C1
Taksony, 42 B5
Talara, 84 B3
Talca, 86 A5
Talcahuano, 86 A5
Taldyqorghan, 53 E2
Talent, OR 134 B2
Taliedo, 40 C1
Taliesin West, AZ 168 D5
Taling Chan, 63 E6
Talladega, AL 120 D4

Talladega NF, AL 120 C4
Tallahassee, FL 113 D3, 120 D2, 122 D6, 179 G2
Tallassee, AL 120 C3
Tallinn, 15 G3, 52 B6
Tallulah, LA 120 A3
Tama, 68 A7
Tamale, 44 C1
Tamanrasset, 44 D3
Tamarac, FL 123 F2, 155 F5
Tambov, 53 B4
Tampa, FL 97 G5, 113 D2, 123 E3, 179 G1
Tampa Bay Downs Racetrack, FL 154 B5
Tampa Intl Arpt, FL 154 C5
Tampa Mus of Art, FL 154 C5
Tampa Stad, FL 154 C5
Tampere, 15 F3, 52 B6
Tampico, 96 D4
Tampines, 63 H2
Tanabe, 70 E6
Tanana R, 100 B6
Tangerang, 64 A7
Tangerine, FL 153 E6
Tangier, 16 A2, 21 B1, 44 B5
Tangshan, 66 B5
Tanjiazhai, 74 D8
Tanjungkarang-Telukbetung, 61 B1
Tanjungpasir, 64 A8
Tanjungpriok, 64 B7
Tannan, 70 A8
Tanshi, 68 B7
Tanshui, 62 B6
Tanta, 45 F4, 48 C5
Tanzania, 47 G5
Taos, NM 127 A1, 131 E3
Taos IR, NM 128 B6
Taoyuan, 62 A4
Tapachula, 97 E2
Tapajós, 85 E3

Tappahannock, VA 119 F2
Taquara, 91 B2
Tara, 53 E3
Tara Hills, CA 174 B7
Tarakan, 61 D3
Taranto, 17 F3, 24 E3
Tarawa, 80 C4
Tarbaek, 36 C7
Taree, 77 F3
Targhee NF, 180 A2, 181 E3
Tarija, 84 D1
Tarnby, 36 C5
Taronga Zoo, 78 F7
Tarpon Springs, FL 154 A6
Tarragona, 16 C3, 21 D3
Tartu, 15 G2
Tashkent, 53 D1, 58 B8
Tasman Sea, 77 G2, 80 B2
Tasmania, 77 E1, 80 B1
Tastrup, 36 A5
Tatabanya, 24 D6
Tatar Str, 55 F4, 66 E8
Tate Gallery, 27 C1
Tatsfield, 26 D6
Tatshenshini-Alsek Wilderness Prov P, AK 136 D6
Tatuapé, 92 C5
Täuffelen, 37 A3
Taunggyi, 58 F5
Taunton, MA 115 C2
Taunton, UK 19 D2
Tauranga, 77 H2
Taurus Mts, 48 D6
Tavannes, 37 A4
Tavares, FL 121 F1
Tavernier, FL 123 F1, 188 F3
Taverny, 28 C8
Tavoy, 59 F4
Tavros, 43 B2
Taylor, MI 156 B5
Taylor Mill, KY 151 D1
Taylors Creek, OH 151 B3
Taylorsport, KY 151 B2

Taylorville, IL 125 C3
Taymyr Pen, 54 A6, 82 C8
Taytay, 62 D2
Tazewell, TN 118 B1
Tbilisi, 45 G6, 53 A2
Teahwhit Head, WA 134 A6
Teaneck, NJ 142 C6
Teaticket, MA 185 E2
Tebessa, 44 D5
Tebet, 64 B7
Tecate, 133 E2
Technical U, 33 A3
Tecolote Canyon Natural Park, CA 169 F5
Tecomán, 96 C3
Tecuseh, 156 F6
Tegel Arpt, 32 C7
Tegucigalpa, 84 A6, 97 F2
Tehachapi, CA 133 D3
Tehran, 45 H5, 49 F6, 53 A1
Tel Aviv-Yafo, 48 D5, 50 A6
Telegraph Creek, 101 B4
Telegraph Hill, CA 173 D3
Telford, 19 D3
Telluride, CO 131 D4
Telok Blangah, 63 F1
Teltow, 32 C6
Teluknaga, 64 A8
Tembisa, 51 H4
Temmangu Shrine, 71 B3
Tempe, AZ 131 B2, 168 C2
Tempe Park, AZ 168 C3
Tempelhof, 32 D6
Tempelhof Arpt, 32 D6
Temple, TX 129 E3
Temple City, CA 170 D5
Temple Hill, MD 148 E5
Temple of Heaven, 73 E1
Temple of the Moon Park, 73 C2
Temple of the Sun, 73 F2
Temple of 1000 Lights, 63 F2
Temple Terrace, FL 154 D5

Temple U, PA 145 E3

Templestowe, 79 E3

Templeton, 105 C4

Temse, 31 F5

Temuco, 86 A4

10 Downing Street, 27 C2

Tena, 90 A2

Tenaya Lake, CA 182 C3

Tenjo, 90 C3

Tennant Creek, 76 C5

Tennessee, 113 C4, 120 C6, 179 F3

Tennessee R, 113 C4, 179 F3, 120 B5

Tennoji-Ku, 71 C1

Tenri, 70 F5

Tensas River NWR, LA 120 A3

Teófilo Otoni, 85 G1

Tepepan, 98 B1

Tepexpan, 98 D5

Tepie, 96 C4

Teramo, 24 C4

Teresina, 85 G3

Termini Sta, 41 E3

Termiz, 53 D1

Ternat, 31 F5

Ternate, 61 F3

Ternes, 29 B4

Terni, 24 C4

Terra Bella, CA 133 D4

Terrace, 136 F5

Terrace Park, OH 151 F2

Terrassa, 38 D7

Terre Haute, IN 112 C5, 125 E3

Terrebonne, 106 C5

Terrytown, LA 163 G4

Teruel, 21 D3

Tervuren, 31 H2

Teslin, 136 E6

Tete, 47 F4

Teterboro Arpt, NJ 142 C3

Tetlin NWR, AK 136 D6

Teton Canyon Campground, WY 181 E3

Teton Creek, WY 181 E3

Teton Range, WY 181 E4

Teton Science School, WY 181 G2

Teton Village, WY 181 F2

Teton Wilderness Area, WY 180 C1, 181 H5

Tétouan, 21 B1, 44 B5

Tetuán, 39 C4

Tewksbury, MA 138 B7

Texarkana, AR 129 G5

Texarkana, TX 113 A3, 129 F5

Texas, 96 D6, 111 F3, 128 E4, 178 D2

Texas City, TX 129 F2

Texas Stad, TX 165 F4

Texas at Arlington, U of, TX 164 D3

Texas at Dallas, U of, TX 165 G5

Teyahualco, 98 B6

Thailand, 61 A4

Thailang Tobacco Monopoly, 63 G5

Thalwil, 37 E1

Thames Barrier, 26 D7

Thames R, 19 E2, 20 C7

Thane, 65 C3

Theatre of Marcellus, 41 D2

Theodore Roosevelt NP, ND 126 B7, 178 D5

Theodore Wirth RP, MN 161 B3

Thermalito, CA 132 B6

Thermopolis, WY 130 D7, 135 H3

Thessaloníki, 17 G3, 25 F4

Thetford, 114 C7

Thibodaux, LA 120 A4

Thief River Falls, MN 124 A7, 126 E8

Thiès, 44 A2

Thimphu, 58 E6

Thohoyandou, 47 F3

Thomas Isl, ME 186 B6

Thomaston, GA 120 D3

Thomastown, 79 C4

Thomasville, GA 120 D2

Thompson, Can 101 F3

Thompson, UT 130 C5

Thompson Falls, MT 135 E5

Thompson Isl Info Ctr, ME 186 A6

Thompsons, TX 166 A1

Thomson, GA 121 E4

Thon Buri, 63 F5

Thon Buri, 63 F5

Thonon-les-Bains, 23 B1

Thonotosassa, FL 154 D6

Thornbury, 79 C3

Thornhill, 104 E8

Thousand Islands, 117 E5

Three Rivers, NM 131 E2

Three Rivers Stad, PA 146 C6

Throgs Neck Brdg, NY 143 F5

Thun, 37 C1

Thunder Basin NG, WY 126 A5

Thunder Bay, 103 A2, 112 B7, 124 D7

Thunder Hole, ME 186 D4

Thunderbird Park, AZ 168 A6

Thunderer, The, WY 180 D5

Thurso, 14 C2, 18 D7

Thurston Isl, 83 C4

Tiananmen Sq, 73 D2

Tiancunzhen, 73 B2

Tiangizo, 73 D2

Tianjin, 55 E1, 60 C8, 66 B5

Tianmen, 96 A6, 111 A4, 133 E2, 169 F1

Tiber R, 17 E3, 24 B4

Tibesti, 45 E3

Tibet, 59 D6

Tiburon, CA 174 B6

Tiburon Angel Isl Ferry, CA 173 D4

Tiburtino, 40 C5

Ticoman, 98 B4

Ticonderoga, NY 115 A4, 117 H5

Tieling, 66 C3

Tien Shan, 53 F1, 58 D8

Tiergarten, 32 C7, 33 C3

Tierpark Berlin, 32 E7

Tierra Ceia, FL 154 C2

Tierra del Fuego, 86 B2

Tierra Verde, FL 154 B3

Tierrasanta, CA 169 G4

Tieton, WA 134 C5

Tieying, 73 E1

Tiffany & Co, NY 141 G5

Tiffin, OH 118 B5

Tifton, GA 121 E2

Tigaon, 64 F5

Tigard, OR 177 F4

Tiger Stad, MI 156 C6

Tigre, 88 C8

Tigris R, 45 G5, 49 E5, 53 A1

Tijuana, 96 A6, 111 A4, 133 E2, 169 F1

Tiksi, 54 C6, 82 B8

Tilbury, 26 F7

Tilden RP, CA 174 C6

Tillamook, OR 134 A4

Tillamook Head, OR 134 A4

Timaru, 77 G1

Times Square, NY 141 E4

Timisoara, 17 G5

Timmins, 103 B2

Timonium, MD 147 D4

Timor, 61 F1, 76 B6

Timor Sea, 61 F1, 76 B6

Timucuan Ecological & Hist Pres, FL 121 F2

Tinley Park, IL 159 C1

Tiny Town, CO 167 E2

Tioga Pass, CA 182 D4

Tioga R, PA 116 D1

Tioga SF, PA 119 F6

Tirana, 25 E5

Tiranë, 17 G3

Tírnavos, 25 F4

Tirosh, 50 B4

Tiruchchirappalli, 59 C3
Tisdale, 101 E3
Tisselt, 31 G4
Tisza R, 17 G5
Titagarh, 65 F3
Titusville, FL 121 F1, 123 F4
Titusville, PA 116 A1
Tivoli, 36 C6
Tizi Ouzou, 21 E2
Tláhuac, 98 D1
Tlajomulco de Zúñiga, 99 F3
Tlalnepantla, 98 B5
Tlalpan, 98 B1
Tlalpitzahuac, 98 D2
Tlaquepaque, 99 G5
Tlemcen, 21 C1
Toapayoh, 63 F2
Toamasina, 47 H4
Tobago, 95 H1
Tobolsk, 53 E4
Tobong, 72 D8
Tobruk, 45 E4, 48 B5
Tocantins R, 85 F2
Toccoa, GA 121 E5
Toco Hills, GA 152 C4
Toda, 68 B8
Toffen, 31 B4
Toga, PA 145 E3
Togane, 68 F6
Togiak NWR, AK 136 B6
Togo, 44 C1
Tohono O'odham Nation IR, AZ 131 B2
Toiyabe NF, CA 132 C5, 182 D6
Toiyabe NF, NV 132 E6
Tokelau, 80 D4
Tokol, 42 A5
Tokorozawa, 68 A8
Tokoza, 51 G1
Tokyo, 60 F8, 66 F5, 68 C7, 69, 80 A6
Tokyo Central Wholesale Market, 69 E1
Tokyo Disneyland, 68 D7

Tokyo Metropolitan Govt Office, 69 D2
Tokyo Sta, 69 D3
Tokyo Stock Exchange, 69 F3
Tolanaro, 47 H3
Toledo, OH 103 C1, 112 C5
Toledo, Spain 16 B3, 21 C3
Toledo Bend Reservoir, TX 129 F4, 118 B6, 125 F4
Toliara, 47 H3
Tolleson, AZ 168 A3
Toluca, 96 D3
Toluquilla, 99 F4
Tolyatti, 53 C4
Tom Bass RP, TX 166 C2
Tom Price, 76 A4
Tombigbee NF, MS 120 B4
Tombouctou, 44 C2
Tombstone, AZ 131 C1
Tomilino, 56 D3
Tomisato, 68 F7
Tomkins Square, NY 141 G2
Toms R, NJ 119 H4
Tomsk, 53 F3
Tonalá, 99 G4
Tonasket, WA 134 C6
Tonbridge, 26 E5
Tone, 68 E8
Tong, 72 A6
Tonga, 80 D3
Tongass, AK 136 E5
Tongbu, 72 E7
Tongdae Mun, 72 D7
Tongjak, 72 C6
Tongliao, 66 C2
Tongling, NV 132 E5
Tonto NF, AZ 130 B2
Tooele, UT 130 B6
Toongabbie, 78 C8
Toowoomba, 77 E4
Topanga, CA 170 A5
Topeka, KS 112 A5, 125 A3, 127 F3, 179 E3

Topkapi Palace, 43 E2
Topsfield, ME 114 F6
Topsfield, MA 138 E7
Tor de Cenci, 40 C4
Tor di Quinto, 40 C6
Tor Sapienza, 40 D5
Toranomon, 69 B1
Torignimmun, 72 C7
Törökbálint, 42 A6
Toronto, 103 C1, 104 D6, 112 D6, 116 B4
Toronto, U of, 104 D6
Toronto Island Park, 104 D5
Toronto Stock Exchange, 104 E6
Torrance, CA 170 B3
Torre Gaia, 40 D5
Torre Lupara, 40 D6
Torrenova, 40 D5
Torreón, 96 C4, 111 E1
Torres Str, 76 B1
Torresdale, PA 145 G4
Torrimpietra, 40 A6
Torrington, CT 115 A2, 117 H1
Torrington, WY 127 B4, 130 E6
Tórshavn, 14 C3
Tortosa, 21 D3
Tortuga Isl, 95 F1
Tortuguitas, 88 B8
Toshima-Ku, 68 C7
Totowa, NJ 142 A6
Totsuka-Ku, 68 B5
Tottenham, 26 D8
Touggourt, 44 D4
Toulon, 16 D4, 21 F4
Toulouse, 16 C4, 21 D4
Touraine, 105 A4
Tournament Players Club of Scottsdale, AZ 168 D5
Tournan-en-Brie, 28 F6
Tours, 16 C5, 20 D6
Towanda, PA 117 E1, 119 F6
Tower Fall, WY 180 C5

Tower Junction, WY 130 C8
Tower Lakes, IL 158 A6
Tower of London, 27 F2
Town & Country, FL 154 C5
Town & Country, MO 162 A2
Town Hill, ME 186 B5
Townsend, MT 135 G4
Townsville, 77 E5
Towson, MD 119 G4, 147 D4
Toyama, 66 E5
Toyonaka, 70 C6
Toyono, 70 C7
Trabrennbahn Volkspark, 32 E6
Trabuco Canyon, CA 171 F2
Trafalgar Sq, 27 C2
Trafaria, 38 A6
Tragliata, 40 A6
Trail, 101 C2
Traiskirchen, 42 D5
Trajan's Forum, 41 D3
Trakvista, 36 D6
Tralee, 19 A3, 20 A8
Transantarctic Mts, 83 C3
Transcona, 107 H5
Trapani, 24 B2
Trastevere, 41 C2
Traverse City, MI 112 C6, 124 E5
Treasure Isl, FL 154 A3
Trejos, 99 H6
Trelew, 86 B4
Trelleborg, 22 E6
Tremonton, UT 135 F1
Trent R, 19 E3
Trento, 23 D1, 24 B6
Trenton, FL 123 E5
Trenton, MO 125 B3
Trenton, NJ 112 E6, 119 H4
Treptow, 32 E7
Tres de Febrero, 88 C7
Trevi, The Fountains of 41 D3

Treviso, 24 **B5**

Trevose, PA 145 **G6**

Trezzano sul Vaviglio, 40 **B1**

Tri-City, OR 132 **A8**

Triangle X Ranch, WY 181 **G3**

Triborough Brdg, NY 143 **E4**

Trident Thorofare Plateau, WY 180 **D1**

Triel-sur-Seine, 28 **B8**

Trier, 23 **B3**

Trieste, 17 **E4**, 23 **E1**, 24 **C5**, 40 **C6**

Trikala, 25 **E4**

Trincomalee, 59 **C3**

Trinidad, Bol 84 **D2**

Trinidad, CA 132 **A7**

Trinidad, CO 111 **E4**, 127 **B2**, 128 **C6**, 131 **E4**

Trinidad & Tobago, 85 **E6**, 95 **H1**

Trinity Islands, AK 136 **C5**

Trinity NF, CA 134 **B1**

Trinity River, TX 129 **F3**

Trinity River Greenbelt Park, TX 165 **F4**

Trionfale, 40 **B6**, 41 **A4**

Triple Creek Park, OH 151 **C4**

Triple Divide Pk, CA 182 **D2**

Tripoli, 44 **D4**, 48 **A5**

Trivandrum, 59 **B3**

Trocadero Gdns, 29 **B2**

Trois-Rivieres, 103 **D2**, 114 **A7**

Troitsk, 56 **A1**

Trolleyville USA, OH 150 **B6**

Trollhättan, 22 **D7**

Trombay, 65 **C2**

Tromsø, 15 **F5**, 52 **C7**, 82 **E7**

Trondheim, 15 **E4**

Trooper, PA 144 **B6**

Trophy Club, TX 164 **C6**

Tropicana, 30 **B2**

Troutdale, OR 177 **H5**

Troy, AL 120 **C3**

Troy, NH 115 **B3**

Troy, NY 115 **A3**, 117 **H3**

Troy, OH 118 **A4**

Troyes, 23 **D6**, 23 **A2**

Truckee, CA 132 **C6**

Trujillo, 84 **B3**

Trujillo Adobe HS, CA 171 **G4**

Trujillo Alto, 122 **C2**

Truman NHS, Harry S, MO 162 **D5**

Truman Sports Complex, Harry S, MO 162 **D5**

Trumbull, CT 116 **B6**

Truro, MA 184 **E7**

Truro, UK 19 **C2**, 103 **E2**

Truth or Consequences, NM 128 **A4**, 131 **D2**

Tshikapa, 47 **E5**

Tsim Sha Tsui, 75 **C2**

Tsing Yi, 75 **A4**

Tsuen Wan, 75 **A4**

Tsukiji, 69 **E1**

Tsukuda, 69 **F1**

Tsumeb, 47 **E4**

Tsurumi-Ku, 68 **C6**

Tsz Wan Shan, 75 **D4**

Tualatin, OR 177 **F4**

Tuamotu Archipelago, 81 **E3**

Tuba City, AZ 131 **C3**

Tucheng, 62 **B4**

Tuchomerice, 35 **D3**

Tuckemuck Isl, MA 185 **G4**

Tucker, GA 152 **D5**

Tuckup Canyon, AZ 183 **B3**

Tucson, AZ 96 **B6**, 111 **C3**, 131 **C2**, 178 **B2**

Tucumcari, NM 111 **E4**, 128 **C5**, 131 **F3**

Tucuruvi, 92 **B5**

Tuktoyaktuk, 136 **E8**

Tukwila, WA 176 **C3**

Tula, 53 **B4**

Tulane U, LA 163 **F5**

Tulare, CA 133 **C4**

Tulelake, CA 132 **B7**

Tullamarine Intl Arpt, 79 **A4**

Tullamore, 19 **B3**, 104 **A7**

Tullinge, 36 **D5**

Tulsa, OK 113 **A4**, 125 **A1**, 127 **F1**, 129 **E6**, 179 **E3**

Tultepec, 98 **C6**

Tultitlán, 98 **B6**

Tulun, 55 **B3**

Tulyehualco, 98 **C1**

Tumba, 36 **D5**

Tumbes, 84 **B3**

Tune, 36 **A5**

Tunis, 17 **E2**, 24 **B1**, 44 **D5**

Tunisia, 17 **E1**, 24 **A1**, 44 **D5**

Tunja, 84 **C5**

Tunjuelito, 90 **C1**

Tunxi, 67 **B3**

Tuolumne Grove, CA 182 **A3**

Tuolumne Meadows, CA 182 **D4**

Tuolumne Pk, CA 182 **C4**

Tuolumne R, CA 182 **A4**

Tupelo, MS 113 **B4**, 120 **B4**, 129 **H5**

Tupper Lake, NY 117 **G5**

Tura, 50 **C1**, 55 **B4**

Turbat, 58 **A6**

Turgutlu, 25 **H3**

Turin, 16 **D4**, 20 **F5**, 24 **A5**

Turkey, 17 **H3**, 25 **H4**, 45 **F5**, 48 **D6**

Turkey Run Park, VA 148 **B7**

Turkmenistan, 45 **H5**, 45 **G6**, 49 **G6**, 58 **A8**

Turks & Caicos Islands, 95 **E5**

Turku, 15 **F3**

Turlock, CA 132 **C5**

Turner Ridge, CA 182 **B1**

Turnu Magurele, 25 **G6**

Turpan Depression, 58 **E8**

Turpin Hills, OH 151 **E2**

Turret Mt, WY 180 **D2**

Turtle Creek, PA 146 **E6**

Turtle Mt Prov P, 126 **D8**

Turumo, 90 **D4**

Tusayan, AZ 183 **E1**

Tusayan Ruin & Mus, AZ 183 **F1**

Tuscaloosa, AL 113 **C3**, 120 **C4**

Tuscarora, NV 132 **E7**

Tuscolano, 40 **C5**

Tushino, 56 **B5**

Tuskegee, AL 120 **D3**

Tustin, CA 171 **E2**

Tuvalu, 80 **C4**

Tuxtla Gutiérrez, 97 **E2**

Tuz Golu, 48 **D6**

Tuzla, 24 **D5**

Tver, 15 **H2**, 52 **B5**

Tweed R, 18 **D5**

Tweedsmuir Prov P, 136 **F5**

Twentynine Palms, CA 133 **F3**

Twentynine Palms Marine Corps Base, CA 133 **E3**

Twickenham, 26 **B7**

Twin Bridges, MT 135 **F4**

Twin City Racetrack, FL 154 **B7**

Twin Falls, ID 110 **C6**, 130 **A7**, 132 **F8**, 135 **E2**

Twin Lakes, CA 182 **D6**

Twin Pks, CA 171 **H6**

Twinsburg, OH 150 **F5**

Two Ocean Lake, WY 181 **G5**

Two Ocean Plateau, WY 180 **C2**

Tyler, TX 113 **A3**, 129 **F4**

Tyler Arboretum, PA 144 **A2**

Tynda, 55 **D4**

Tyreso, 36 **F6**

Tyrrhenian Sea, 17 **E3**, 24 **C2**

Tysons Corner, VA 148 **A7**

Tyumen, 53 **D4**

U

Ubangi R, 45 **E1**

Ubaque, 90 **D1**

Uberlândia, 85 **F1**

Ucayali R, 84 **C2**

Uccle, 31 **G1**

Uchikanda, 69 **D4**

UCLA, CA 170 **B5**

Uddevalla, 22 **D7**

Udel'naya, 57 **G3**

Udine, 17 **E4**, 23 **E1**, 24 **C6**

Uelzen, 23 **D4**

Uetliberg, 37 **D1**

Ufa, 53 **D4**

Uganda, 45 **F1**, 47 **G6**

Uherské Hradiste, 23 **F2**

Uhrineves, 35 **F2**

Uijongbu, 72 **D8**

Uinkaret Plateau, AZ 183 **A4**

Uintah and Ouray IR, UT 130 **C5**

Uithoorn, 30 **D4**

Uiwang, 72 **D5**

Uji, 70 **F7**

Újpest, 42 **B8**

Ujungpandang, 61 **E2**

Ukhta, 52 **D5**

Ukiah, CA 132 **A6**

Ukraine, 17 **H6**, 45 **F6**

Ukyo-Ku, 71 **D3**

Ulaanbaatar, 55 **C2**

Ulan-Ude, 55 **C3**

Ullnasjon, 36 **E7**

Úllo, 42 **C6**

Ulm, 23 **C2**

Ulsan, 66 **D5**

Uluberia, 65 **D1**

Ulyanovsk, 53 **C4**

Ulysses, KS 127 **C2**

Umatilla, OR 134 **C4**

Umatilla NF, OR 134 **D4**

Umeå, 15 **F4**

Umeda-Koma Theater, 71 **A4**

Umnak Isl, AK 136 **A5**

Umpqua NF, OR 134 **B3**

Umraniye, 43 **F2**

Umtata, 47 **F2**

Unadilla R, NY 117 **F3**

Unalaska Isl, AK 136 **A5**

Underground Atlanta, GA 152 **B3**

UNESCO, 29 **C1**

Unga Isl, AK 136 **B5**

Ungava Bay, 103 **C4**

Ungava Pen, 102 **B5**

Unhos, 38 **B8**

Union, NJ 142 **A3**

Union, SC 121 **F5**

Union, WV 118 **D2**

Union City, CA 175 **D4**

Union City, NJ 141 **E6**, 142 **C4**

Union City, PA 116 **A1**

Union City, TN 120 **B6**

Union Park, FL 153 **H4**

Union Square, CA 173 **E2**

Union Square, NY 141 **F3**

Union Sta, CA 172 **E6**

Union Sta, Can 104 **E6**

Union Sta, DC 149 **F3**

Union Sta, IL 160 **B5**

Union Sta, MO 162 **C2**

Uniondale, NY 143 **H3**

Uniontown, PA 118 **D4**

Unionville, NV 132 **D7**

United Arab Emirates, 49 **G3**

United Ctr, IL 159 **D4**

United Kingdom, 16 **C6**

United Nations, NY 141 **G4**

United States, 81 **H6**, 96 **D6**

US Air Arena, MD 148 **F6**

US Air Force Academy, CO 127 **B3**

US Customs, CA 169 **G1**

US Intl U, CA 169 **G5**

US Holocaust Mem Mus, DC 149 **C2**

US Mint, CO 167 **G3**

US Supreme Court, DC 149 **F2**

USS Arizona N Mem, HI 177 **F3**, 178 **C1**

USS Constitution, MA 140 **D6**

Universal Studios, FL 153 **F3**

University City, MO 162 **B2**

University Hts, OH 150 **E7**

University Park, TX 165 **F4**

University Place, WA 176 **A1**

Unp'yong, 72 **C7**

Úpalota, 42 **B7**

Upington, 47 **E2**

Upland, CA 171 **F5**

Upland, PA 144 **B1**

Upolu Pt, HI 137 **E2**

Upper Darby, PA 144 **D3**

Upper Falls, MD 147 **F4**

Upper Hadlock Pond, ME 186 **C4**

Upper Klamath Lake, OR 132 **B8**

Upper/Lower Falls, WY 180 **B4**

Upper Matecumbe Key, FL 188 **F3**

Upper Montclair, NJ 142 **B5**

Upper Red Lake, MN 124 **B7**

Upper River Rouge, MI 156 **A8**

Upper Sandusky, OH 118 **B5**

Upper Saranac Lake, NY 117 **G5**

Upplands-Vasby, 36 **D7**

Uppsala, 15 **F3**, 22 **F8**

Ural Mts, 53 **D4**

Ural R, 53 **C3**

Uran, 65 **B1**

Uranium City, 101 **E4**

Urawa, 68 **B8**

Urayasu, 68 **D7**

Urbana, IL 125 **D3**

Urbana, OH 118 **B4**

Urench, 58 **A8**

Urganch, 53 **C2**

Uruapán, 96 **C3**

Uruguaiana, 86 **C5**

Uruguay, 86 **C5**

Uruguay R, 86 **B5**

Urumqi, 55 **A1**, 58 **E8**

Usak, 25 **H3**

Usáquen, 90 **C3**

Usera, 39 **C2**

Ushuaia, 86 **B2**

Uskudar, 43 **E2**

Uskumrukoy, 43 **E1**

Usme, 90 **C1**

Ussuriysk, 55 **F3**, 66 **C6**

Ust-Ilimsk, 55 **B3**

Ust'-Izora, 57 **H1**

Ust-Kut, 55 **C3**

Uster, 37 **F1**

Usti nad Labem, 23 **E3**

Ustyurt Plateau, 53 **C2**

Usumacinta R, 97 **E2**

Utah, 110 **C5**, 130 **B5**, 135 **F1**, 178 **B4**

Utan, 65 **A4**

Ute Mountain IR, CO 131 **D4**

Utica, NY 112 **E6**, 117 **F3**

Utrecht, 23 **B4**

Utsubo Park, 71 **A3**

Utsunomiya, 66 **F5**

Uttarpara, 65 **E2**

Utuado, 122 **B2**

Utukok R, AK 136 **C8**

Uvalde, TX 128 **D2**

Uwharrie NF, NC 121 **F5**

Uxbridge, 26 **B7**

Uzbekistan, 45 **G6**, 58 **A8**

Uzice, 25 **E6**

Uzumasa, 71 **D3**

Uzunkopru, 25 **G5**

V

Vaca Key, FL 188 D2
Vacaville, CA 132 B5
Vadnais Hts, MN 161 E4
Vadodara, 58 B5
Vaerlose, 36 B7
Vail, CO 127 A3, 130 E5
Val de Grace, 29 E1
Val-d'Or, 103 C2
Valby, 36 B6
Valdés Pen, 86 B4
Valdez, AK 100 A5, 136 D6
Valdez, FL 153 G6
Valdivia, 86 A4
Valdosta, GA 113 D3,
  121 E2, 122 D6
Vale, OR 134 D3
Valence, 20 F5
Valencia, Spain 16 C3,
  21 D3
Valencia, Venez 84 D6,
  95 F1
Valentine, NE 126 D5
Valentine NWR, NE
  127 D4
Valenzuela, 62 B3
Valera, 84 C5
Valhalla, 51 G5
Valjevo, 25 E6
Valladolid, 16 B3, 21 B3
Valladupar, 84 C5
Valle de Aragón, 98 C4
Vallejo, CA 132 B5, 174 C8
Vallentuna, 36 E8
Valleranello, 40 C4
Vallersville, MA 184 B6
Valletta, 17 F1, 24 C1
Valley City, ND 126 E7
Valley Falls, OR 132 C8
Valley Forge, PA 144 A5
Valley Forge NHP, PA
  144 A5, 179 H4
Valley Stream, NY 143 G3
Valley View, OH 150 B6
Valparaíso, Chile 86 A5

Valparaiso, FL 122 C6
Van Buren, ME 114 E8
Van Cortlandt Park, NY
  143 E6
Van Dusen Botanical Gdns,
  107 F2
Van Gogh Mus, 30 D6
Van Horn, TX 131 E1
Van Kleef Aquarium,
  63 F1
Van Riebeeck Nature
  Reserve, 51 H5
Van Wert, OH 118 A5
Van Wyksrust, 51 E1
Vanceburg, KY 118 B3
Vancouver, Can 101 C2,
  107 F2, 110 B8
Vancouver, WA 134 B4,
  177 H5
Vancouver Intl Arpt,
  107 F1
Vancouver Isl, 101 B2
Vandalia, IL 125 D3
Vandenberg Village, CA
  133 B3
Vänern, 15 E2, 22 D7
Vanier, Can 105 B3
Vankaren, 136 A8
Vanuatu, 80 B3
Vanzago, 40 A2
Varanasi, 58 D5
Varazdin, 23 F1, 24 D6
Varberg, 22 D7
Vardø, 15 G6
Varedo, 40 B3
Varennes, 106 D4
Varese, 24 A5
Vari, 43 C1
Varimbombi, 43 C4
Varna, 17 H4, 25 H6
Värnamo, 22 E7
Varsta, 36 D5
Vasai, 65 B4
Vashon Hts, WA 176 B4
Vassa, 15 F4
Västerås, 22 E8
Vasterhaninge, 36 E5

Vastervik, 22 F7
Vatican City, 17 E3,
  24 B4, 40 C5, 41 A4
Vatican Mus, 41 B4
Vättern, 15 E2, 22 E7
Vaxholm, 36 F7
Växjö, 15 E2, 22 E6
Vecses, 42 C6
Vedbaek, 36 C7
Vega Baja, 122 B2
Vejle, 22 C6
Vekso, 36 A6
Velbert, 34 D6
Veld, 30 D6
Velen, 35 F3
Velké Prílepy, 35 D3
Velten, 32 C8
Vendelsö, 36 F5
Veneta, OR 134 B3
Venezuela, 84 D5, 95 F1
Venice, FL 123 E3
Venice, IL 162 C2
Venice, Italy 17 E4, 24 C5
Ventas, 39 D3
Ventspils, 15 F2
Ventura, CA 133 C3
Vénustiano Carranza,
  98 B3
Veracruz, 96 D3
Verazzano Narrows Brdg,
  NY 142 C2
Verbania, 20 F5
Verdun, 106 C2
Vereeniging, 47 F3
Vereseghyáz, 42 C4
Vergennes, VT 117 H5
Verkhoyansk, 54 D5
Verkhoyansk Range,
  54 D5, 82 B8
Vermillion, SD 126 E5
Vermillion R, 114 A8
Vermont, 103 D2, 112 E6,
  115 A3, 179 H5
Vernal, UT 110 D5, 130 C6
Vernon, CA 172 F5
Vernon, TX 128 D5
Vernon Hills, IL 158 B6

Vero Beach, FL 123 F3
Véroia, 25 F4
Verona, Italy 17 E4,
  23 D1, 24 B5
Verona, NJ 142 A5
Verona, PA 146 E7
Versailles, Fr 28 C6
Versailles, IL 118 A2
Verwoerdburg, 51 H6
Vesuvius, 24 C3
Veszprem, 24 D6
Veterans Mem Coliseum,
  AZ 168 B3
Veterans Mem CP, MO
  162 C3
Veterans Stad, PA 145 E2
Vialonga, 38 C8
Viareggio, 24 B4
Viborg, 22 C6
Vicálvaro, 39 E2
Vicente Guerrero, 133 F1
Vicente López, 88 D8
Vicenza, 24 B5
Vichy, 20 E5
Vicksburg, MS 120 A3,
  129 H4
Vicksburg NMP MS 179 E2
Victoria, Austral 77 E2
Victoria, Can 101 B2,
  110 A8, 134 B6
Victoria, Hong Kong
  67 A2, 75 C2
Victoria, KS 127 D2
Victoria, TX 111 F2,
  129 E2
Victoria Arts Ctr, 79 B2
Victoria Conv & Exh Ctr,
  75 D2
Victoria de las Tunas,
  94 C4
Victoria Gdns, 65 B2
Victoria Isl, 82 C5, 100 E6
Victoria Land, 83 B2
Victoria Pk, 75 B2
Victoria Rail Sta, 65 B1
Victoria Sta, 27 B1
Victoriaville, 114 B7

Victorville, CA 133 E3

Vidalia, GA 121 E3

Vidin, 25 F6

Vidnoye, 56 C2

Viedma, 86 B4

Vienna, Aust 17 F5, 23 F2, 42 E7

Vienna, VA 148 A6

Vienna-Schwechat Arpt, 42 F6

Vienne R, 20 D6

Vientiane, 61 A4

Vietnam, 61 B4

Vietnam Veterans Mem, DC 149 B2

View Bank, 79 D3

Vigentino, 40 C1

Vigny, 28 B8

Vigo, 16 A4, 21 A4

Vijayawada, 59 C4

Vila Formosa, 92 C4

Vila Madelena, 92 A5

Vila Maria, 92 B5

Vila Prudente, 92 C4

Viladecans, 38 D5

Villa Abemelek, 41 A2

Villa Ahumada, 96 C6, 128 A3

Villa Ballester, 88 C7

Villa Borghese, 40 C6, 41 D4

Villa Celimontana, 41 E2

Villa Coapa, 98 B1

Villa Crespo, 89 A3

Villa de Las Flores, 98 C6

Villa de Mayo, 88 B8

Villa Dominico, 88 E6

Villa Doria Pamphili, 41 A2

Villa Hills, KY 151 C1

Villa María del Triunfo, 87 H4

Villa Park, CA 171 E3

Villa Sciarra, 41 B1

Villach, 23 E1, 24 C6

Village Green, PA 144 A1

Village of Indian Hill, OH 151 F3

Villahermosa, 97 E3

Villanova, PA 144 B4

Villanova U, PA 144 C4

Villaverde, 39 C1

Villavicencio, 84 C4

Ville de Vallecas, 39 D2

Villeneuve le Comte, 28 F6

Villeneuve St-Georges, 28 D6

Vilnius, 15 G1, 52 A5

Vilvoorde, 31 G3

Vilyuy R, 55 C4

Vilyuysk, 54 D5

Vimodrone, 40 C2

Vimont, 106 B4

Viña del Mar, 86 A5

Vincennes, Fr 28 D7

Vincennes, IN 125 E2

Vincente Calderón Stad, 39 B2

Vincente de Carvalho, 92 D2

Vine Hill, CA 174 D7

Vineland, NJ 119 G4

Vineyard Haven, MA 185 G2

Vineyard Sd, MA 185 F1

Vinh, 61 B4

Vinings, GA 152 A5

Vinita, OK 127 F1

Vinkeveen, 30 D4

Vinnitsa, 17 H6

Vinnytsya, 53 A4

Vinor, 35 F3

Vinson Massif, 83 C4

Violet, LA 163 H4

Virden, 126 D8

Virgin Islands, 95 G4

Virginia, 112 E5, 119 F2, 179 G3

Virginia, MN 112 A7

Virginia Beach, VA 119 G1

Virginia Canyon, CA 182 C5

Virginia City, MT 135 G4

Virginia Gdns, FL 155 F2

Virginia Hills, VA 148 C5

Virginia Pk, CA 182 D5

Víron, 43 C2

Virum, 36 B7

Visalia, CA 133 D4

Visby, 22 F7

Viscount Melville Sd, 100 E7

Vishakhapatnam, 59 D4

Vishnu Temple, AZ 183 E2

Vista, CA 133 E2

Vista Encantadora, AZ 183 E2

Vista Hermosa, 98 A4

Vistula R, 17 F6

Vitacura, 87 G3

Vitarte, 87 H5

Vitebsk, 15 H2, 52 B5

Viterbo, 24 B4

Vitim R, 55 D3

Vitinia, 40 B4

Vitória, Bra 85 G1

Vitoria, Spain 16 B4, 21 C4

Vitoria da Conquista, 85 G2

Vittoria, 24 C1

Vlaardingen, 30 A2

Vladivostok, 55 F2, 66 C6

Vlorë, 17 G3, 25 E4

Vnukovo, 56 A3

Vnukovo Arpt, 56 A3

Voerde, 34 A8

Vol Irazú, 97 G1

Vol Tajumulco, 97 E2

Volga R, 45 G6, 53 B3, 53 C4

Volgograd, 53 B3

Volo, IL 158 A7

Volo Bog State Natural Area, IL 158 A7

Volodarskiy, 56 D1, 57 F1

Vologda, 52 C5

Vólos, 17 G3, 25 F3

Volta Redonda, 86 C6

Volusia, 40 C6

Voorberg, 30 A3

Voorheesville, NY 117 G3

Voorschoten, 30 B4

Vorkuta, 52 E5

Voronezh, 53 B4

Vosendorf, 42 D6

Vosloorus, 51 G1

Vostochnyy, 56 D5

Voula, 43 B1

Vouliagmeni, 43 C1

Voyageurs NP, MN 124 B7, 179 E6

Vrane, 35 E1

Vranje, 25 F5

Vrasene, 31 F6

Vratsa, 25 F6

Vrsovice, 35 E3

Vsevolozhsk, 57 H3

Vulcans Throne, AZ 183 A2

Vyborg, 15 G3

Vysocany, 35 F3

W

Waarder, 30 C3

Waasmunster, 31 E5

Wabash R, IL 125 D2

Wabu, 72 E7

Waco, TX 111 F3, 129 E4, 178 D2

Wad Madani, 45 F2, 48 D1

Waddinxveen, 30 C3

Wade Park, OH 150 E7

Wadsworth, IL 158 C8

Wagga Wagga, 77 E3

Waggaman, LA 163 E5

Wagon Wheel Canyon Wilderness Park, CA 171 F3

Wah Fu, 75 B1

Wahiawa, HI 137 C3

Wahpeton, ND 124 A6, 126 E7

Waialeale, HI 137 A4

Waianae, HI 137 C3

Waidmannslust, 32 C8
Waikiki Beach, HI 177 H1
Wailing Wall, 50 D4
Wailuku, HI 137 D3
Waimalu, HI 177 F3
Waimea, HI 137 E2
Waingapu, 61 E1
Waipahu, HI 177 E3
Wakayama, 66 E5
Wake Isl, 80 C5
Wakeby, MA 184 B5
Wakefield, MA 138 D5
Wakkanai, 66 E7
Wako, 68 B8
Walbrzych, 17 F6, 23 F3
Walden, NY 117 G1
Waldo, IL 123 E5
Waldoboro, ME 115 D4
Waldport, OR 134 A3
Wales, 16 B6, 19 D3,
 20 C8
Walhalla Glades, AZ
 183 E2
Walker Art Ctr, MN 161 C2
Walker Lake, NV 132 C4
Walker Mill RP, MD
 148 F6
Walkerville, 51 F1
Walla Walla, WA 134 D4
Wallace, ID 135 E5
Wallace, KS 127 C2
Walldorf, 35 A1
Wallington, NJ 142 C5
Wallis & Futuna, 80 C3
Wallisellen, 37 F2
Walnut, CA 171 E4
Walnut Creek, CA 174 E6
Walpole, MA 139 B1
Walsenburg, CO 127 A2
Walsum, 34 A8
Walt Disney World, FL
 153 F3
Walterboro, SC 121 F3
Waltham, MA 115 C3,
 139 B4
Waltham Forest, 26 D7

Walton, NY 117 F2
Walton, UK 26 B6
Walton Hills, OH 150 E5
Wambel, 34 F8
Wamesit, MA 138 B7
Wamsutter, WY 135 H1
Wan Chai, 75 C2
Wanchese, NC 187 G5
Wandsworth, 26 C7
Wanli, 62 D6
Wanne-Eicke, 34 D8
Wantirna, 79 E2
Wapato, WA 134 C5
Wappingers Falls, NY
 117 H1
Waquoit Village, MA
 185 E2
Warabi, 68 B8
Wards Chapel, MD 147 A4
Wareham, MA 184 A5
Warlingham, 26 D6
Warm Springs, NV 132 E5
Warm Springs IR, OR
 134 B3
Warner Robins, GA 121 E3
Warnimont Park, WI
 157 C1
Warrandyte, 79 E3
Warranwood, 79 F3
Warraq El Arab, 50 B3
Warren, MI 156 E8
Warren, OH 118 D5
Warren, PA 116 B1, 119 E6
Warren Park, IN 157 F2
Warrensburg, NY 117 G4
Warrensville Hts, OH
 150 E6
Warrenton, VA 119 F3
Warrenville, IL 159 A3
Warrington, FL 122 B6
Warrnambool, 76 D2
Warsaw, IN 125 E4
Warsaw, NY 116 C3
Warsaw, Poland 17 G6,
 52 A5
Warsaw, VA 119 G2
Warwick, NY 116 A6

Warwick, RI 115 C2
Wasatch NF, UT 130 C6
Wasco, CA 133 C4
Washakie Wilderness, WY
 180 D3
Washburn Isl SP, MA
 185 E2
Washington, 101 C2,
 110 A8, 134 B5, 178 B6
Washington, DC 112 E5,
 119 F3, 148 D7, 149,
 179 H4
Washington, NC 121 H5
Washington, PA 118 D4
Washington, U of, WA
 176 C5
Washington Coliseum, DC
 149 F4
Washington Mon, DC
 149 C2
Washington Natl Arpt,
 VA 148 D6
Washington Park, IL
 162 D2
Washington Park, IN
 157 E2
Washington Park, OR
 177 F5
Washington Park, WI
 157 B3
Washington Square, IL
 160 C8
Washington Square Park,
 NY 141 F3
Washougal, WA 177 H6
Waskaganish, 103 C3
Wassaw NWR, GA 121 F3
Wassenaar, 30 B4
Watampone, 61 E2
Watauga, TX 164 C4
Watchtower, AZ 183 F2
Water Keys, FL 188 B2
Waterberge, 51 F6
Waterbury, CT 115 A2
Waterfalls, AZ 183 B2
Waterford, Ire 14 B1,
 19 B3, 20 B8

Waterford, PA 116 A1
Watergate Complex, DC
 149 A3
Wateringen, 30 A3
Waterloo, IA 125 B4
Waterloo, MD 147 B1
Waterloo, NY 116 D3
Waterloo Sta, 27 D2
Watertown, MA 139 C3
Watertown, NY 112 E6,
 117 E5
Watertown, SD 110 F6,
 126 E6
Waterville, ME 114 D5
Waterville, WA 134 C5
Waterworks Bldg, 89 C3
Watford, 26 B8
Watkins Glen, NY 116 D2,
 119 F6
Watsoma, 79 D4
Watson Lake, 101 C4,
 136 F6
Watsons Bay, 78 F7
Watsonville, CA 133 B4
Wattenberg, CO 167 H6
Wattenscheid, 34 D7
Wattenwil, 37 C1
Wattle Glen, 79 E4
Wauconda, IL 158 A6
Waukegan, IL 125 D4,
 158 C7
Wausau, WI 112 B6,
 124 D4
Wauseon, OH 118 B6
Wauwatosa, WI 157 A3
Wauwinet, MA 185 G6
Waverly, NY 117 E2
Waverly, OH 118 B3
Waves, NC 187 H3
Waw, 45 F1
Wawa, 103 B2
Wawona, CA 182 B1
Waxahachie, TX 129 F4
Waycross, GA 121 E2,
 123 E6
Wayland, MA 139 A3

Wayne, MI 156 **A5**

Wayne, PA 144 **B4**

Wayne, NE 127 **E4**

Wayne, WV 118 **C2**

Wayne NF, OH 118 **C4**

Wayne / Orange County Arpt, John, CA 171 **E2**

Waynesboro, GA 121 **E4**

Waynesboro, MS 120 **B3**

Weald, The 26 **E5**

Weatherford, OK 127 **E1**

Weaverville, CA 132 **B7**, 134 **B1**

Webster Groves, MO 162 **B1**

Weddell Sea, 83 **E4**

Wedding, 32 **C7**

Weed, CA 132 **B7**, 134 **B1**

Weehawken, NJ 141 **E6**, 142 **D4**

Weesow, 32 **F8**

Wegendorf, 32 **F8**

Weiden, 23 **D3**

Weifang, 66 **B5**

Weigongcum, 73 **C3**

Weihai, 55 **E1**, 60 **C8**, 66 **C5**

Weikiva Springs, FL 153 **G5**

Weipa, 76 **D6**

Weiser, ID 134 **D3**

Weissensee, 32 **D7**

Wejherowo, 22 **F5**

Wekiwa Springs SP, FL 153 **F5**

Welch, WV 118 **C2**

Welkom, 47 **F2**

Welland, 116 **B3**

Wellesley, MA 139 **A3**

Wellesley College, MA 139 **A3**

Wellfleet, MA 184 **F7**

Wellfleet Bay Wilderness Sanctuary, MA 184 **F6**

Wellfleet Harbor, MA 184 **F7**

Wellington, KS 129 **E6**

Wellington, *New Zealand* 80 **C2**

Wells, ME 115 **C4**

Wells, NV 132 **F7**, 135 **E1**, 178 **B4**

Wells Fargo Mus, CA 172 **E6**

Wellsboro, PA 119 **F6**

Wellsville, NY 116 **C2**

Wembley, 26 **C7**

Wembley Stad/Conf Ctr, 26 **C7**

Wemmel, 31 **F3**

Wenatchee, WA 110 **B7**, 134 **C5**

Wenatchee NF, WA 134 **C6**

Wendover, NV 130 **A6**

Wendover, UT 132 **F7**

Wendover Range, UT 130 **B6**, 132 **F7**

Wengi, 37 **B3**

Wenham, MA 138 **F6**

Wenzhou, 60 **D6**, 67 **C3**

Werden, 34 **C7**

Werder, 32 **A5**

Werkendam, 30 **D1**

Werne, 34 **E7**

Werneuchen, 32 **F8**

Wernsdorf, 32 **F5**

Wersten, 34 **B5**

West Allis, WI 157 **A2**

West Bank, 48 **D5**

West Barnstable, MA 184 **C5**

West Bend, WI 124 **D5**

West Boxford, MA 138 **D8**

West Brewster, MA 184 **E5**

West Chester, OH 151 **E4**

West Chester, PA 119 **G4**

West Chicago, IL 159 **A4**

West Conshohoken, PA 144 **C5**

West Covina, CA 170 **D4**

West Dennis, MA 184 **E5**

West Entrance, MT 180 **A4**

West Falmouth, MA 185 **E1**

West Fargo, ND 126 **E7**

West Forks, ME 114 **D6**

West Grand Lake, ME 114 **E6**

West Harrison, IN 151 **A3**

West Haven, CT 115 **A1**, 116 **C6**

West Hempstead, NY 143 **H3**

West Hollywood, CA 170 **B5**, 172 **A7**

West Hoxton, 78 **A6**

West Ice Shelf, 83 **D1**

West Indies, 95 **E4**

West Kildonan, 107 **F6**

West Lake, FL 188 **E4**

West Linn, OR 177 **G4**

West Meadows, 79 **B4**

West Memphis, AR 120 **A5**, 129 **H6**

West Miami, FL 155 **F1**

West Mifflin, PA 146 **D5**

West Milwaukee, WI 157 **B2**

West New York, NJ 141 **F6**, 142 **D4**

West Orange, NJ 142 **A5**

West Palm Beach, FL 113 **E2**, 123 **F2**, 179 **G1**

West Paterson, NJ 142 **B6**

West Peabody, MA 138 **D6**

West Philadelphia, PA 144 **D2**

West Pittsburg, CA 174 **E7**

West Plains, MO 125 **C1**, 129 **G6**

West Point, MS 120 **B4**

West Point, NE 126 **E4**

West Point Military Academy, NY 119 **H6**

West Potomac Park, DC 149 **B2**

West Richland, WA 134 **C4**

West Roxbury, MA 139 **C2**

West St Paul, MN 161 **B2**

West Samoa, 80 **D3**

West Seneca, NY 116 **B3**

West Siberian Plain, 53 **F4**

West Slope, OR 177 **F5**

West Sommerville, MA 139 **C4**

West Springfield, VA 148 **B5**

West Tisbury, MA 185 **G1**

West Tremont, ME 186 **A2**

West Trenton, ME 186 **A6**

West Union, OH 118 **B3**

West University Place, TX 166 **B3**

West Vancouver, 107 **G3**

West View, PA 146 **B7**

West Virginia, 112 **D5**, 118 **D4**, 179 **G4**

West Yarmouth, MA 184 **D5**

West Yellowstone, MT 130 **B8**, 135 **G3**, 180 **A4**

Westboro, 105 **A2**

Westbrook, ME 115 **C4**

Westbury, NY 143 **H4**

Westchester, IL 159 **B4**

Westerham, 26 **D6**

Western Addition, CA 173 **B1**

Western Australia, 76 **B4**

Western Bay, ME 186 **A5**

Western Desert, 48 **C4**

Western Ghats, 57 **B4**

Western Railway Mus, CA 174 **F8**

Western Sahara, 44 **A4**

Western Way, ME 186 **C2**

Westfalenhalle, 34 **F7**

Westfield, MA 115 **A2**

Westfield, NY 116 **A2**

Westfield, PA 116 **D1**

Westlake, OH 150 **A7**

Westlake, TX 164 **C5**

Westland, MI 156 **A6**

Westminster, 27 **B1**

Westminster, CA 170 **D2**

Westminster, CO 167 **F5**

Westminster, MD 119 **F4**

Westminster Abbey, 27 **C1**

Westmont, NJ 145 **F2**

Westmorland, CA 133 **E2**

Weston, Can 104 C6
Weston, FL 155 E4
Weston, MA 139 A3
Westover Hills, TX 164 B3
Westview, MD 147 B2
Westville, NJ 145 E1
Westwago, LA 163 F4
Westwood, CA 132 C6
Westwood, Can 107 F5
Westwood, KS 162 C4
Westwood, MA 139 B2
Westwood Hills, KS 162 C5
Westwood Lakes, FL 155 E1
Westworth, TX 164 A3
Wetherill Park, 78 B7
Wetter, 34 E6
Wettingen, 37 D2
Wewahitchka, FL 122 C5
Wewak, 76 C2
Wexford, 19 C3
Weyburn, 126 B8
Weymouth, MA 139 E2
Whangarei, 77 H2
Wharton SF, NJ 119 H4
Wheat Ridge, CO 167 F3
Wheatland, WY 127 A4,
  130 E6
Wheaton, IL 159 A3
Wheaton, MD 148 D8
Wheeler Pk, NV 130 A5
Wheeling, IL 158 B5
Wheeling, WV 112 D5,
  118 B4
Whitby, 116 B5
White Bear Lake, MN
  161 F4
White Bird, ID 135 E4
White Center, WA 176 B4
White Earth IR, MN
  124 A7, 126 F7
White Horse, PA 144 A3
White Horse Beach, MA
  184 B2
White House, DC 149 C3
White Marsh, MD 147 F4
White Missouri R, SD
  126 D5

White Mountain NF, NH
  115 B4
White Mountain Pk, CA
  132 D5
White Mountains NRA,
  AK 136 D7
White Nile R, 45 F2,
  48 C1
White Oak, MD 148 E8
White Plains, NY 116 B6,
  119 H5
White Ranch CP, CO
  167 E4
White R, 120 A5,
  125 B1, 129 G6, 132 F5
White River NWR, AR
  120 A5, 129 H5
White Rock Lake Park,
  TX 165 G4
White Sands Missile Range,
  NM 128 B4, 131 D2
White Sands NM, NM
  128 B4, 131 D2, 178 C2
White Sea, 15 H5, 52 D6
White Settlement, TX
  164 A3
White Sulphur Springs,
  MT 135 G5
Whitechapel, 27 F3
Whitecourt, 101 D3
Whitehall, NY 117 H4
Whitehall, PA 146 C5
Whitehorse, 100 B5,
  136 E6
Whitesburg, KY 118 B1
Whitesnell PP, 124 A8
Whitestone, NY 143 F5
Whitestone Brdg, NY
  143 E5
Whitewater Bay, FL
  188 D4
Whiting, IN 159 E2
Whiting Ranch Wilderness
  Park, CA 171 F2
Whitley City, KY 118 A1
Whitnall Park, WI 157 A1
Whitney Mus, NY 141 G6

Whittier, CA 170 D4
Whyalla, 76 D3
Wichita, KS 111 F4, 127 E2,
  178 D3
Wichita Falls, TX 111 F3,
  129 E5, 178 D2
Wick, 18 D7
Wicked Pt, 116 D4
Wickliffe, OH 150 F8
Wiener Neustadt, 23 E7
Wierda Park, 51 G5
Wiesbaden, 16 D6, 23 C3
Wijnegem, 31 H6
Wild Water Kingdom,
  104 B7
Wildau, 32 E5
Wildcat Canyon RP, CA
  174 C6
Wilder, KY 151 D1
Wildfield, 104 B8
Wildomar, CA 171 H1
Wildwood Hills, MD
  148 B8
Wilhelmshaven, 22 C5
Wilhemsdorf, 32 A5
Wilkes-Barre, PA 119 G5
Wilkes Land, 83 C1
Wilkins, PA 146 E6
Wilkinsburg, PA 146 D6
Willamette Falls, OR
  177 G4
Willcox, AZ 131 C2
Willebroek, 31 G4
Willemstad, 95 F1
Willernie, MN 161 F4
Williams, AZ 131 B3
Williams Lake, 101 C3
Williamsburg, KY 118 B1,
  125 F2
Williamsburg, NY 141 H1,
  142 D3
Williamsburg, VA 119 G2
Williamson, WV 118 C2
Williamsport, PA 119 F5
Williamston, NC 121 H6
Williamstown, Austral
  79 B2

Williamstown, KY 118 A3
Williamstown, MA 117 H3
Willimantic, CT 115 B2
Willingboro, PA 145 H4
Williston, FL 123 E5
Williston, ND 110 E7,
  126 B8
Williston Park, NY 143 H4
Willits, CA 132 A6
Willmar, MN 126 F6
Willmersdorf, 32 F8
Willmore Park, MO
  162 B1
Willoughby, 78 E8
Willoughby Hills, OH
  150 F8
Willow, FL 154 D2
Willow Brook, CA 170 C3
Willow Creek, CA 132 A7
Willow Grove, PA 145, E6
Willowbrook, IL 159 B3
Willowdale, 104 D7
Willowdale SF, MA 138 F7
Willows, CA 132 B6
Wilmer, TX 165 G1
Wilmersdorf, 32 C6, 33 A1
Wilmette, IL 158 D5
Wilmington, DE 112 E5,
  119 G4, 179 M4
Wilmington, MA 138 C6
Wilmington, NC 113 E4,
  121 H4, 179 G3
Wilmington, OH 118 B4
Wilrijk, 31 G5
Wilson, NC 121 G5
Wilson, WY 181 E1
Wilton Manors, FL 155 G5
Wimauma, FL 154 D3
Wimbledon, 26 C7
Winchester, IN 118 A4
Winchester, KY 118 A2
Winchester, MA 139 C4
Winchester, TN 120 C5
Winchester, VA 119 E3
Winchester Mystery
  House, CA 175 E2

Wind Cave NP, SD 130 E7, 178 D5

Wind River IR, WY 130 C7, 135 H2

Windcrest, TX 163 H3

Windermere, FL 153 F3

Windhoek, 47 E3

Winding Stair Mountain NRA, OK 129 F5

Window Rock, AZ 131 C3

Windsor, CA 132 A5

Windsor, Can 103 B1, 112 D6, 118 B6, 125 F4, 156 E6

Windsor, UK 26 A7

Windsor Castle, 26 A7

Windsor Intl Arpt, 156 E5

Windward Islands, 95 H2

Windward Passage, 94 D4

Winfield, IL 159 A4

Winfield, KS 127 E2, 129 E6

Winisk, 103 A3

Winkler, 126 E8

Winnemucca, NV 110 B6, 132 D7, 134 D1

Winnemucca Lake, NV 132 D6

Winner, SD 126 D5

Winnetka, IL 158 D5

Winnett, MT 135 H5

Winnfield, LA 129 G4

Winnipeg, 101 F2, 107 F4, 110 F7, 124 A8

Winnipeg Intl Arpt, 107 F5

Winnsboro, LA 129 G4

Winona, MN 112 A6, 124 C5

Winona, MS 120 B4, 129 H5

Winslow, AZ 111 C4, 131 C3

Winsted, CT 115 A2, 117 H1

Winston, OR 132 A8

Winston-Salem, NC 113 D4, 121 F6

Winter Garden, FL 153 E4

Winter Haven, FL 123 F4

Winter Park, FL 123 F4

Winter Springs, FL 153 H5

Winterthur, 37 F2

Winthrop, MA 139 E4

Winthrop Harbor, IL 158 C8

Winton Woods, OH 151 D4

Wiscassey, ME 115 D4

Wisconsin, 103 A1, 112 B6, 124 C5, 179 E5

Wisconsin R, WI 124 C5

Wisconsin, U of, at Milwaukee, WI 157 C3

Wismar, 22 D5

Witch Hole Pond, ME 186 C5

Witkoppen, 51 F4

Witten, 34 E7

Wittenberge, 23 D4

Wo Mei, 75 F4

Woburn, MA 139 C5

Woerden, 30 D3

Wohlen, 37 D1

Woking, 26 B6

Wolf Pt, MT 126 A8

Wolfe Isl, 117 E5

Wolfeboro, NH 115 C4

Wolfsberg, 23 E1

Wolfsburg, 23 C4

Wollochet, WA 176 A1

Wollongong, 77 F2

Wonga Park, 79 F3

Woltersdorf, 32 F6

Woluwe-St Pierre, 31 G2

Wolverhampton, 19 D3

Wolvertem, 31 F3

Wompatuck SP, MA 139 F1

Wondang, 72 B8

Wonsan, 66 D5

Wood Ridge, NJ 142 C5

Woodbine Race Track, 104 C6

Woodbridge, 104 C7

Woodbury, MN 161 F2

Woodbury, NJ 119 H4

Woodcrest, CA 171 H3

Woodhaven, NY 143 E3

Woodinville, WA 176 D6

Woodland, CA 132 B5

Woodland Mound Park, OH 151 F1

Woodlands, TX 129 F3

Woodlawn, MD 147 C3

Woodlawn, OH 151 D4

Woodlynne, NJ 145 F2

Woodmere, NY 143 G2

Woodmere, OH 150 F7

Woodmoor, MD 147 B3

Woodridge, IL 159 B3

Woodruff Arts Ctr, GA 152 B4

Woods Hole, MA 185 F1

Woodside, CA 175 C2

Woodside, NY 143 E4

Woodstock, Can 114 F7

Woodstock, MD 147 A3

Woodstock, NY 117 G2

Woodstock, VT 115 B4

Woodstock, VA 119 E3

Woodstream, NJ 145 H2

Woodsville, NH 115 ·B4

Woodville, FL 122 D6

Woodward, OK 127 D1, 128 D6

Woolen's Garden, IN 157 F3

Woollahra, 78 F7

Woolooware Bay, 78 E5

Woomera, 76 D3

Woonsocket, RI 115 B2

Wooster, OH 118 C5

Worb, 37 C2

Worcester, Afr 47 E2

Worcester, MA 112 F6, 115 B2

Worker's Stad, 73 E3

Worland, WY 130 D7, 135 H3

World Diamond Trading Ctr, 31 G6

World Trade Ctr, Austral 79 B2

World Trade Ctr, NY 141 E1

Worth, IL 159 C2

Worthington, MD 147 A2

Worthington, MN 126 F5

Wounded Knee, SD 126 C5, 130 F7

Wrangel Isl, 54 D8, 82 B6

Wrangell-St Elias NP & Pres, AK 136 D6, 178 B1

Wright Brothers Natl Mem, NC 187 G6

Wrigley, 136 F7

Wrigley Bldg, IL 160 C7

Wrigley Field, IL 159 D4

Wroclaw, 17 F6, 23 F4

Wuhan, 60 C6, 67 A3

Wuhu, 60 C7, 67 B3

Wujiaochang, 74 E8

Wuku, 62 B5

Wülfrath, 34 C6

Wupatki Natl Mon, AZ 131 B3, 178 B3

Wuppertal, 34 D5

Würzburg, 23 D3

Wutoschingen, 37 D4

Wuxi, 67 B4

Wuyi Shan, 67 B3

Wuzhou, 60 C5, 67 A4

Wyandotte, MI 156 C5

Wyandotte NWR, MI 156 C5

Wye R, 19 D3

Wylie, TX 165 H6

Wyndham, 76 B6

Wyndmoor, PA 144 D5

Wynndale, IN 157 E3

Wyoming, 101 D1, 110 D6, 130 D7, 135 H2, 178 C4

Wyoming, OH 151 D3

Wysocking Bay, NC 187 F3

Wytheville, VA 118 D1, 121 F6

X

Xai-Xai, 47 **G3**
Xalapa, 96 **D3**
Xenia, OH 118 **B4**
Xi R, 60 **B5**
Xiamen, 67 **B2**
Xian, 60 **B7**
Xiangfan, 60 **B7**, 67 **A4**
Xianghongoi, 73 **A4**
Xiangtan, 67 **A3**
Xiannongtan Stad, 73 **E1**
Xiao Hinggan Ling, 66 **C7**
Xiaotun, 73 **A4**
Xiaoqiaoli, 74 **E6**
Xichang, 60 **A6**
Xicheng District, 73 **C3**
Xigaze, 58 **E6**
Xingtai, 66 **A5**
Xingu R, 85 **F3**
Xining, 60 **A7**
Xinyang, 67 **A4**
Xiqiao Park & Zoo, 74 **A5**
Xiyuan, 73 **B4**
Xizhuang, 73 **D1**
Xochimilco, 98 **C1**
Xuanwu District, 73 **C1**
Xuhui District, 74 **C5**
Xuijiahui, 74 **C5**
Xujiazhai, 74 **C7**
Xuzhou, 55 **E1**, 60 **C7**, 67 **B4**

Y

Yablonovvy Range, 55 **D3**, 66 **A8**
Yabucoa, 122 **C1**
Yachats, OR 134 **A3**
Yachimata, 68 **F7**
Yachiyo, 68 **E7**
Yaesu, 69 **E3**
Yaki Pt, AZ 183 **E2**
Yakima, WA 110 **B7**, 134 **C5**
Yakima IR, WA 134 **C4**
Yakutat, AK 100 **A5**

Yakutsk, 54 **D5**, 82 **B8**
Yalova, 25 **H4**
Yam, 56 **C1**
Yamagata, 66 **F6**
Yamal Pen, 52 **F5**
Yamashina-Ku, 71 **F2**
Yamashiro, 70 **F6**
Yamato, 68 **A6**
Yamato-Koriyama, 70 **F5**
Yambol, 25 **G5**
Yamenkou, 73 **A2**
Yamontovo, 56 **B2**
Yamoussoukro, 44 **B1**
Yamsay Mt, OR 132 **B8**, 134 **B2**
Yan Kit, 63 **H2**
Yan Nawn, 63 **G4**
Yanan, 55 **D1**, 60 **B7**
Yancheng, 67 **B4**
Yangch'on, 72 **C6**
Yangfangdian, 73 **C2**
Yangmingshan NP, 62 **C6**
Yangpu, 74 **F7**
Yangquan, 66 **A5**
Yangzhou, 67 **B4**
Yankee Stad, NY 143 **E5**
Yankton, SD 126 **E5**
Yantai, 66 **B5**
Yao, 70 **D5**
Yaojiazhai, 74 **F7**
Yaoundé, 44 **D1**
Yap Isl, 80 **A5**
Yaqui, 96 **B6**
Yaren, 80 **C4**
Yarmouth, Can 103 **E2**
Yarmouth, MA 184 **D5**
Yarmouth Port, MA 184 **D4**
Yaroslavl, 52 **C5**
Yarraville, 79 **B2**
Yarrow Pt, WA 176 **C5**
Yashio, 68 **C8**
Yau Tong, 75 **E2**
Yauco, 122 **B1**
Yavapai Pt, AZ 183 **E2**
Yavne, 50 **A5**
Yawata, 70 **E7**
Yazd, 49 **G5**

Yazoo City, MS 120 **A4**, 129 **H4**
Yazoo NWR, MS 120 **A4**
Yeadon, PA 144 **D2**
Yehod, 50 **B6**
Yekaterinburg, 53 **E4**
Yellow Sea, 55 **F1**, 60 **D8**, 66 **C5**
Yellowknife, 100 **D5**
Yellowstone Lake, WY 180 **D3**
Yellowstone NP, WY 130 **C7**, 135 **G3**, 178 **C5**, 180 **B4**
Yellowstone R, MT 126 **B7**, 135 **H4**, 180 **A6**
Yemen, 45 **H2**, 49 **F1**
Yenikoy, 43 **E3**
Yenisey R, 55 **A4**, 82 **D8**
Yeovil, 19 **D2**
Yerevan, 53 **A2**
Yesilkoy, 43 **D2**
Yesilkoy Arpt, 43 **D2**
Yichang, 60 **B6**, 67 **A3**
Yichun, 55 **E3**, 66 **C7**
Yinchuan, 55 **C1**, 60 **A7**
Yingko, 62 **A4**
Yingkou, 66 **B5**
Yining, 53 **F1**, 58 **D8**
Yogyakarta, 61 **C1**
Yokohama, 60 **F8**, 66 **F5**, 68 **B6**
Yokosuka, 68 **B5**
Yongsan, 72 **C6**
Yongzhou, 67 **A2**
Yonkers, NY 116 **B6**
Yorba Linda, CA 171 **E3**
York, Can 19 **E4**
York, PA 119 **F4**
York, UK 104 **D6**
York Factory, 101 **A3**
York Mills, 104 **E7**
Yorkton, 101 **E2**
Yorktowne Hts, NY 116 **B6**
Yosemite Falls, CA 182 **B3**
Yosemite NP, CA 132 **C5**, 178 **A4**, 182 **B4**
Yosemite Valley, CA 182 **B3**

Yosemite Village, CA 182 **B3**
Yosemite West, CA 182 **E2**
Yoshida, 71 **F4**
Yotsukaido, 68 **E7**
Young Heroes Mon, 99 **F5**
Youngstown, NY 116 **B3**
Youngstown, OH 112 **D5**, 118 **D5**
Yreka, CA 132 **B7**, 134 **B1**
Ystad, 22 **E6**
Yu Shan, 67 **C2**
Yu Yuan Gdn, 74 **E6**
Yuba City, CA 132 **B6**
Yucatan Chan, 97 **F4**
Yucatan Pen, 97 **F3**
Yueyang, 67 **A3**
Yugoslavia, 17 **G4**, 25 **E6**, 45 **E6**
Yukon-Charley Rivers Natural Pres, AK 136 **D7**, 178 **B2**
Yukon Delta NWR, AK 136 **B6**
Yukon Flats NWR, AK 136 **D7**
Yukon Plateau, 100 **B5**
Yukon R, 82 **B5**, 100 **A6**, 136 **C7**, 178 **A2**
Yukon Terr, 100 **B5**
Yulee, FL 123 **F6**
Yuma, AZ 131 **A2**, 133 **F2**
Yuma Proving Ground, AZ 131 **A2**
Yumen, 55 **B1**, 58 **F7**
Yungho, 62 **C5**
Yurakucho, 69 **D2**
Yurimaguas, 84 **C3**
Yurlovo, 56 **A5**
Yuzhno-Sakhalinsk, 66 **F8**

Z

Zaandam, 30 **C6**
Zabol, 49 **H5**
Zacatecas, 96 **C4**
Zadar, 24 **C5**
Zagreb, 17 **F4**, 23 **F1**, 24 **D5**, 45 **E6**

Zagros Mts, 45 H5, 49 F5
Zahedan, 49 H5, 58 A6
Zaire, 45 F1, 47 E6
Zajecar, 25 F6
Zalaegerszeg, 23 F1, 24 D6
Zalatitán, 99 G5
Zama, 68 A6
Zambezi R, 47 F4
Zambia, 47 F4
Zamboanga, 61 E3
Zamora, 21 B3
Zandar, 17 F4
Zandvoort, 30 B6
Zanesville, OH 112 D5, 118 C4
Zanzibar, 47 G5
Zanzibar Isl, 47 G5
Zapata, TX 128 D1
Zapopan, 99 F5
Zaporizhya, 53 A4
Zapote de Santa Cruz del Valle, 99 G3
Zapotitán de Hidalgo, 99 E1
Zapotitlán, 98 C2
Zaragoza, 16 C3, 21 D4
Zaria, 44 D2

Zdiby, 35 E3
Zehlendorf, 32 C6
Zelafon, 50 B4
Zele, 31 E4
Zellwood, FL 153 E5
Zemst, 31 G3
Zenica, 24 D5
Zepernick, 32 E8
Zephyrhills, FL 123 E4
Zeppelinheim, 35 A1
Zero Milestone, DC 149 C3
Zeuthen, 32 E5
Zeytinburnu, 43 E2
Zhabel District, 74 D8
Zhambyl, 53 E1
Zhangjiakou, 66 A5
Zhangjiazhai, 74 A6
Zhangye, 55 C1, 58 F8
Zhangzhou, 67 B2
Zhanjiang, 60 C5
Zhaojiahuayuan, 74 C7
Zhaojiajiao, 74 B7
Zheleznodorozhnyy, 56 D4
Zhengbaiqi, 73 A4
Zhengzhou, 60 B7, 67 A4
Zhenru, 74 B7

Zhezqarghan, 53 E2
Zhitomir, 17 H6
Zhongxinjingzhen, 74 A6
Zhoujiajiao, 74 B6
Zhoujiazhai, 74 F7
Zhoushenxiang, 74 B5
Zhuzhou, 67 A3
Ziamen, 60 C6
Zibo, 66 B5
Zielona Gora, 23 F4
Zigong, 60 A6
Zimbabwe, 47 F4
Zinder, 44 D2
Zinguinchor, 44 A2
Zion, IL 158 C8
Zion NP, UT 131 B4, 178 B3
Zionsville, IN 157 D4
Zipacón, 90 A3
Ziyyon, 50 D4
Zizhuyuan, 73 B3
Znojmo, 23 F2
Zoetermeer, 30 B3
Zográfos, 43 C3
Zollikerberg, 37 F1
Zollikofen, 37 B2
Zollikon, 37 F1

Zoological Gdns, Arg 89 A4
Zoological Gdns, Czech Rep 35 E3
Zoological Gdns, Den 36 C6
Zoological Gdn, Ger 35 B3
Zoological Gdns, Ger 33 B2
Zuchwil, 37 C4
Zuglo, 42 B7
Zuid-Beijerland, 30 A1
Zuidland, 30 A1
Zuni IR, NM 128 A6, 131 C3
Zuni Pueblo, NM 131 C3
Zunyi, 60 B6
Zuojiazhuang, 73 F3
Zürich, 16 D5, 20 F6, 23 C1, 24 A6, 37 E1
Zurich-Kloten Arpt, 37 E2
Zurzach, 37 D3
Zushi, 68 B5
Zwickau, 23 E3
Zwijndrecht, 30 C1
Zyryanka, 54 E6

Record of Personal Data

Name: _____

Address: _____

_____ Home Telephone: _____

Office Telephone: _____ Facsimile: _____

E-Mail: _____ Social Security No. _____

Passport No. _____ Frequent Flyer No. _____

Notable Numbers

Emergency   Personal

_____   _____

_____   _____

_____   _____

_____   _____

_____

                                     ### Financial/Credit

Medical   _____

_____

_____   _____

                                     ### Legal

_____   _____

_____   _____

_____   _____